The AMAZING SPIDER-MAN

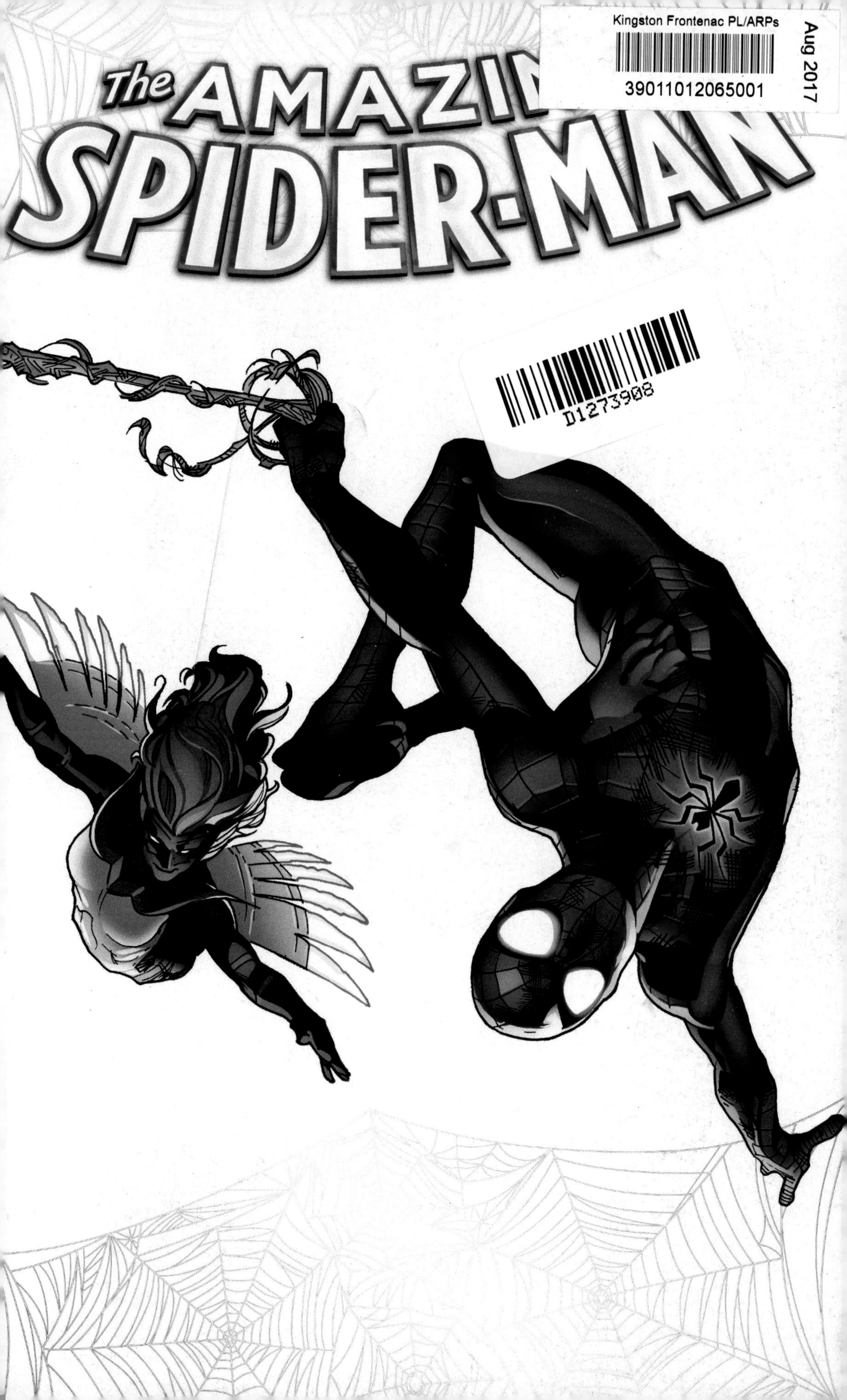

AMAZING SPIDER-MAN: WORLDWIDE VOL. 6. Contains material originally published in magazine form as AMAZING SPIDER-MAN #25-28. First printing 2017. ISBN# 978-1-302-90293-3. Published by MARVEL WORLDWIDE, INC., a subsidiary of MARVEL ENTERTAINMENT, LLC. OFFICE OF PUBLICATION: 135 West 50th Street, New York, NY 10020. Copyright © 2017 MARVEL No similarity between any of the names, characters, persons, and/or institutions in this magazine with those of any living or dead person or institution is intended, and any such similarity which may exist is purely coincidental. **Printed in the U.S.A.** DAN BUCKLEY, President, Marvel Entertainment; JOE QUESADA, Chief Creative Officer; TOM BREVOORT, SVP of Publishing; DAVID BOGART, SVP of Business Affairs & Operations, Publishing & Partnership; C.B. CEBULSKI, VP of Brand Management & Development, Asia; DAVID GABRIEL, SVP of Sales & Marketing, Publishing; JEFF YOUNGQUIST, VP of Production & Special Projects; DAN CARR, Executive Director of Publishing Technology; ALEX MORALES, Director of Publishing Operations; SUSAN CRESPI, Production Manager; STAN LEE, Chairman Emeritus. For information regarding advertising in Marvel Comics or on Marvel.com, please contact Vit DeBellis, Integrated Sales Manager, at vdebellis@marvel.com. For Marvel subscription inquiries, please call 888-511-5480. **Manufactured between 5/26/2017 and 6/26/2017 by QUAD/GRAPHICS WASECA, WASECA, MN, USA.**

10 9 8 7 6 5 4 3 2 1

THE AMAZING SPIDER-MAN

WORLDWIDE

DAN SLOTT
WRITER

STUART IMMONEN
PENCILER

WADE VON GRAWBADGER
INKER

MARTE GRACIA
WITH **ANDRES MOSSA** (#28)
INKER

VC'S JOE CARAMAGNA
LETTERER

ALEX ROSS
COVER ART

AMAZING SPIDER-MAN #25 BACK-UP STORIES

CHRISTOS GAGE, JACOB CHABOT, JAMES ASMUS, HANNAH BLUMENREICH, CALE ATKINSON AND DAN SLOTT
WRITERS

TODD NAUCK, RAY-ANTHONY HEIGHT & WALDEN WONG, TANA FORD, JORDAN GIBSON, CALE ATKINSON AND GIUSEPPI CAMUNCOLI & CAM SMITH
ARTISTS

RACHELLE ROSENBERG, JIM CAMPBELL, ANDRES MOSSA, JORDIE BELLAIRE, CALE ATKINSON AND JASON KEITH
COLOR ARTISTS

VC'S TRAVIS LANHAM, VC'S CORY PETIT, VC'S CLAYTON COWLES, CALE ATKINSON AND VC'S JOE CARAMAGNA
LETTERERS

ALLISON STOCK
ASSISTANT EDITOR

DEVIN LEWIS
ASSOCIATE EDITOR

NICK LOWE
EDITOR

SPIDER-MAN CREATED BY
STAN LEE & STEVE DITKO

COLLECTION EDITOR: **JENNIFER GRÜNWALD**
ASSISTANT EDITOR: **CAITLIN O'CONNELL**
ASSOCIATE MANAGING EDITOR: **KATERI WOODY**

EDITOR, SPECIAL PROJECTS: **MARK D. BEAZLEY**
VP PRODUCTION & SPECIAL PROJECTS: **JEFF YOUNGQUIST**
SVP PRINT, SALES & MARKETING: **DAVID GABRIEL**

EDITOR IN CHIEF: **AXEL ALONSO**
CHIEF CREATIVE OFFICER: **JOE QUESADA**

PRESIDENT: **DAN BUCKLEY**
EXECUTIVE PRODUCER: **ALAN FINE**

P R E V I O U S L Y

THINGS HAVE BEEN BUSIER THAN EVER FOR PETER PARKER. HIS COMPANY,
PARKER INDUSTRIES, NOW HAS OFFICES IN SHANGHAI, LONDON AND SAN
FRANCISCO, AND ITS SIGNATURE PRODUCT, WEBWARE, IS THE MUST-HAVE
GADGET ON THE MARKET.

RECENTLY, IN ORDER TO STOP ONE OF HIS ENEMY'S SCHEMES, SPIDER-MAN
HAD NO CHOICE BUT TO HACK INTO EVERY WEBWARE UNIT ON THE PLANET AND
BROADCAST A SPECIFIC, HIGH-PITCHED SIGNAL. WHILE DOING THIS SAVED
COUNTLESS LIVES, THE WORLD AT LARGE NOW BELIEVES THAT WEBWARE IS A
MALFUNCTIONING PIECE OF JUNK.

BUT THAT'S A SECONDARY CONCERN TO SPIDER-MAN RIGHT NOW, BECAUSE HE
RECENTLY GOT A TIP ON THE LOCATION OF HIS ARCHENEMY: NORMAN OSBORN!

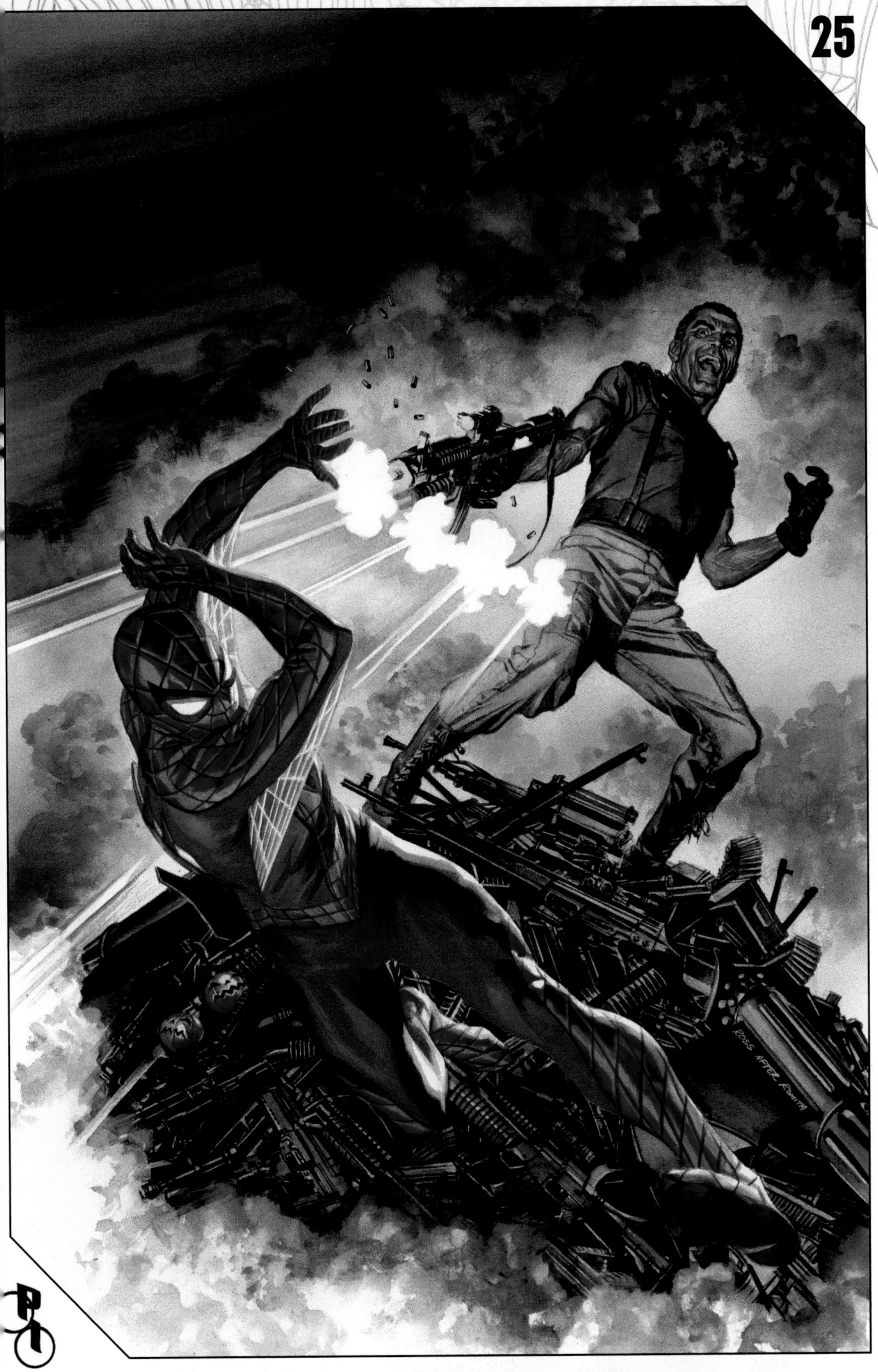
25
ROSS AFTER ROMITA

THE OSBORN IDENTITY PART ONE: "BUG HUNT"

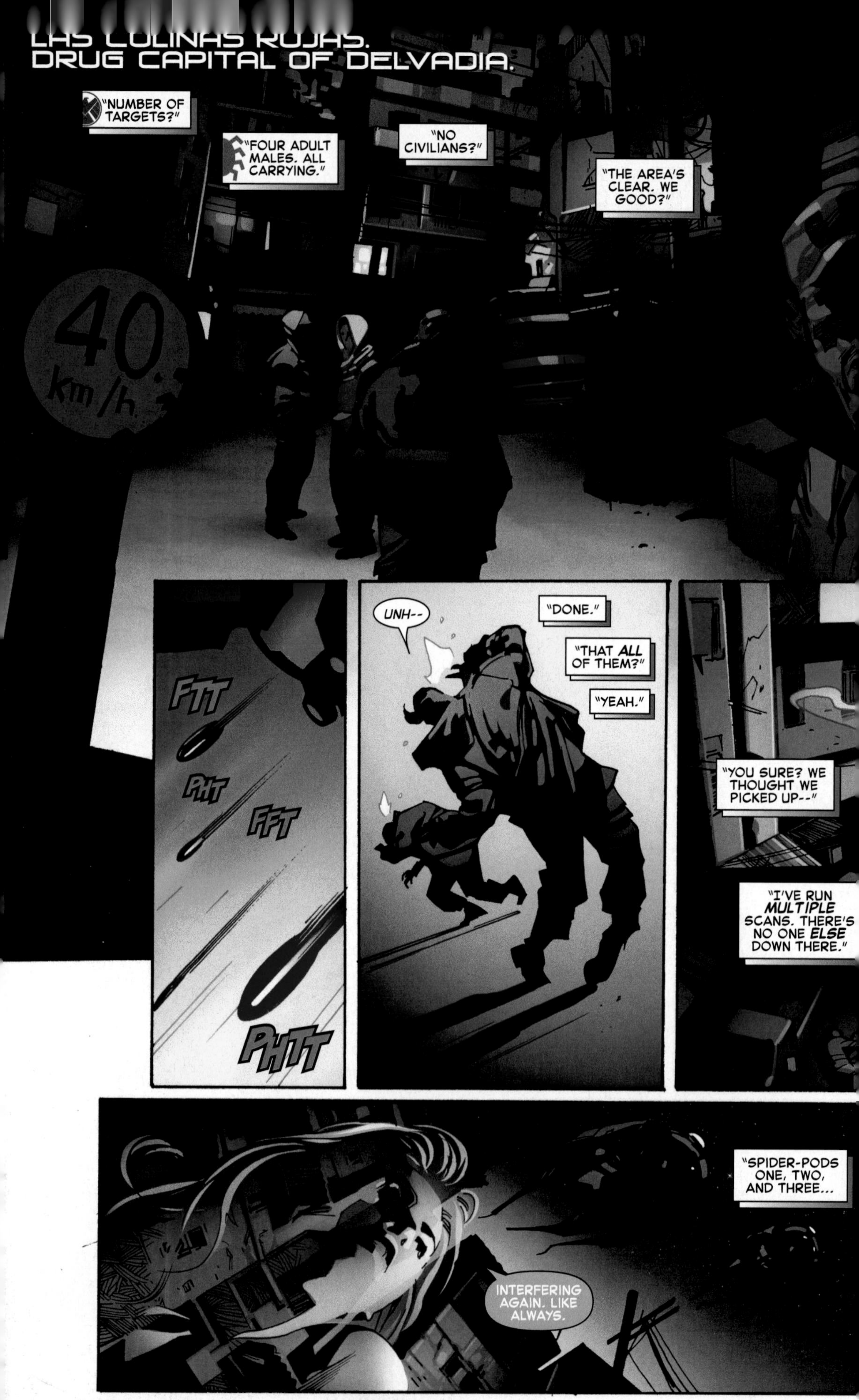
LAS COLINAS ROJAS.
DRUG CAPITAL OF DELVADIA.
"NUMBER OF TARGETS?"
"FOUR ADULT MALES. ALL CARRYING."
"NO CIVILIANS?"
"THE AREA'S CLEAR. WE GOOD?"
40 km/h
FTT
PHT
FFT
PHTT
UNH--
"DONE."
"THAT *ALL* OF THEM?"
"YEAH."
"YOU SURE? WE THOUGHT WE PICKED UP--"
"I'VE RUN *MULTIPLE* SCANS. THERE'S NO ONE *ELSE* DOWN THERE."
"SPIDER-PODS ONE, TWO, AND THREE...
INTERFERING AGAIN. LIKE ALWAYS.

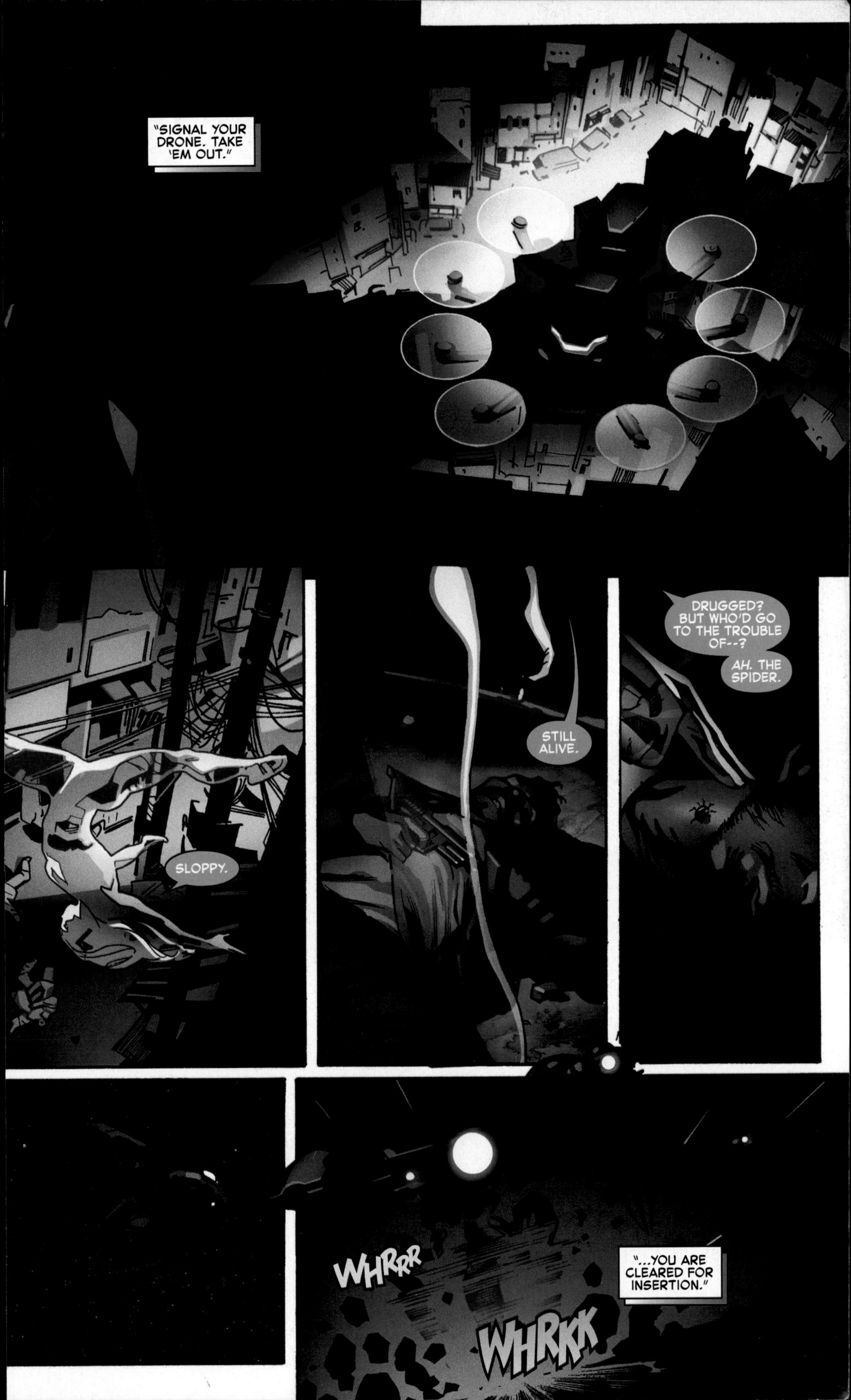
"SIGNAL YOUR DRONE. TAKE 'EM OUT."
SLOPPY.
STILL ALIVE.
DRUGGED? BUT WHO'D GO TO THE TROUBLE OF--?
AH. THE SPIDER.
WHRRR
"...YOU ARE CLEARED FOR INSERTION."
WHRKK

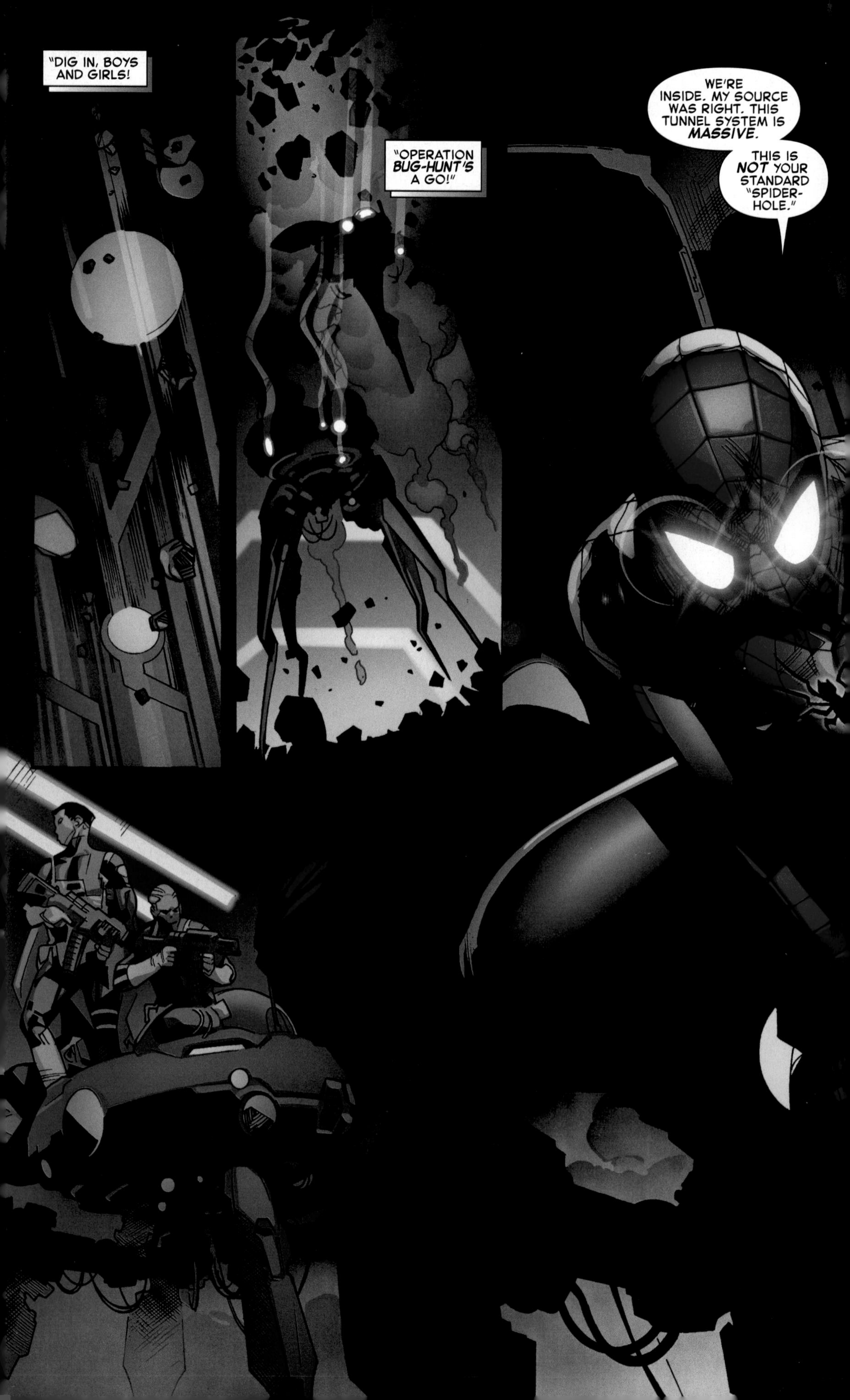
"DIG IN, BOYS AND GIRLS!
"OPERATION BUG-HUNT'S A GO!"
WE'RE INSIDE. MY SOURCE WAS RIGHT. THIS TUNNEL SYSTEM IS MASSIVE.
THIS IS NOT YOUR STANDARD "SPIDER-HOLE."

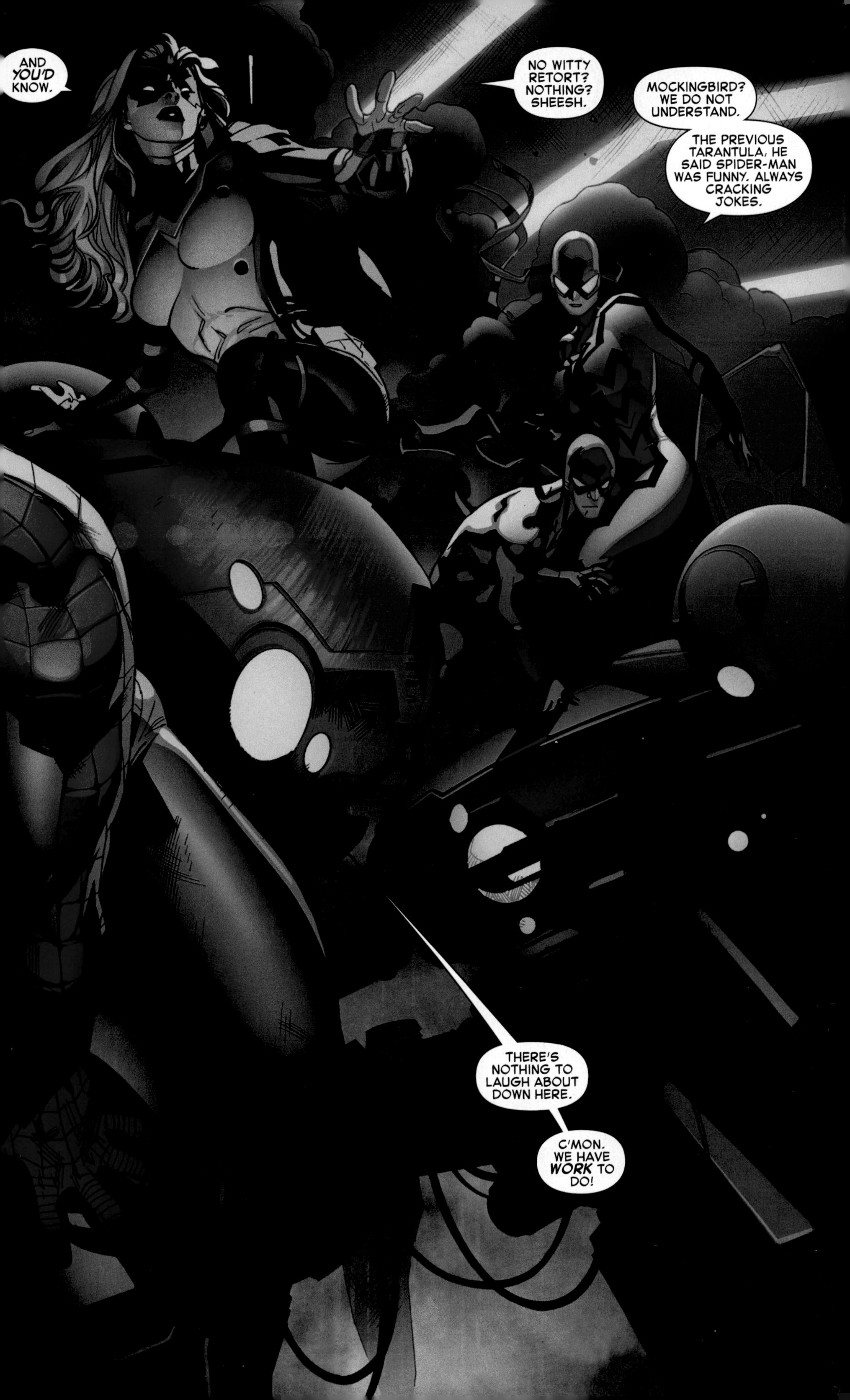
AND YOU'D KNOW.
NO WITTY RETORT? NOTHING? SHEESH.
MOCKINGBIRD? WE DO NOT UNDERSTAND.
THE PREVIOUS TARANTULA, HE SAID SPIDER-MAN WAS FUNNY. ALWAYS CRACKING JOKES.
THERE'S NOTHING TO LAUGH ABOUT DOWN HERE.
C'MON. WE HAVE WORK TO DO!

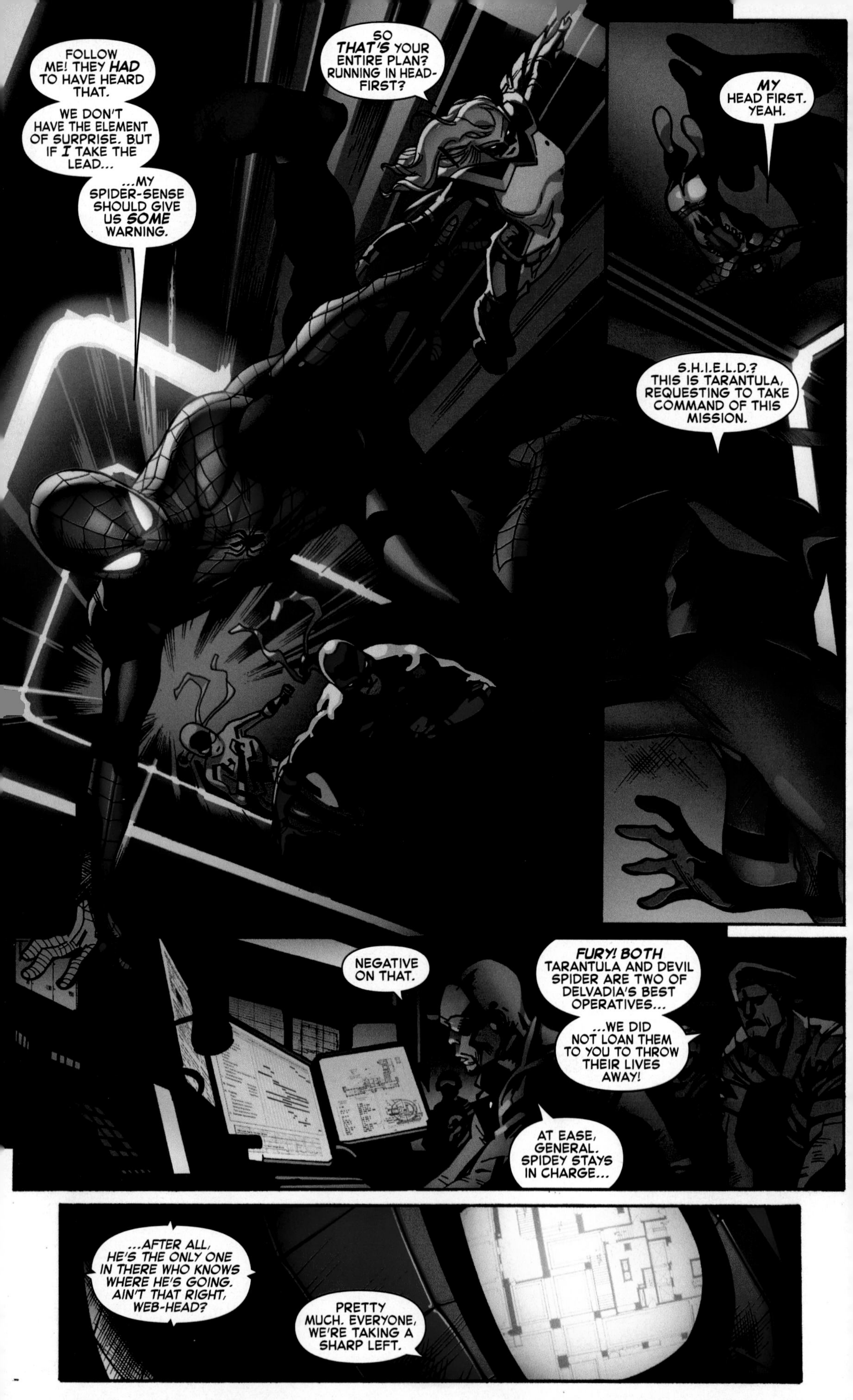
FOLLOW ME! THEY HAD TO HAVE HEARD THAT.
WE DON'T HAVE THE ELEMENT OF SURPRISE. BUT IF I TAKE THE LEAD...
...MY SPIDER-SENSE SHOULD GIVE US SOME WARNING.
SO THAT'S YOUR ENTIRE PLAN? RUNNING IN HEAD-FIRST?
MY HEAD FIRST. YEAH.
S.H.I.E.L.D.? THIS IS TARANTULA, REQUESTING TO TAKE COMMAND OF THIS MISSION.
NEGATIVE ON THAT.
FURY! BOTH TARANTULA AND DEVIL SPIDER ARE TWO OF DELVADIA'S BEST OPERATIVES...
...WE DID NOT LOAN THEM TO YOU TO THROW THEIR LIVES AWAY!
AT EASE, GENERAL. SPIDEY STAYS IN CHARGE...
...AFTER ALL, HE'S THE ONLY ONE IN THERE WHO KNOWS WHERE HE'S GOING. AIN'T THAT RIGHT, WEB-HEAD?
PRETTY MUCH. EVERYONE, WE'RE TAKING A SHARP LEFT.

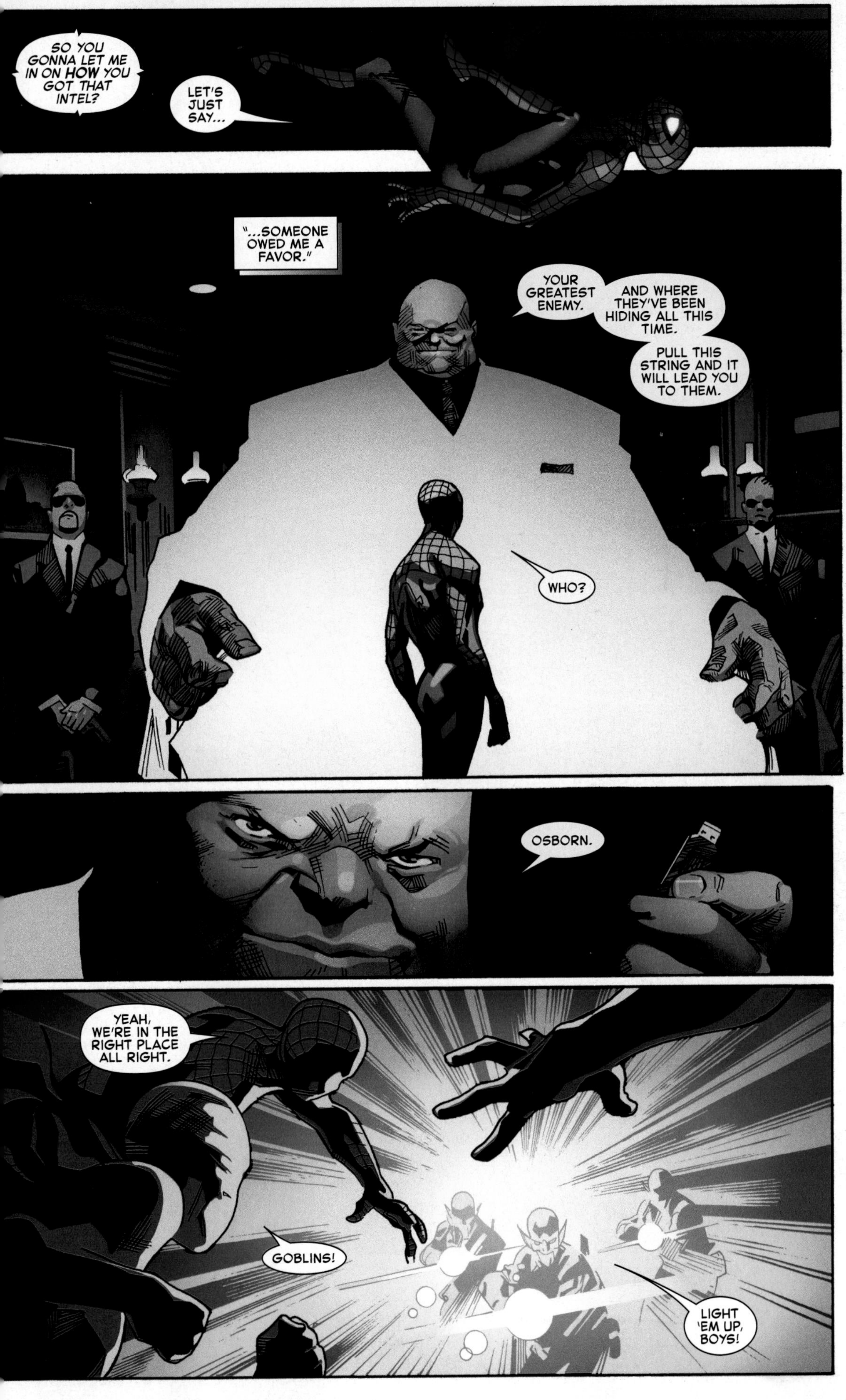
SO YOU GONNA LET ME IN ON HOW YOU GOT THAT INTEL?
LET'S JUST SAY...
"...SOMEONE OWED ME A FAVOR."
YOUR GREATEST ENEMY.
AND WHERE THEY'VE BEEN HIDING ALL THIS TIME.
PULL THIS STRING AND IT WILL LEAD YOU TO THEM.
WHO?
OSBORN.
YEAH, WE'RE IN THE RIGHT PLACE ALL RIGHT.
GOBLINS!
LIGHT 'EM UP, BOYS!

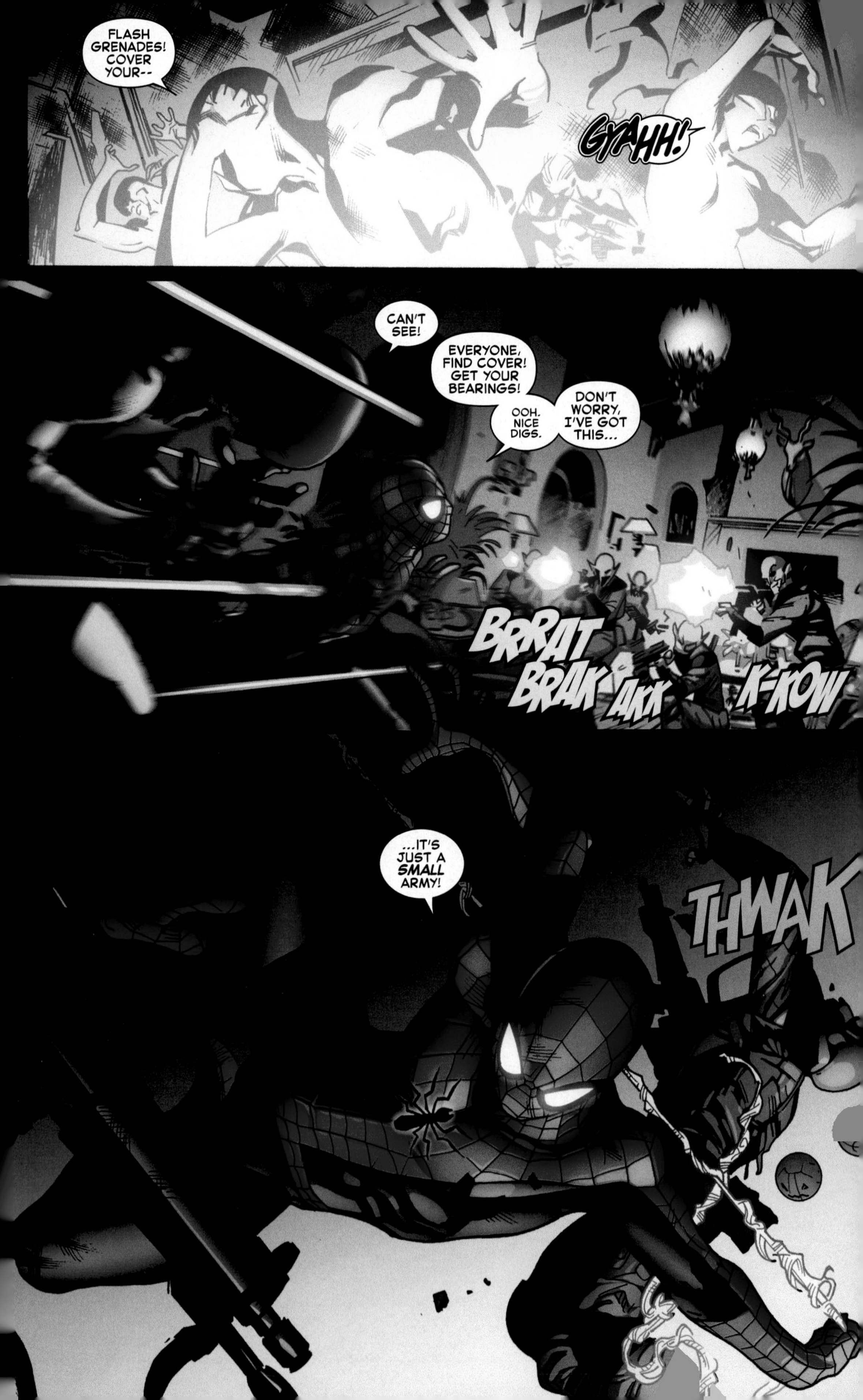
FLASH GRENADES! COVER YOUR--
GYAHH!
CAN'T SEE!
EVERYONE, FIND COVER! GET YOUR BEARINGS!
OOH. NICE DIGS.
DON'T WORRY, I'VE GOT THIS...
BRRAT
BRAK AKK
K-KOW
...IT'S JUST A SMALL ARMY!
THWAK

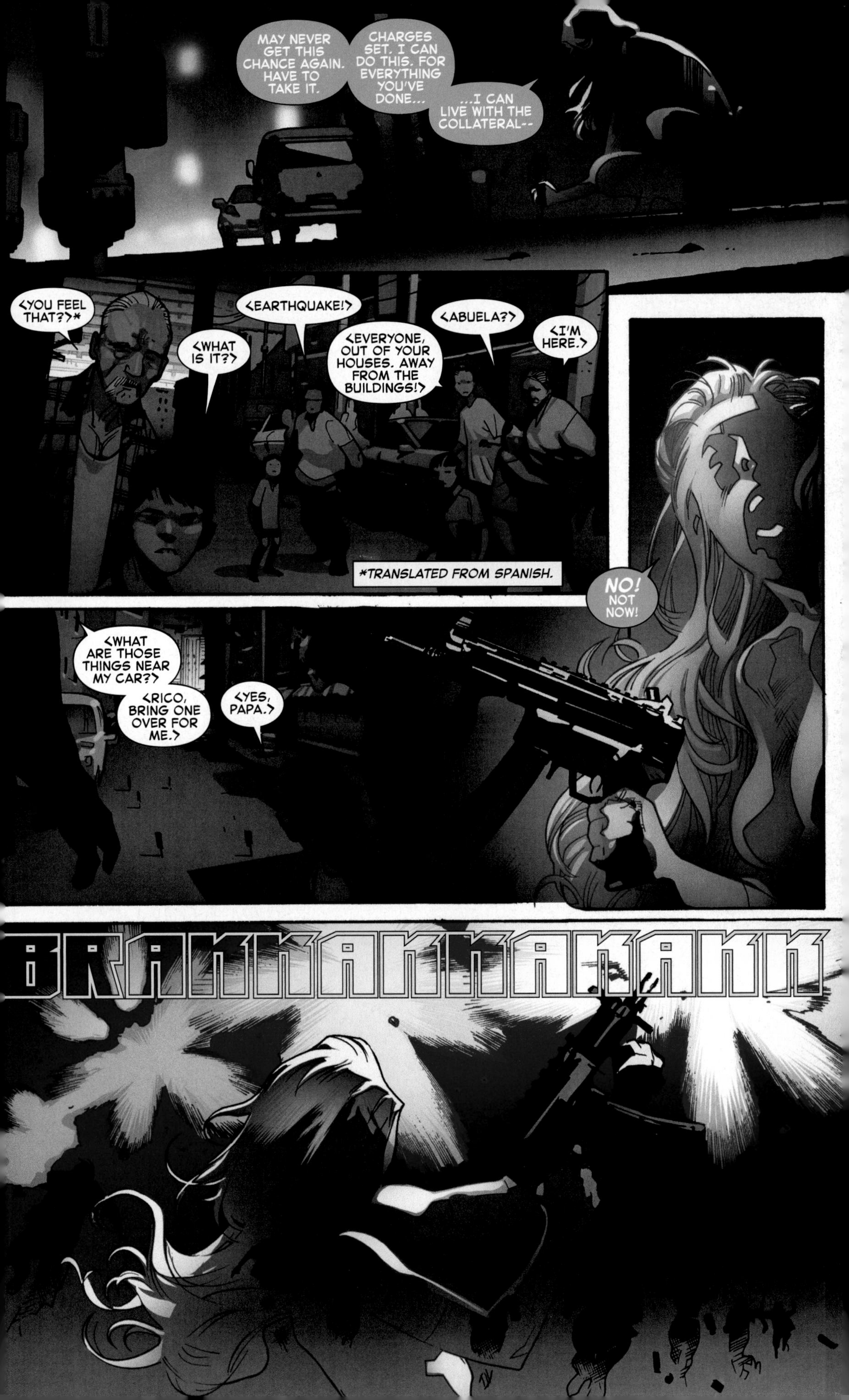
MAY NEVER GET THIS CHANCE AGAIN. HAVE TO TAKE IT.
CHARGES SET. I CAN DO THIS. FOR EVERYTHING YOU'VE DONE...
...I CAN LIVE WITH THE COLLATERAL--
<YOU FEEL THAT?>*
<WHAT IS IT?>
<EARTHQUAKE!>
<EVERYONE, OUT OF YOUR HOUSES. AWAY FROM THE BUILDINGS!>
<ABUELA?>
<I'M HERE.>
*TRANSLATED FROM SPANISH.
NO! NOT NOW!
<WHAT ARE THOSE THINGS NEAR MY CAR?>
<RICO, BRING ONE OVER FOR ME.>
<YES, PAPA.>
BRAKKAKKAKAKK

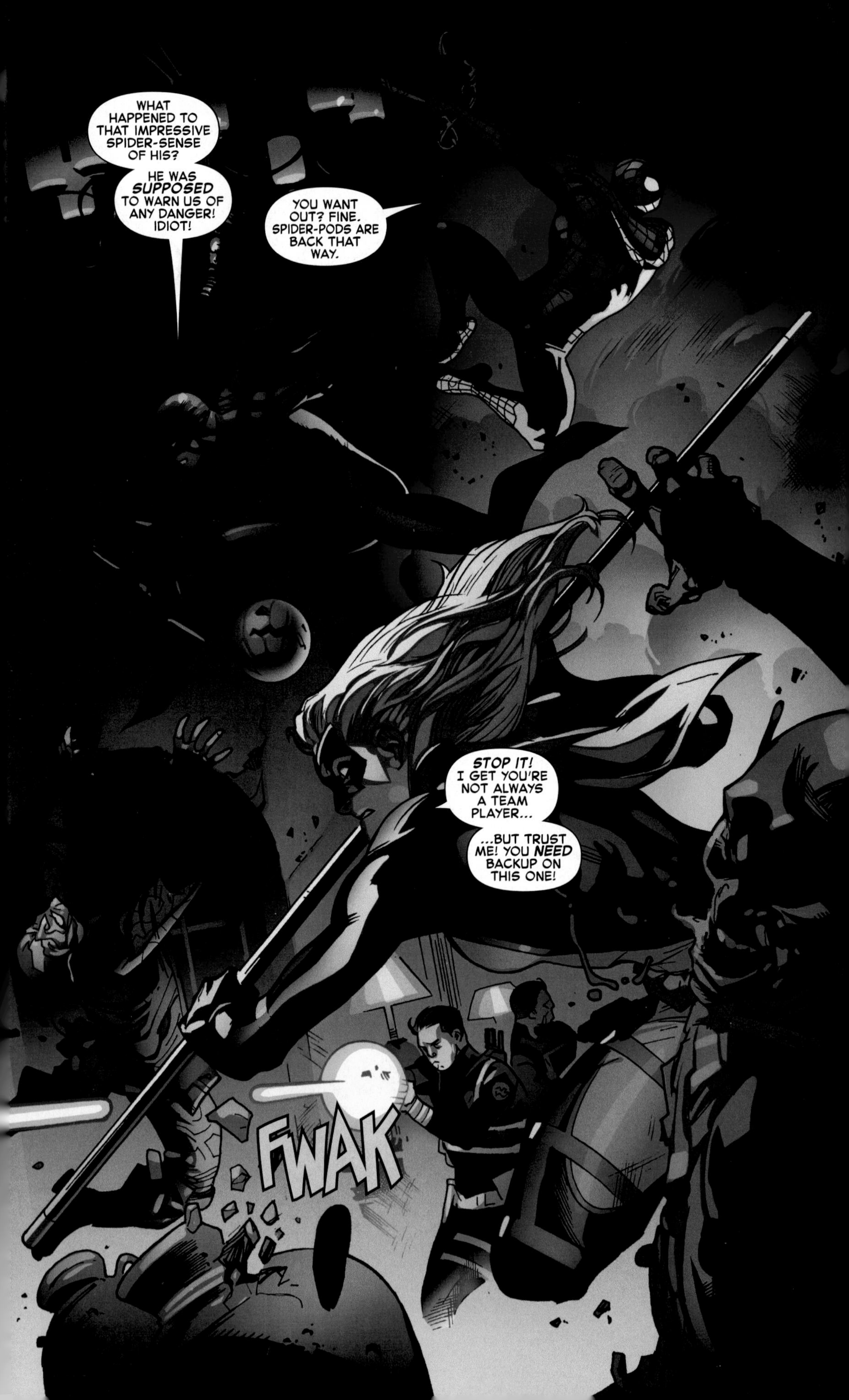
WHAT HAPPENED TO THAT IMPRESSIVE SPIDER-SENSE OF HIS?
HE WAS *SUPPOSED* TO WARN US OF ANY DANGER! IDIOT!
YOU WANT OUT? FINE. SPIDER-PODS ARE BACK THAT WAY.
STOP IT! I GET YOU'RE NOT ALWAYS A TEAM PLAYER...
...BUT TRUST ME! YOU *NEED* BACKUP ON THIS ONE!
FWAK

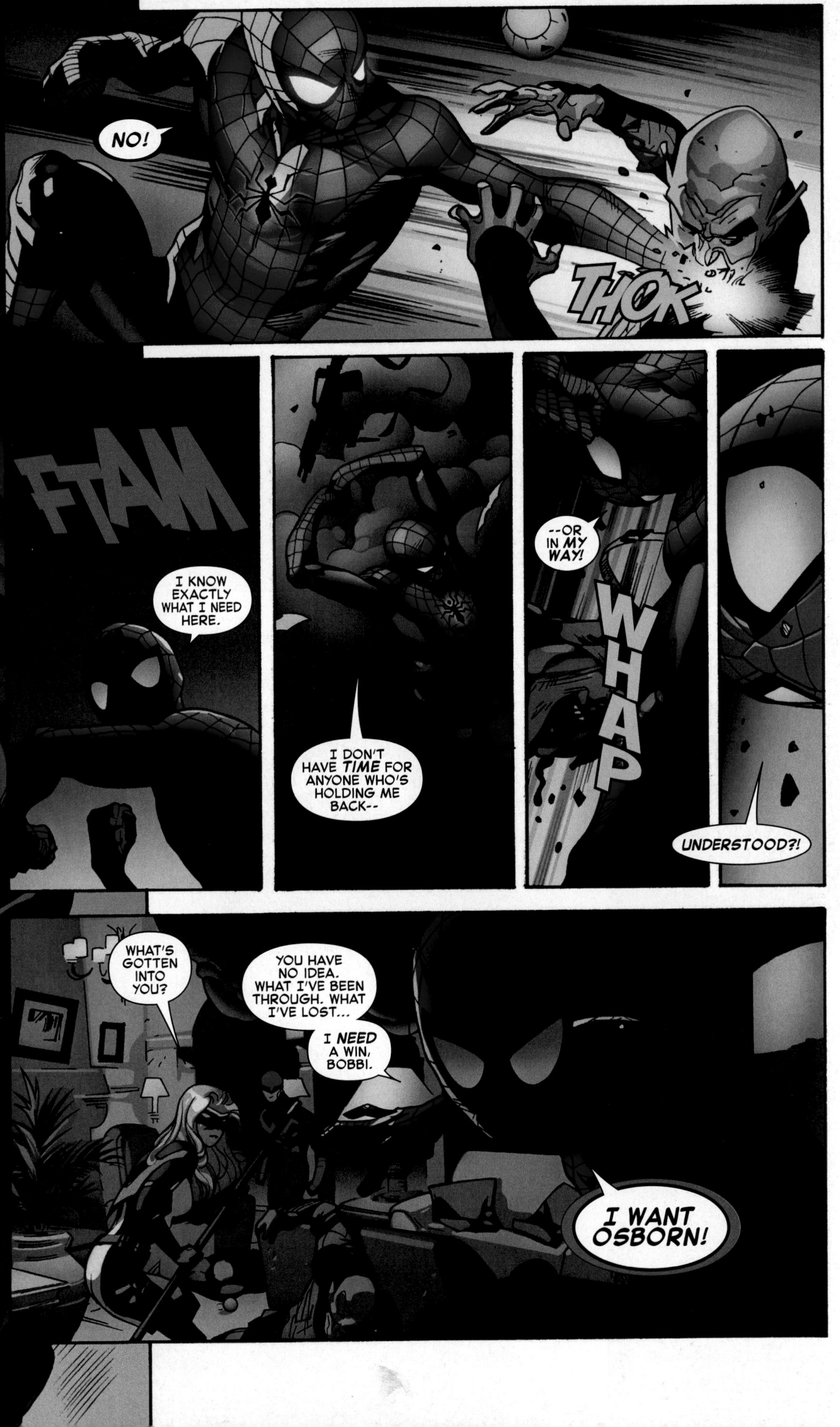
NO!
THOK
FTAM
I KNOW EXACTLY WHAT I NEED HERE.
I DON'T HAVE TIME FOR ANYONE WHO'S HOLDING ME BACK--
--OR IN MY WAY!
WHAP
UNDERSTOOD?!
WHAT'S GOTTEN INTO YOU?
YOU HAVE NO IDEA. WHAT I'VE BEEN THROUGH. WHAT I'VE LOST...
I NEED A WIN, BOBBI.
I WANT OSBORN!

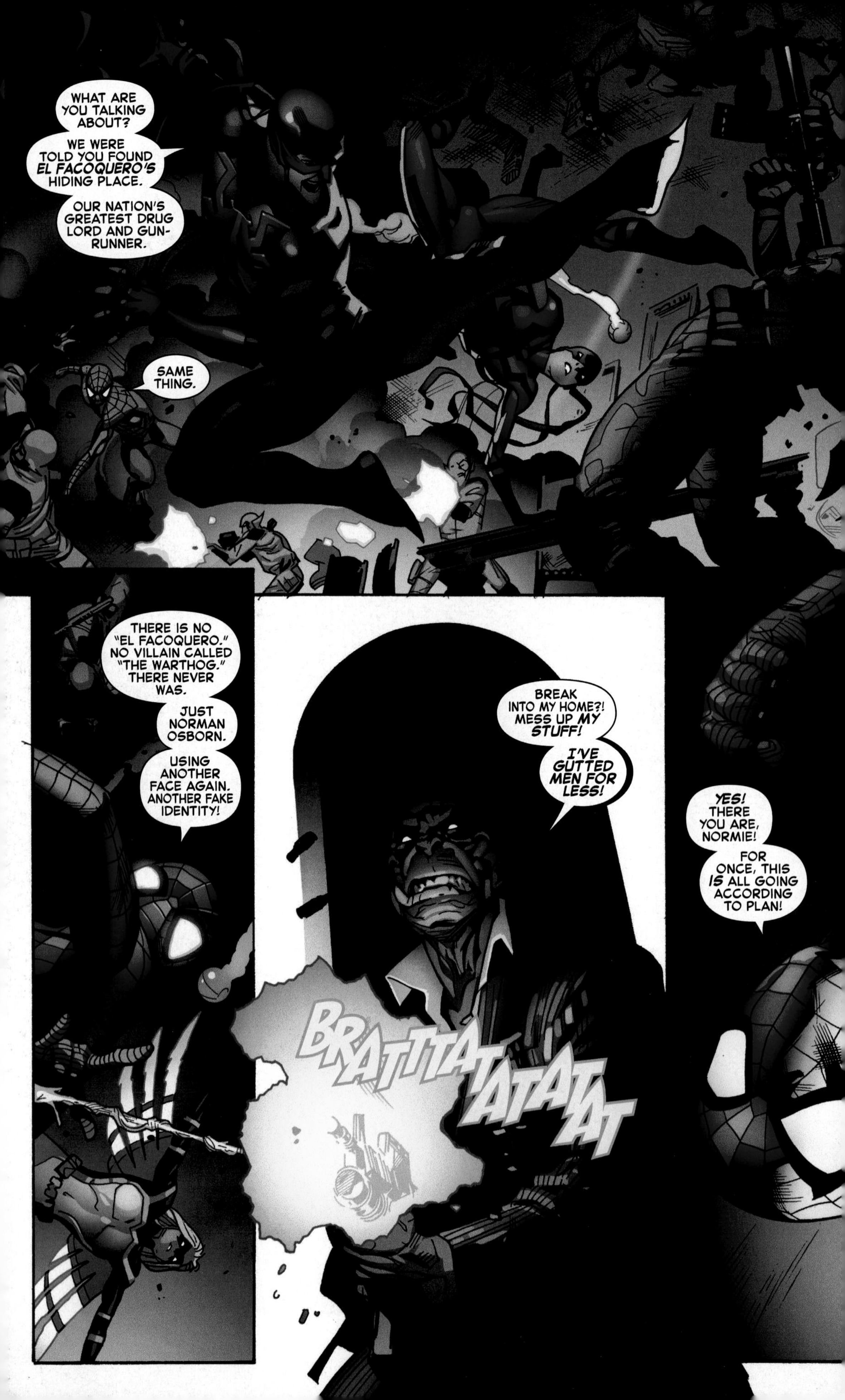
WHAT ARE YOU TALKING ABOUT?
WE WERE TOLD YOU FOUND *EL FACOQUERO'S* HIDING PLACE.
OUR NATION'S GREATEST DRUG LORD AND GUN-RUNNER.
SAME THING.
THERE IS NO "EL FACOQUERO." NO VILLAIN CALLED "THE WARTHOG." THERE NEVER WAS.
JUST NORMAN OSBORN.
USING ANOTHER FACE AGAIN. ANOTHER FAKE IDENTITY!
BREAK INTO MY HOME?! MESS UP *MY STUFF!*
I'VE GUTTED MEN FOR LESS!
YES! THERE YOU ARE, NORMIE!
FOR ONCE, THIS *IS* ALL GOING ACCORDING TO PLAN!
BRATTTATATATAT

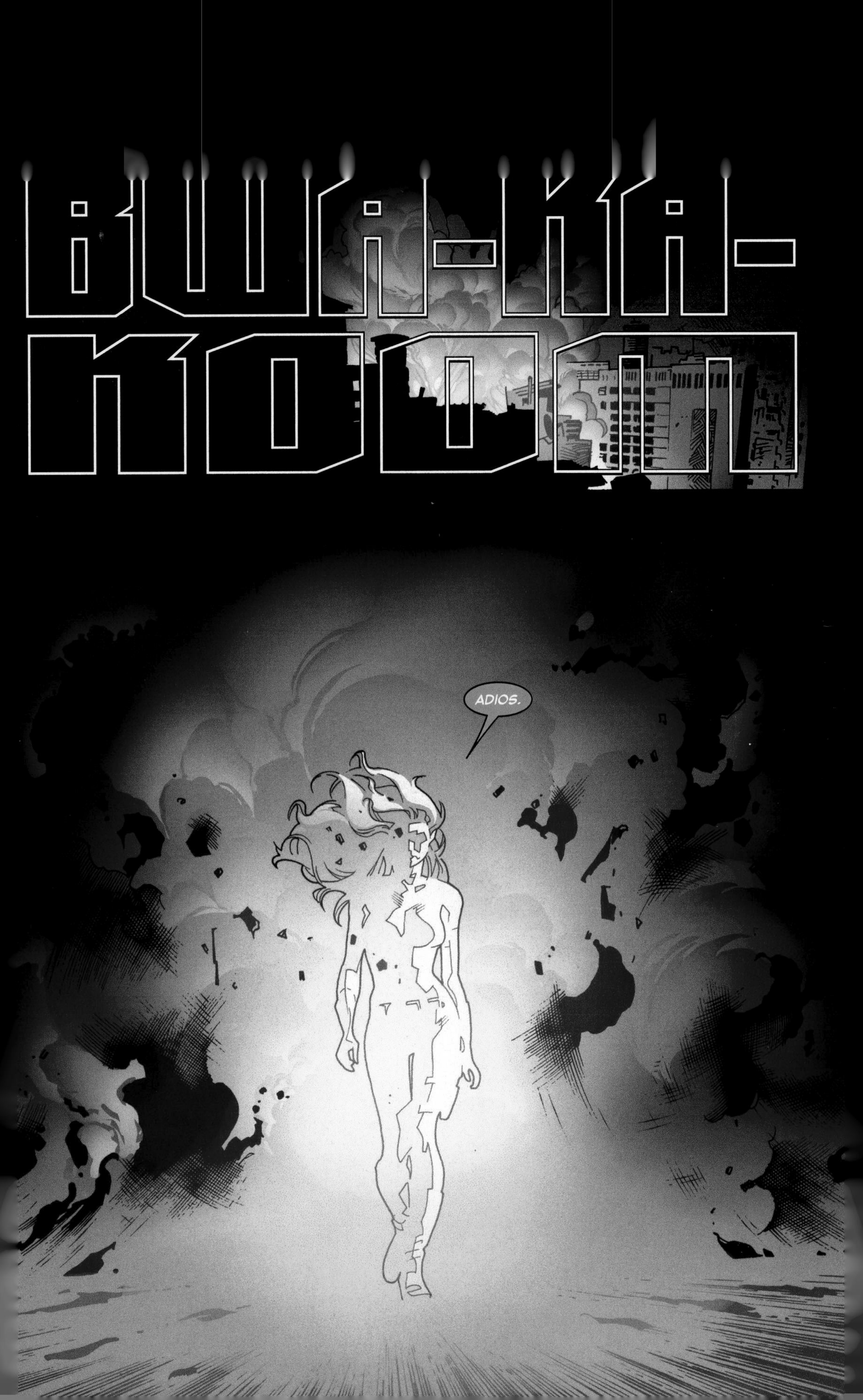
BWA-KA-
NOOM
ADIOS.

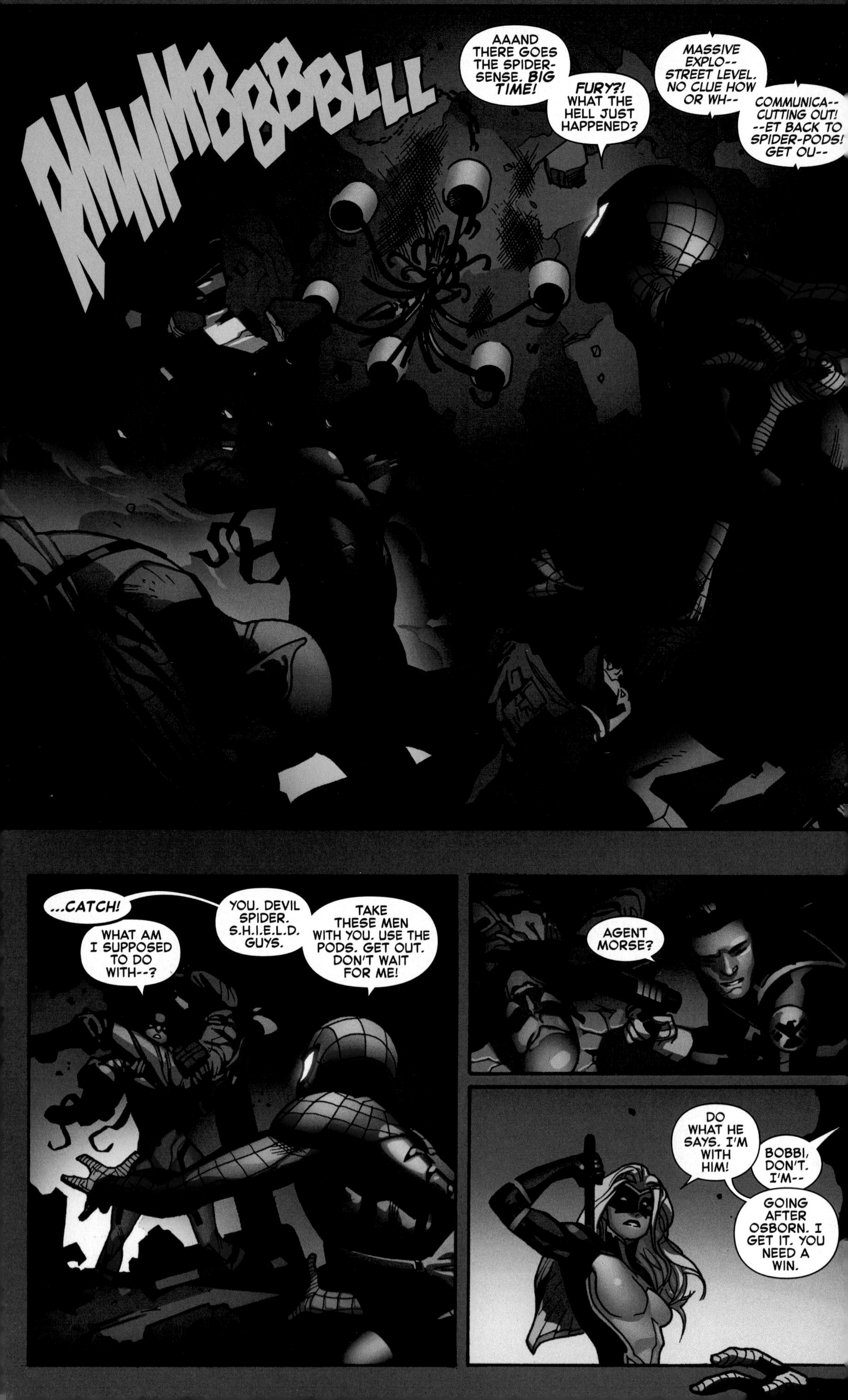

RHUMBBBBLLL
AAAND THERE GOES THE SPIDER-SENSE. BIG TIME!
FURY?! WHAT THE HELL JUST HAPPENED?
MASSIVE EXPLO-- STREET LEVEL. NO CLUE HOW OR WH--
COMMUNICA-- CUTTING OUT! --ET BACK TO SPIDER-PODS! GET OU--
...CATCH!
WHAT AM I SUPPOSED TO DO WITH--?
YOU. DEVIL SPIDER. S.H.I.E.L.D. GUYS.
TAKE THESE MEN WITH YOU. USE THE PODS. GET OUT. DON'T WAIT FOR ME!
AGENT MORSE?
DO WHAT HE SAYS. I'M WITH HIM!
BOBBI, DON'T. I'M--
GOING AFTER OSBORN. I GET IT. YOU NEED A WIN.

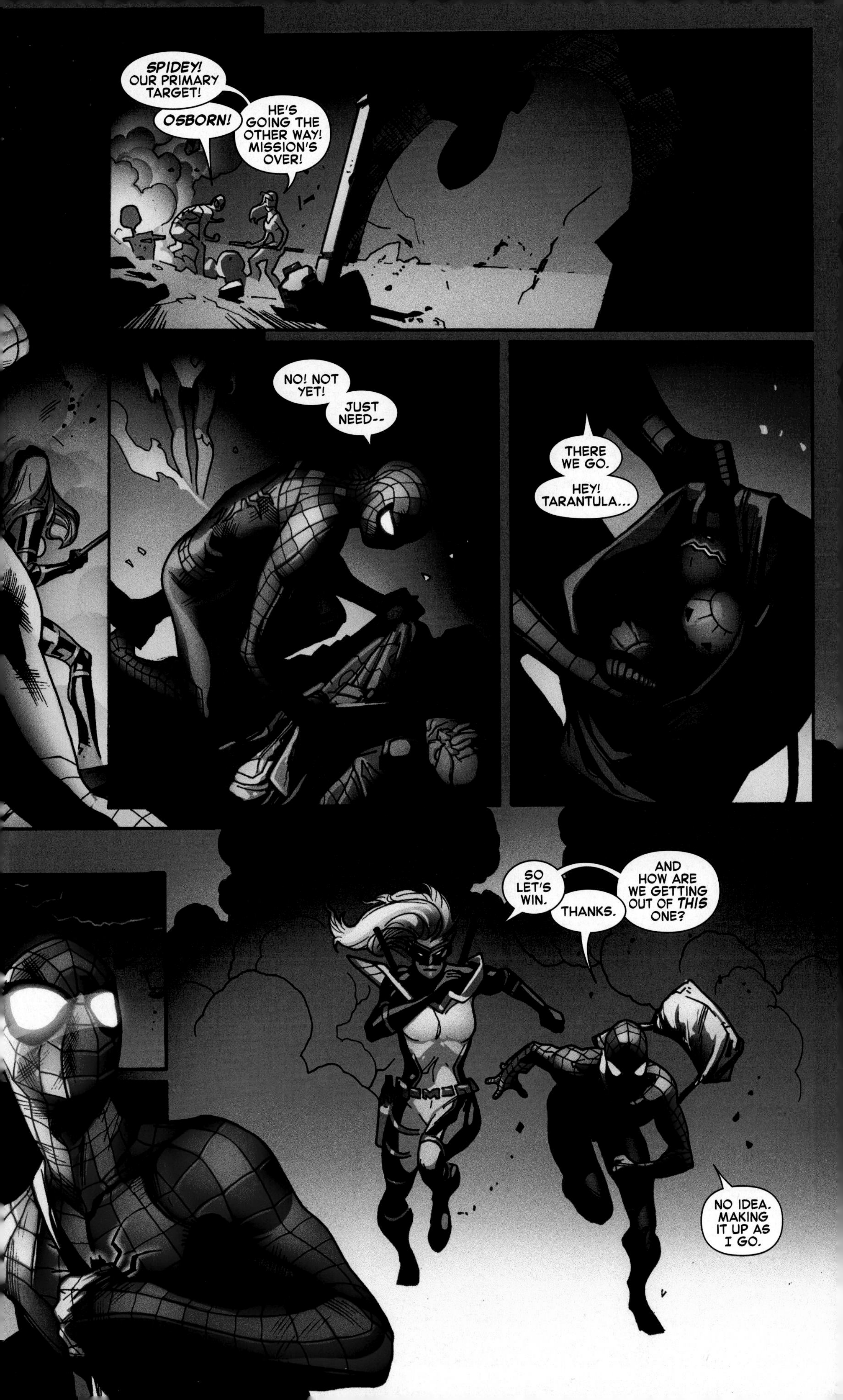
SPIDEY! OUR PRIMARY TARGET!
OSBORN!
HE'S GOING THE OTHER WAY! MISSION'S OVER!
NO! NOT YET!
JUST NEED--
THERE WE GO.
HEY! TARANTULA...
SO LET'S WIN.
AND HOW ARE WE GETTING OUT OF THIS ONE?
THANKS.
NO IDEA. MAKING IT UP AS I GO.

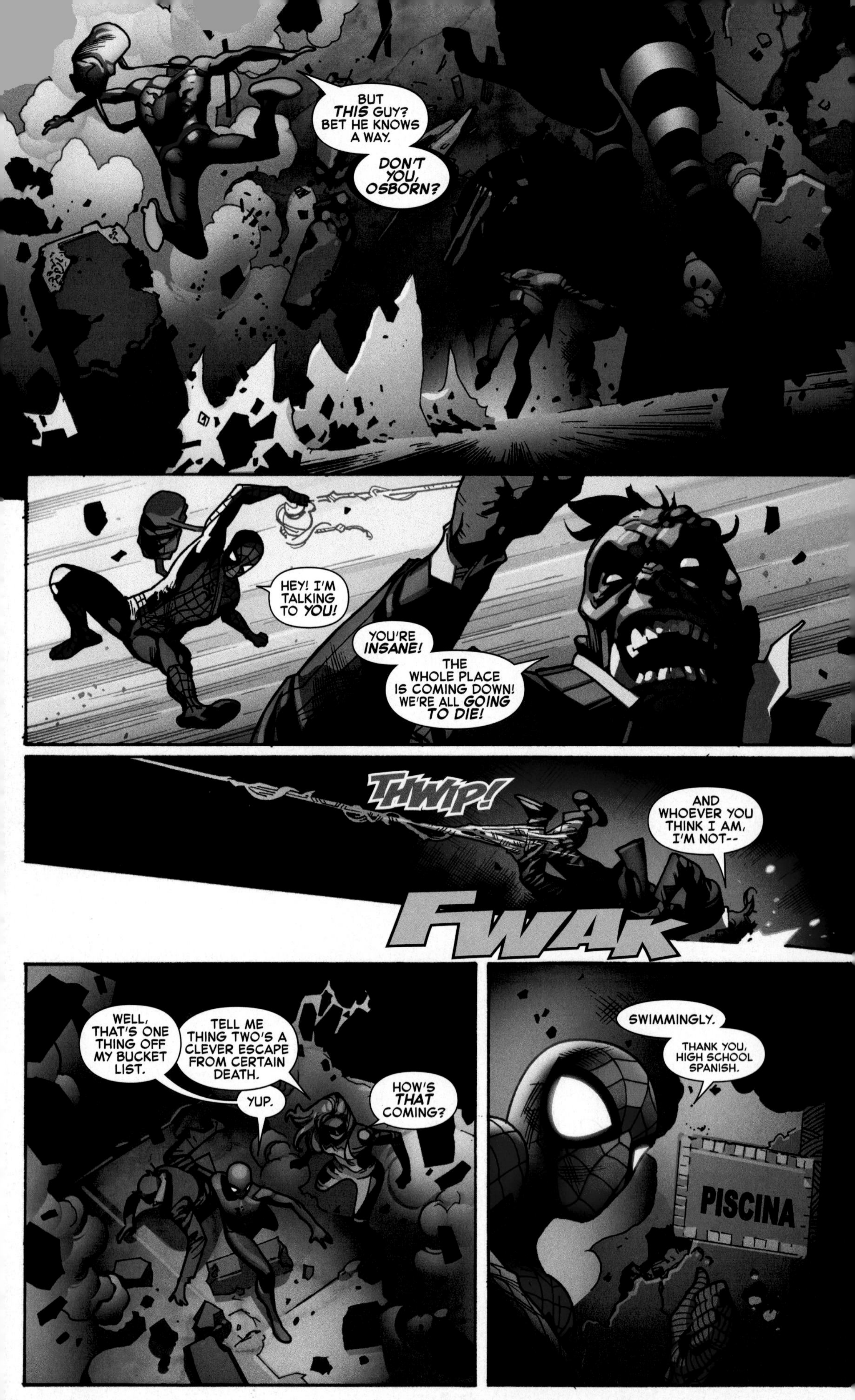
BUT THIS GUY? BET HE KNOWS A WAY.
DON'T YOU, OSBORN?
HEY! I'M TALKING TO YOU!
YOU'RE INSANE!
THE WHOLE PLACE IS COMING DOWN! WE'RE ALL GOING TO DIE!
THWIP!
AND WHOEVER YOU THINK I AM, I'M NOT--
FWAK
WELL, THAT'S ONE THING OFF MY BUCKET LIST.
TELL ME THING TWO'S A CLEVER ESCAPE FROM CERTAIN DEATH.
YUP.
HOW'S THAT COMING?
SWIMMINGLY.
THANK YOU, HIGH SCHOOL SPANISH.
PISCINA

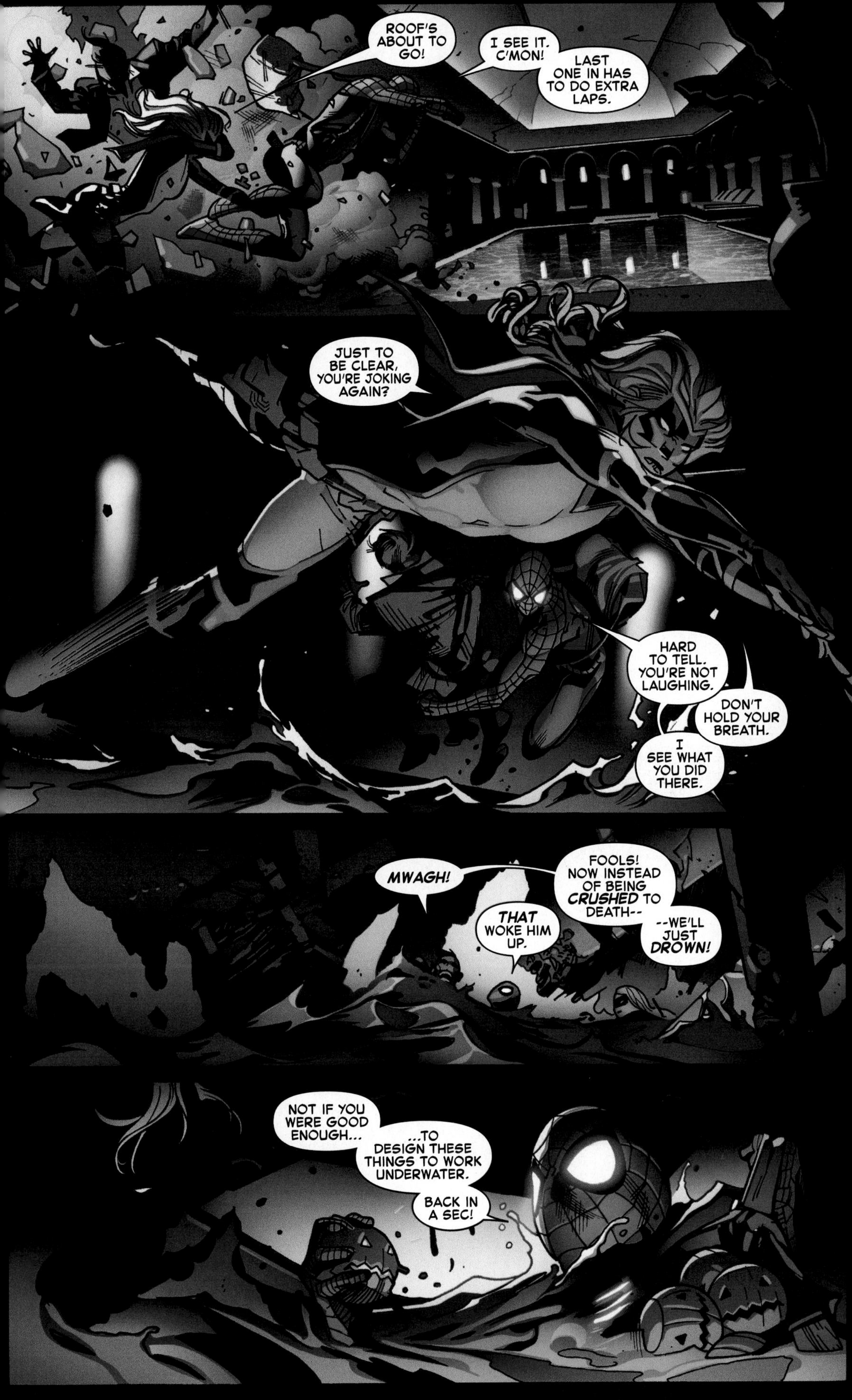
ROOF'S ABOUT TO GO!
I SEE IT. C'MON!
LAST ONE IN HAS TO DO EXTRA LAPS.
JUST TO BE CLEAR, YOU'RE JOKING AGAIN?
HARD TO TELL. YOU'RE NOT LAUGHING.
DON'T HOLD YOUR BREATH.
I SEE WHAT YOU DID THERE.
MWAGH!
FOOLS! NOW INSTEAD OF BEING CRUSHED TO DEATH--
THAT WOKE HIM UP.
--WE'LL JUST DROWN!
NOT IF YOU WERE GOOD ENOUGH...
...TO DESIGN THESE THINGS TO WORK UNDERWATER.
BACK IN A SEC!

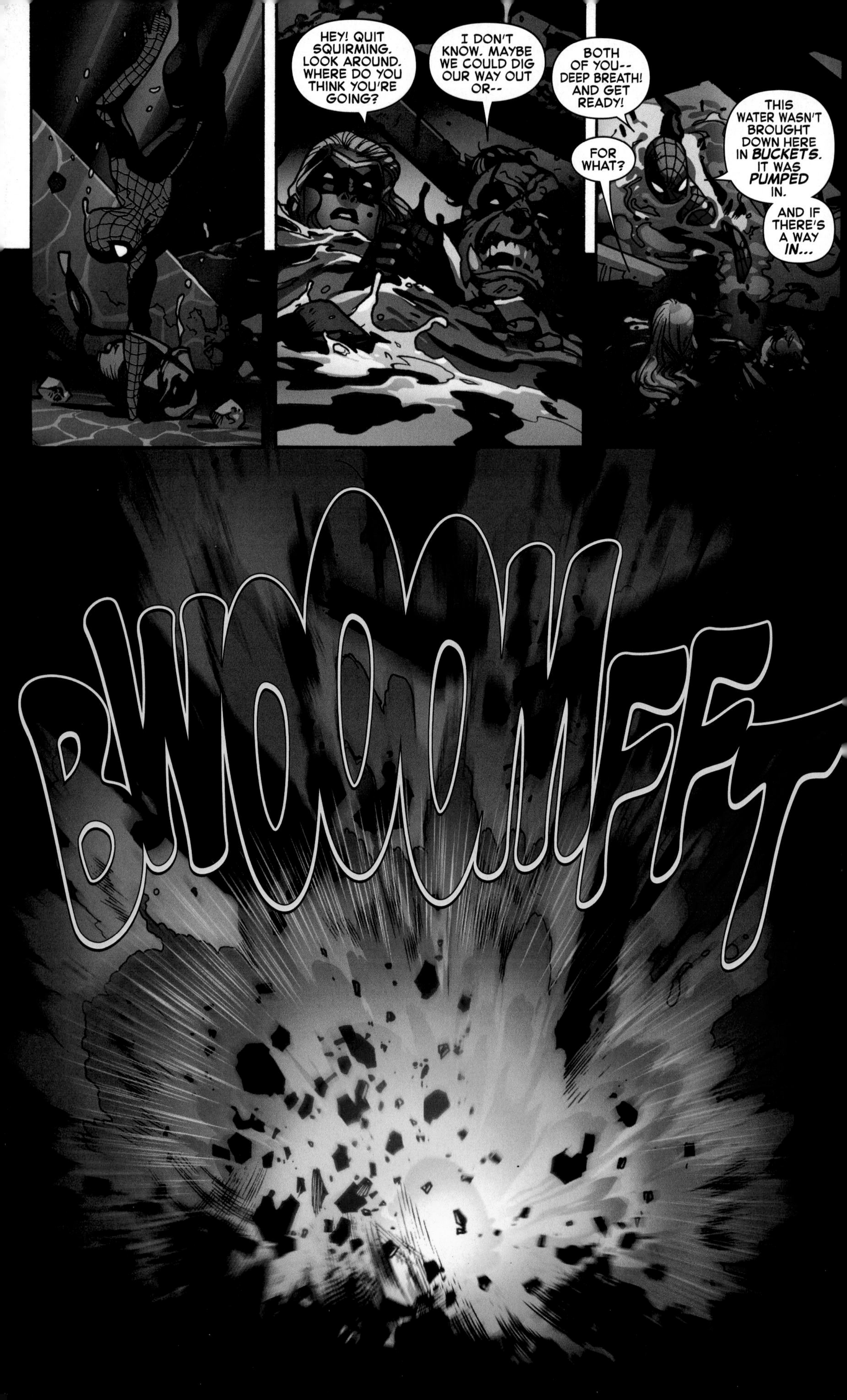
HEY! QUIT SQUIRMING. LOOK AROUND. WHERE DO YOU THINK YOU'RE GOING?
I DON'T KNOW. MAYBE WE COULD DIG OUR WAY OUT OR--
BOTH OF YOU-- DEEP BREATH! AND GET READY!
FOR WHAT?
THIS WATER WASN'T BROUGHT DOWN HERE IN BUCKETS. IT WAS PUMPED IN.
AND IF THERE'S A WAY IN...
BWOOOMFFT

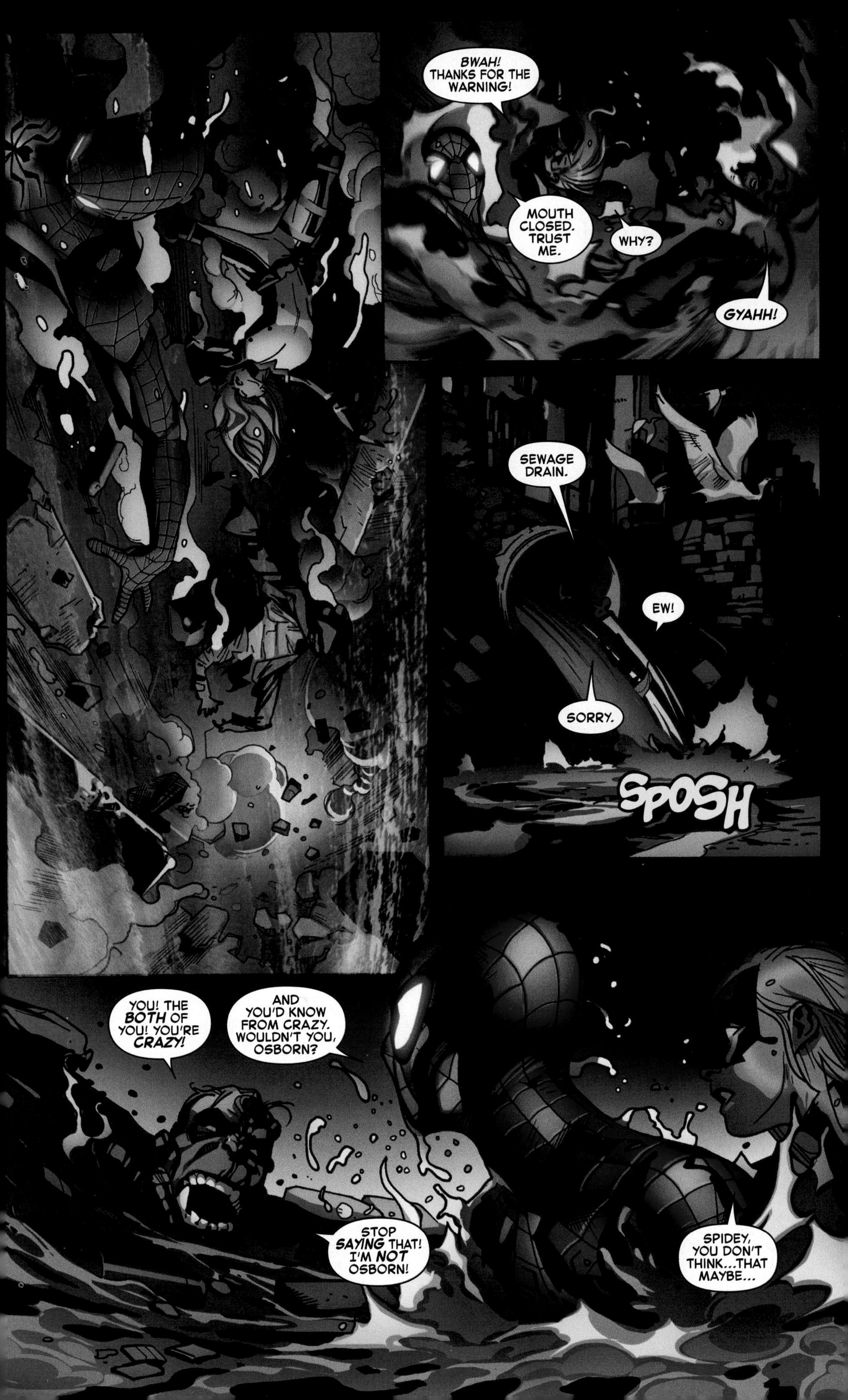
BWAH! THANKS FOR THE WARNING!
MOUTH CLOSED. TRUST ME.
WHY?
GYAHH!
SEWAGE DRAIN.
EW!
SORRY.
SPOSH
YOU! THE BOTH OF YOU! YOU'RE CRAZY!
AND YOU'D KNOW FROM CRAZY. WOULDN'T YOU, OSBORN?
STOP SAYING THAT! I'M NOT OSBORN!
SPIDEY, YOU DON'T THINK...THAT MAYBE...

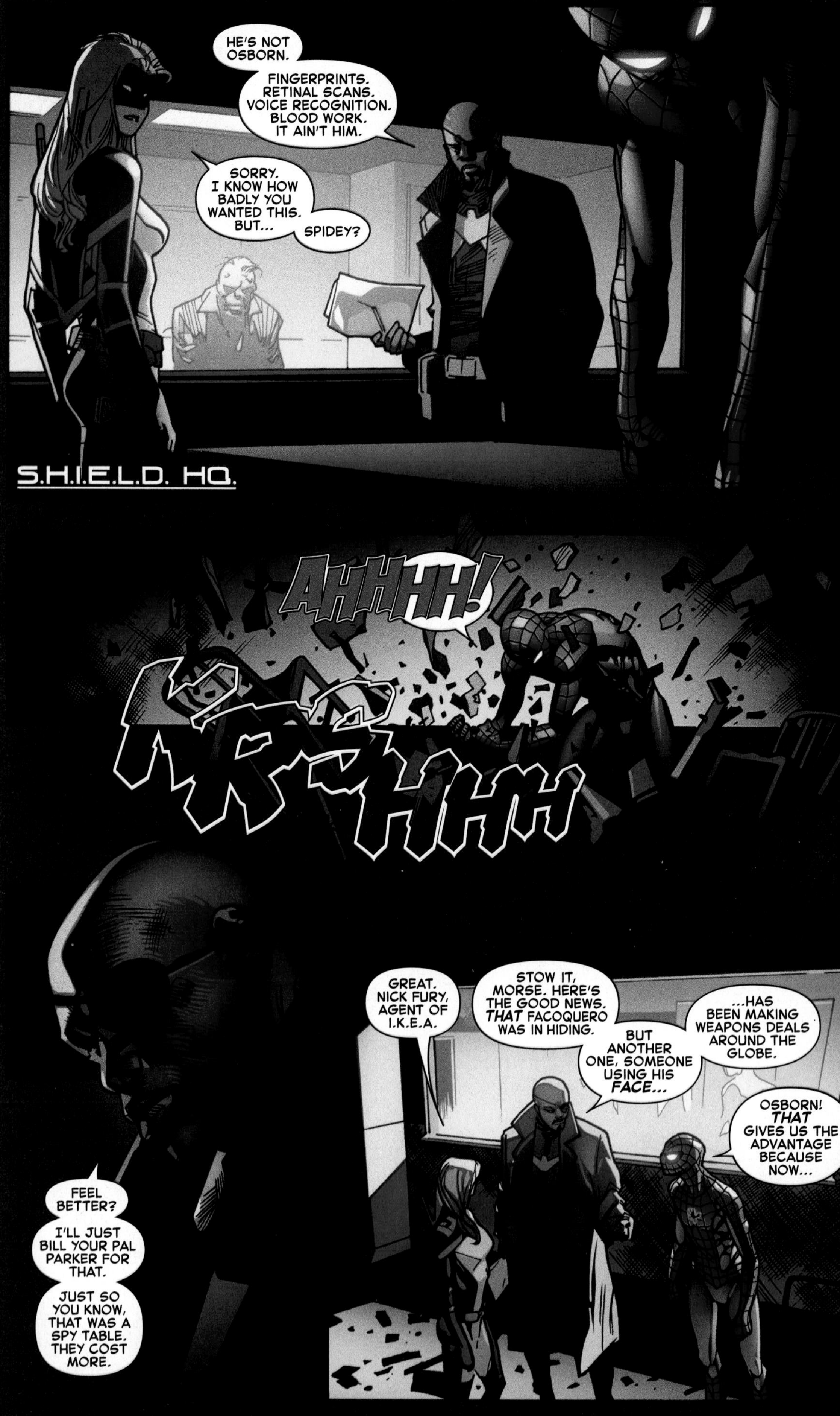
S.H.I.E.L.D. HQ.
HE'S NOT OSBORN.
FINGERPRINTS. RETINAL SCANS. VOICE RECOGNITION. BLOOD WORK. IT AIN'T HIM.
SORRY. I KNOW HOW BADLY YOU WANTED THIS. BUT...
SPIDEY?
AHHHH!
KRRSHHH
FEEL BETTER?
I'LL JUST BILL YOUR PAL PARKER FOR THAT.
JUST SO YOU KNOW, THAT WAS A SPY TABLE. THEY COST MORE.
GREAT. NICK FURY, AGENT OF I.K.E.A.
STOW IT, MORSE. HERE'S THE GOOD NEWS. *THAT* FACOQUERO WAS IN HIDING.
BUT ANOTHER ONE, SOMEONE USING HIS *FACE*...
...HAS BEEN MAKING WEAPONS DEALS AROUND THE GLOBE.
OSBORN! *THAT* GIVES US THE ADVANTAGE BECAUSE NOW...

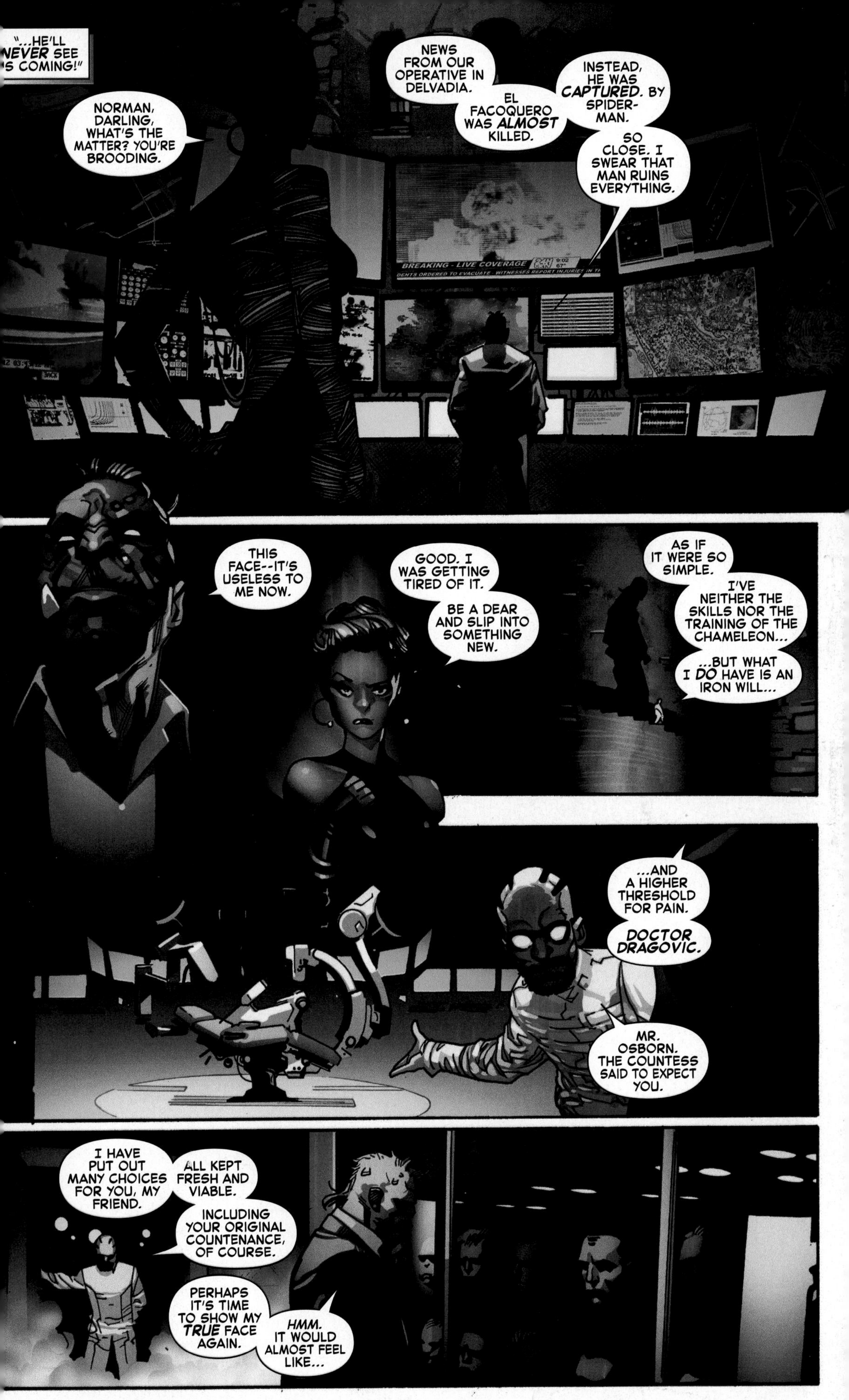

"...HE'LL NEVER SEE S COMING!"
NORMAN, DARLING, WHAT'S THE MATTER? YOU'RE BROODING.
NEWS FROM OUR OPERATIVE IN DELVADIA.
EL FACOQUERO WAS ALMOST KILLED.
INSTEAD, HE WAS CAPTURED. BY SPIDER-MAN.
SO CLOSE. I SWEAR THAT MAN RUINS EVERYTHING.
BREAKING - LIVE COVERAGE
THIS FACE--IT'S USELESS TO ME NOW.
GOOD. I WAS GETTING TIRED OF IT.
BE A DEAR AND SLIP INTO SOMETHING NEW.
AS IF IT WERE SO SIMPLE.
I'VE NEITHER THE SKILLS NOR THE TRAINING OF THE CHAMELEON...
...BUT WHAT I DO HAVE IS AN IRON WILL...
...AND A HIGHER THRESHOLD FOR PAIN.
DOCTOR DRAGOVIC.
MR. OSBORN. THE COUNTESS SAID TO EXPECT YOU.
I HAVE PUT OUT MANY CHOICES FOR YOU, MY FRIEND.
ALL KEPT FRESH AND VIABLE.
INCLUDING YOUR ORIGINAL COUNTENANCE, OF COURSE.
PERHAPS IT'S TIME TO SHOW MY TRUE FACE AGAIN.
HMM. IT WOULD ALMOST FEEL LIKE...

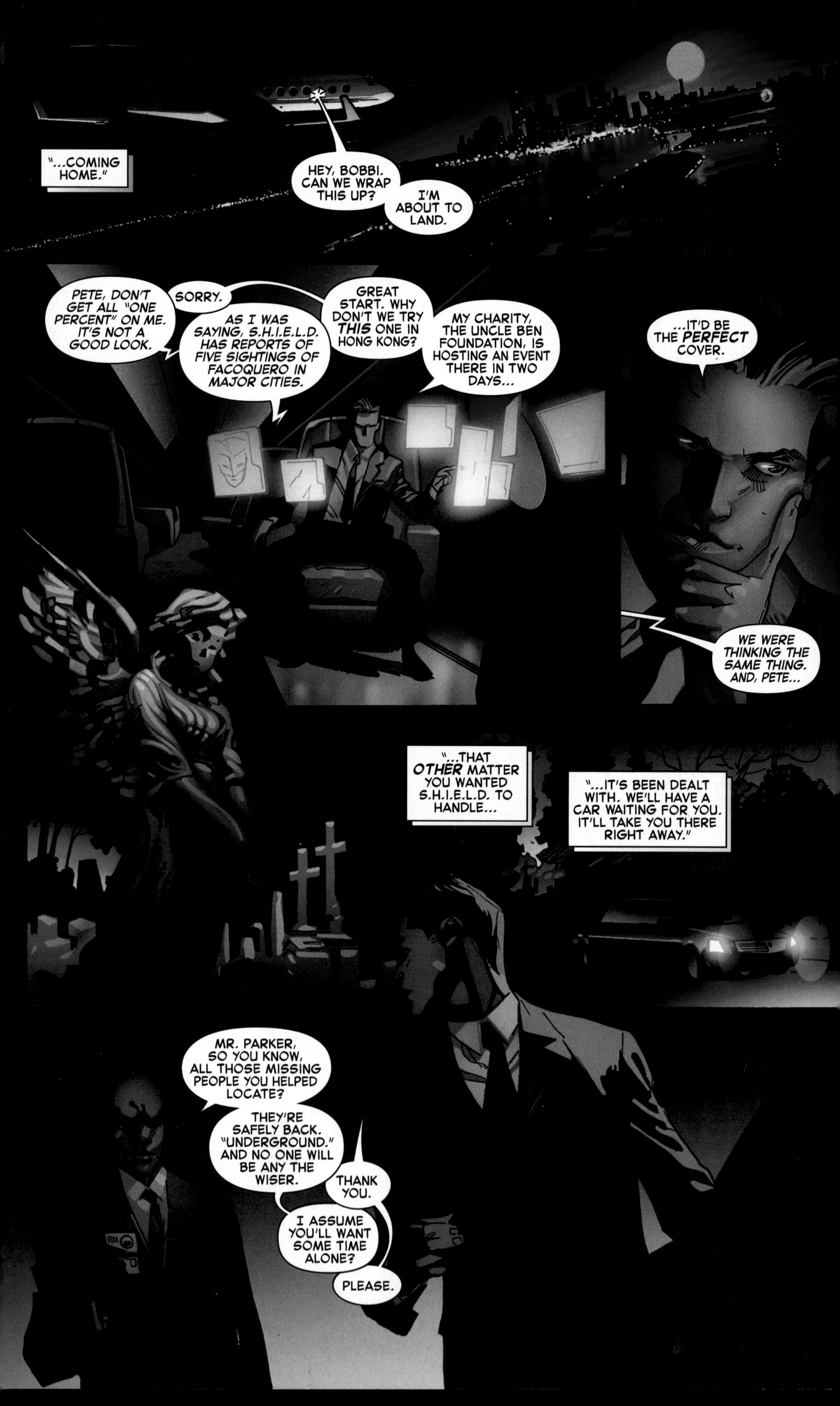
"...COMING HOME."
HEY, BOBBI. CAN WE WRAP THIS UP?
I'M ABOUT TO LAND.
PETE, DON'T GET ALL "ONE PERCENT" ON ME. IT'S NOT A GOOD LOOK.
SORRY.
AS I WAS SAYING, S.H.I.E.L.D. HAS REPORTS OF FIVE SIGHTINGS OF FACOQUERO IN MAJOR CITIES.
GREAT START. WHY DON'T WE TRY THIS ONE IN HONG KONG?
MY CHARITY, THE UNCLE BEN FOUNDATION, IS HOSTING AN EVENT THERE IN TWO DAYS...
...IT'D BE THE PERFECT COVER.
WE WERE THINKING THE SAME THING. AND, PETE...
"...THAT OTHER MATTER YOU WANTED S.H.I.E.L.D. TO HANDLE...
"...IT'S BEEN DEALT WITH. WE'LL HAVE A CAR WAITING FOR YOU. IT'LL TAKE YOU THERE RIGHT AWAY."
MR. PARKER, SO YOU KNOW, ALL THOSE MISSING PEOPLE YOU HELPED LOCATE?
THEY'RE SAFELY BACK. "UNDERGROUND." AND NO ONE WILL BE ANY THE WISER.
THANK YOU.
I ASSUME YOU'LL WANT SOME TIME ALONE?
PLEASE.

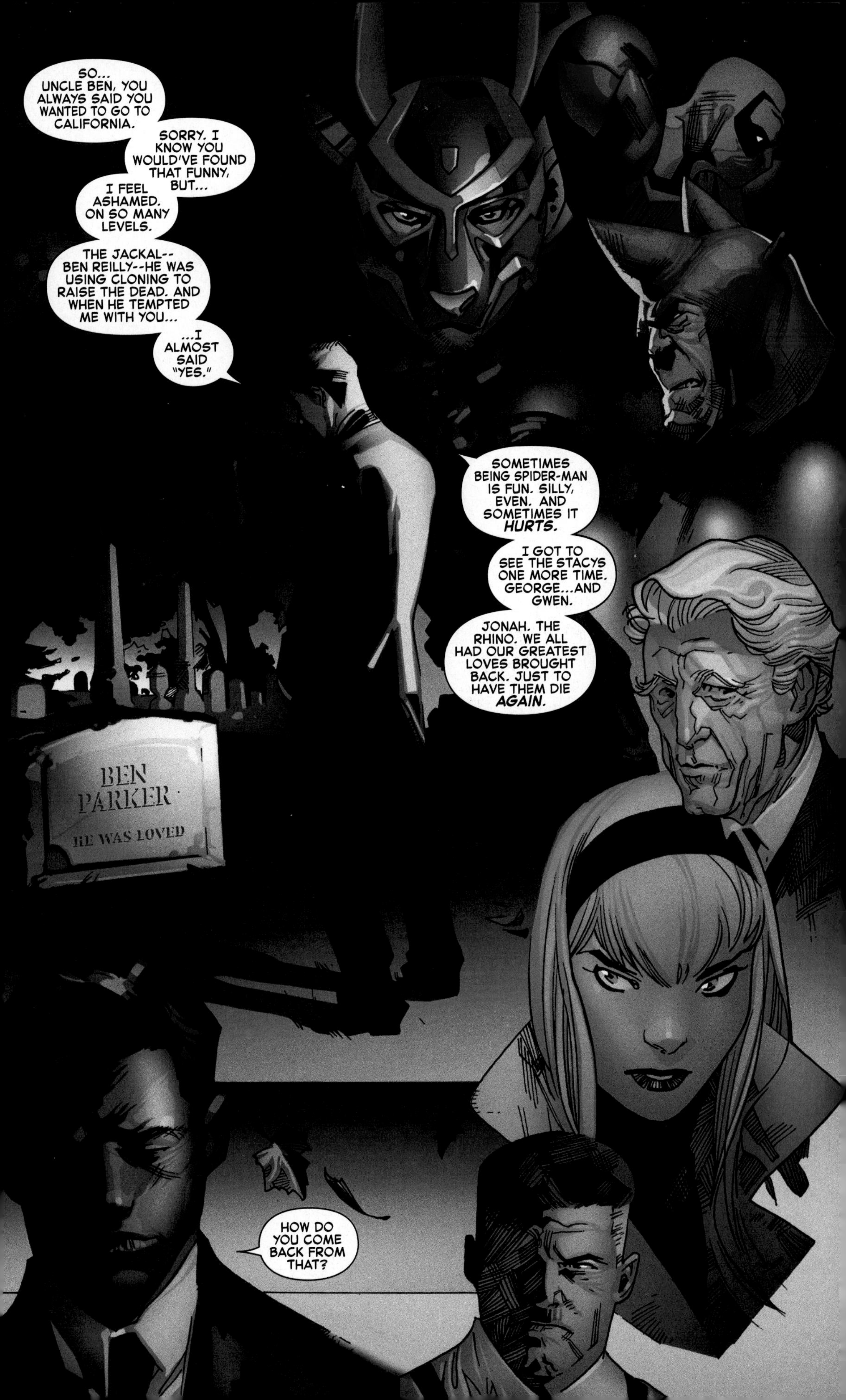
SO... UNCLE BEN, YOU ALWAYS SAID YOU WANTED TO GO TO CALIFORNIA.
SORRY. I KNOW YOU WOULD'VE FOUND THAT FUNNY, BUT...
I FEEL ASHAMED. ON SO MANY LEVELS.
THE JACKAL-- BEN REILLY--HE WAS USING CLONING TO RAISE THE DEAD. AND WHEN HE TEMPTED ME WITH YOU...
...I ALMOST SAID "YES."
SOMETIMES BEING SPIDER-MAN IS FUN. SILLY, EVEN. AND SOMETIMES IT *HURTS.*
I GOT TO SEE THE STACYS ONE MORE TIME. GEORGE...AND GWEN.
JONAH. THE RHINO. WE ALL HAD OUR GREATEST LOVES BROUGHT BACK. JUST TO HAVE THEM DIE *AGAIN.*
BEN PARKER
HE WAS LOVED
HOW DO YOU COME BACK FROM THAT?

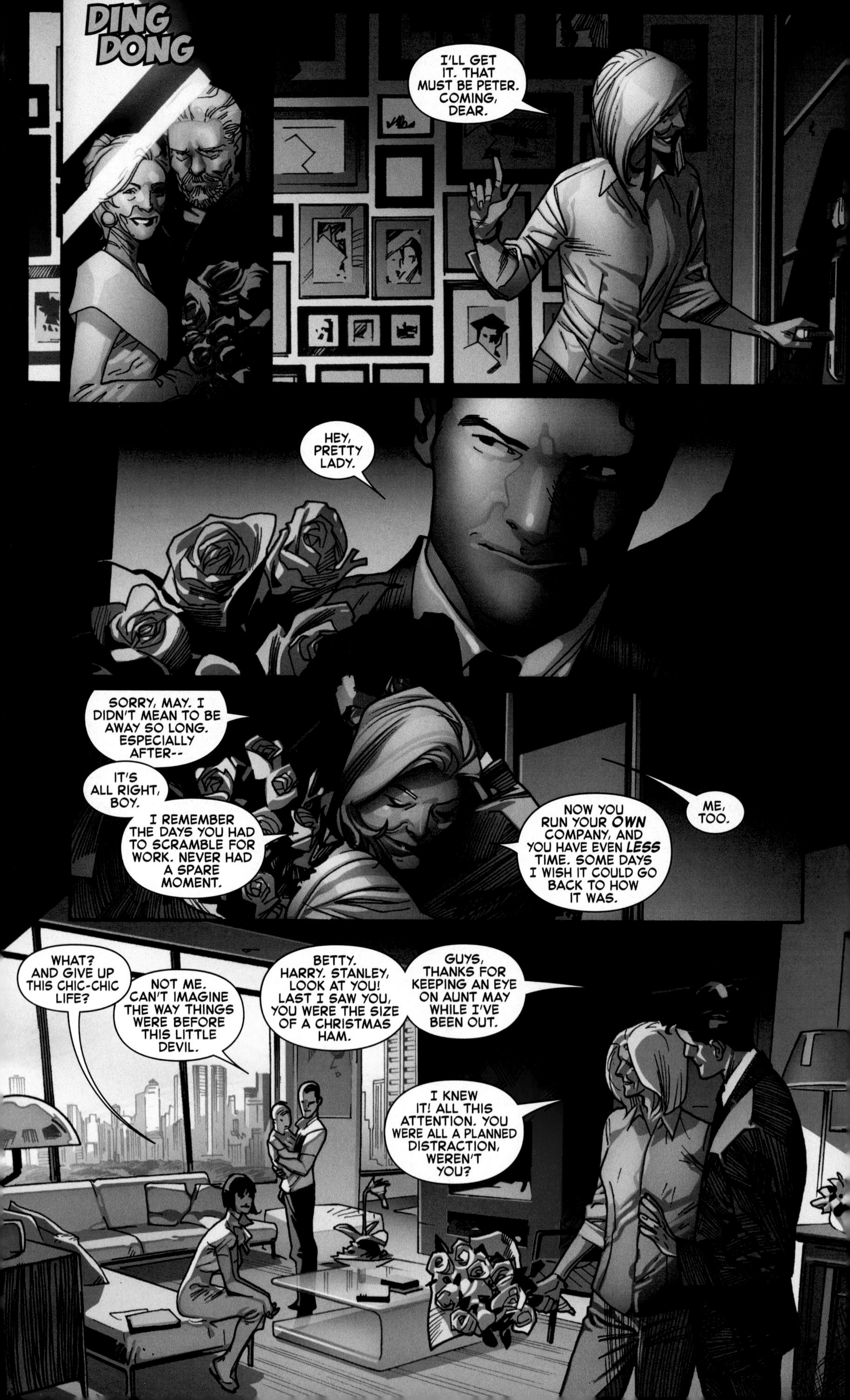

DING DONG
I'LL GET IT. THAT MUST BE PETER. COMING, DEAR.
HEY, PRETTY LADY.
SORRY, MAY. I DIDN'T MEAN TO BE AWAY SO LONG. ESPECIALLY AFTER--
IT'S ALL RIGHT, BOY.
I REMEMBER THE DAYS YOU HAD TO SCRAMBLE FOR WORK. NEVER HAD A SPARE MOMENT.
NOW YOU RUN YOUR OWN COMPANY, AND YOU HAVE EVEN LESS TIME. SOME DAYS I WISH IT COULD GO BACK TO HOW IT WAS.
ME, TOO.
WHAT? AND GIVE UP THIS CHIC-CHIC LIFE?
NOT ME. CAN'T IMAGINE THE WAY THINGS WERE BEFORE THIS LITTLE DEVIL.
BETTY. HARRY. STANLEY, LOOK AT YOU! LAST I SAW YOU, YOU WERE THE SIZE OF A CHRISTMAS HAM.
GUYS, THANKS FOR KEEPING AN EYE ON AUNT MAY WHILE I'VE BEEN OUT.
I KNEW IT! ALL THIS ATTENTION. YOU WERE ALL A PLANNED DISTRACTION, WEREN'T YOU?

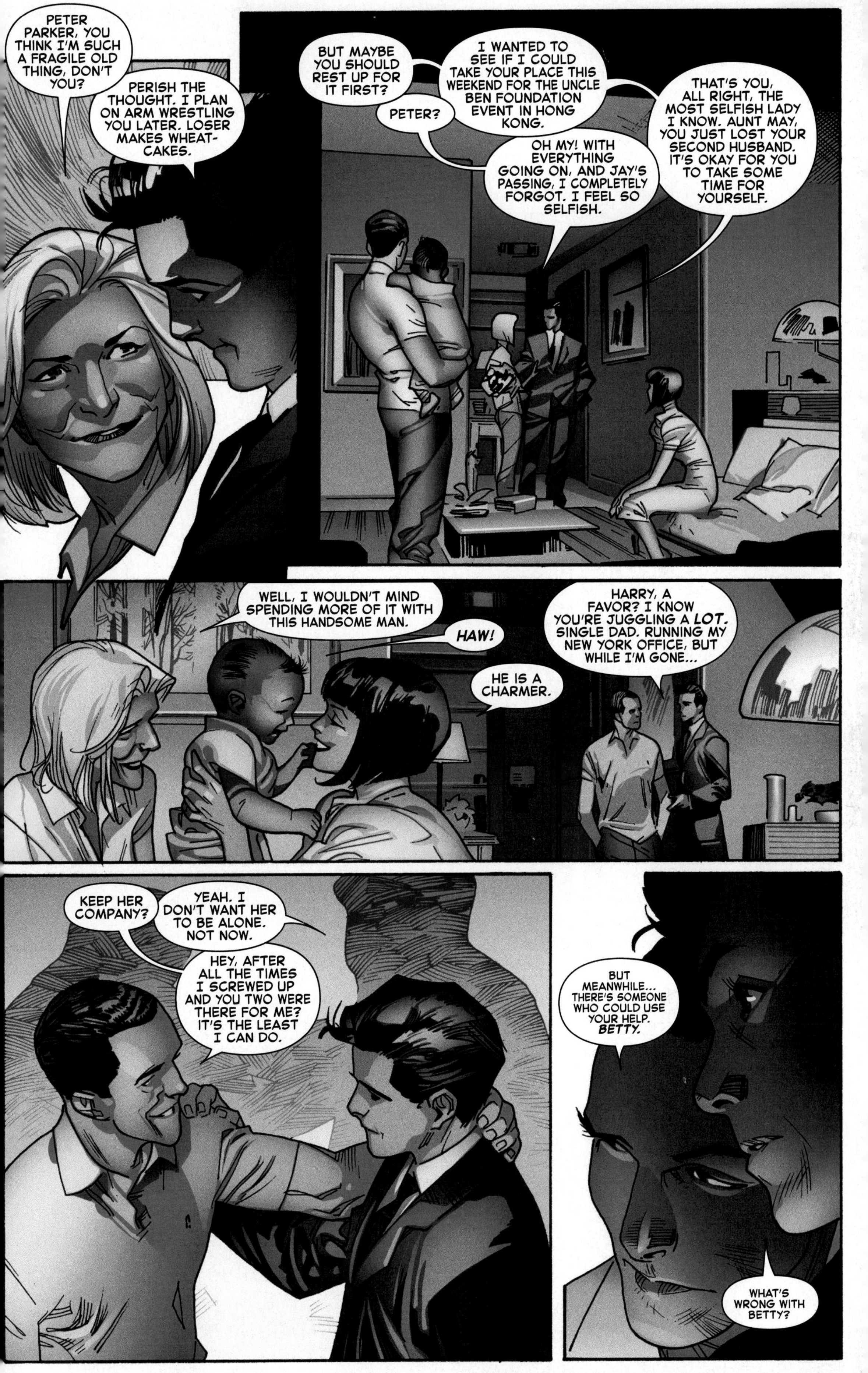

PETER PARKER, YOU THINK I'M SUCH A FRAGILE OLD THING, DON'T YOU?
PERISH THE THOUGHT. I PLAN ON ARM WRESTLING YOU LATER. LOSER MAKES WHEAT-CAKES.
BUT MAYBE YOU SHOULD REST UP FOR IT FIRST?
I WANTED TO SEE IF I COULD TAKE YOUR PLACE THIS WEEKEND FOR THE UNCLE BEN FOUNDATION EVENT IN HONG KONG.
PETER?
OH MY! WITH EVERYTHING GOING ON, AND JAY'S PASSING, I COMPLETELY FORGOT. I FEEL SO SELFISH.
THAT'S YOU, ALL RIGHT, THE MOST SELFISH LADY I KNOW. AUNT MAY, YOU JUST LOST YOUR SECOND HUSBAND. IT'S OKAY FOR YOU TO TAKE SOME TIME FOR YOURSELF.
WELL, I WOULDN'T MIND SPENDING MORE OF IT WITH THIS HANDSOME MAN.
HAW!
HE IS A CHARMER.
HARRY, A FAVOR? I KNOW YOU'RE JUGGLING A LOT. SINGLE DAD. RUNNING MY NEW YORK OFFICE, BUT WHILE I'M GONE...
KEEP HER COMPANY?
YEAH. I DON'T WANT HER TO BE ALONE. NOT NOW.
HEY, AFTER ALL THE TIMES I SCREWED UP AND YOU TWO WERE THERE FOR ME? IT'S THE LEAST I CAN DO.
BUT MEANWHILE... THERE'S SOMEONE WHO COULD USE YOUR HELP. BETTY.
WHAT'S WRONG WITH BETTY?

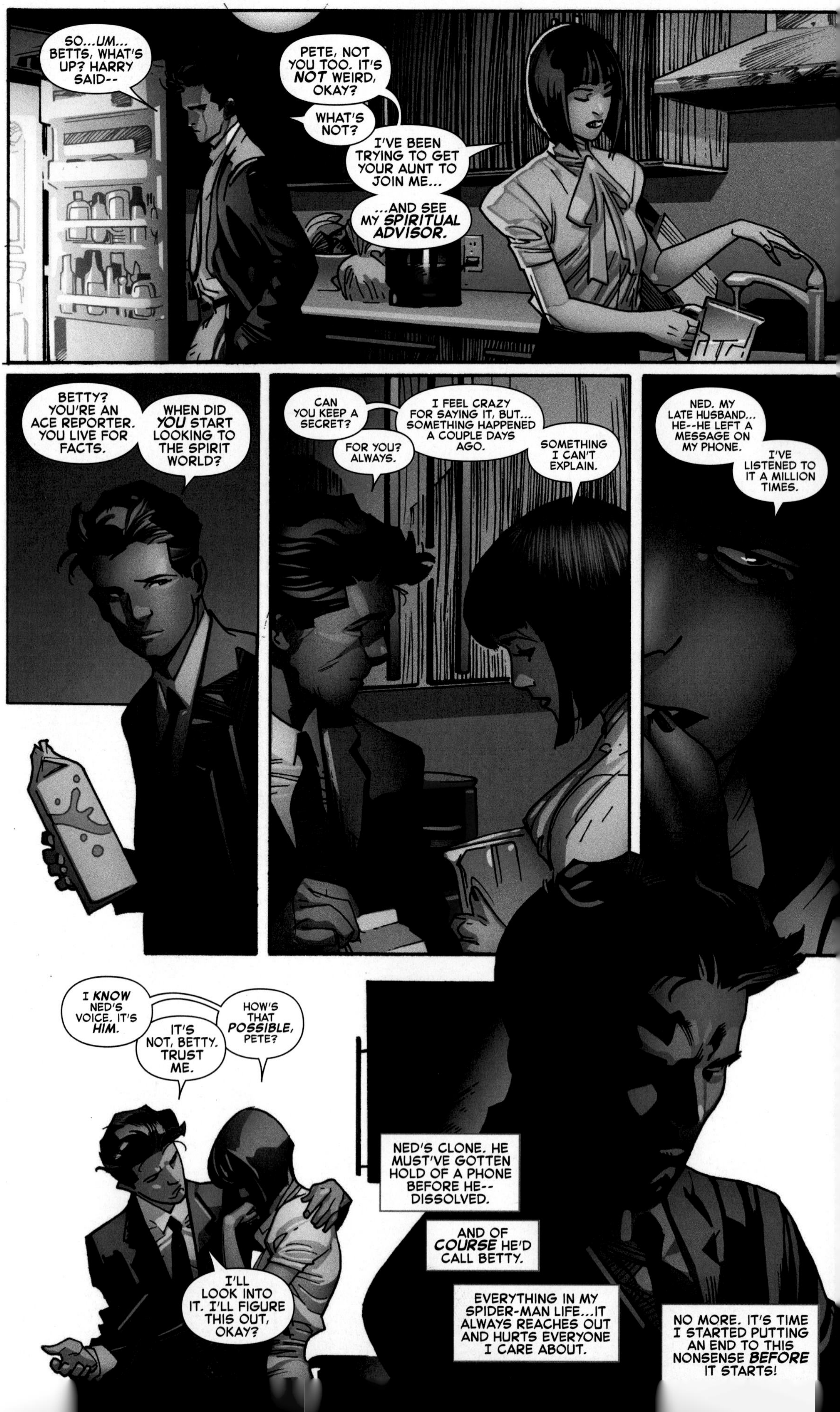

SO...UM... BETTS, WHAT'S UP? HARRY SAID--
PETE, NOT YOU TOO. IT'S NOT WEIRD, OKAY?
WHAT'S NOT?
I'VE BEEN TRYING TO GET YOUR AUNT TO JOIN ME...
...AND SEE MY SPIRITUAL ADVISOR.
BETTY? YOU'RE AN ACE REPORTER. YOU LIVE FOR FACTS.
WHEN DID YOU START LOOKING TO THE SPIRIT WORLD?
CAN YOU KEEP A SECRET?
FOR YOU? ALWAYS.
I FEEL CRAZY FOR SAYING IT, BUT... SOMETHING HAPPENED A COUPLE DAYS AGO.
SOMETHING I CAN'T EXPLAIN.
NED. MY LATE HUSBAND... HE--HE LEFT A MESSAGE ON MY PHONE.
I'VE LISTENED TO IT A MILLION TIMES.
I KNOW NED'S VOICE. IT'S HIM.
HOW'S THAT POSSIBLE, PETE?
IT'S NOT, BETTY. TRUST ME.
I'LL LOOK INTO IT. I'LL FIGURE THIS OUT, OKAY?
NED'S CLONE. HE MUST'VE GOTTEN HOLD OF A PHONE BEFORE HE--DISSOLVED.
AND OF COURSE HE'D CALL BETTY.
EVERYTHING IN MY SPIDER-MAN LIFE...IT ALWAYS REACHES OUT AND HURTS EVERYONE I CARE ABOUT.
NO MORE. IT'S TIME I STARTED PUTTING AN END TO THIS NONSENSE BEFORE IT STARTS!

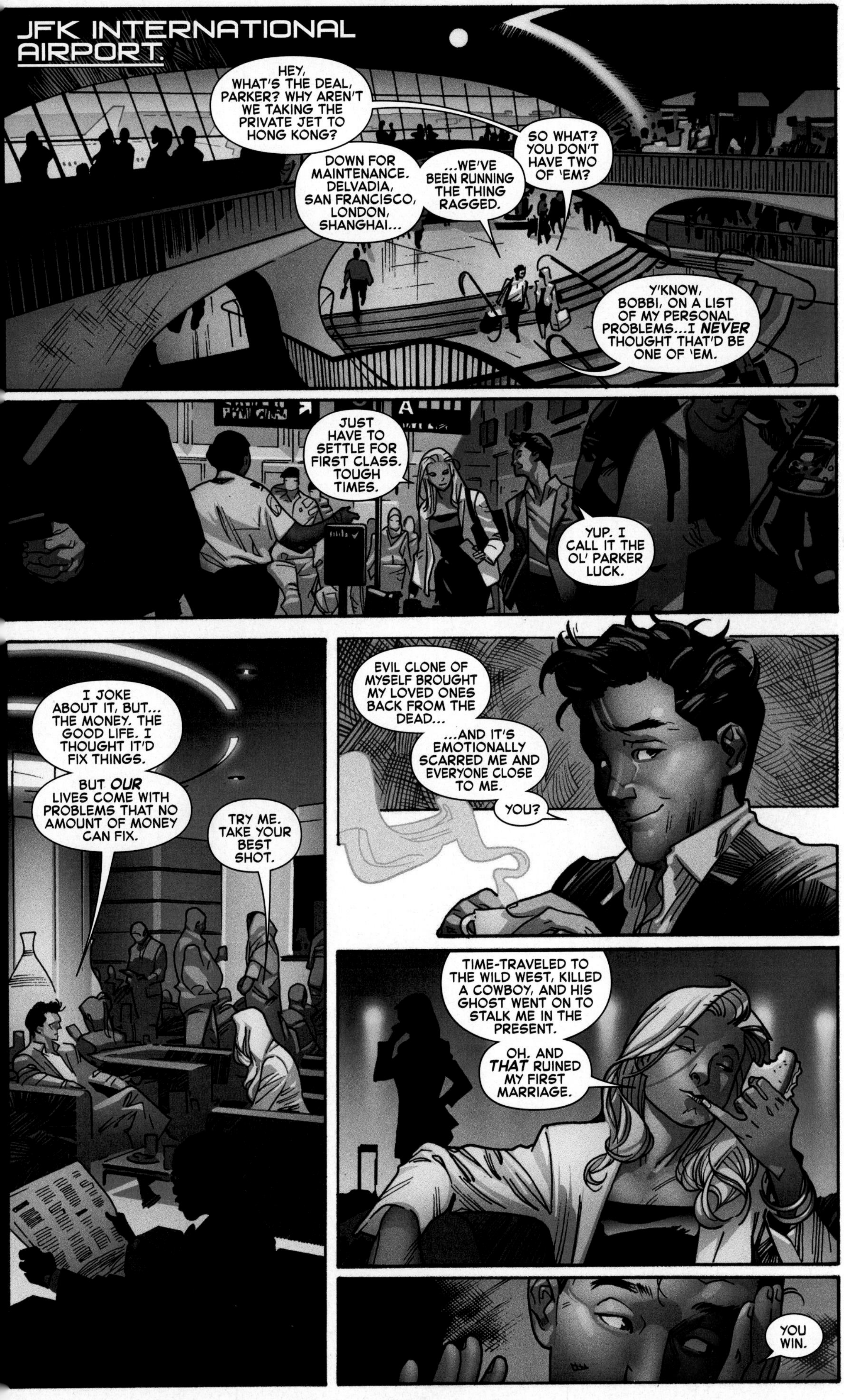
JFK INTERNATIONAL AIRPORT.
HEY, WHAT'S THE DEAL, PARKER? WHY AREN'T WE TAKING THE PRIVATE JET TO HONG KONG?
DOWN FOR MAINTENANCE. DELVADIA, SAN FRANCISCO, LONDON, SHANGHAI...
...WE'VE BEEN RUNNING THE THING RAGGED.
SO WHAT? YOU DON'T HAVE TWO OF 'EM?
Y'KNOW, BOBBI, ON A LIST OF MY PERSONAL PROBLEMS...I NEVER THOUGHT THAT'D BE ONE OF 'EM.
JUST HAVE TO SETTLE FOR FIRST CLASS. TOUGH TIMES.
YUP. I CALL IT THE OL' PARKER LUCK.
I JOKE ABOUT IT, BUT... THE MONEY. THE GOOD LIFE. I THOUGHT IT'D FIX THINGS.
BUT OUR LIVES COME WITH PROBLEMS THAT NO AMOUNT OF MONEY CAN FIX.
TRY ME. TAKE YOUR BEST SHOT.
EVIL CLONE OF MYSELF BROUGHT MY LOVED ONES BACK FROM THE DEAD...
...AND IT'S EMOTIONALLY SCARRED ME AND EVERYONE CLOSE TO ME.
YOU?
TIME-TRAVELED TO THE WILD WEST, KILLED A COWBOY, AND HIS GHOST WENT ON TO STALK ME IN THE PRESENT.
OH. AND THAT RUINED MY FIRST MARRIAGE.
YOU WIN.

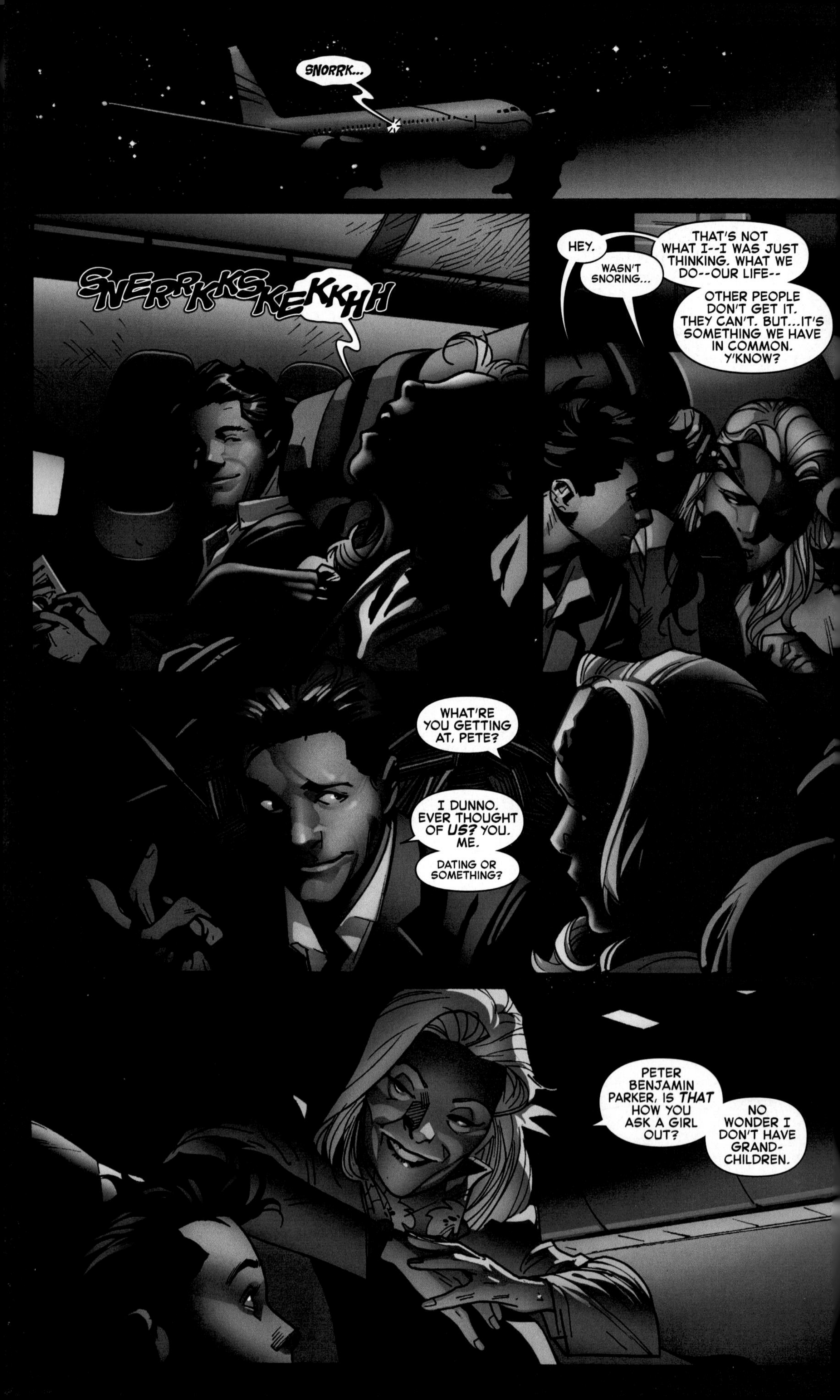
SNORRK...
SNERRKKKSKEKKHH
HEY.
WASN'T SNORING...
THAT'S NOT WHAT I--I WAS JUST THINKING. WHAT WE DO--OUR LIFE--
OTHER PEOPLE DON'T GET IT. THEY CAN'T. BUT...IT'S SOMETHING WE HAVE IN COMMON. Y'KNOW?
WHAT'RE YOU GETTING AT, PETE?
I DUNNO. EVER THOUGHT OF US? YOU. ME.
DATING OR SOMETHING?
PETER BENJAMIN PARKER, IS THAT HOW YOU ASK A GIRL OUT?
NO WONDER I DON'T HAVE GRAND-CHILDREN.

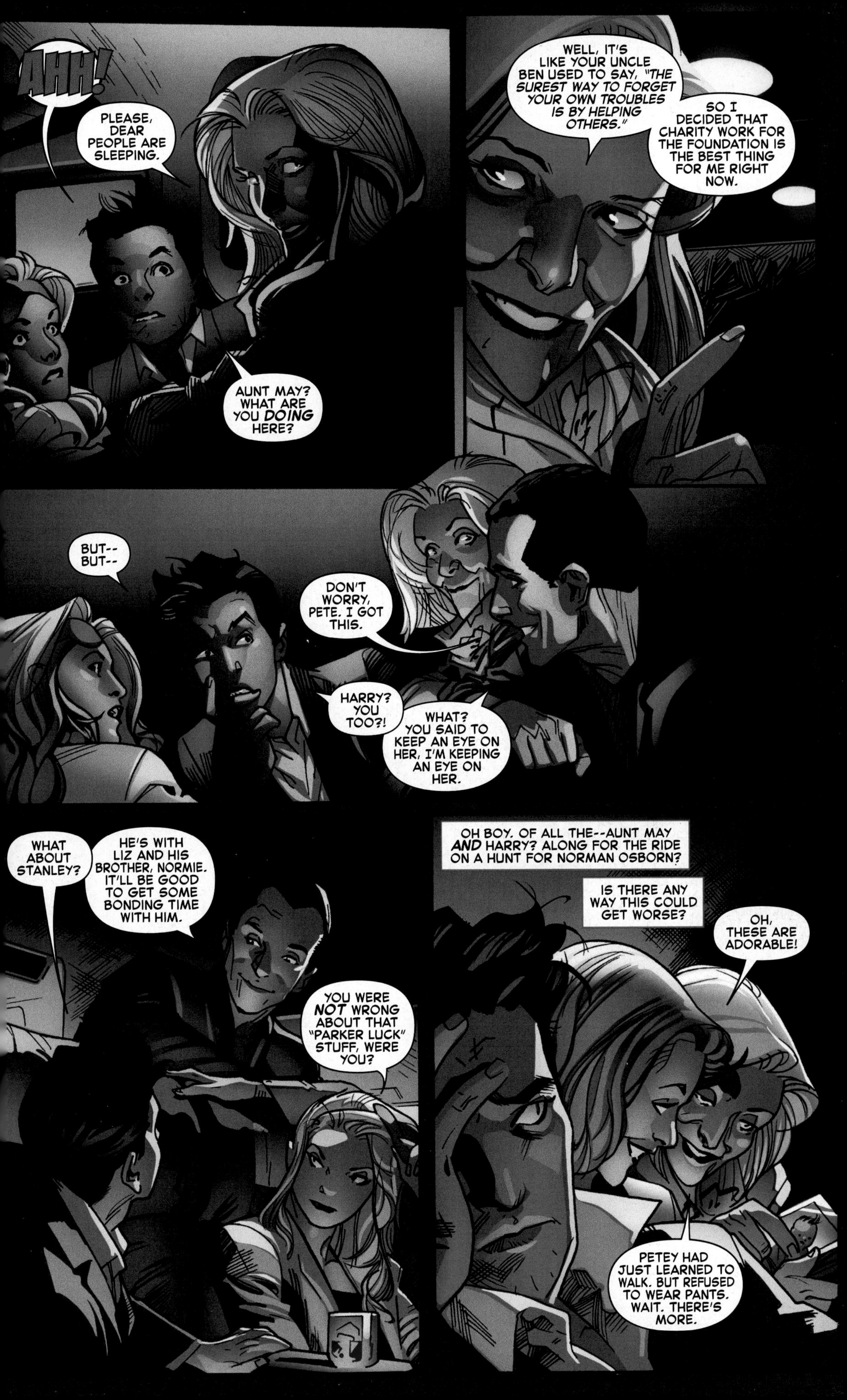
AHH!
PLEASE, DEAR PEOPLE ARE SLEEPING.
AUNT MAY? WHAT ARE YOU DOING HERE?
WELL, IT'S LIKE YOUR UNCLE BEN USED TO SAY, "THE SUREST WAY TO FORGET YOUR OWN TROUBLES IS BY HELPING OTHERS."
SO I DECIDED THAT CHARITY WORK FOR THE FOUNDATION IS THE BEST THING FOR ME RIGHT NOW.
BUT-- BUT--
DON'T WORRY, PETE. I GOT THIS.
HARRY? YOU TOO?!
WHAT? YOU SAID TO KEEP AN EYE ON HER, I'M KEEPING AN EYE ON HER.
WHAT ABOUT STANLEY?
HE'S WITH LIZ AND HIS BROTHER, NORMIE. IT'LL BE GOOD TO GET SOME BONDING TIME WITH HIM.
YOU WERE NOT WRONG ABOUT THAT "PARKER LUCK" STUFF, WERE YOU?
OH BOY. OF ALL THE--AUNT MAY AND HARRY? ALONG FOR THE RIDE ON A HUNT FOR NORMAN OSBORN?
IS THERE ANY WAY THIS COULD GET WORSE?
OH, THESE ARE ADORABLE!
PETEY HAD JUST LEARNED TO WALK. BUT REFUSED TO WEAR PANTS. WAIT. THERE'S MORE.

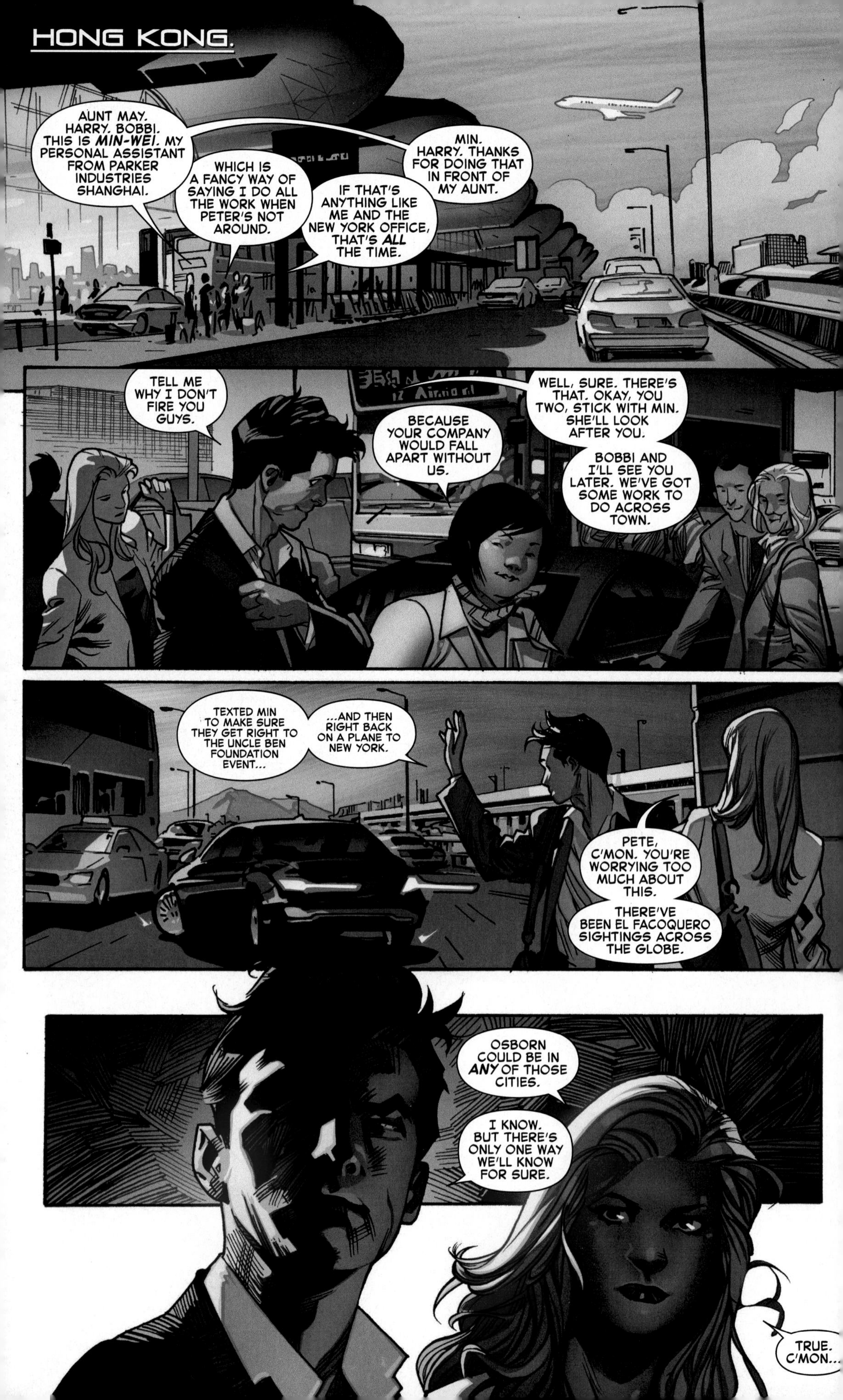
HONG KONG.
AUNT MAY. HARRY. BOBBI. THIS IS MIN-WEI. MY PERSONAL ASSISTANT FROM PARKER INDUSTRIES SHANGHAI.
WHICH IS A FANCY WAY OF SAYING I DO ALL THE WORK WHEN PETER'S NOT AROUND.
IF THAT'S ANYTHING LIKE ME AND THE NEW YORK OFFICE, THAT'S ALL THE TIME.
MIN. HARRY. THANKS FOR DOING THAT IN FRONT OF MY AUNT.
TELL ME WHY I DON'T FIRE YOU GUYS.
BECAUSE YOUR COMPANY WOULD FALL APART WITHOUT US.
WELL, SURE. THERE'S THAT. OKAY, YOU TWO, STICK WITH MIN. SHE'LL LOOK AFTER YOU.
BOBBI AND I'LL SEE YOU LATER. WE'VE GOT SOME WORK TO DO ACROSS TOWN.
TEXTED MIN TO MAKE SURE THEY GET RIGHT TO THE UNCLE BEN FOUNDATION EVENT...
...AND THEN RIGHT BACK ON A PLANE TO NEW YORK.
PETE, C'MON. YOU'RE WORRYING TOO MUCH ABOUT THIS.
THERE'VE BEEN EL FACOQUERO SIGHTINGS ACROSS THE GLOBE.
OSBORN COULD BE IN ANY OF THOSE CITIES.
I KNOW. BUT THERE'S ONLY ONE WAY WE'LL KNOW FOR SURE.
TRUE. C'MON...

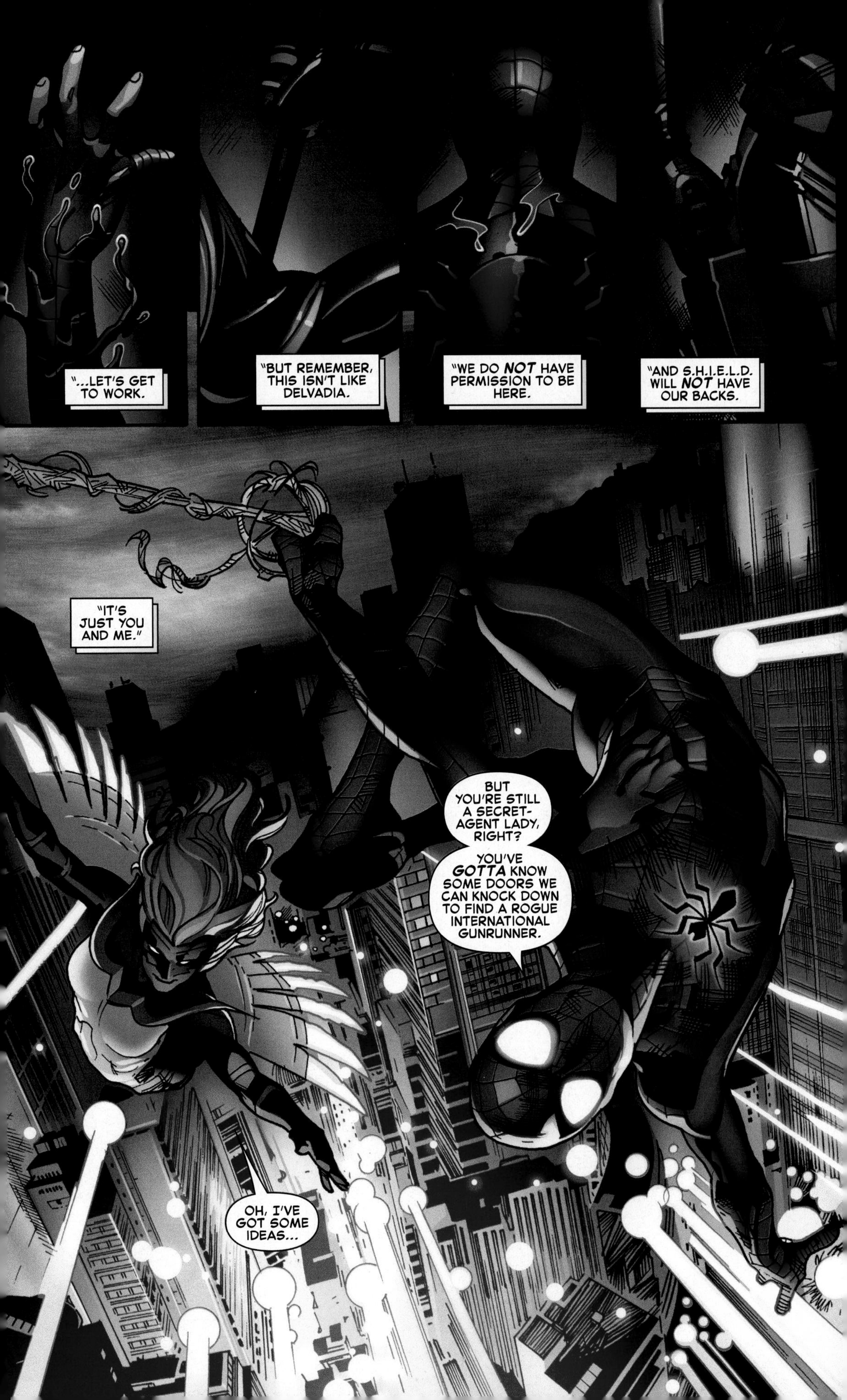
"...LET'S GET TO WORK.
"BUT REMEMBER, THIS ISN'T LIKE DELVADIA.
"WE DO NOT HAVE PERMISSION TO BE HERE.
"AND S.H.I.E.L.D. WILL NOT HAVE OUR BACKS.
"IT'S JUST YOU AND ME."
BUT YOU'RE STILL A SECRET-AGENT LADY, RIGHT?
YOU'VE GOTTA KNOW SOME DOORS WE CAN KNOCK DOWN TO FIND A ROGUE INTERNATIONAL GUNRUNNER.
OH, I'VE GOT SOME IDEAS...

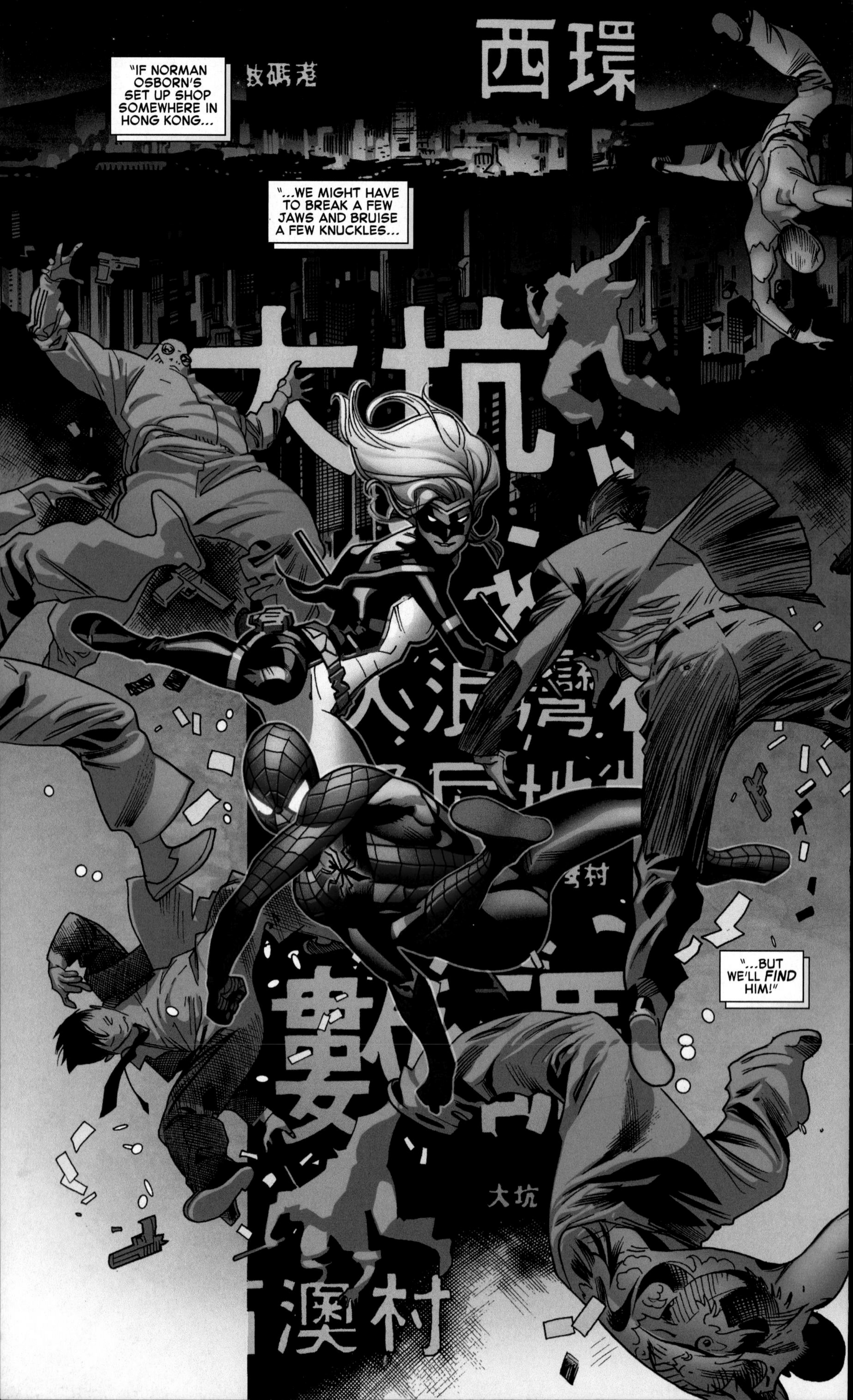
"IF NORMAN OSBORN'S SET UP SHOP SOMEWHERE IN HONG KONG...
"...WE MIGHT HAVE TO BREAK A FEW JAWS AND BRUISE A FEW KNUCKLES...
"...BUT WE'LL *FIND* HIM!"
西環
大坑
澳村

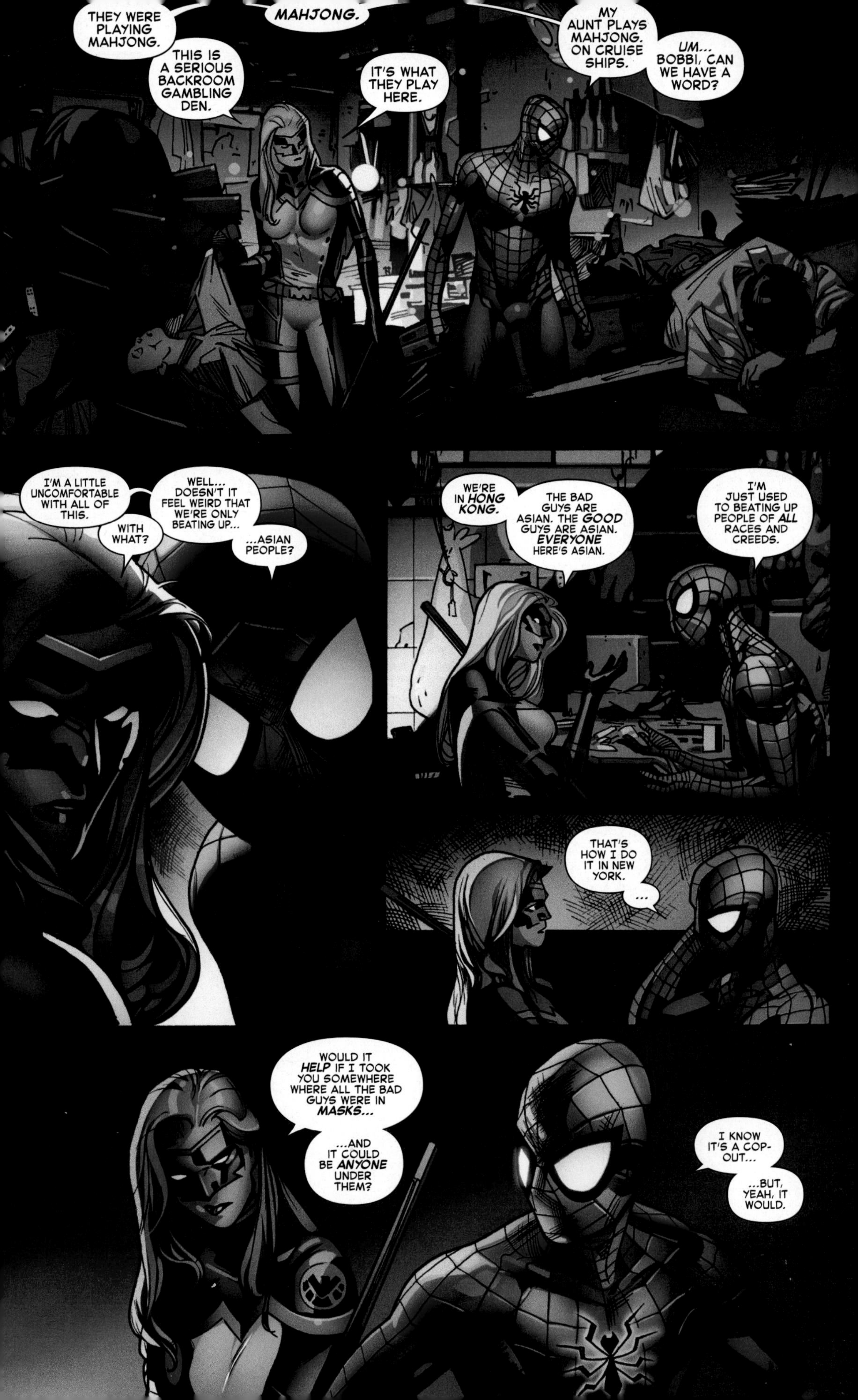
THEY WERE PLAYING MAHJONG.
MAHJONG.
MY AUNT PLAYS MAHJONG. ON CRUISE SHIPS.
THIS IS A SERIOUS BACKROOM GAMBLING DEN.
IT'S WHAT THEY PLAY HERE.
UM... BOBBI, CAN WE HAVE A WORD?
I'M A LITTLE UNCOMFORTABLE WITH ALL OF THIS.
WITH WHAT?
WELL... DOESN'T IT FEEL WEIRD THAT WE'RE ONLY BEATING UP...
...ASIAN PEOPLE?
WE'RE IN HONG KONG.
THE BAD GUYS ARE ASIAN. THE GOOD GUYS ARE ASIAN. EVERYONE HERE'S ASIAN.
I'M JUST USED TO BEATING UP PEOPLE OF ALL RACES AND CREEDS.
THAT'S HOW I DO IT IN NEW YORK.
...
WOULD IT HELP IF I TOOK YOU SOMEWHERE WHERE ALL THE BAD GUYS WERE IN MASKS...
...AND IT COULD BE ANYONE UNDER THEM?
I KNOW IT'S A COP-OUT...
...BUT, YEAH, IT WOULD.

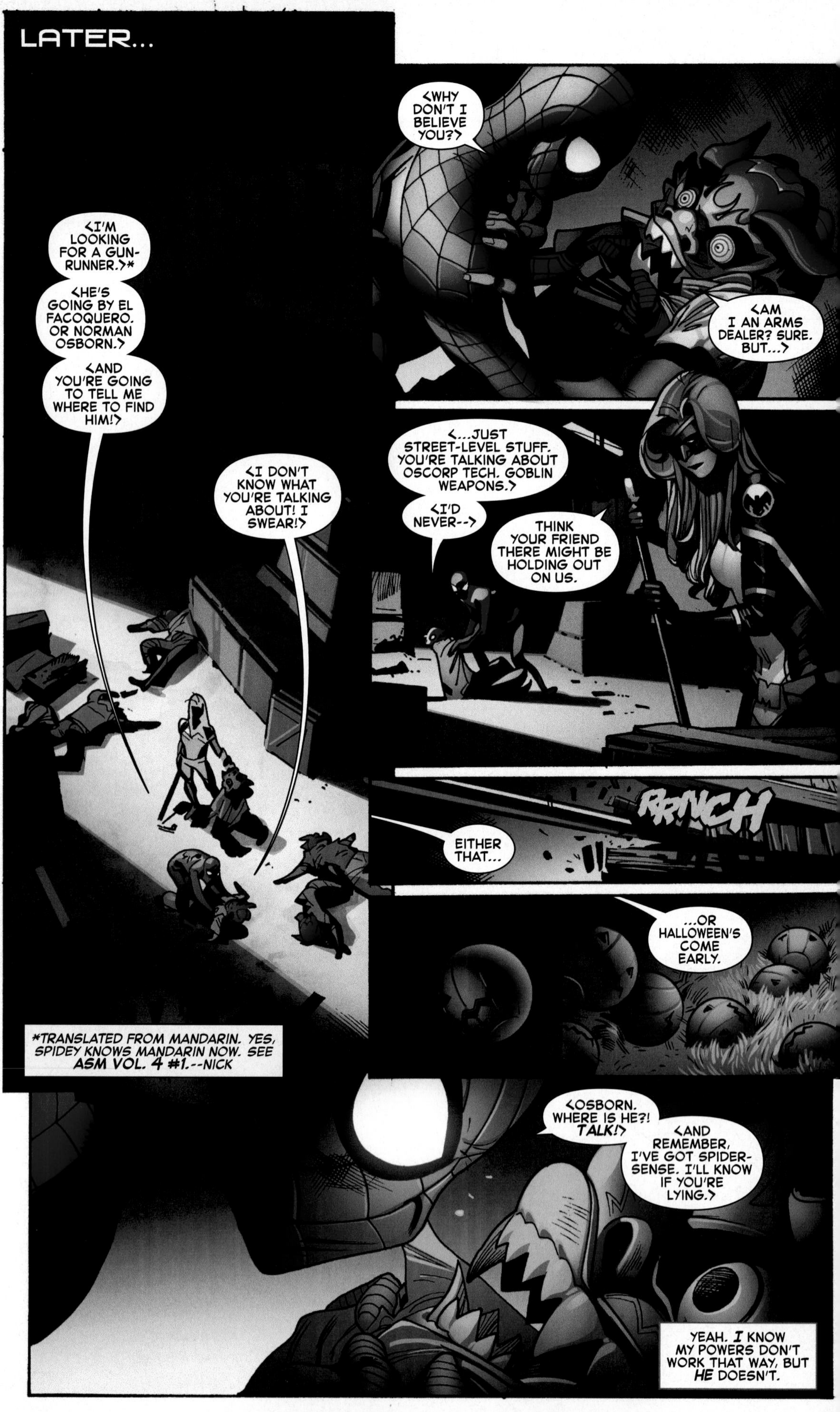
LATER...
<WHY DON'T I BELIEVE YOU?>
<AM I AN ARMS DEALER? SURE. BUT...>
<I'M LOOKING FOR A GUN-RUNNER.>*
<HE'S GOING BY EL FACOQUERO. OR NORMAN OSBORN.>
<AND YOU'RE GOING TO TELL ME WHERE TO FIND HIM!>
<I DON'T KNOW WHAT YOU'RE TALKING ABOUT! I SWEAR!>
*TRANSLATED FROM MANDARIN. YES, SPIDEY KNOWS MANDARIN NOW. SEE ASM VOL. 4 #1.--NICK
<...JUST STREET-LEVEL STUFF. YOU'RE TALKING ABOUT OSCORP TECH. GOBLIN WEAPONS.>
<I'D NEVER-->
THINK YOUR FRIEND THERE MIGHT BE HOLDING OUT ON US.
RRNCH
EITHER THAT...
...OR HALLOWEEN'S COME EARLY.
<OSBORN. WHERE IS HE?! TALK!>
<AND REMEMBER, I'VE GOT SPIDER-SENSE. I'LL KNOW IF YOU'RE LYING.>
YEAH. I KNOW MY POWERS DON'T WORK THAT WAY, BUT HE DOESN'T.

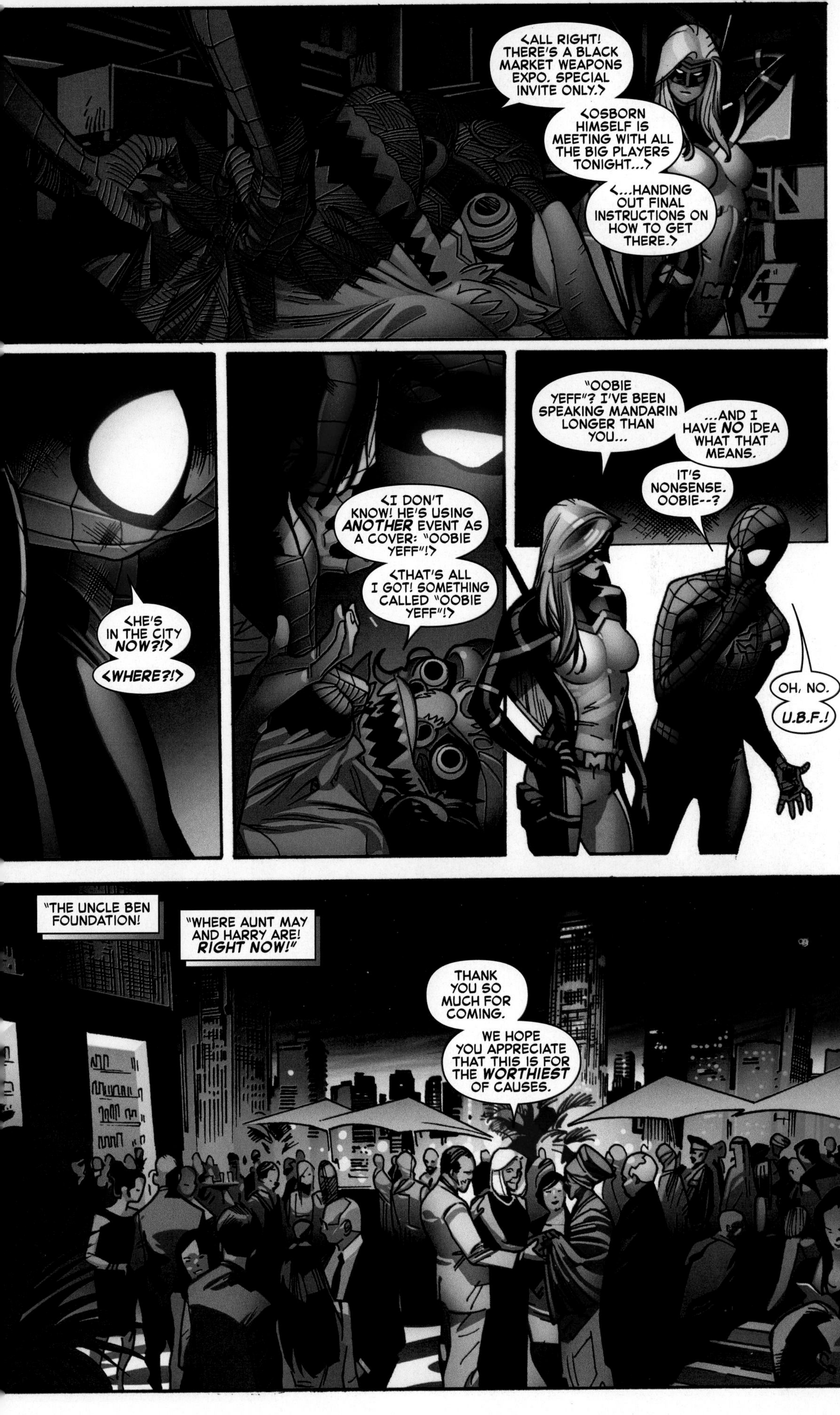

<ALL RIGHT! THERE'S A BLACK MARKET WEAPONS EXPO. SPECIAL INVITE ONLY.>
<OSBORN HIMSELF IS MEETING WITH ALL THE BIG PLAYERS TONIGHT...>
<...HANDING OUT FINAL INSTRUCTIONS ON HOW TO GET THERE.>
<HE'S IN THE CITY NOW?!>
<WHERE?!>
<I DON'T KNOW! HE'S USING ANOTHER EVENT AS A COVER: "OOBIE YEFF"!>
<THAT'S ALL I GOT! SOMETHING CALLED "OOBIE YEFF"!>
"OOBIE YEFF"? I'VE BEEN SPEAKING MANDARIN LONGER THAN YOU...
...AND I HAVE NO IDEA WHAT THAT MEANS.
IT'S NONSENSE. OOBIE--?
OH, NO.
U.B.F.!
"THE UNCLE BEN FOUNDATION!
"WHERE AUNT MAY AND HARRY ARE! RIGHT NOW!"
THANK YOU SO MUCH FOR COMING.
WE HOPE YOU APPRECIATE THAT THIS IS FOR THE WORTHIEST OF CAUSES.

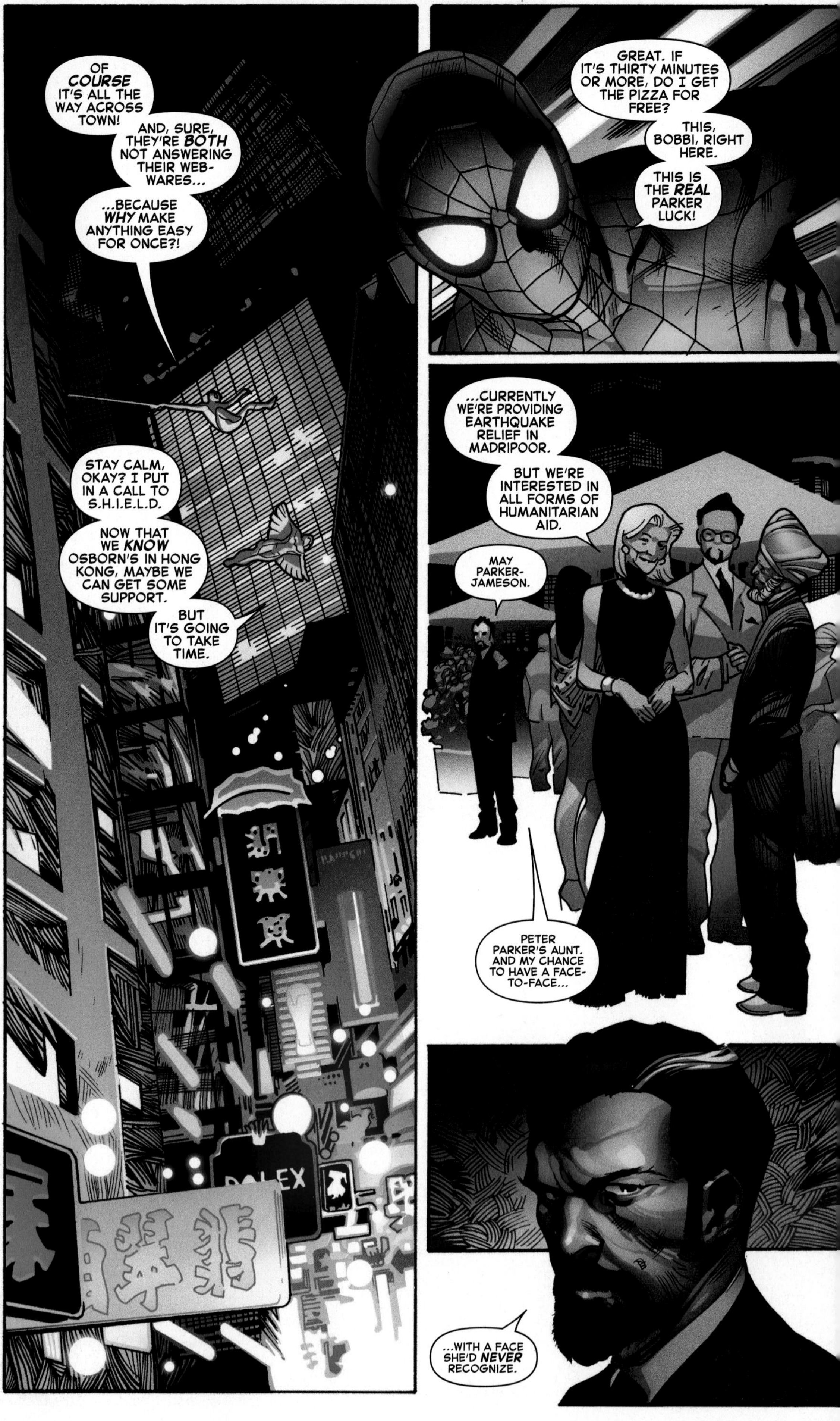
OF COURSE IT'S ALL THE WAY ACROSS TOWN!
AND, SURE, THEY'RE BOTH NOT ANSWERING THEIR WEB-WARES...
...BECAUSE WHY MAKE ANYTHING EASY FOR ONCE?!
STAY CALM, OKAY? I PUT IN A CALL TO S.H.I.E.L.D.
NOW THAT WE KNOW OSBORN'S IN HONG KONG, MAYBE WE CAN GET SOME SUPPORT.
BUT IT'S GOING TO TAKE TIME.
GREAT. IF IT'S THIRTY MINUTES OR MORE, DO I GET THE PIZZA FOR FREE?
THIS, BOBBI, RIGHT HERE.
THIS IS THE REAL PARKER LUCK!
...CURRENTLY WE'RE PROVIDING EARTHQUAKE RELIEF IN MADRIPOOR.
BUT WE'RE INTERESTED IN ALL FORMS OF HUMANITARIAN AID.
MAY PARKER-JAMESON.
PETER PARKER'S AUNT. AND MY CHANCE TO HAVE A FACE-TO-FACE...
...WITH A FACE SHE'D NEVER RECOGNIZE.

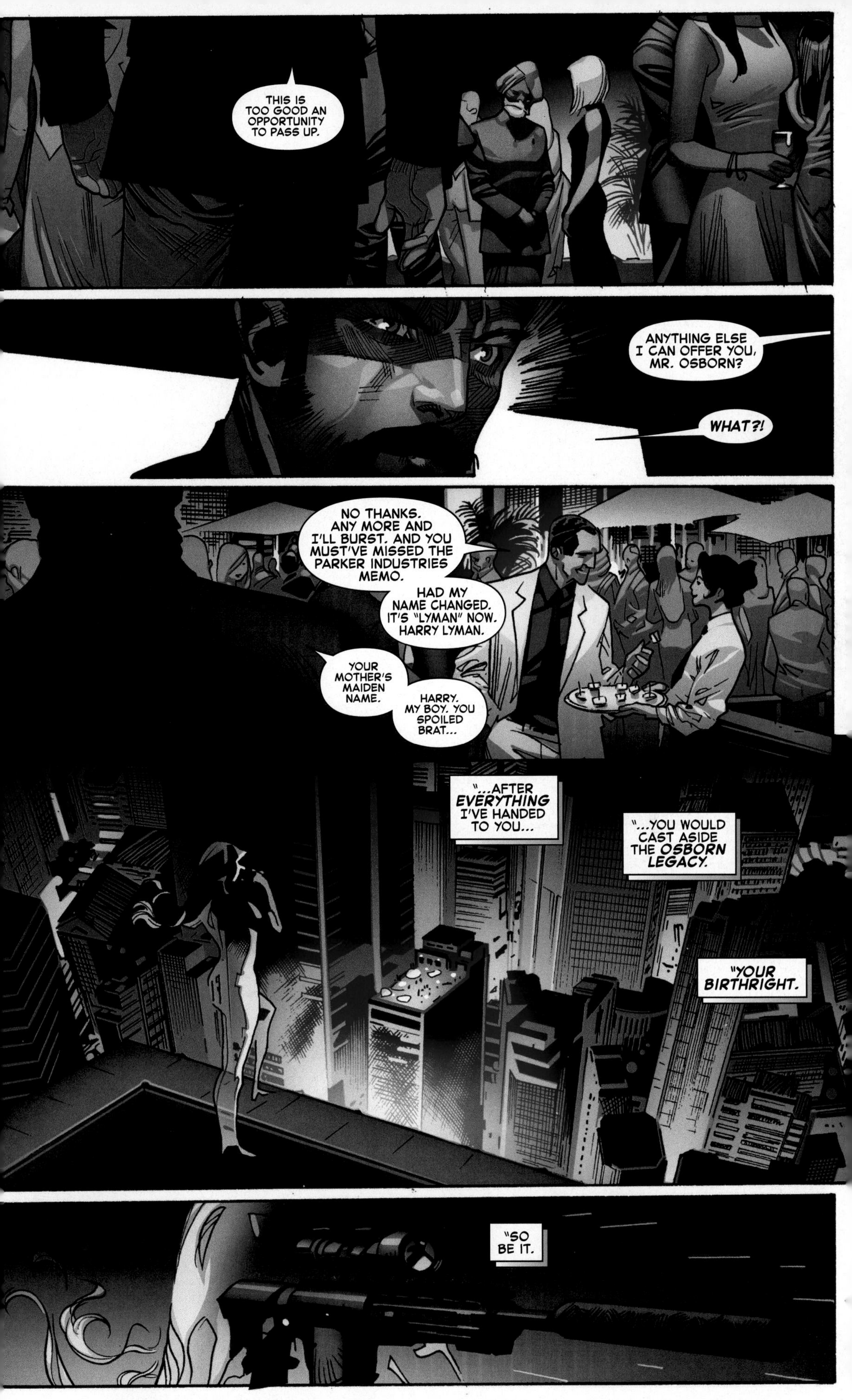

THIS IS TOO GOOD AN OPPORTUNITY TO PASS UP.
ANYTHING ELSE I CAN OFFER YOU, MR. OSBORN?
WHAT?!
NO THANKS. ANY MORE AND I'LL BURST. AND YOU MUST'VE MISSED THE PARKER INDUSTRIES MEMO.
HAD MY NAME CHANGED. IT'S "LYMAN" NOW. HARRY LYMAN.
YOUR MOTHER'S MAIDEN NAME.
HARRY. MY BOY. YOU SPOILED BRAT...
"...AFTER EVERYTHING I'VE HANDED TO YOU...
"...YOU WOULD CAST ASIDE THE OSBORN LEGACY.
"YOUR BIRTHRIGHT.
"SO BE IT.

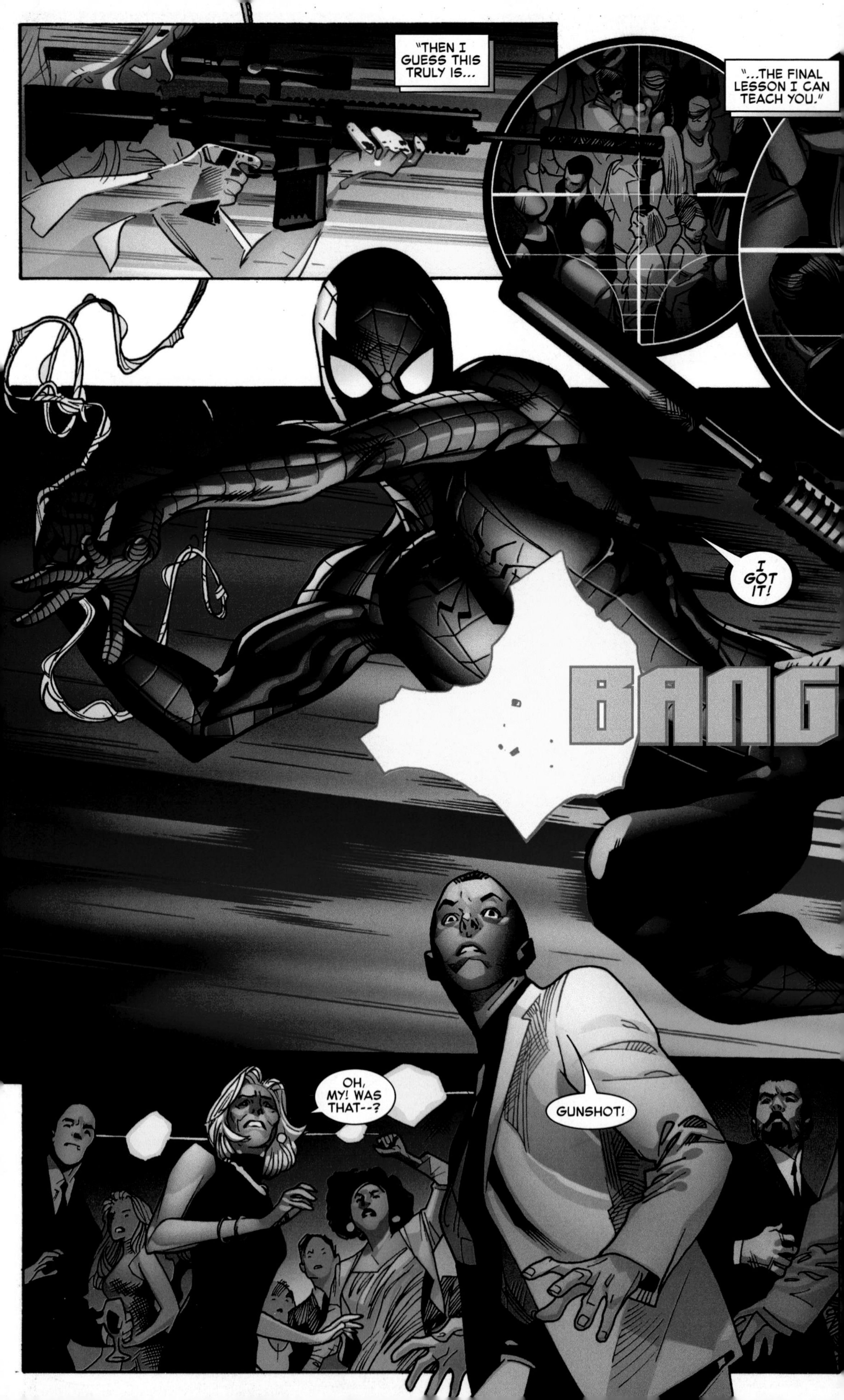
"THEN I GUESS THIS TRULY IS...
"...THE FINAL LESSON I CAN TEACH YOU."
I GOT IT!
BANG
OH, MY! WAS THAT--?
GUNSHOT!

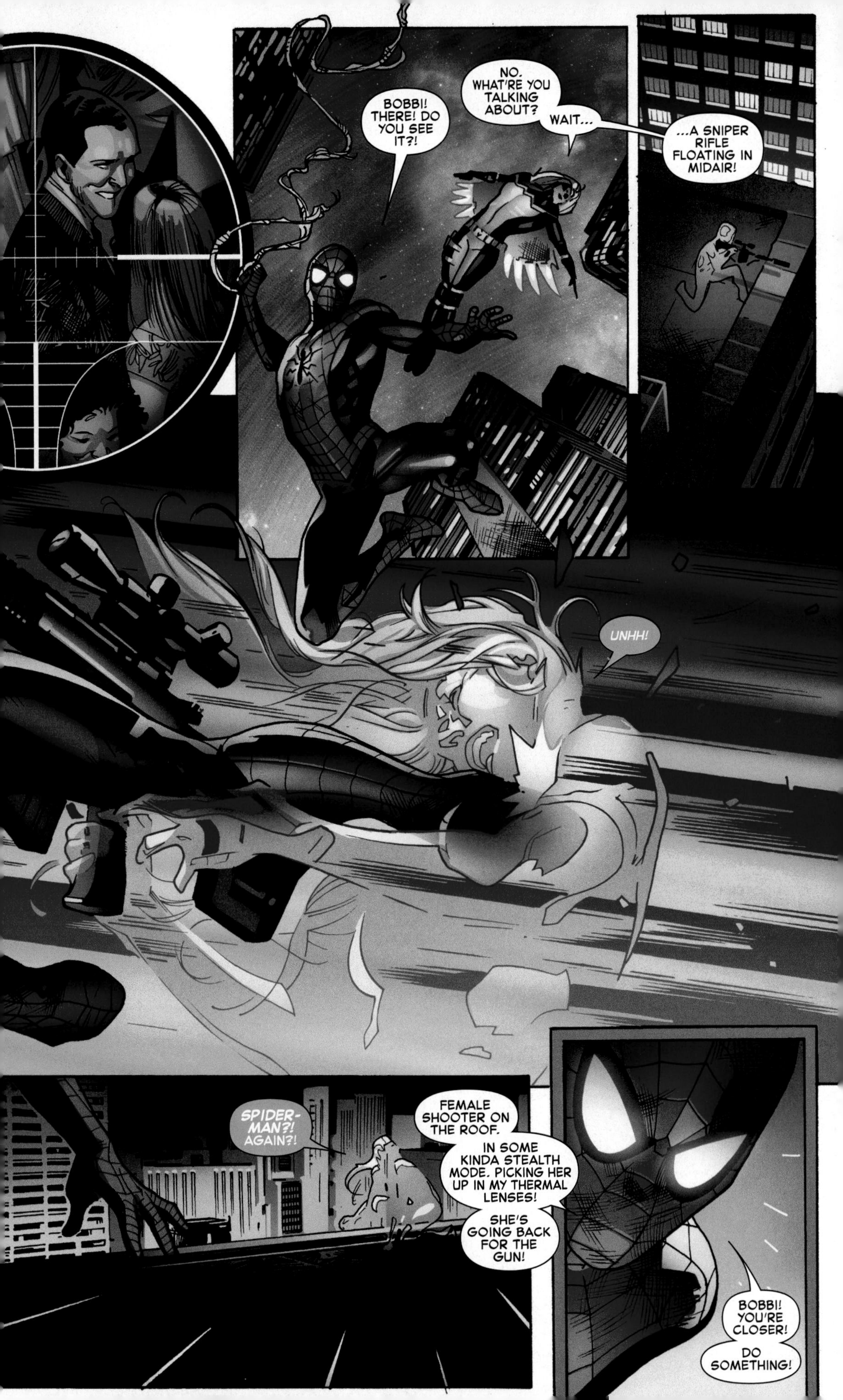

BOBBI! THERE! DO YOU SEE IT?!
NO. WHAT'RE YOU TALKING ABOUT?
WAIT...
...A SNIPER RIFLE FLOATING IN MIDAIR!
UNHH!
SPIDER-MAN?! AGAIN?!
FEMALE SHOOTER ON THE ROOF.
IN SOME KINDA STEALTH MODE. PICKING HER UP IN MY THERMAL LENSES!
SHE'S GOING BACK FOR THE GUN!
BOBBI! YOU'RE CLOSER!
DO SOMETHING!

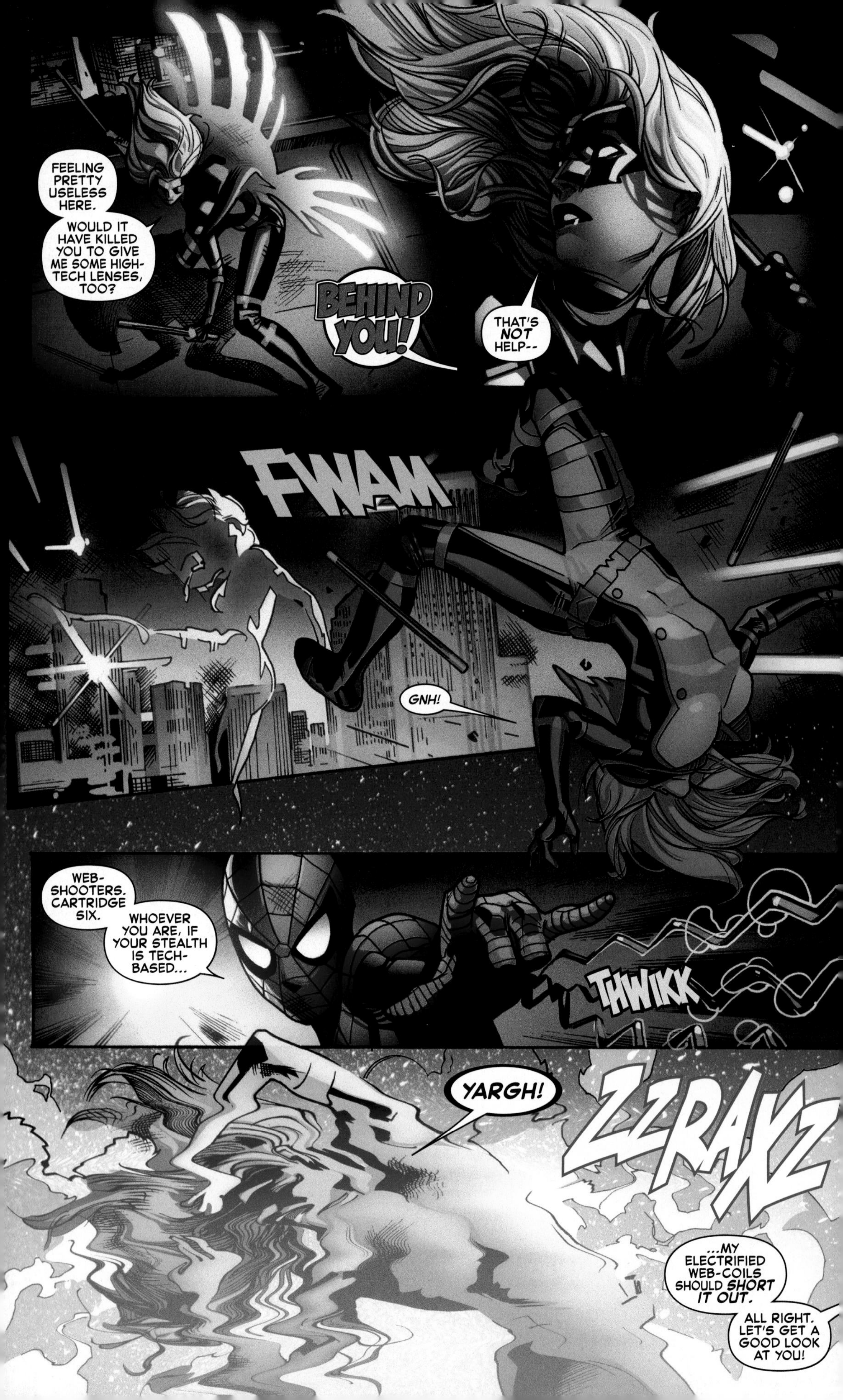

FEELING PRETTY USELESS HERE.
WOULD IT HAVE KILLED YOU TO GIVE ME SOME HIGH-TECH LENSES, TOO?
BEHIND YOU!
THAT'S NOT HELP--
FWAM
GNH!
WEB-SHOOTERS. CARTRIDGE SIX.
WHOEVER YOU ARE, IF YOUR STEALTH IS TECH-BASED...
THWIKK
YARGH!
ZZRAKZ
...MY ELECTRIFIED WEB-COILS SHOULD SHORT IT OUT.
ALL RIGHT. LET'S GET A GOOD LOOK AT YOU!

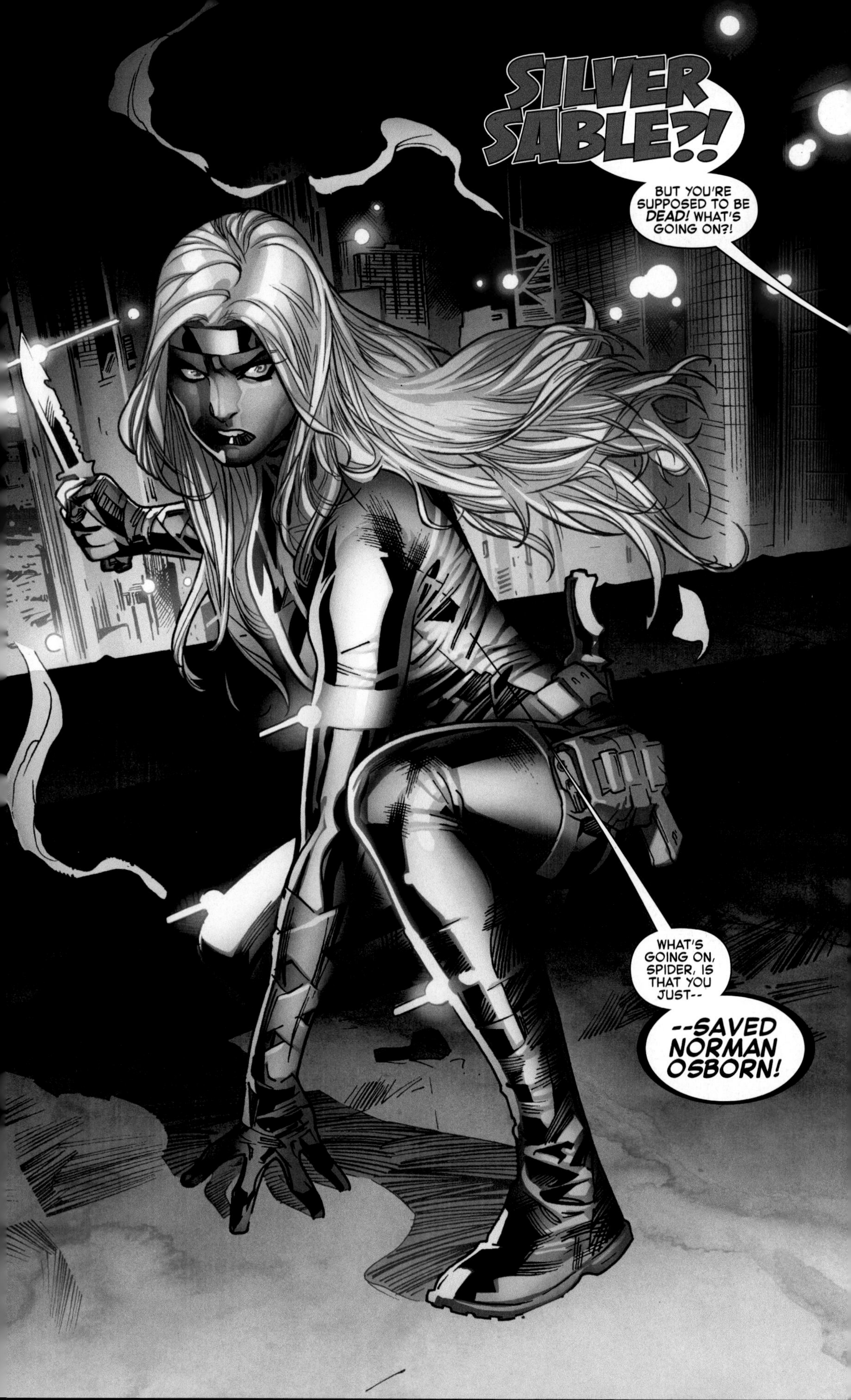
SILVER SABLE?!
BUT YOU'RE SUPPOSED TO BE DEAD! WHAT'S GOING ON?!
WHAT'S GOING ON, SPIDER, IS THAT YOU JUST--
--SAVED NORMAN OSBORN!

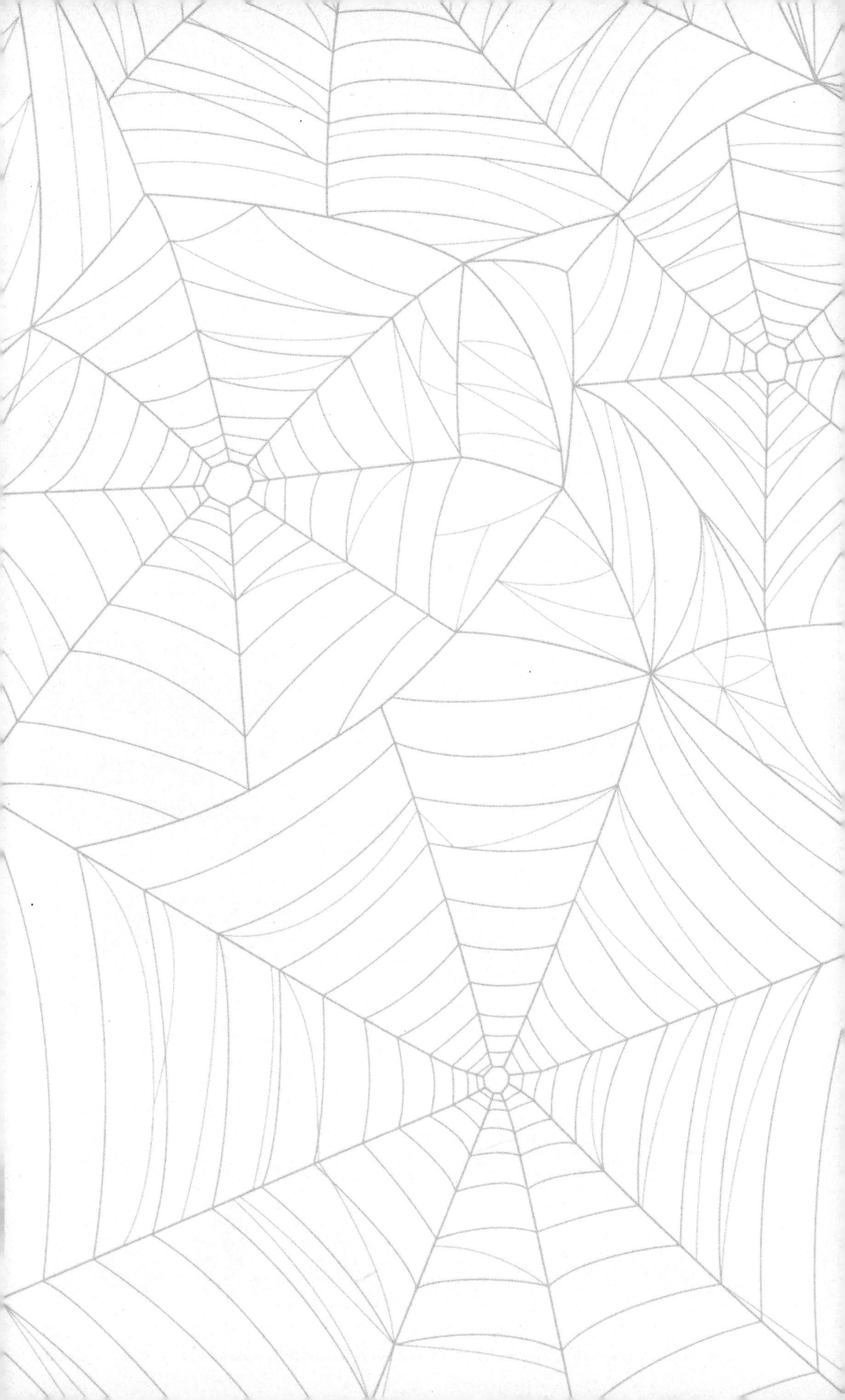

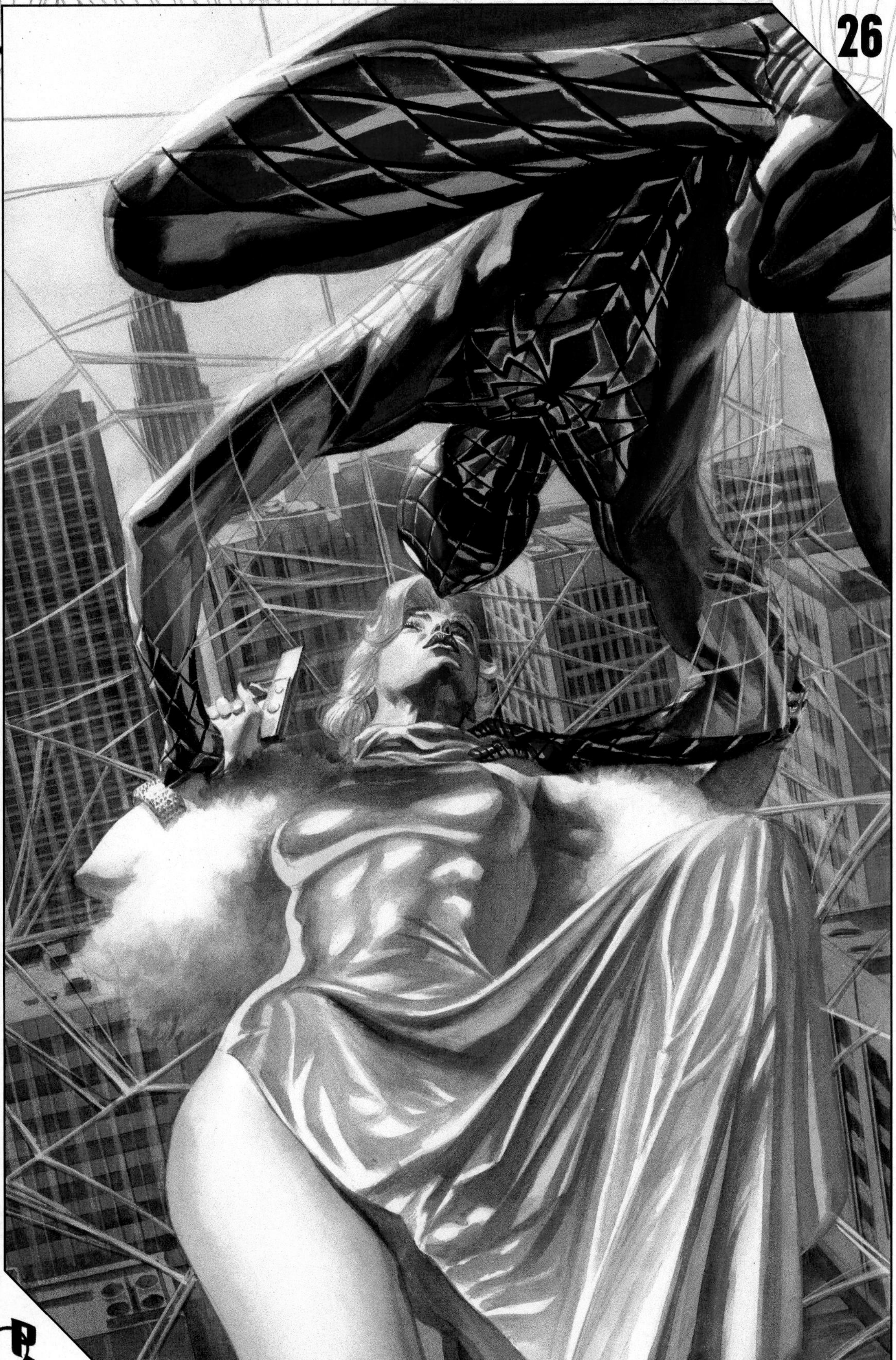

THE OSBORN IDENTITY PART TWO: "FIGHT OR FLIGHT"

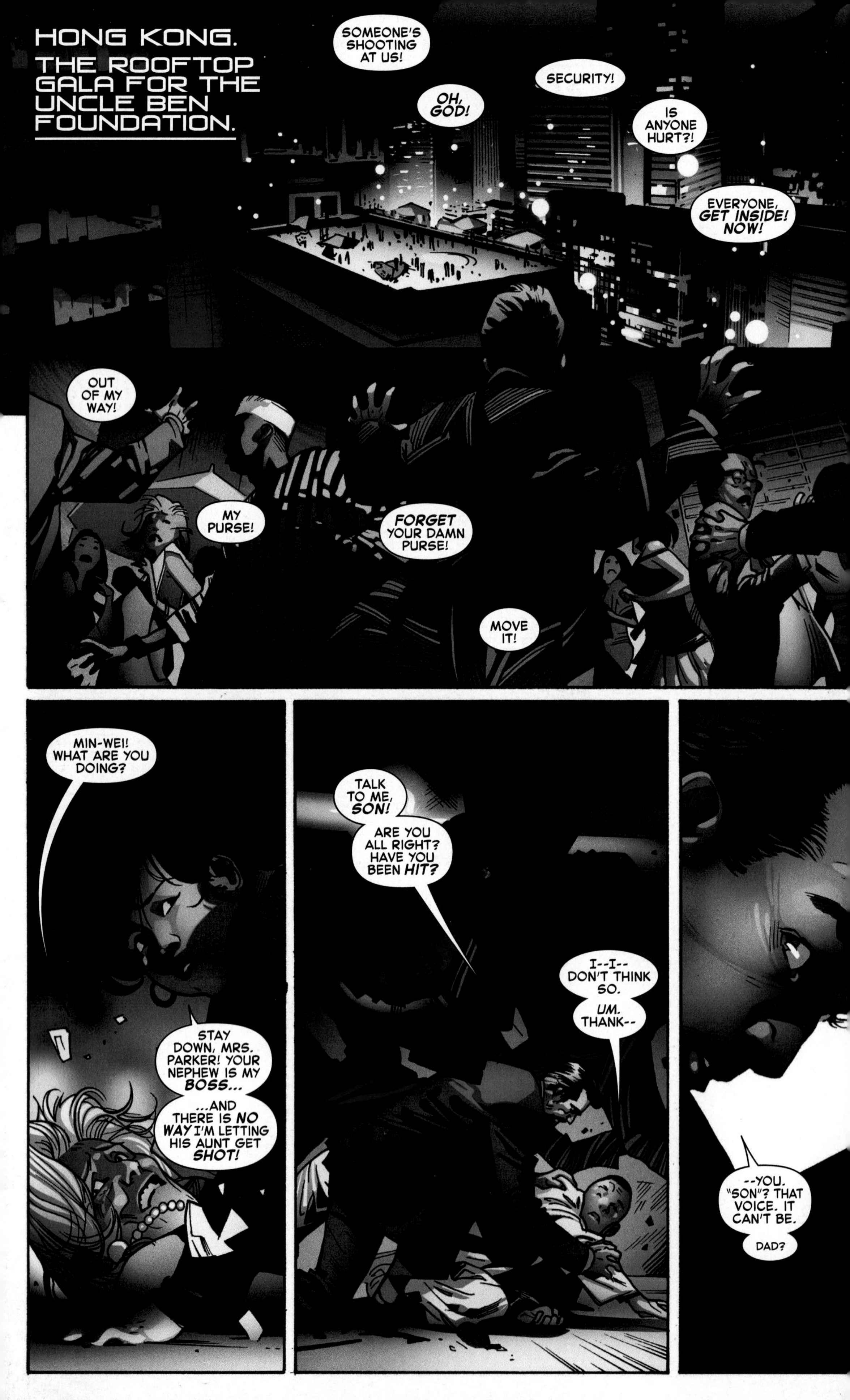
HONG KONG.
THE ROOFTOP GALA FOR THE UNCLE BEN FOUNDATION.
SOMEONE'S SHOOTING AT US!
OH, GOD!
SECURITY!
IS ANYONE HURT?!
EVERYONE, GET INSIDE! NOW!
OUT OF MY WAY!
MY PURSE!
FORGET YOUR DAMN PURSE!
MOVE IT!
MIN-WEI! WHAT ARE YOU DOING?
STAY DOWN, MRS. PARKER! YOUR NEPHEW IS MY BOSS...
...AND THERE IS NO WAY I'M LETTING HIS AUNT GET SHOT!
TALK TO ME, SON!
ARE YOU ALL RIGHT? HAVE YOU BEEN HIT?
I--I-- DON'T THINK SO.
UM. THANK--
--YOU. "SON"? THAT VOICE. IT CAN'T BE.
DAD?

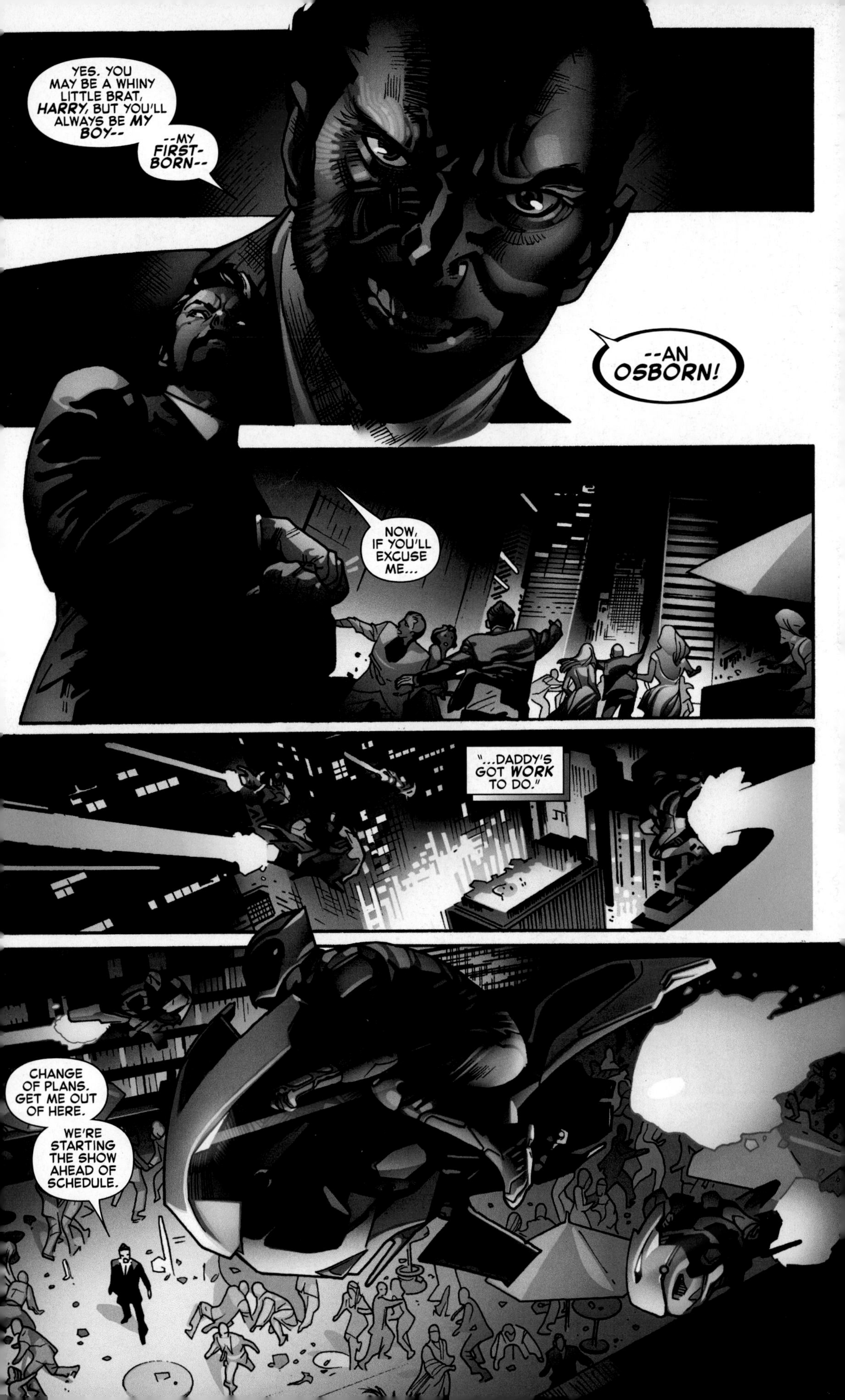
YES. YOU MAY BE A WHINY LITTLE BRAT, HARRY, BUT YOU'LL ALWAYS BE MY BOY--
--MY FIRST-BORN--
--AN OSBORN!
NOW, IF YOU'LL EXCUSE ME...
"...DADDY'S GOT WORK TO DO."
CHANGE OF PLANS. GET ME OUT OF HERE.
WE'RE STARTING THE SHOW AHEAD OF SCHEDULE.

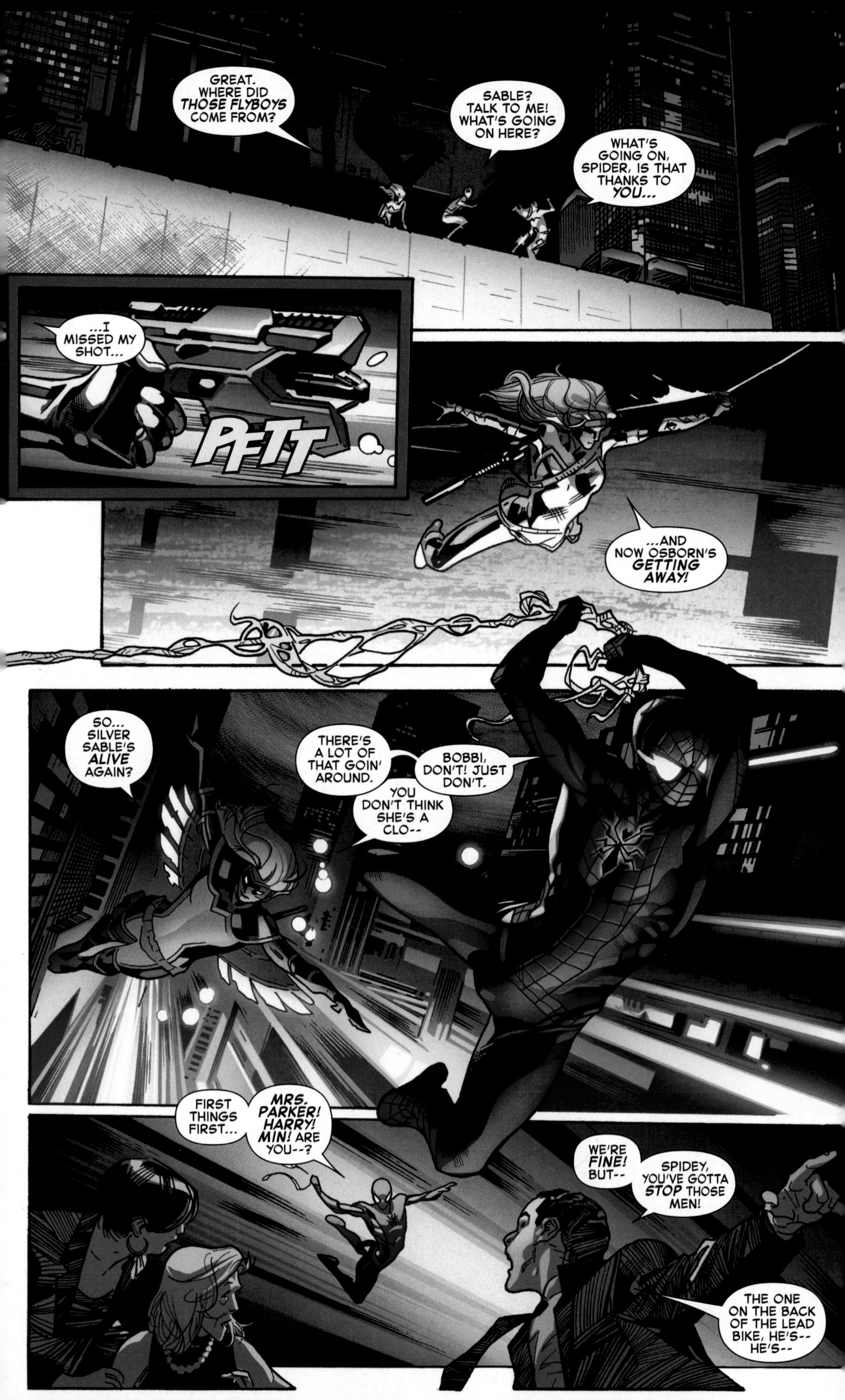
GREAT. WHERE DID THOSE FLYBOYS COME FROM?
SABLE? TALK TO ME! WHAT'S GOING ON HERE?
WHAT'S GOING ON, SPIDER, IS THAT THANKS TO YOU...
...I MISSED MY SHOT...
PFTT
...AND NOW OSBORN'S GETTING AWAY!
SO... SILVER SABLE'S ALIVE AGAIN?
THERE'S A LOT OF THAT GOIN' AROUND.
BOBBI, DON'T! JUST DON'T.
YOU DON'T THINK SHE'S A CLO--
FIRST THINGS FIRST...
MRS. PARKER! HARRY! MIN! ARE YOU--?
WE'RE FINE! BUT--
SPIDEY, YOU'VE GOTTA STOP THOSE MEN!
THE ONE ON THE BACK OF THE LEAD BIKE, HE'S-- HE'S--

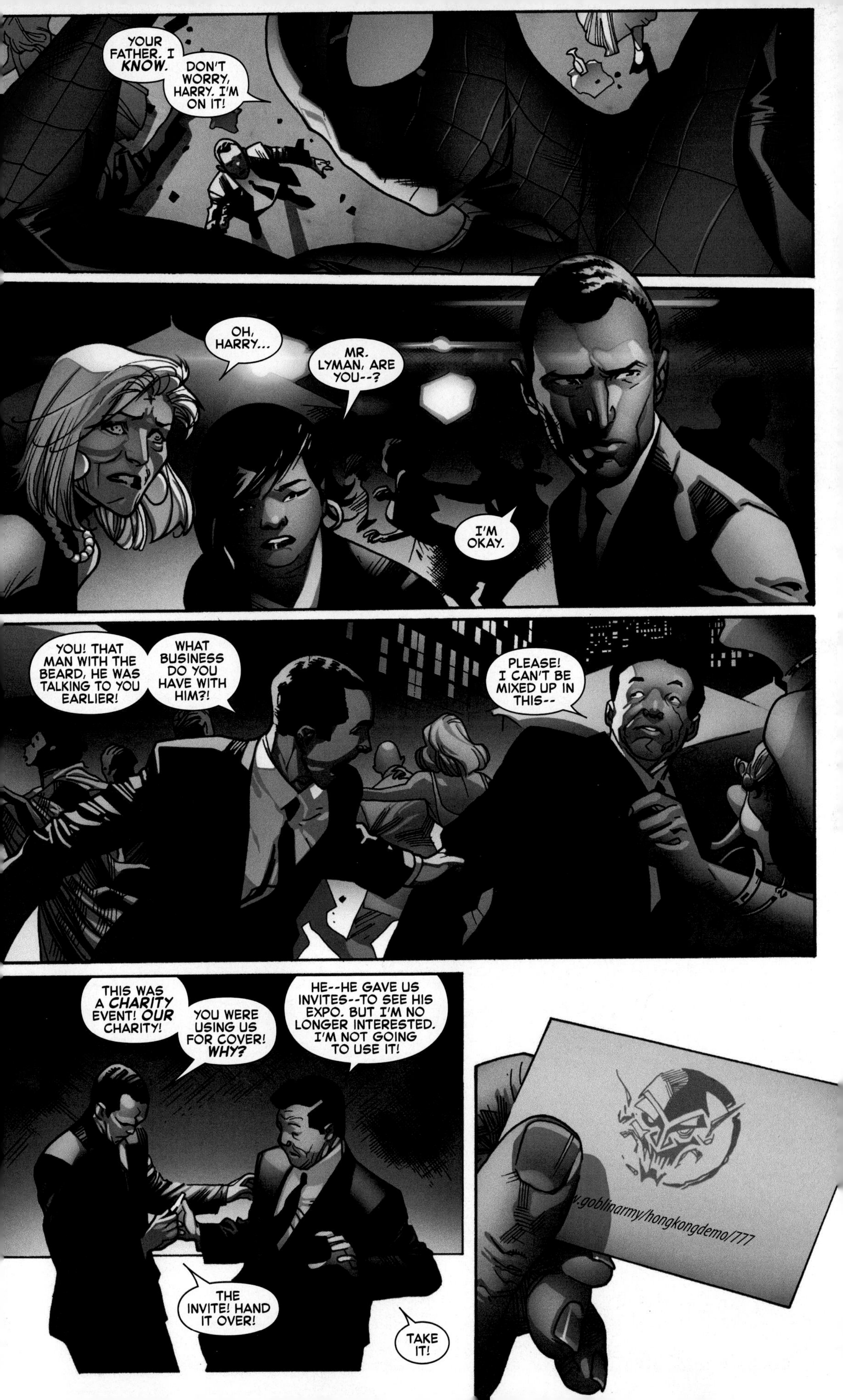

YOUR FATHER. I KNOW.
DON'T WORRY, HARRY. I'M ON IT!
OH, HARRY...
MR. LYMAN, ARE YOU--?
I'M OKAY.
YOU! THAT MAN WITH THE BEARD, HE WAS TALKING TO YOU EARLIER!
WHAT BUSINESS DO YOU HAVE WITH HIM?!
PLEASE! I CAN'T BE MIXED UP IN THIS--
THIS WAS A CHARITY EVENT! OUR CHARITY!
YOU WERE USING US FOR COVER! WHY?
HE--HE GAVE US INVITES--TO SEE HIS EXPO. BUT I'M NO LONGER INTERESTED. I'M NOT GOING TO USE IT!
THE INVITE! HAND IT OVER!
TAKE IT!
.goblinarmy/hongkongdemo/777

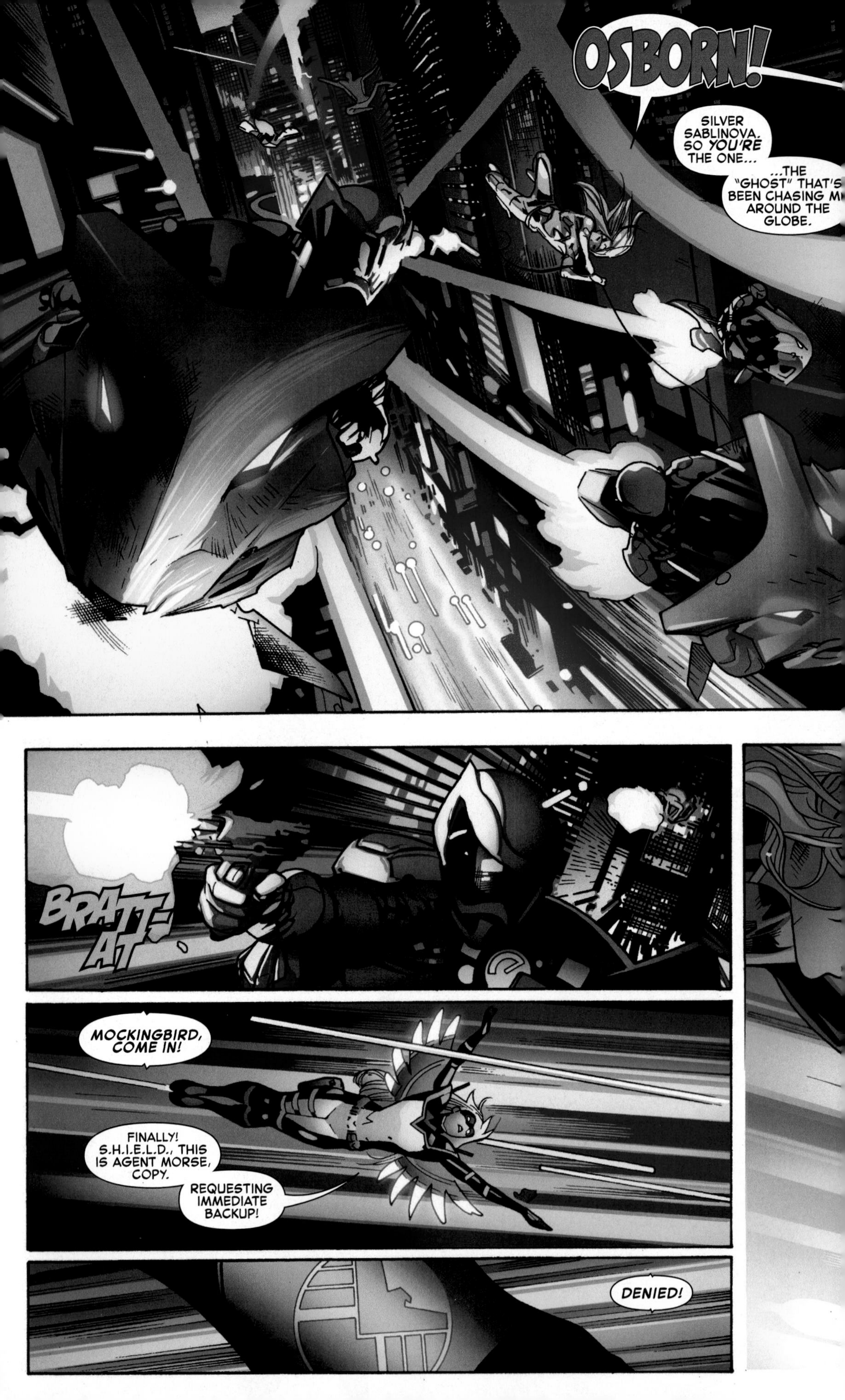
OSBORN!
SILVER SABLINOVA. SO YOU'RE THE ONE...
...THE "GHOST" THAT'S BEEN CHASING M AROUND THE GLOBE.
BRATT-AT
MOCKINGBIRD, COME IN!
FINALLY! S.H.I.E.L.D., THIS IS AGENT MORSE, COPY.
REQUESTING IMMEDIATE BACKUP!
DENIED!

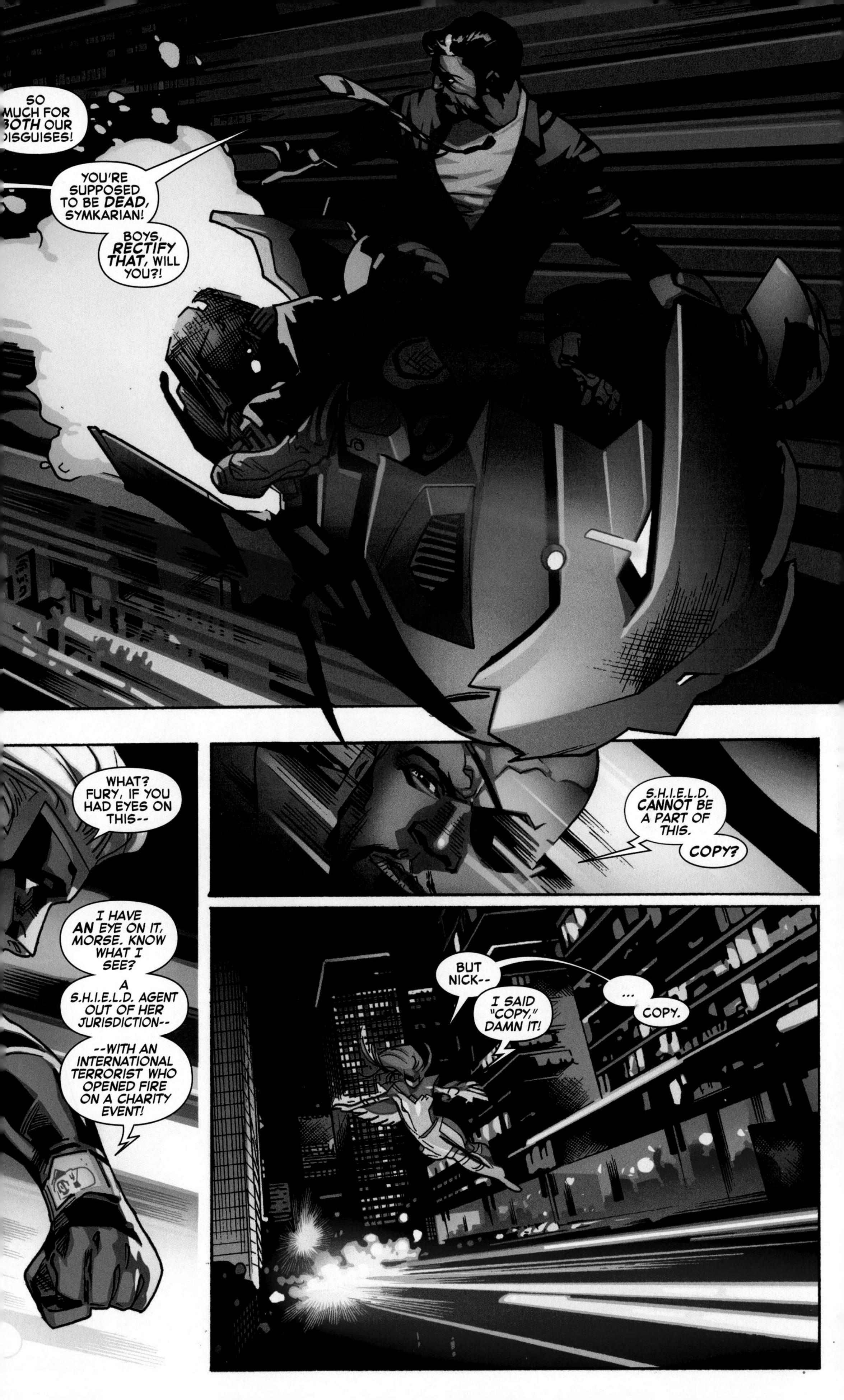
SO MUCH FOR BOTH OUR DISGUISES!
YOU'RE SUPPOSED TO BE DEAD, SYMKARIAN!
BOYS, RECTIFY THAT, WILL YOU?!
WHAT? FURY, IF YOU HAD EYES ON THIS--
S.H.I.E.L.D. CANNOT BE A PART OF THIS.
COPY?
I HAVE AN EYE ON IT, MORSE. KNOW WHAT I SEE?
A S.H.I.E.L.D. AGENT OUT OF HER JURISDICTION--
--WITH AN INTERNATIONAL TERRORIST WHO OPENED FIRE ON A CHARITY EVENT!
BUT NICK--
I SAID "COPY," DAMN IT!
...
COPY.

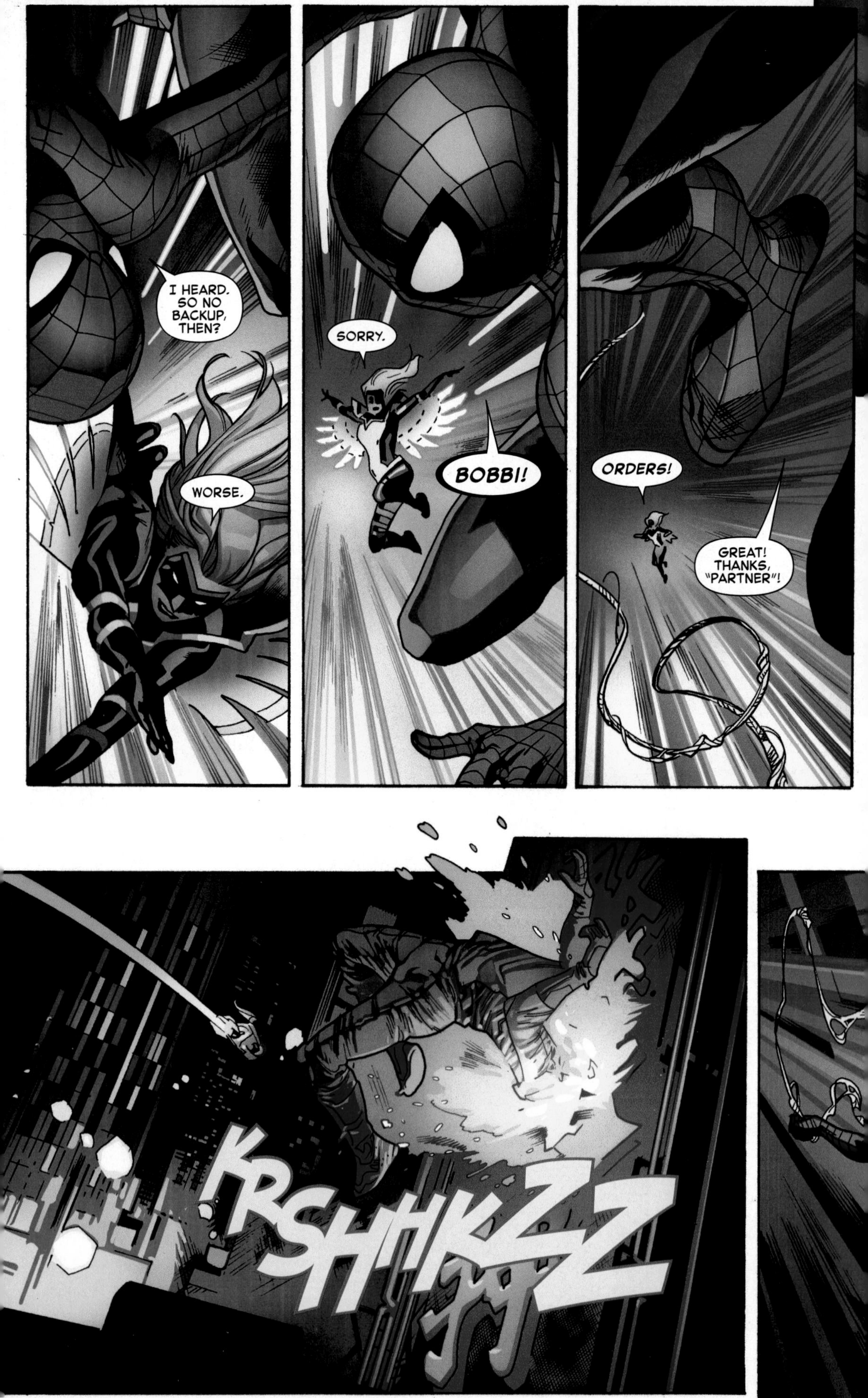
I HEARD. SO NO BACKUP, THEN?
WORSE.
SORRY.
BOBBI!
ORDERS!
GREAT! THANKS, "PARTNER"!
KRSHKZZ

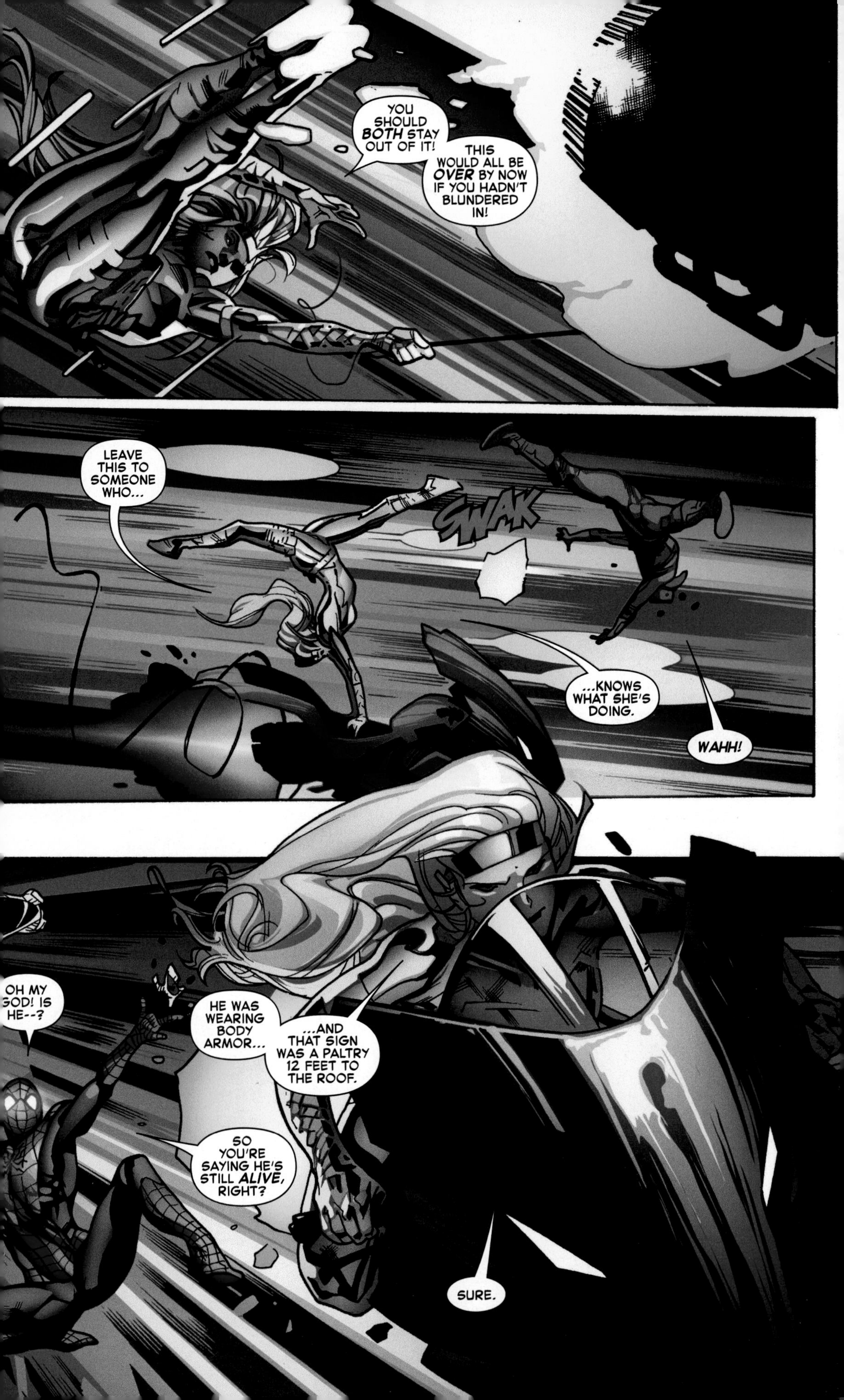
YOU SHOULD BOTH STAY OUT OF IT!
THIS WOULD ALL BE OVER BY NOW IF YOU HADN'T BLUNDERED IN!
LEAVE THIS TO SOMEONE WHO...
SWAK
...KNOWS WHAT SHE'S DOING.
WAHH!
OH MY GOD! IS HE--?
HE WAS WEARING BODY ARMOR...
...AND THAT SIGN WAS A PALTRY 12 FEET TO THE ROOF.
SO YOU'RE SAYING HE'S STILL ALIVE, RIGHT?
SURE.

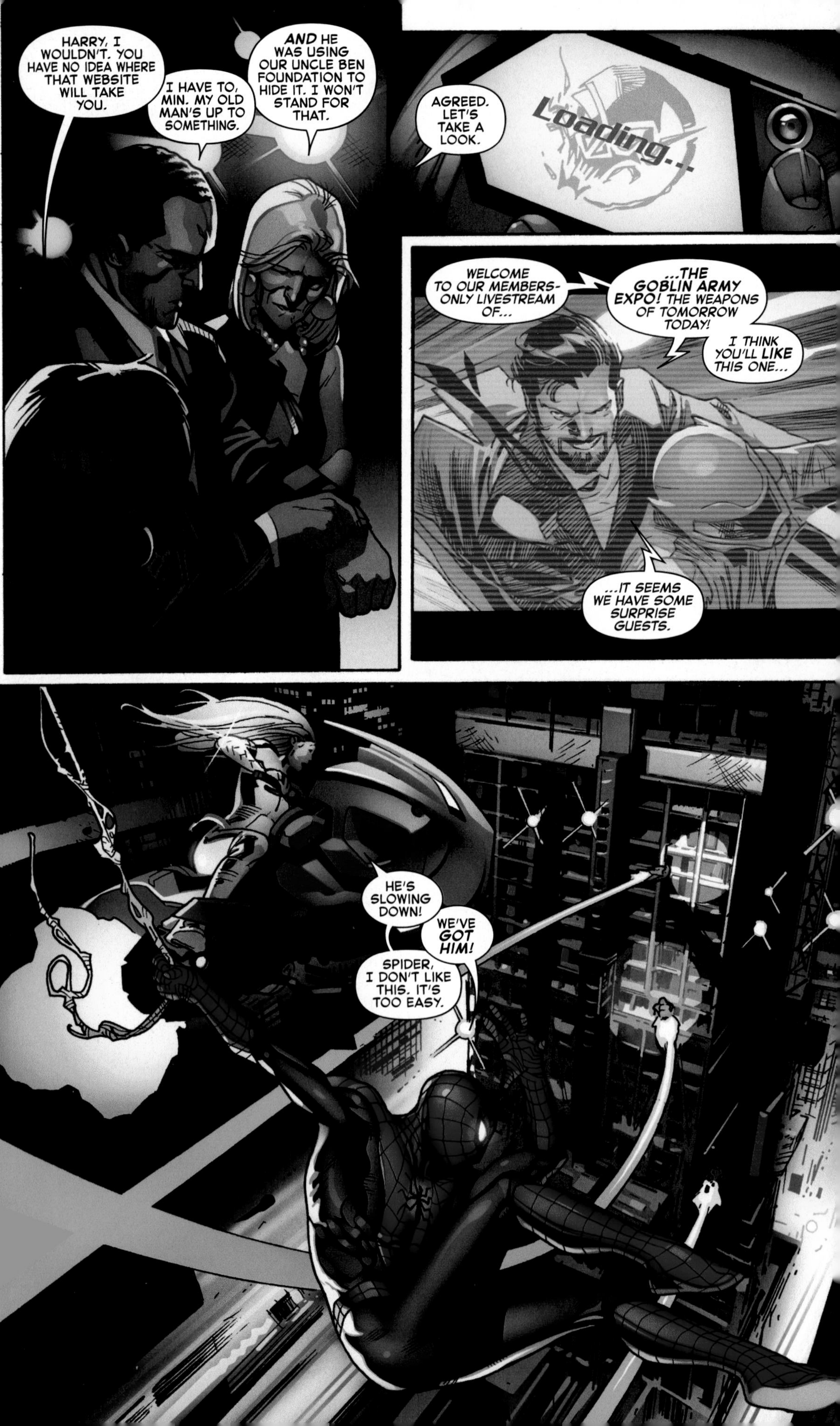
HARRY, I WOULDN'T. YOU HAVE NO IDEA WHERE THAT WEBSITE WILL TAKE YOU.
I HAVE TO, MIN. MY OLD MAN'S UP TO SOMETHING.
AND HE WAS USING OUR UNCLE BEN FOUNDATION TO HIDE IT. I WON'T STAND FOR THAT.
AGREED. LET'S TAKE A LOOK.
Loading...
WELCOME TO OUR MEMBERS-ONLY LIVESTREAM OF...
...THE GOBLIN ARMY EXPO! THE WEAPONS OF TOMORROW TODAY!
I THINK YOU'LL LIKE THIS ONE...
...IT SEEMS WE HAVE SOME SURPRISE GUESTS.
HE'S SLOWING DOWN!
WE'VE GOT HIM!
SPIDER, I DON'T LIKE THIS. IT'S TOO EASY.

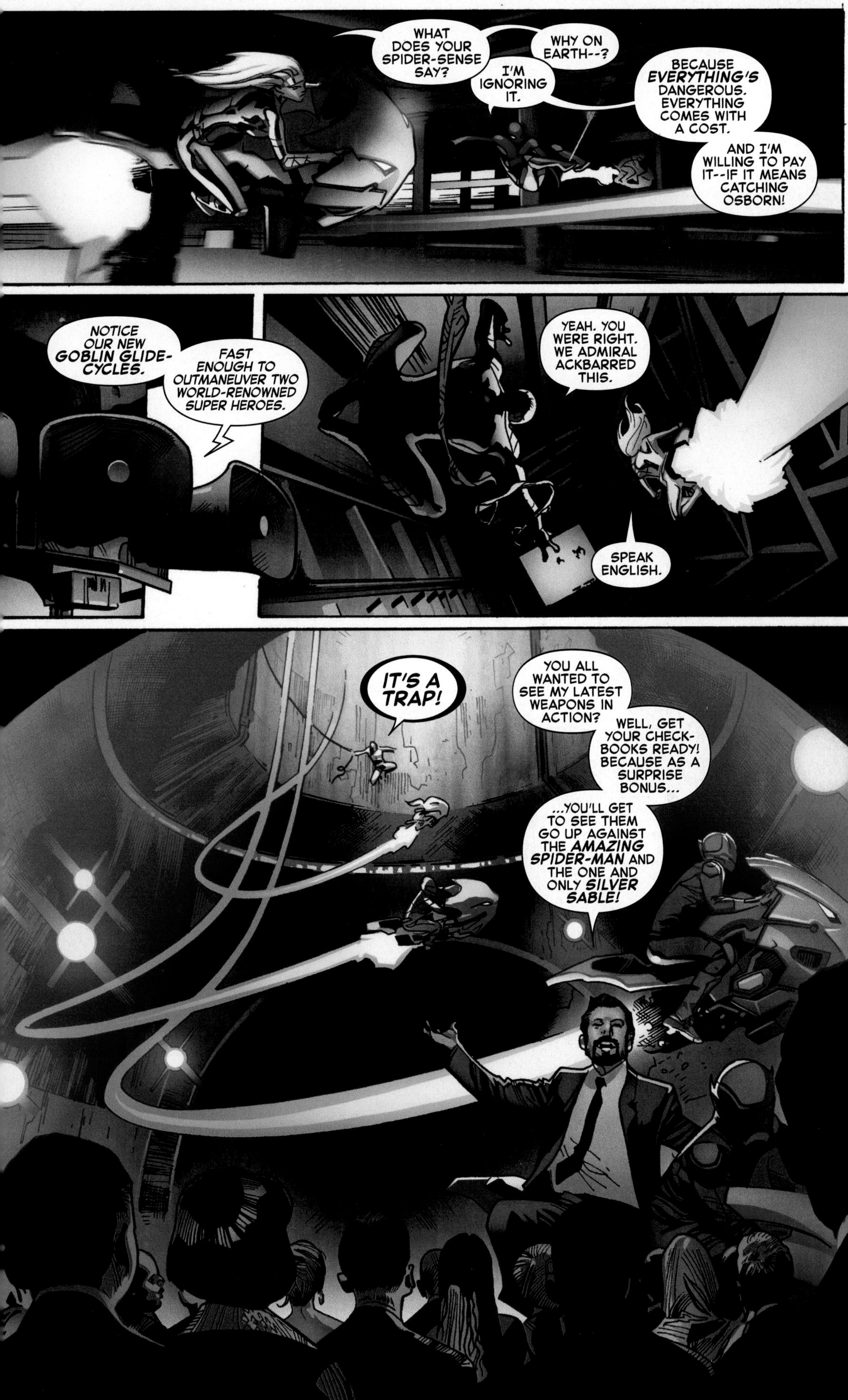

WHAT DOES YOUR SPIDER-SENSE SAY?
WHY ON EARTH--?
I'M IGNORING IT.
BECAUSE EVERYTHING'S DANGEROUS. EVERYTHING COMES WITH A COST.
AND I'M WILLING TO PAY IT--IF IT MEANS CATCHING OSBORN!
NOTICE OUR NEW GOBLIN GLIDE-CYCLES.
FAST ENOUGH TO OUTMANEUVER TWO WORLD-RENOWNED SUPER HEROES.
YEAH. YOU WERE RIGHT. WE ADMIRAL ACKBARRED THIS.
SPEAK ENGLISH.
IT'S A TRAP!
YOU ALL WANTED TO SEE MY LATEST WEAPONS IN ACTION?
WELL, GET YOUR CHECK-BOOKS READY! BECAUSE AS A SURPRISE BONUS...
...YOU'LL GET TO SEE THEM GO UP AGAINST THE AMAZING SPIDER-MAN AND THE ONE AND ONLY SILVER SABLE!

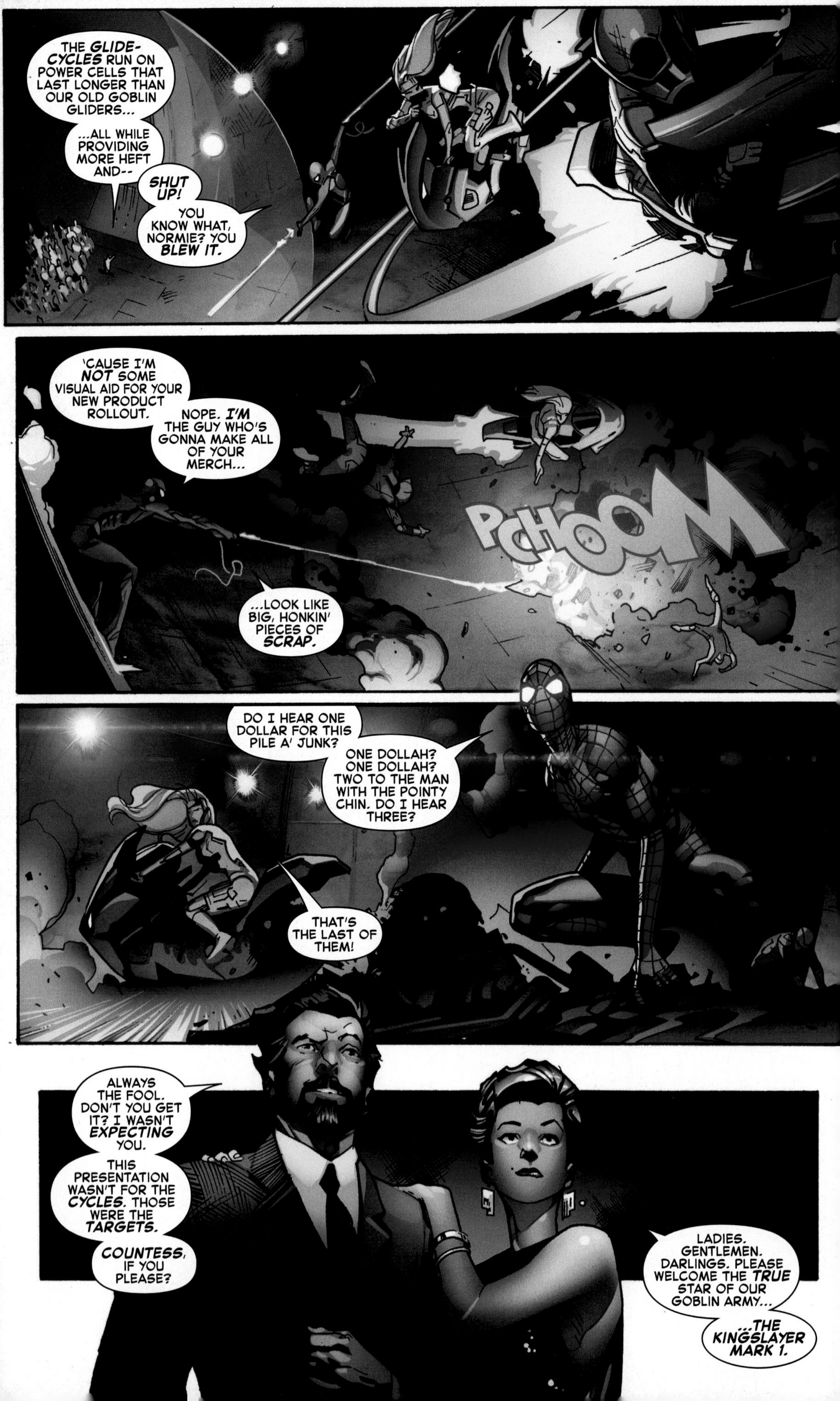
THE GLIDE-CYCLES RUN ON POWER CELLS THAT LAST LONGER THAN OUR OLD GOBLIN GLIDERS...
...ALL WHILE PROVIDING MORE HEFT AND--
SHUT UP!
YOU KNOW WHAT, NORMIE? YOU BLEW IT.
'CAUSE I'M NOT SOME VISUAL AID FOR YOUR NEW PRODUCT ROLLOUT.
NOPE. I'M THE GUY WHO'S GONNA MAKE ALL OF YOUR MERCH...
PCHOOM
...LOOK LIKE BIG, HONKIN' PIECES OF SCRAP.
DO I HEAR ONE DOLLAR FOR THIS PILE A' JUNK?
ONE DOLLAH? ONE DOLLAH? TWO TO THE MAN WITH THE POINTY CHIN. DO I HEAR THREE?
THAT'S THE LAST OF THEM!
ALWAYS THE FOOL. DON'T YOU GET IT? I WASN'T EXPECTING YOU.
THIS PRESENTATION WASN'T FOR THE CYCLES. THOSE WERE THE TARGETS.
COUNTESS, IF YOU PLEASE?
LADIES. GENTLEMEN. DARLINGS. PLEASE WELCOME THE TRUE STAR OF OUR GOBLIN ARMY...
...THE KINGSLAYER MARK 1.

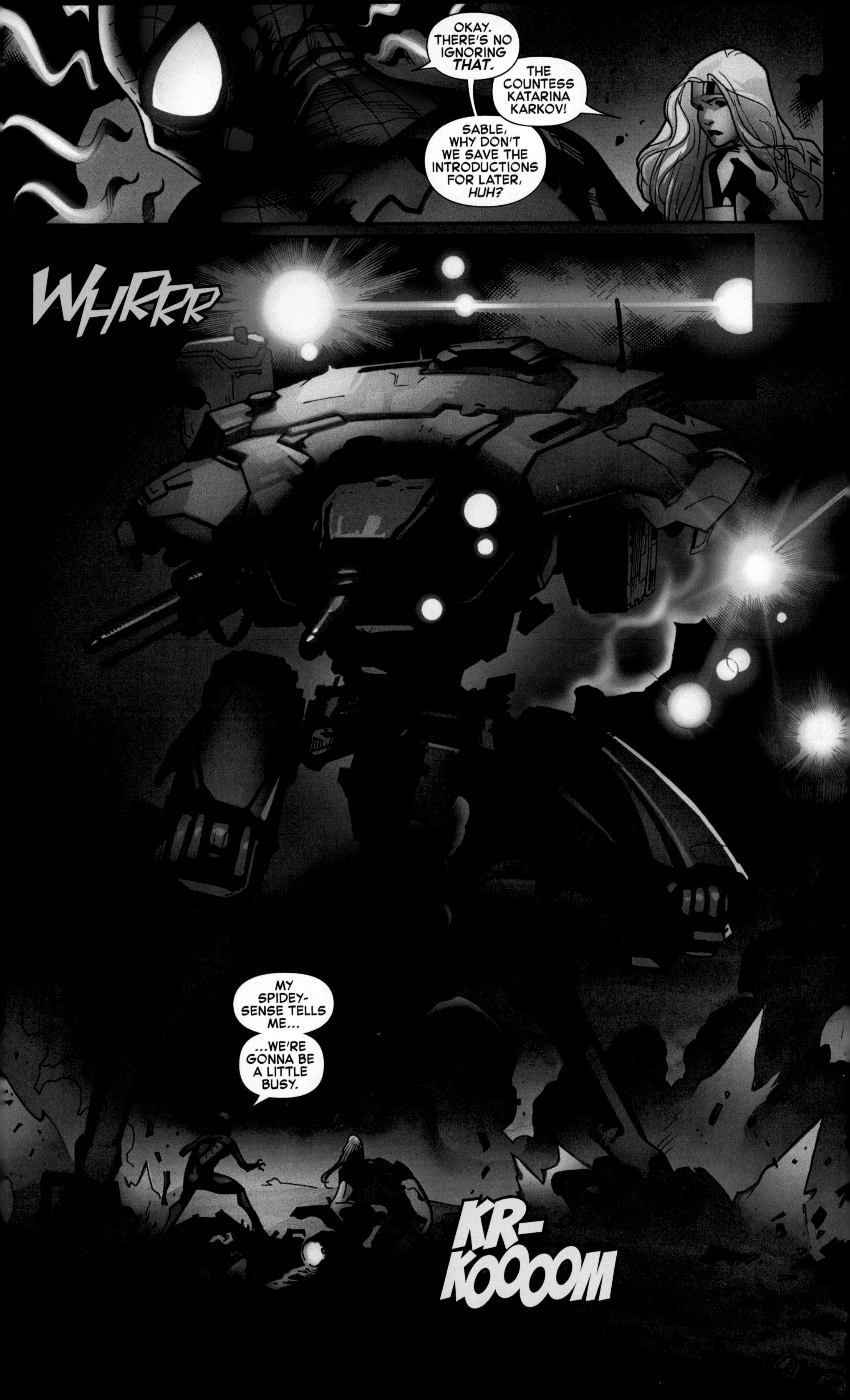

OKAY. THERE'S NO IGNORING THAT.
THE COUNTESS KATARINA KARKOV!
SABLE, WHY DON'T WE SAVE THE INTRODUCTIONS FOR LATER, HUH?
WHRRR
MY SPIDEY-SENSE TELLS ME...
...WE'RE GONNA BE A LITTLE BUSY.
KR-KOOOOM

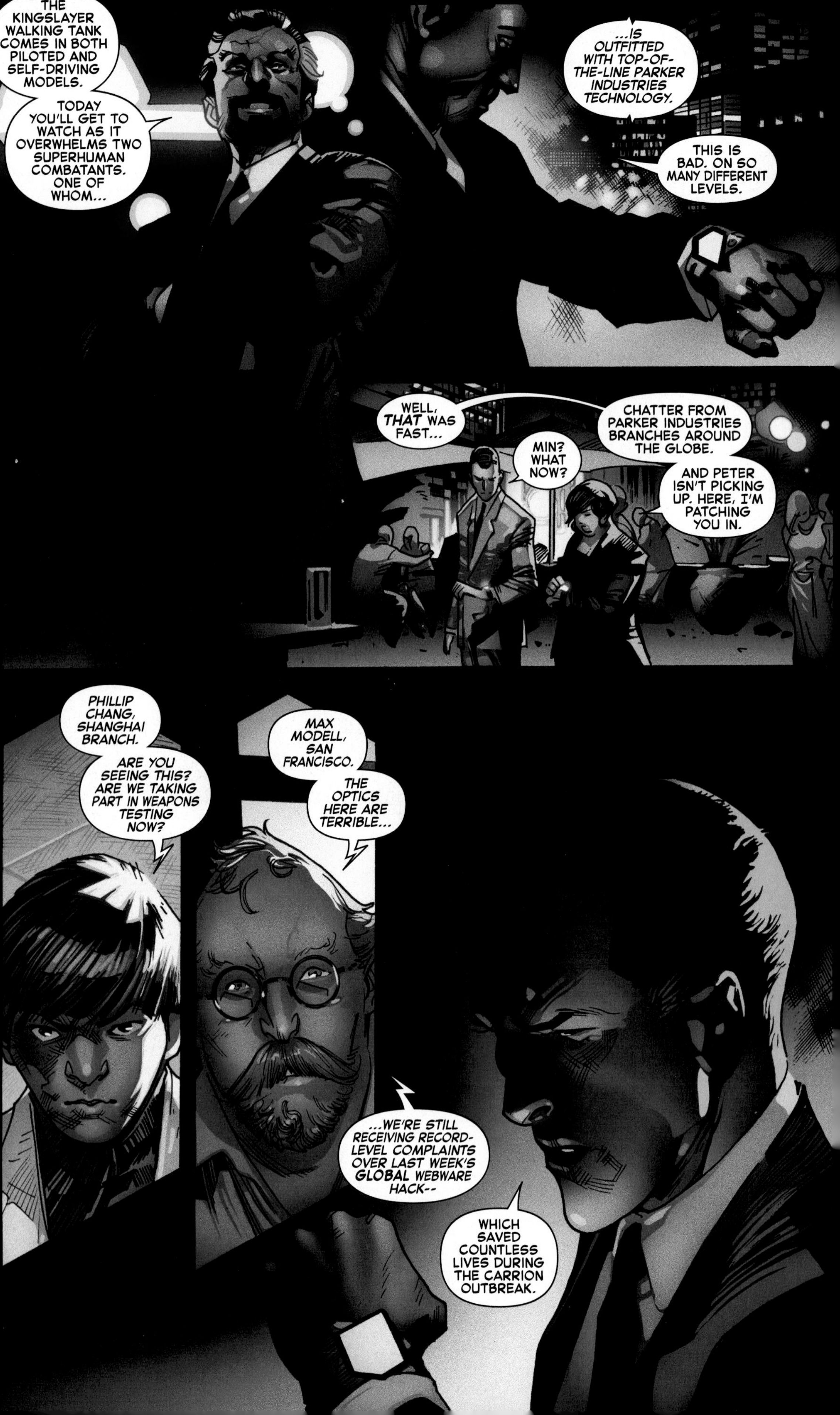
THE KINGSLAYER WALKING TANK COMES IN BOTH PILOTED AND SELF-DRIVING MODELS.
TODAY YOU'LL GET TO WATCH AS IT OVERWHELMS TWO SUPERHUMAN COMBATANTS. ONE OF WHOM...
...IS OUTFITTED WITH TOP-OF-THE-LINE PARKER INDUSTRIES TECHNOLOGY.
THIS IS BAD. ON SO MANY DIFFERENT LEVELS.
WELL, THAT WAS FAST...
MIN? WHAT NOW?
CHATTER FROM PARKER INDUSTRIES BRANCHES AROUND THE GLOBE.
AND PETER ISN'T PICKING UP. HERE, I'M PATCHING YOU IN.
PHILLIP CHANG, SHANGHAI BRANCH.
ARE YOU SEEING THIS? ARE WE TAKING PART IN WEAPONS TESTING NOW?
MAX MODELL, SAN FRANCISCO.
THE OPTICS HERE ARE TERRIBLE...
...WE'RE STILL RECEIVING RECORD-LEVEL COMPLAINTS OVER LAST WEEK'S GLOBAL WEBWARE HACK--
WHICH SAVED COUNTLESS LIVES DURING THE CARRION OUTBREAK.

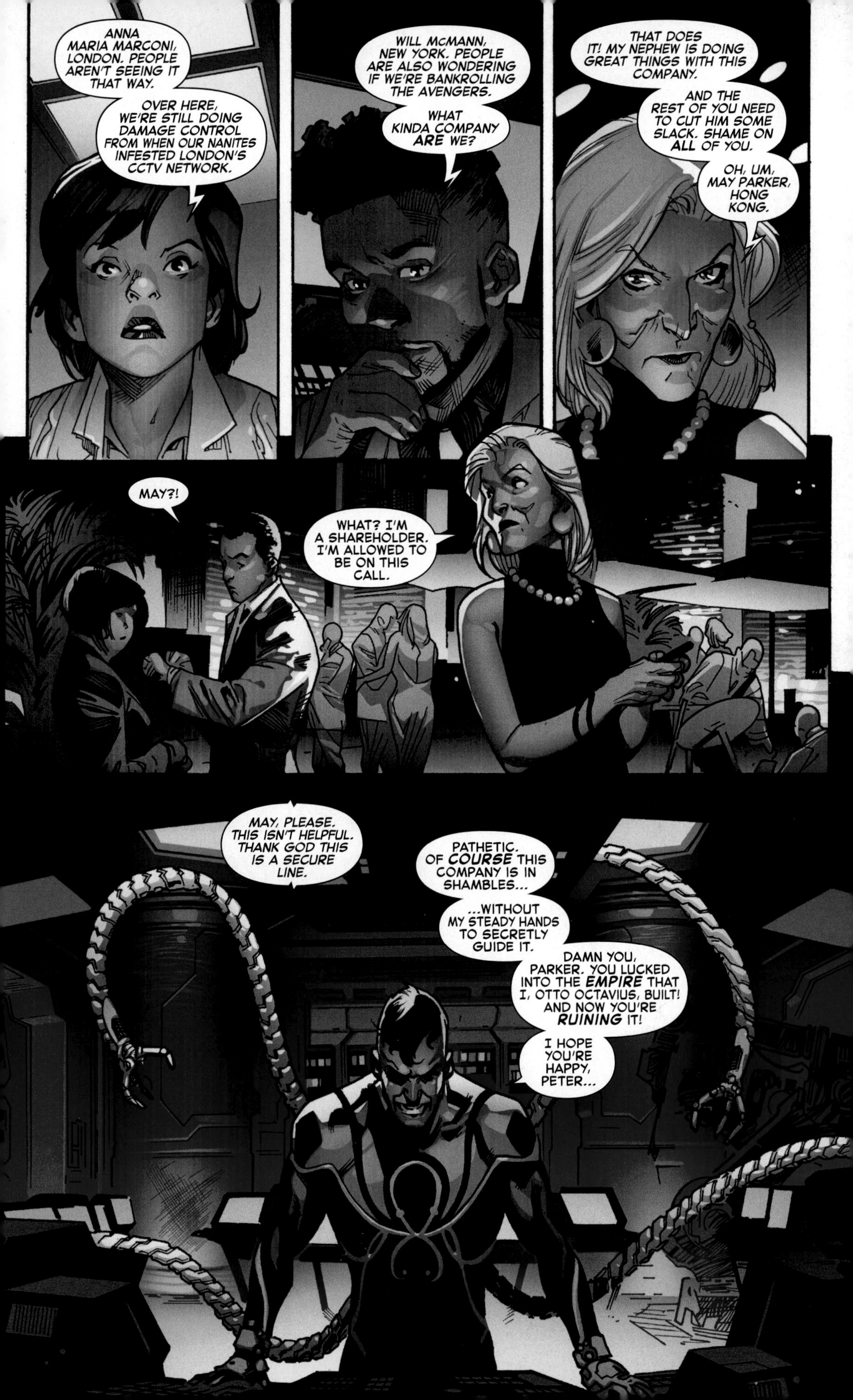
ANNA MARIA MARCONI, LONDON. PEOPLE AREN'T SEEING IT THAT WAY.
OVER HERE, WE'RE STILL DOING DAMAGE CONTROL FROM WHEN OUR NANITES INFESTED LONDON'S CCTV NETWORK.
WILL McMANN, NEW YORK. PEOPLE ARE ALSO WONDERING IF WE'RE BANKROLLING THE AVENGERS.
WHAT KINDA COMPANY ARE WE?
THAT DOES IT! MY NEPHEW IS DOING GREAT THINGS WITH THIS COMPANY.
AND THE REST OF YOU NEED TO CUT HIM SOME SLACK. SHAME ON ALL OF YOU.
OH, UM, MAY PARKER, HONG KONG.
MAY?!
WHAT? I'M A SHAREHOLDER. I'M ALLOWED TO BE ON THIS CALL.
MAY, PLEASE. THIS ISN'T HELPFUL. THANK GOD THIS IS A SECURE LINE.
PATHETIC. OF COURSE THIS COMPANY IS IN SHAMBLES...
...WITHOUT MY STEADY HANDS TO SECRETLY GUIDE IT.
DAMN YOU, PARKER. YOU LUCKED INTO THE EMPIRE THAT I, OTTO OCTAVIUS, BUILT! AND NOW YOU'RE RUINING IT!
I HOPE YOU'RE HAPPY, PETER...

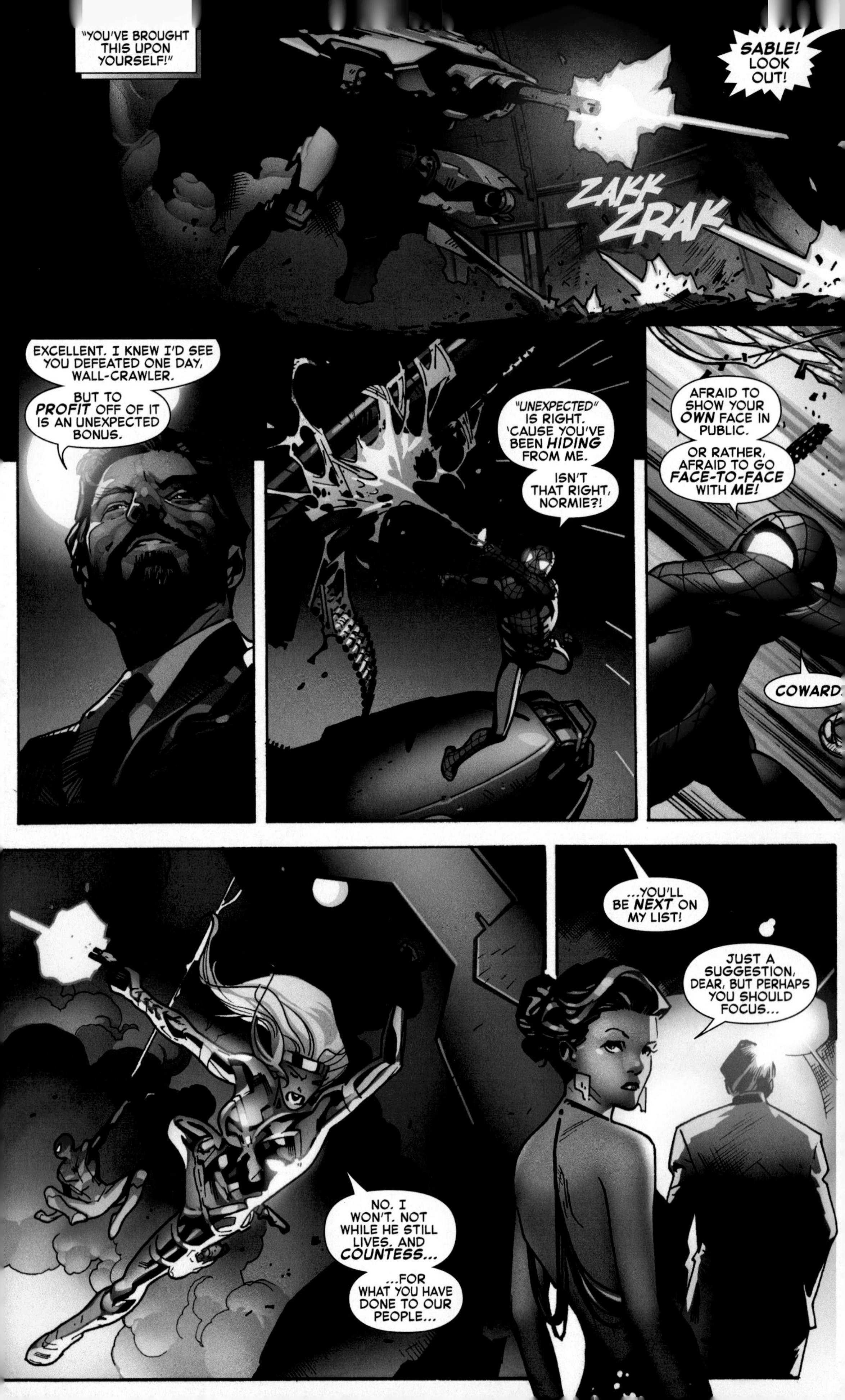
"YOU'VE BROUGHT THIS UPON YOURSELF!"
SABLE! LOOK OUT!
ZAKK ZRAK
EXCELLENT. I KNEW I'D SEE YOU DEFEATED ONE DAY, WALL-CRAWLER.
BUT TO PROFIT OFF OF IT IS AN UNEXPECTED BONUS.
"UNEXPECTED" IS RIGHT. 'CAUSE YOU'VE BEEN HIDING FROM ME.
ISN'T THAT RIGHT, NORMIE?!
AFRAID TO SHOW YOUR OWN FACE IN PUBLIC.
OR RATHER, AFRAID TO GO FACE-TO-FACE WITH ME!
COWARD.
NO. I WON'T. NOT WHILE HE STILL LIVES. AND COUNTESS...
...FOR WHAT YOU HAVE DONE TO OUR PEOPLE...
...YOU'LL BE NEXT ON MY LIST!
JUST A SUGGESTION, DEAR, BUT PERHAPS YOU SHOULD FOCUS...

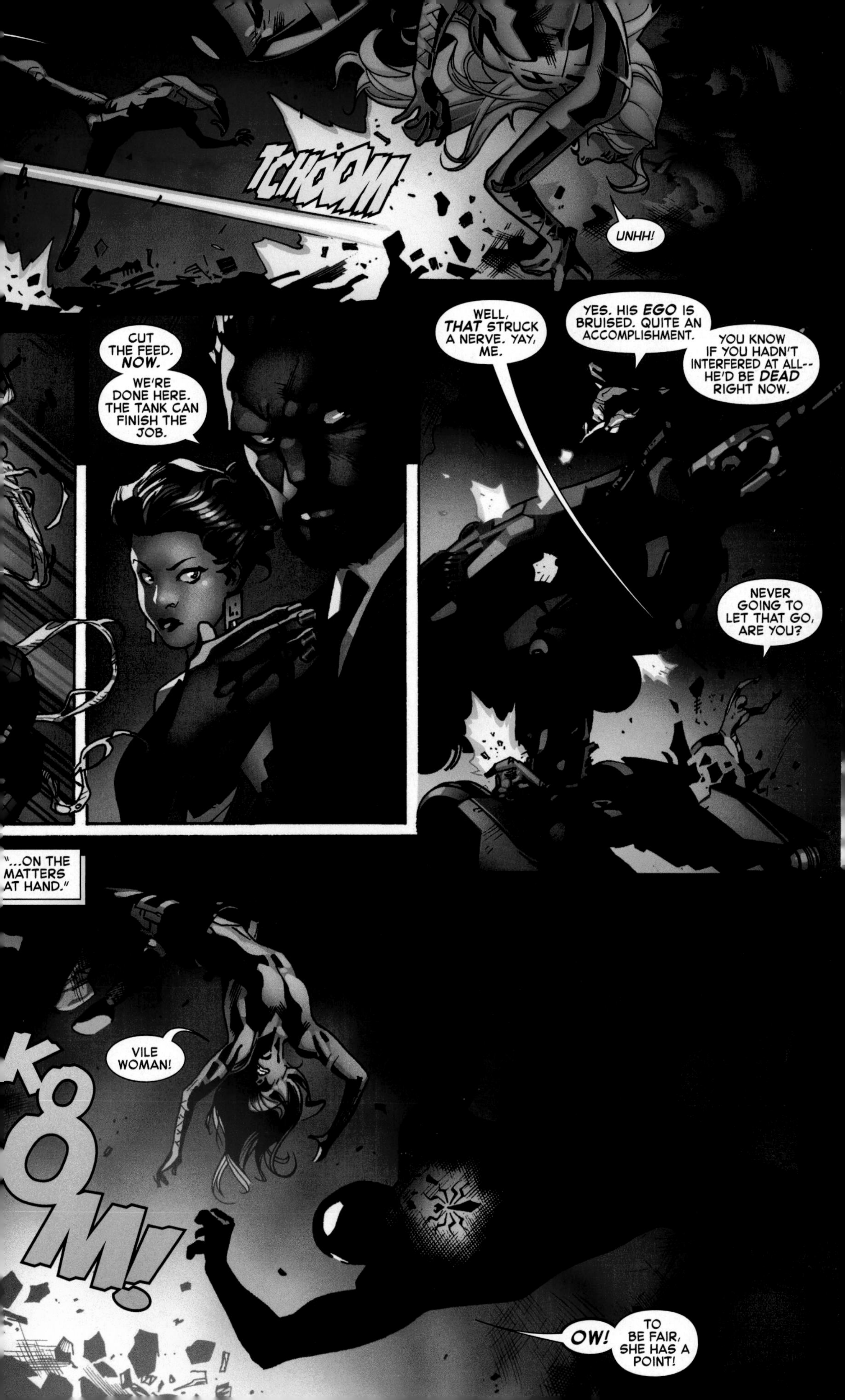
TCHOOM
UNHH!
CUT THE FEED. NOW.
WE'RE DONE HERE. THE TANK CAN FINISH THE JOB.
WELL, THAT STRUCK A NERVE. YAY, ME.
YES. HIS EGO IS BRUISED. QUITE AN ACCOMPLISHMENT.
YOU KNOW IF YOU HADN'T INTERFERED AT ALL-- HE'D BE DEAD RIGHT NOW.
NEVER GOING TO LET THAT GO, ARE YOU?
"...ON THE MATTERS AT HAND."
VILE WOMAN!
KBOOM!
OW!
TO BE FAIR, SHE HAS A POINT!

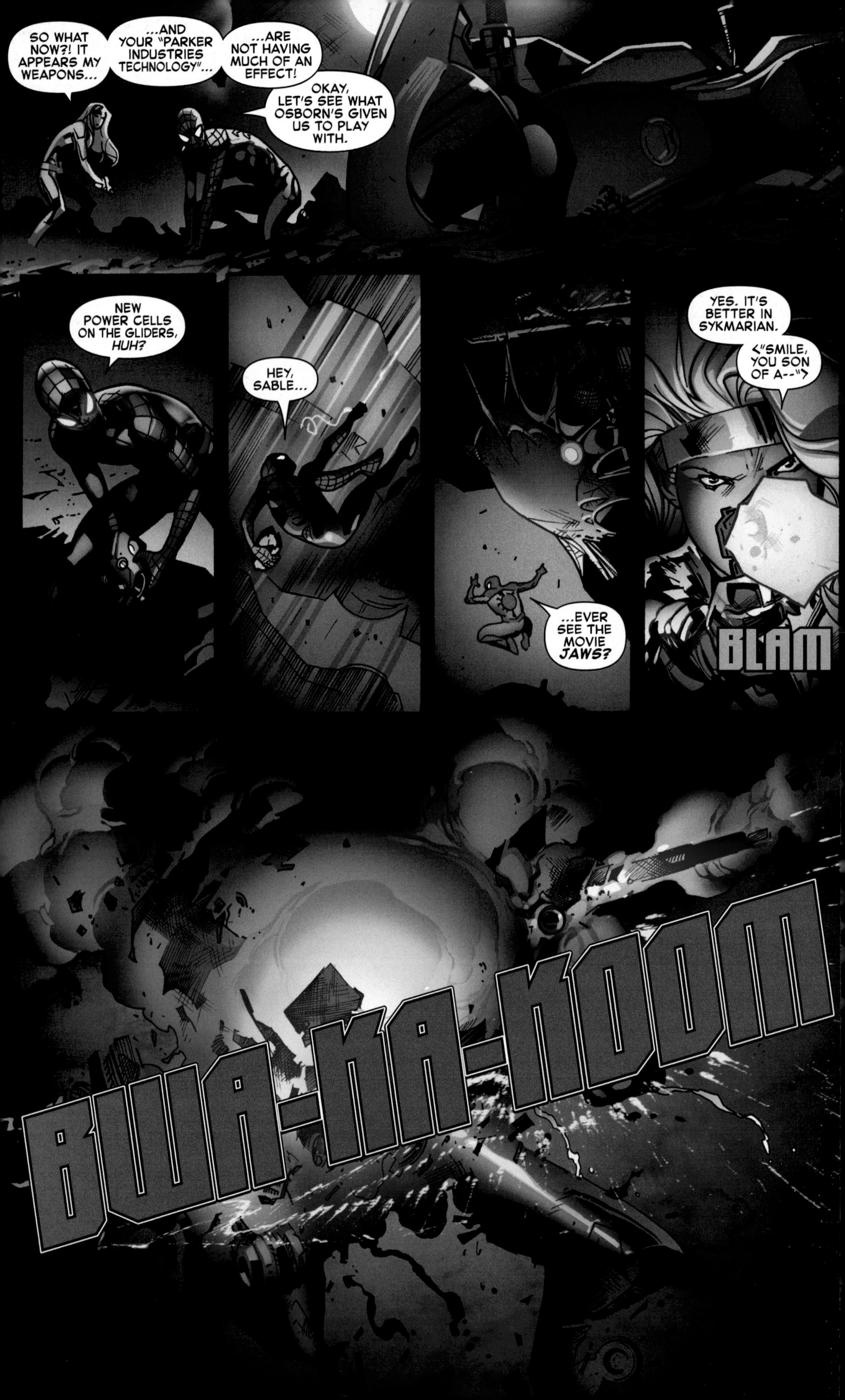
SO WHAT NOW?! IT APPEARS MY WEAPONS...
...AND YOUR "PARKER INDUSTRIES TECHNOLOGY"...
...ARE NOT HAVING MUCH OF AN EFFECT!
OKAY, LET'S SEE WHAT OSBORN'S GIVEN US TO PLAY WITH.
NEW POWER CELLS ON THE GLIDERS, *HUH?*
HEY, SABLE...
...EVER SEE THE MOVIE *JAWS?*
YES. IT'S BETTER IN SYKMARIAN.
<"SMILE, YOU SON OF A--">
BLAM
BWA-KA-KOOM

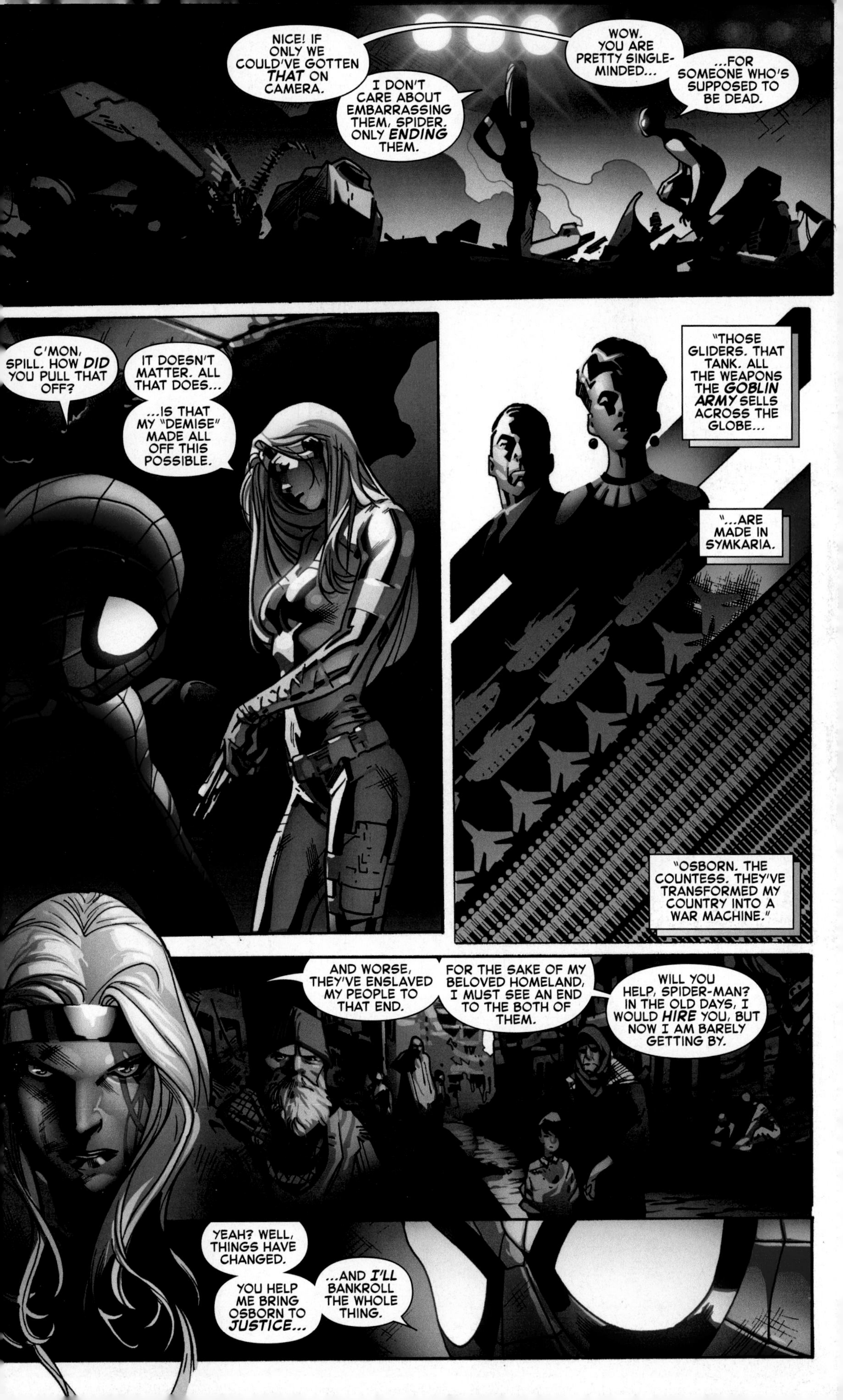
NICE! IF ONLY WE COULD'VE GOTTEN THAT ON CAMERA.
I DON'T CARE ABOUT EMBARRASSING THEM, SPIDER. ONLY ENDING THEM.
WOW. YOU ARE PRETTY SINGLE-MINDED...
...FOR SOMEONE WHO'S SUPPOSED TO BE DEAD.
C'MON, SPILL. HOW DID YOU PULL THAT OFF?
IT DOESN'T MATTER. ALL THAT DOES...
...IS THAT MY "DEMISE" MADE ALL OFF THIS POSSIBLE.
"THOSE GLIDERS. THAT TANK. ALL THE WEAPONS THE GOBLIN ARMY SELLS ACROSS THE GLOBE...
"...ARE MADE IN SYMKARIA.
"OSBORN. THE COUNTESS. THEY'VE TRANSFORMED MY COUNTRY INTO A WAR MACHINE."
AND WORSE, THEY'VE ENSLAVED MY PEOPLE TO THAT END.
FOR THE SAKE OF MY BELOVED HOMELAND, I MUST SEE AN END TO THE BOTH OF THEM.
WILL YOU HELP, SPIDER-MAN? IN THE OLD DAYS, I WOULD HIRE YOU, BUT NOW I AM BARELY GETTING BY.
YEAH? WELL, THINGS HAVE CHANGED.
YOU HELP ME BRING OSBORN TO JUSTICE...
...AND I'LL BANKROLL THE WHOLE THING.

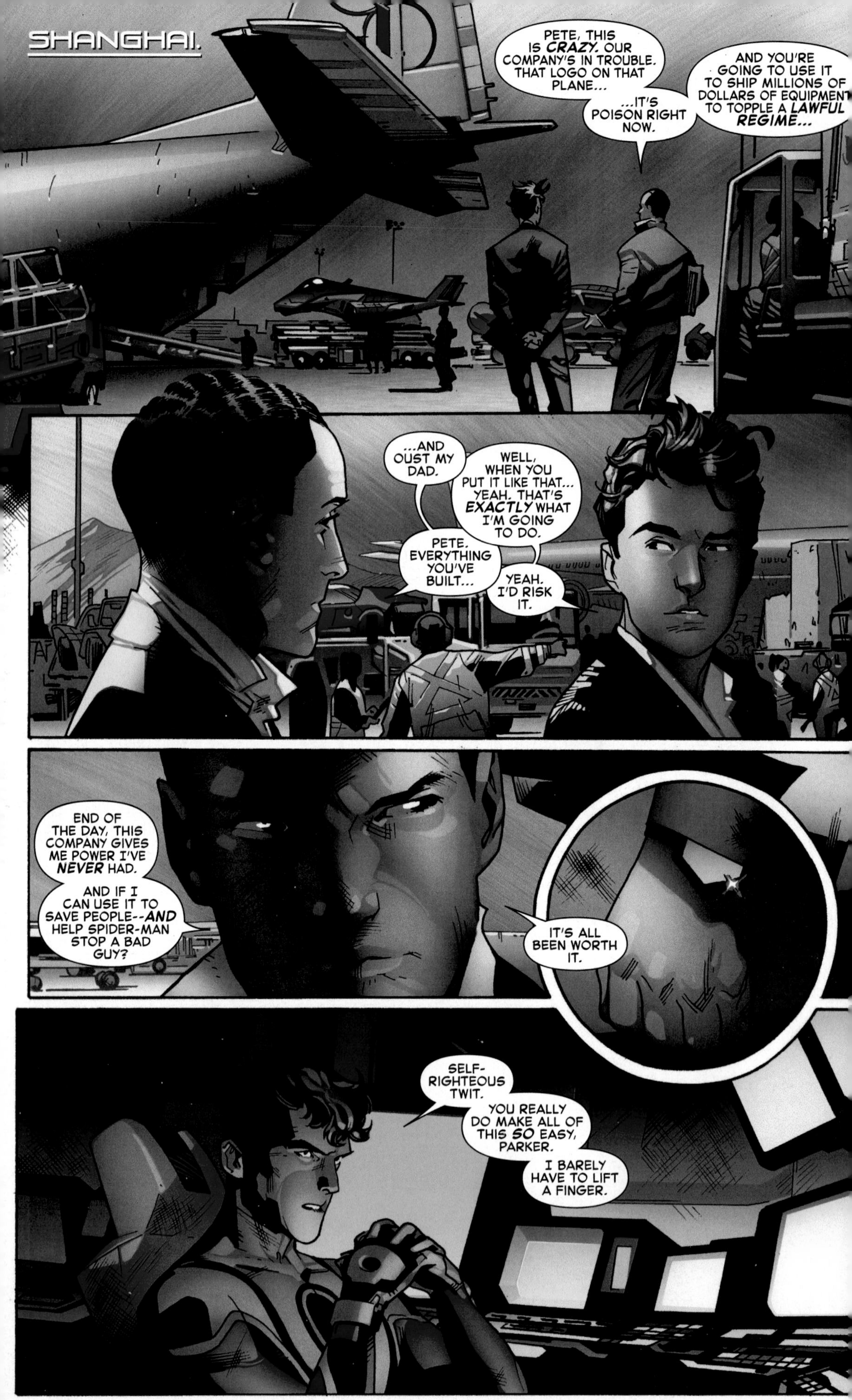
SHANGHAI.
PETE, THIS IS CRAZY. OUR COMPANY'S IN TROUBLE. THAT LOGO ON THAT PLANE...
...IT'S POISON RIGHT NOW.
AND YOU'RE GOING TO USE IT TO SHIP MILLIONS OF DOLLARS OF EQUIPMENT TO TOPPLE A LAWFUL REGIME...
...AND OUST MY DAD.
WELL, WHEN YOU PUT IT LIKE THAT... YEAH. THAT'S EXACTLY WHAT I'M GOING TO DO.
PETE. EVERYTHING YOU'VE BUILT...
YEAH. I'D RISK IT.
END OF THE DAY, THIS COMPANY GIVES ME POWER I'VE NEVER HAD.
AND IF I CAN USE IT TO SAVE PEOPLE--AND HELP SPIDER-MAN STOP A BAD GUY?
IT'S ALL BEEN WORTH IT.
SELF-RIGHTEOUS TWIT.
YOU REALLY DO MAKE ALL OF THIS SO EASY, PARKER.
I BARELY HAVE TO LIFT A FINGER.

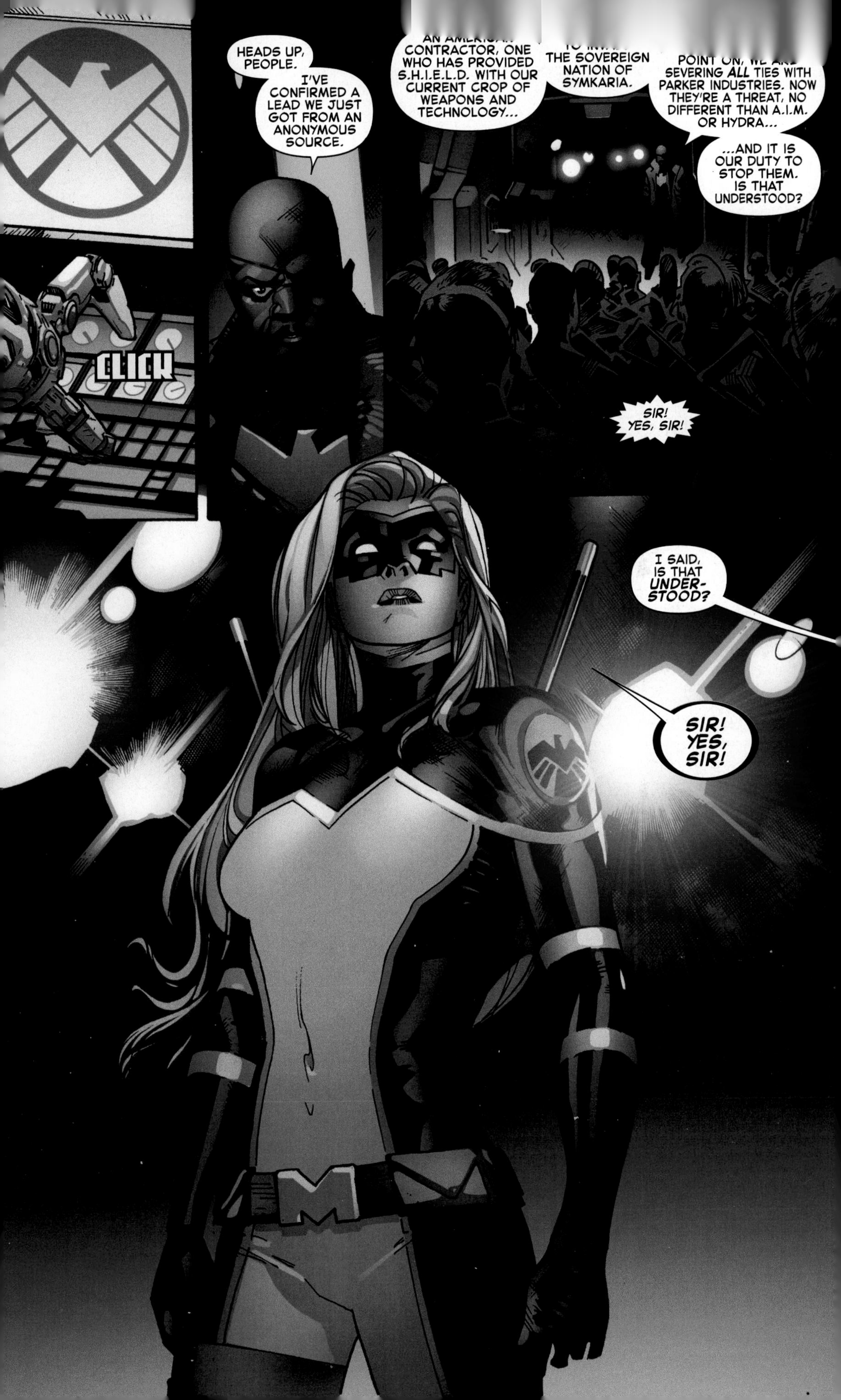
CLICK
HEADS UP, PEOPLE.
I'VE CONFIRMED A LEAD WE JUST GOT FROM AN ANONYMOUS SOURCE.
CONTRACTOR, ONE WHO HAS PROVIDED S.H.I.E.L.D. WITH OUR CURRENT CROP OF WEAPONS AND TECHNOLOGY...
THE SOVEREIGN NATION OF SYMKARIA.
SEVERING **ALL** TIES WITH PARKER INDUSTRIES. NOW THEY'RE A THREAT, NO DIFFERENT THAN A.I.M. OR HYDRA...
...AND IT IS OUR DUTY TO STOP THEM. IS THAT UNDERSTOOD?
SIR! YES, SIR!
I SAID, IS THAT **UNDER-STOOD?**
SIR! YES, SIR!

27

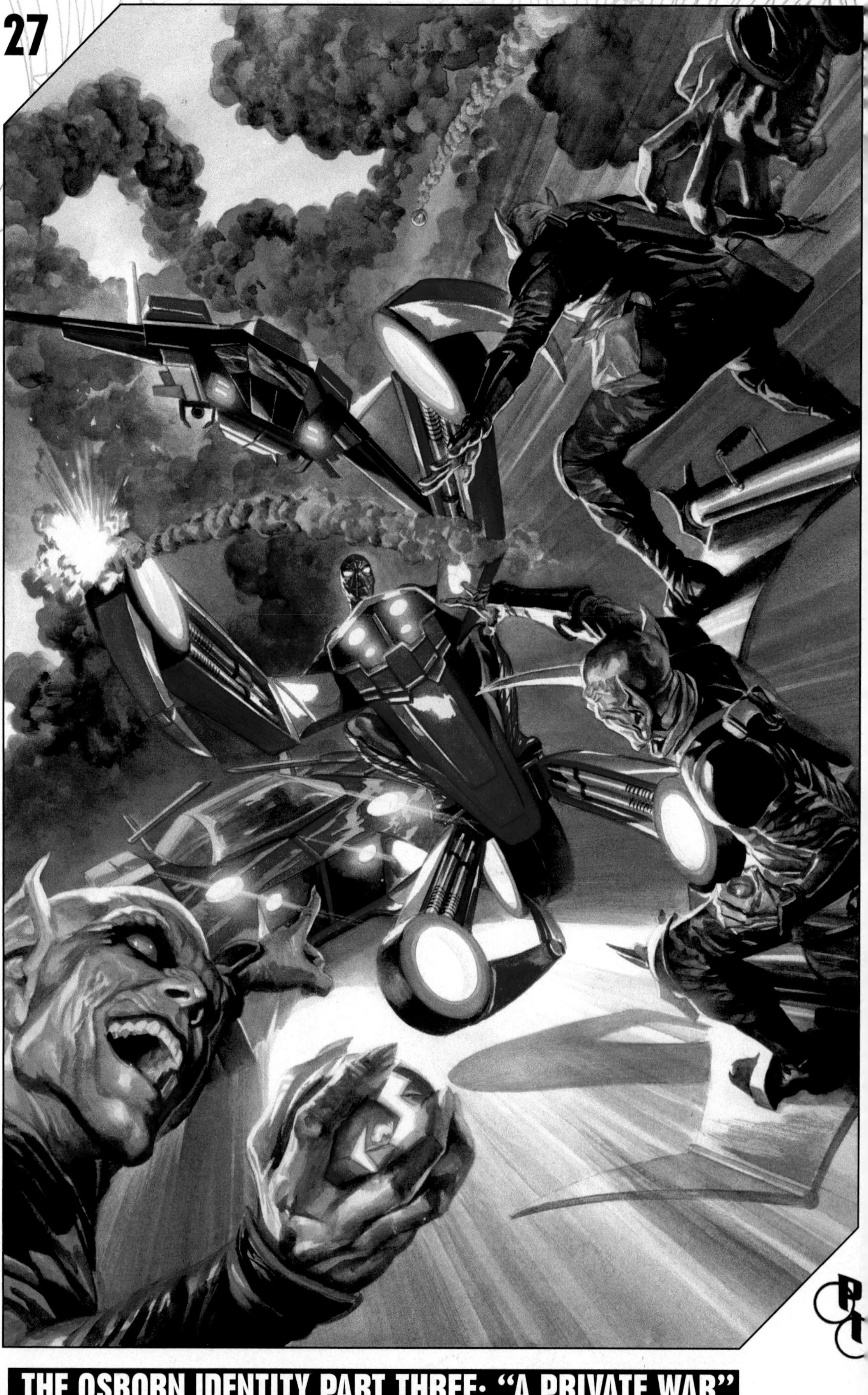

THE OSBORN IDENTITY PART THREE: "A PRIVATE WAR"

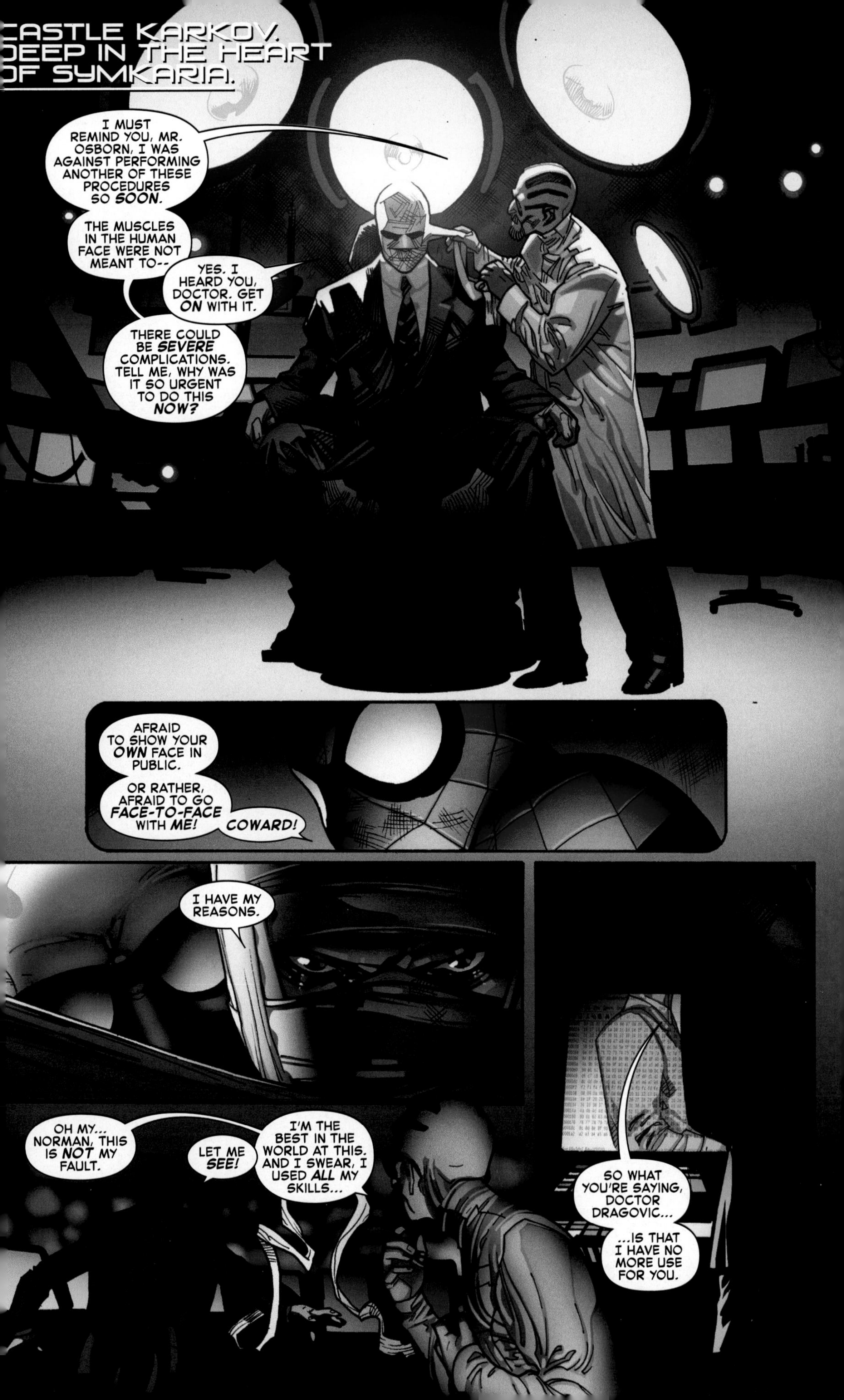
CASTLE KARKOV. DEEP IN THE HEART OF SYMKARIA.
I MUST REMIND YOU, MR. OSBORN, I WAS AGAINST PERFORMING ANOTHER OF THESE PROCEDURES SO SOON.
THE MUSCLES IN THE HUMAN FACE WERE NOT MEANT TO--
YES. I HEARD YOU, DOCTOR. GET ON WITH IT.
THERE COULD BE SEVERE COMPLICATIONS. TELL ME, WHY WAS IT SO URGENT TO DO THIS NOW?
AFRAID TO SHOW YOUR OWN FACE IN PUBLIC.
OR RATHER, AFRAID TO GO FACE-TO-FACE WITH ME!
COWARD!
I HAVE MY REASONS.
OH MY... NORMAN, THIS IS NOT MY FAULT.
LET ME SEE!
I'M THE BEST IN THE WORLD AT THIS. AND I SWEAR, I USED ALL MY SKILLS...
SO WHAT YOU'RE SAYING, DOCTOR DRAGOVIC...
...IS THAT I HAVE NO MORE USE FOR YOU.

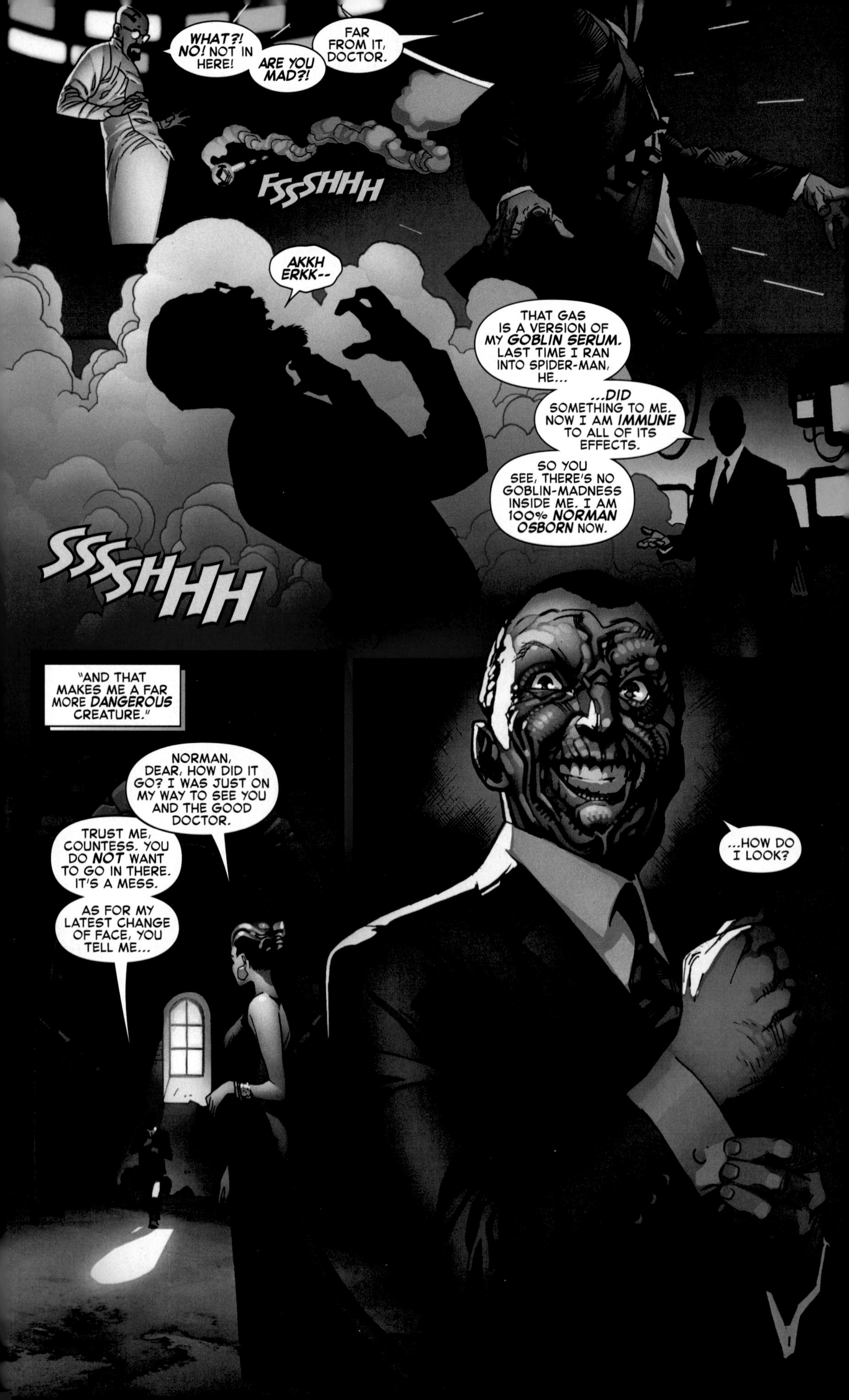

WHAT?! NO! NOT IN HERE!
ARE YOU MAD?!
FAR FROM IT, DOCTOR.
FSSSHHH
AKKH ERKK--
THAT GAS IS A VERSION OF MY GOBLIN SERUM. LAST TIME I RAN INTO SPIDER-MAN, HE...
...DID SOMETHING TO ME. NOW I AM IMMUNE TO ALL OF ITS EFFECTS.
SO YOU SEE, THERE'S NO GOBLIN-MADNESS INSIDE ME. I AM 100% NORMAN OSBORN NOW.
SSSSHHHH
"AND THAT MAKES ME A FAR MORE DANGEROUS CREATURE."
NORMAN, DEAR, HOW DID IT GO? I WAS JUST ON MY WAY TO SEE YOU AND THE GOOD DOCTOR.
TRUST ME, COUNTESS. YOU DO NOT WANT TO GO IN THERE. IT'S A MESS.
AS FOR MY LATEST CHANGE OF FACE, YOU TELL ME...
...HOW DO I LOOK?

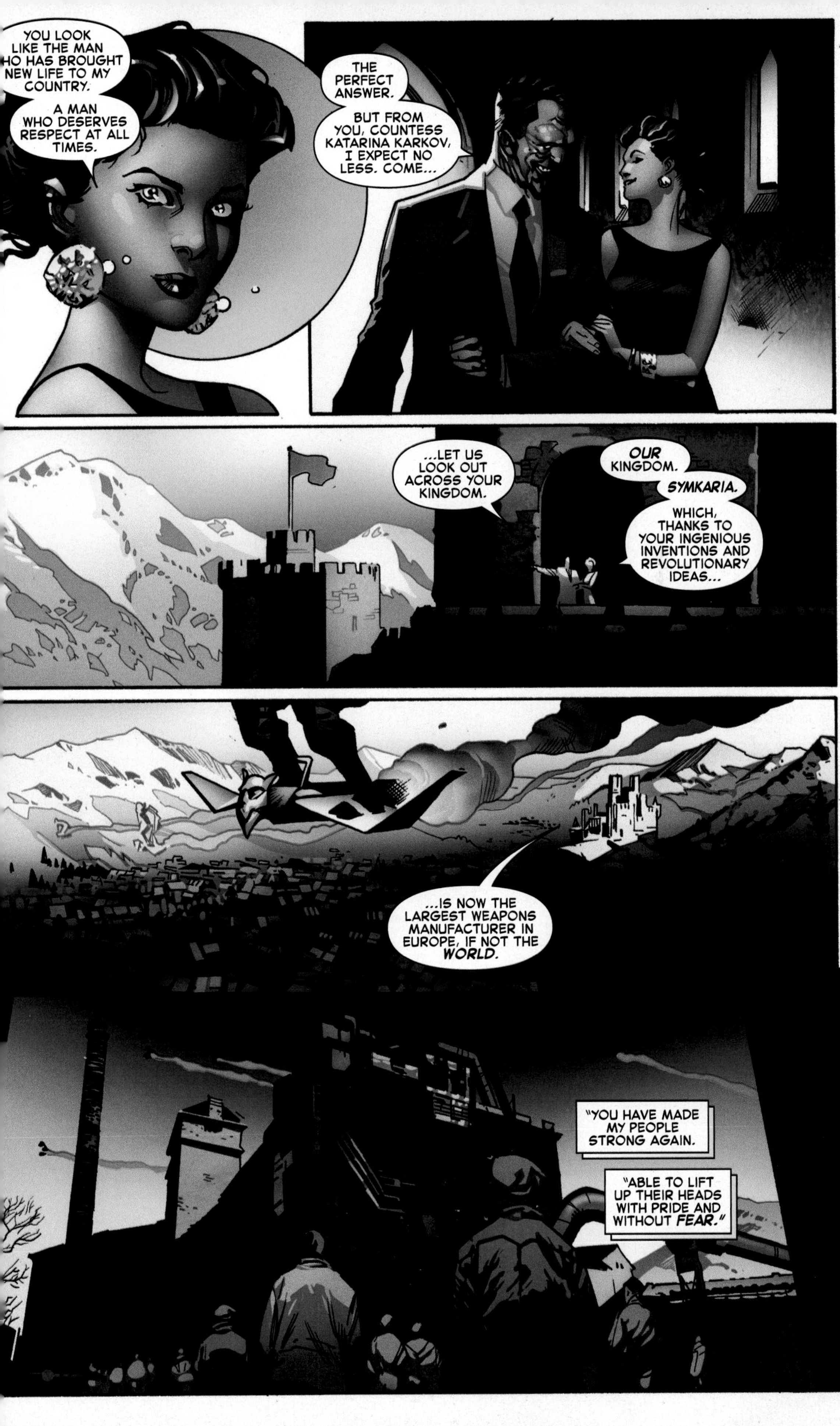
YOU LOOK LIKE THE MAN HO HAS BROUGHT NEW LIFE TO MY COUNTRY.
A MAN WHO DESERVES RESPECT AT ALL TIMES.
THE PERFECT ANSWER.
BUT FROM YOU, COUNTESS KATARINA KARKOV, I EXPECT NO LESS. COME...
...LET US LOOK OUT ACROSS YOUR KINGDOM.
OUR KINGDOM.
SYMKARIA.
WHICH, THANKS TO YOUR INGENIOUS INVENTIONS AND REVOLUTIONARY IDEAS...
...IS NOW THE LARGEST WEAPONS MANUFACTURER IN EUROPE, IF NOT THE WORLD.
"YOU HAVE MADE MY PEOPLE STRONG AGAIN.
"ABLE TO LIFT UP THEIR HEADS WITH PRIDE AND WITHOUT FEAR."

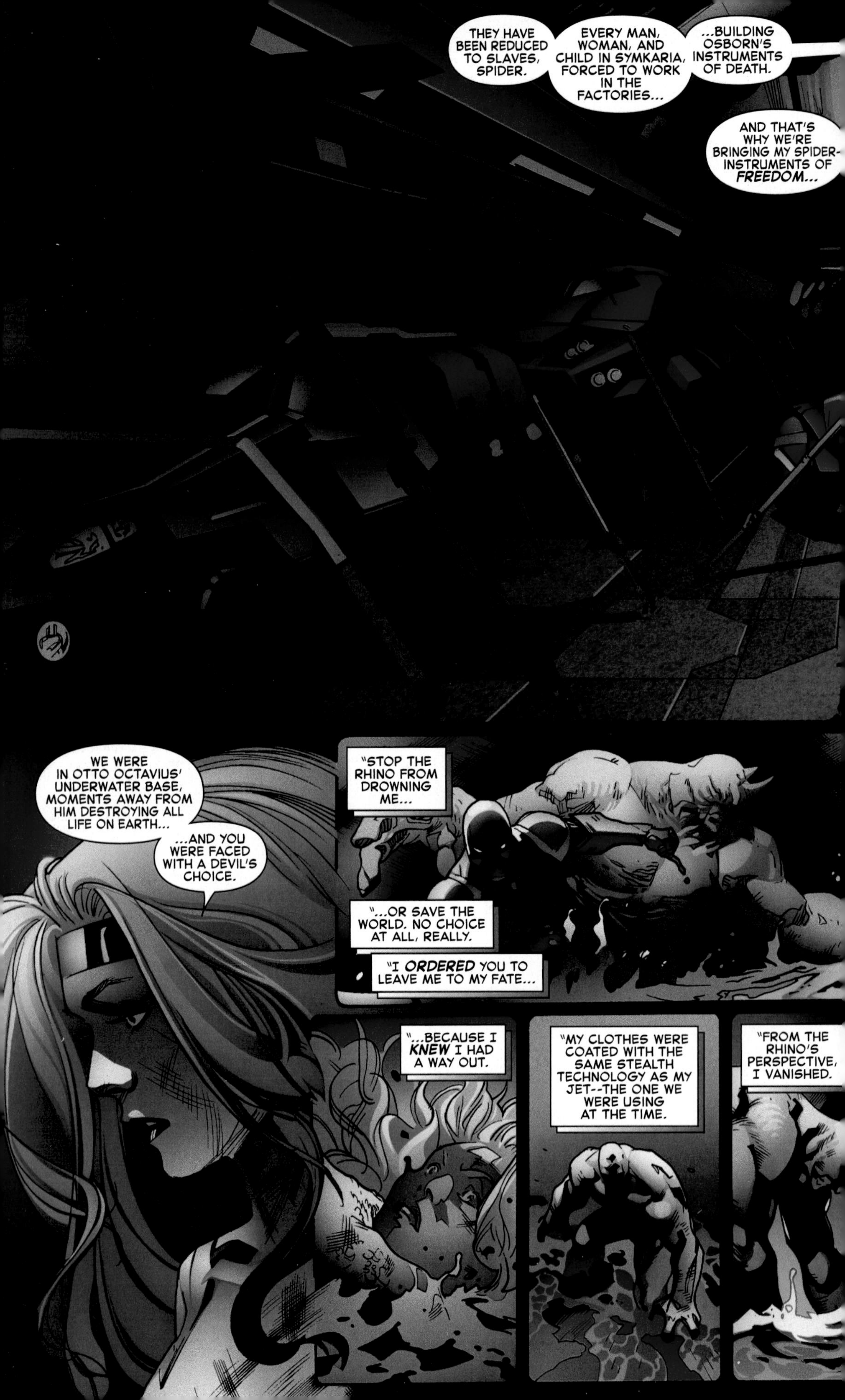
THEY HAVE BEEN REDUCED TO SLAVES, SPIDER.
EVERY MAN, WOMAN, AND CHILD IN SYMKARIA, FORCED TO WORK IN THE FACTORIES...
...BUILDING OSBORN'S INSTRUMENTS OF DEATH.
AND THAT'S WHY WE'RE BRINGING MY SPIDER-INSTRUMENTS OF FREEDOM...
WE WERE IN OTTO OCTAVIUS' UNDERWATER BASE, MOMENTS AWAY FROM HIM DESTROYING ALL LIFE ON EARTH...
...AND YOU WERE FACED WITH A DEVIL'S CHOICE.
"STOP THE RHINO FROM DROWNING ME...
"...OR SAVE THE WORLD. NO CHOICE AT ALL, REALLY.
"I ORDERED YOU TO LEAVE ME TO MY FATE...
"...BECAUSE I KNEW I HAD A WAY OUT.
"MY CLOTHES WERE COATED WITH THE SAME STEALTH TECHNOLOGY AS MY JET--THE ONE WE WERE USING AT THE TIME.
"FROM THE RHINO'S PERSPECTIVE, I VANISHED.

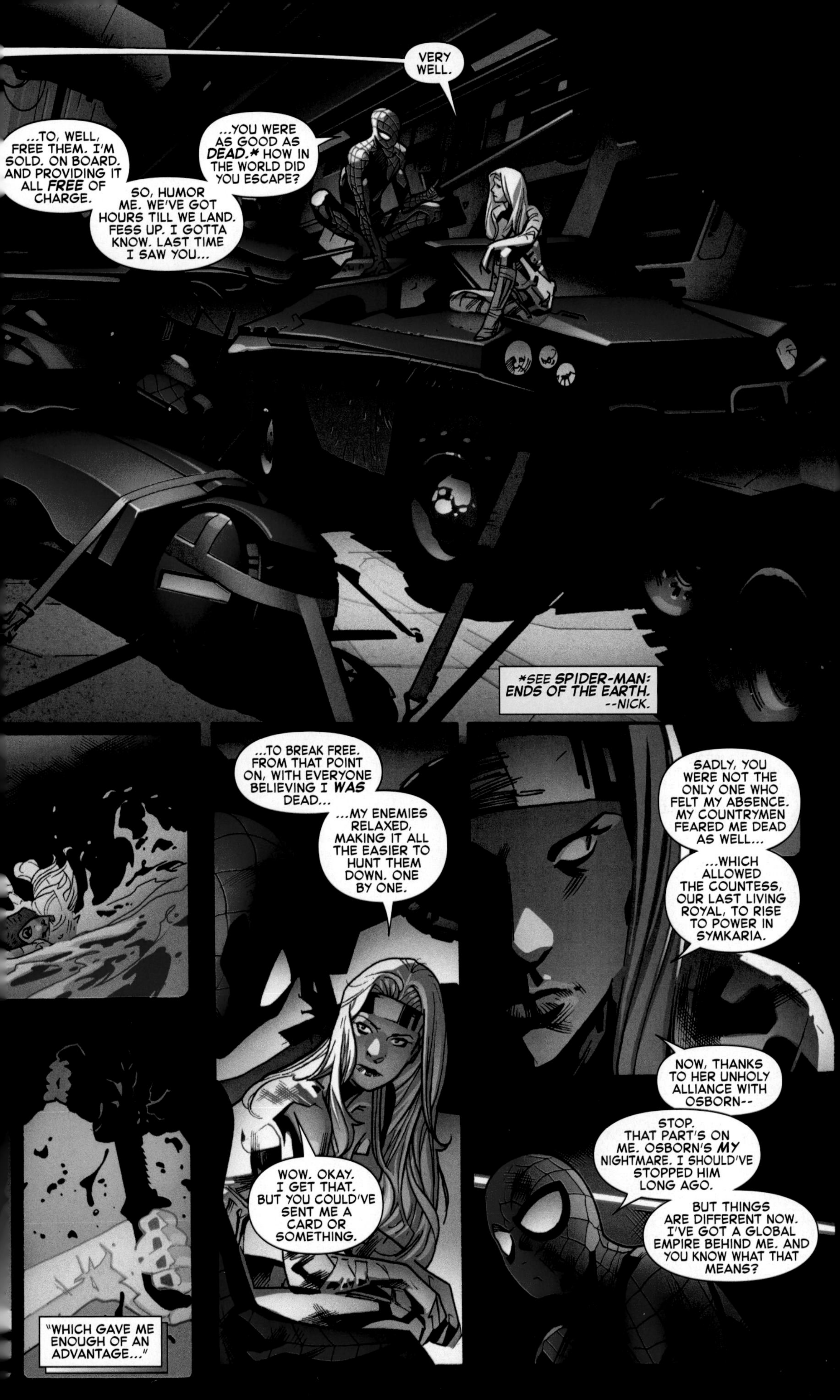

VERY WELL.
...TO, WELL, FREE THEM. I'M SOLD. ON BOARD. AND PROVIDING IT ALL FREE OF CHARGE.
SO, HUMOR ME. WE'VE GOT HOURS TILL WE LAND. FESS UP. I GOTTA KNOW. LAST TIME I SAW YOU...
...YOU WERE AS GOOD AS DEAD.* HOW IN THE WORLD DID YOU ESCAPE?
*SEE SPIDER-MAN: ENDS OF THE EARTH. --NICK.
"WHICH GAVE ME ENOUGH OF AN ADVANTAGE..."
...TO BREAK FREE. FROM THAT POINT ON, WITH EVERYONE BELIEVING I WAS DEAD...
...MY ENEMIES RELAXED, MAKING IT ALL THE EASIER TO HUNT THEM DOWN. ONE BY ONE.
WOW. OKAY. I GET THAT. BUT YOU COULD'VE SENT ME A CARD OR SOMETHING.
SADLY, YOU WERE NOT THE ONLY ONE WHO FELT MY ABSENCE. MY COUNTRYMEN FEARED ME DEAD AS WELL...
...WHICH ALLOWED THE COUNTESS, OUR LAST LIVING ROYAL, TO RISE TO POWER IN SYMKARIA.
NOW, THANKS TO HER UNHOLY ALLIANCE WITH OSBORN--
STOP. THAT PART'S ON ME. OSBORN'S MY NIGHTMARE. I SHOULD'VE STOPPED HIM LONG AGO.
BUT THINGS ARE DIFFERENT NOW. I'VE GOT A GLOBAL EMPIRE BEHIND ME. AND YOU KNOW WHAT THAT MEANS?

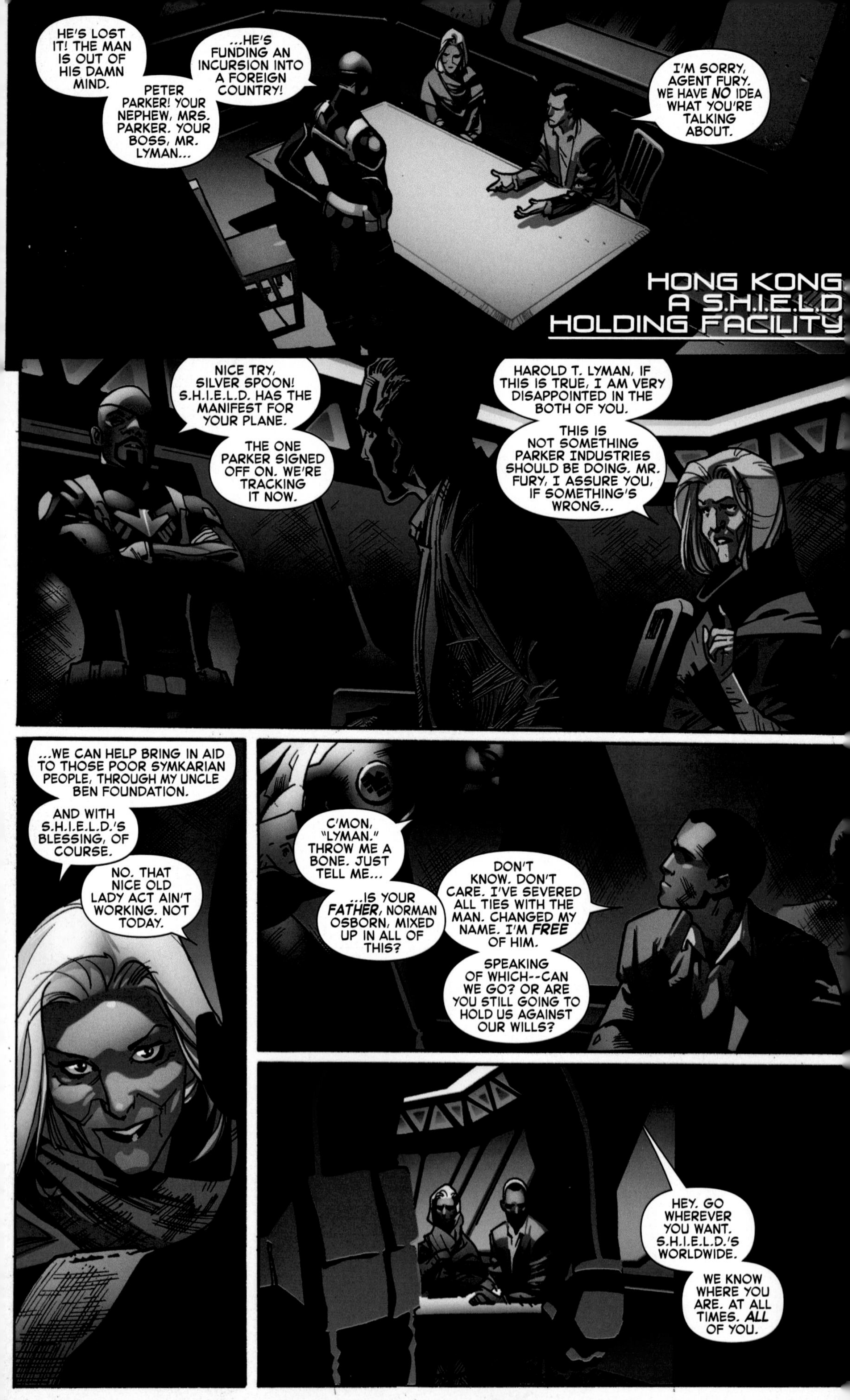
HE'S LOST IT! THE MAN IS OUT OF HIS DAMN MIND.
...HE'S FUNDING AN INCURSION INTO A FOREIGN COUNTRY!
PETER PARKER! YOUR NEPHEW, MRS. PARKER. YOUR BOSS, MR. LYMAN...
I'M SORRY, AGENT FURY. WE HAVE NO IDEA WHAT YOU'RE TALKING ABOUT.
HONG KONG
A S.H.I.E.L.D HOLDING FACILITY
NICE TRY, SILVER SPOON! S.H.I.E.L.D. HAS THE MANIFEST FOR YOUR PLANE.
THE ONE PARKER SIGNED OFF ON. WE'RE TRACKING IT NOW.
HAROLD T. LYMAN, IF THIS IS TRUE, I AM VERY DISAPPOINTED IN THE BOTH OF YOU.
THIS IS NOT SOMETHING PARKER INDUSTRIES SHOULD BE DOING. MR. FURY, I ASSURE YOU, IF SOMETHING'S WRONG...
...WE CAN HELP BRING IN AID TO THOSE POOR SYMKARIAN PEOPLE, THROUGH MY UNCLE BEN FOUNDATION.
AND WITH S.H.I.E.L.D.'S BLESSING, OF COURSE.
NO. THAT NICE OLD LADY ACT AIN'T WORKING. NOT TODAY.
C'MON, "LYMAN." THROW ME A BONE. JUST TELL ME...
...IS YOUR FATHER, NORMAN OSBORN, MIXED UP IN ALL OF THIS?
DON'T KNOW. DON'T CARE. I'VE SEVERED ALL TIES WITH THE MAN. CHANGED MY NAME. I'M FREE OF HIM.
SPEAKING OF WHICH--CAN WE GO? OR ARE YOU STILL GOING TO HOLD US AGAINST OUR WILLS?
HEY. GO WHEREVER YOU WANT. S.H.I.E.L.D.'S WORLDWIDE.
WE KNOW WHERE YOU ARE. AT ALL TIMES. ALL OF YOU.

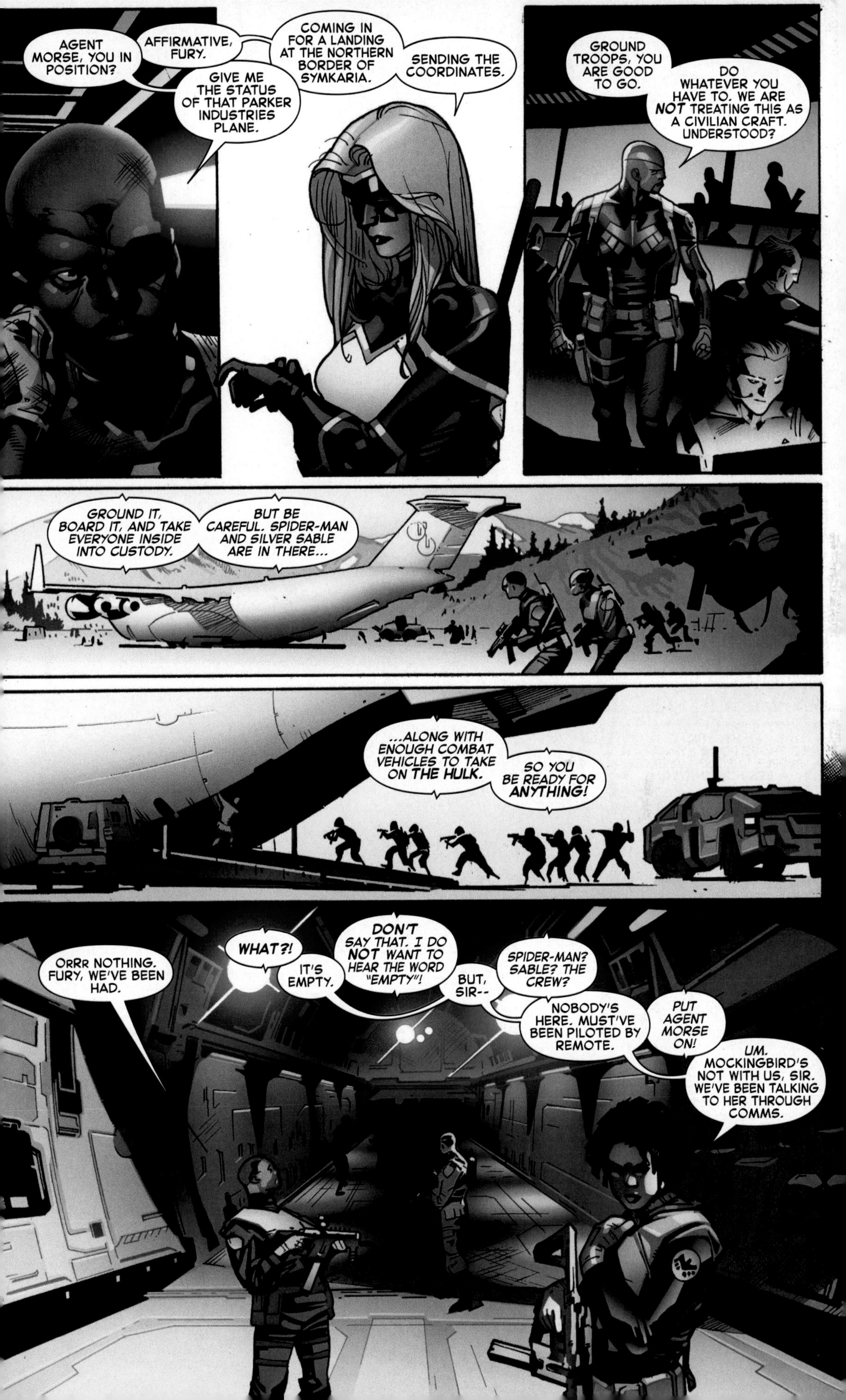

AGENT MORSE, YOU IN POSITION?
AFFIRMATIVE, FURY.
GIVE ME THE STATUS OF THAT PARKER INDUSTRIES PLANE.
COMING IN FOR A LANDING AT THE NORTHERN BORDER OF SYMKARIA.
SENDING THE COORDINATES.
GROUND TROOPS, YOU ARE GOOD TO GO.
DO WHATEVER YOU HAVE TO. WE ARE NOT TREATING THIS AS A CIVILIAN CRAFT. UNDERSTOOD?
GROUND IT, BOARD IT, AND TAKE EVERYONE INSIDE INTO CUSTODY.
BUT BE CAREFUL. SPIDER-MAN AND SILVER SABLE ARE IN THERE...
...ALONG WITH ENOUGH COMBAT VEHICLES TO TAKE ON THE HULK.
SO YOU BE READY FOR ANYTHING!
ORRR NOTHING. FURY, WE'VE BEEN HAD.
WHAT?!
IT'S EMPTY.
DON'T SAY THAT. I DO NOT WANT TO HEAR THE WORD "EMPTY"!
BUT, SIR--
SPIDER-MAN? SABLE? THE CREW?
NOBODY'S HERE. MUST'VE BEEN PILOTED BY REMOTE.
PUT AGENT MORSE ON!
UM. MOCKINGBIRD'S NOT WITH US, SIR. WE'VE BEEN TALKING TO HER THROUGH COMMS.

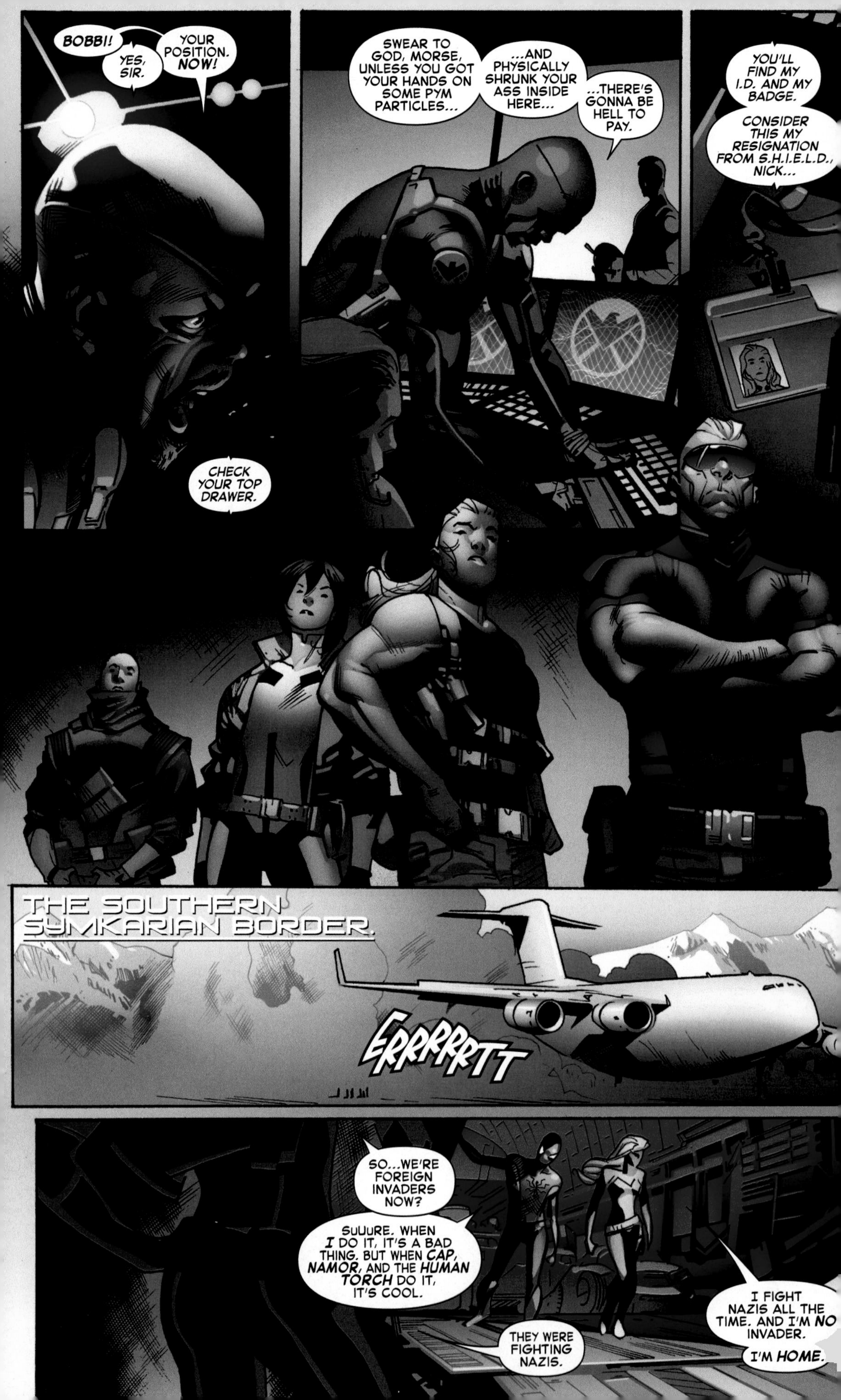
BOBBI!
YES, SIR.
YOUR POSITION. NOW!
CHECK YOUR TOP DRAWER.
SWEAR TO GOD, MORSE, UNLESS YOU GOT YOUR HANDS ON SOME PYM PARTICLES...
...AND PHYSICALLY SHRUNK YOUR ASS INSIDE HERE...
...THERE'S GONNA BE HELL TO PAY.
YOU'LL FIND MY I.D. AND MY BADGE.
CONSIDER THIS MY RESIGNATION FROM S.H.I.E.L.D., NICK...
THE SOUTHERN SYMKARIAN BORDER.
ERRRRRTT
SO...WE'RE FOREIGN INVADERS NOW?
SUUURE. WHEN I DO IT, IT'S A BAD THING. BUT WHEN CAP, NAMOR, AND THE HUMAN TORCH DO IT, IT'S COOL.
THEY WERE FIGHTING NAZIS.
I FIGHT NAZIS ALL THE TIME. AND I'M NO INVADER.
I'M HOME.

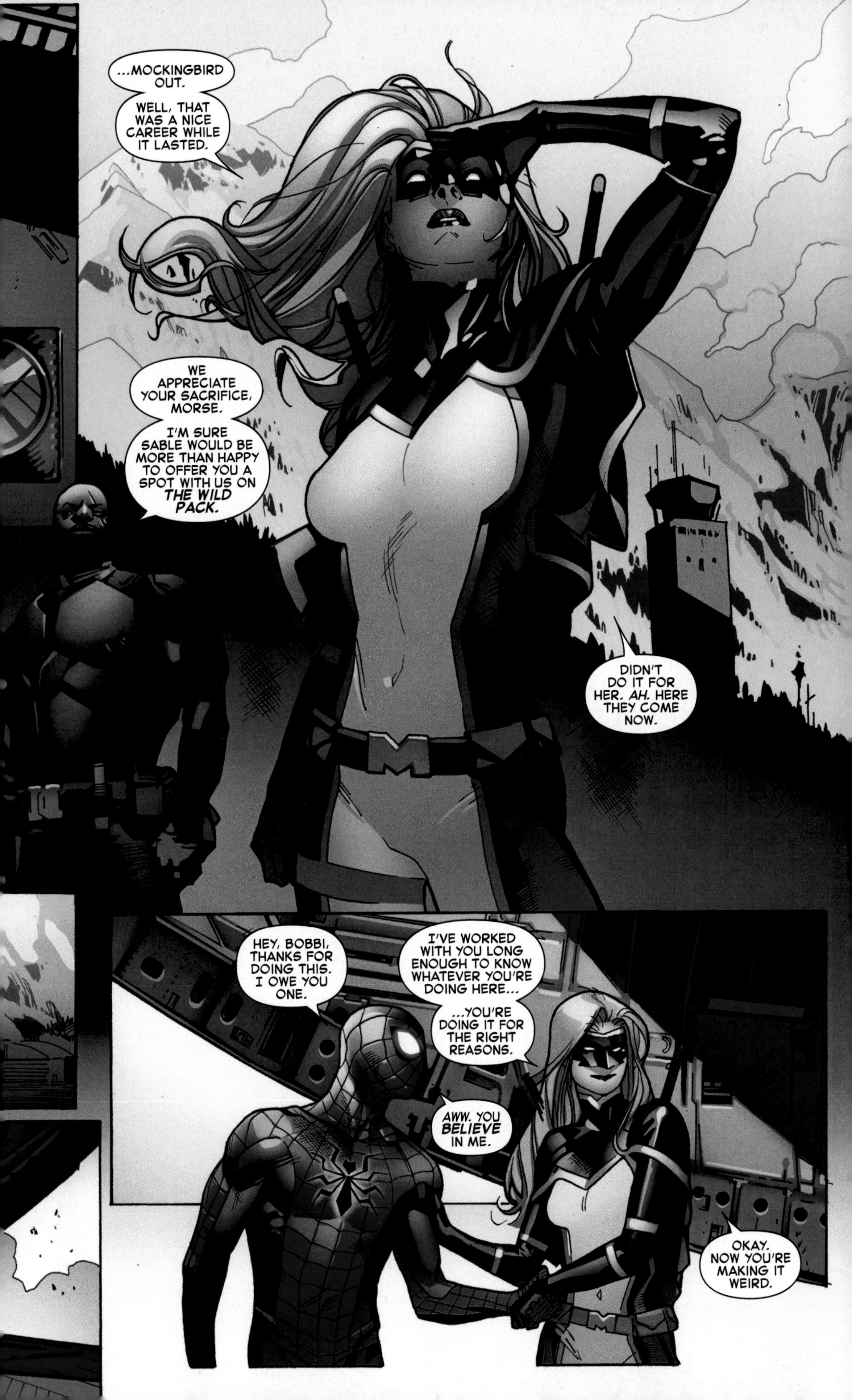
...MOCKINGBIRD OUT.
WELL, THAT WAS A NICE CAREER WHILE IT LASTED.
WE APPRECIATE YOUR SACRIFICE, MORSE.
I'M SURE SABLE WOULD BE MORE THAN HAPPY TO OFFER YOU A SPOT WITH US ON *THE WILD PACK.*
DIDN'T DO IT FOR HER. *AH.* HERE THEY COME NOW.
HEY, BOBBI, THANKS FOR DOING THIS. I OWE YOU ONE.
I'VE WORKED WITH YOU LONG ENOUGH TO KNOW WHATEVER YOU'RE DOING HERE...
...YOU'RE DOING IT FOR THE RIGHT REASONS.
AWW. YOU *BELIEVE* IN ME.
OKAY. NOW YOU'RE MAKING IT WEIRD.

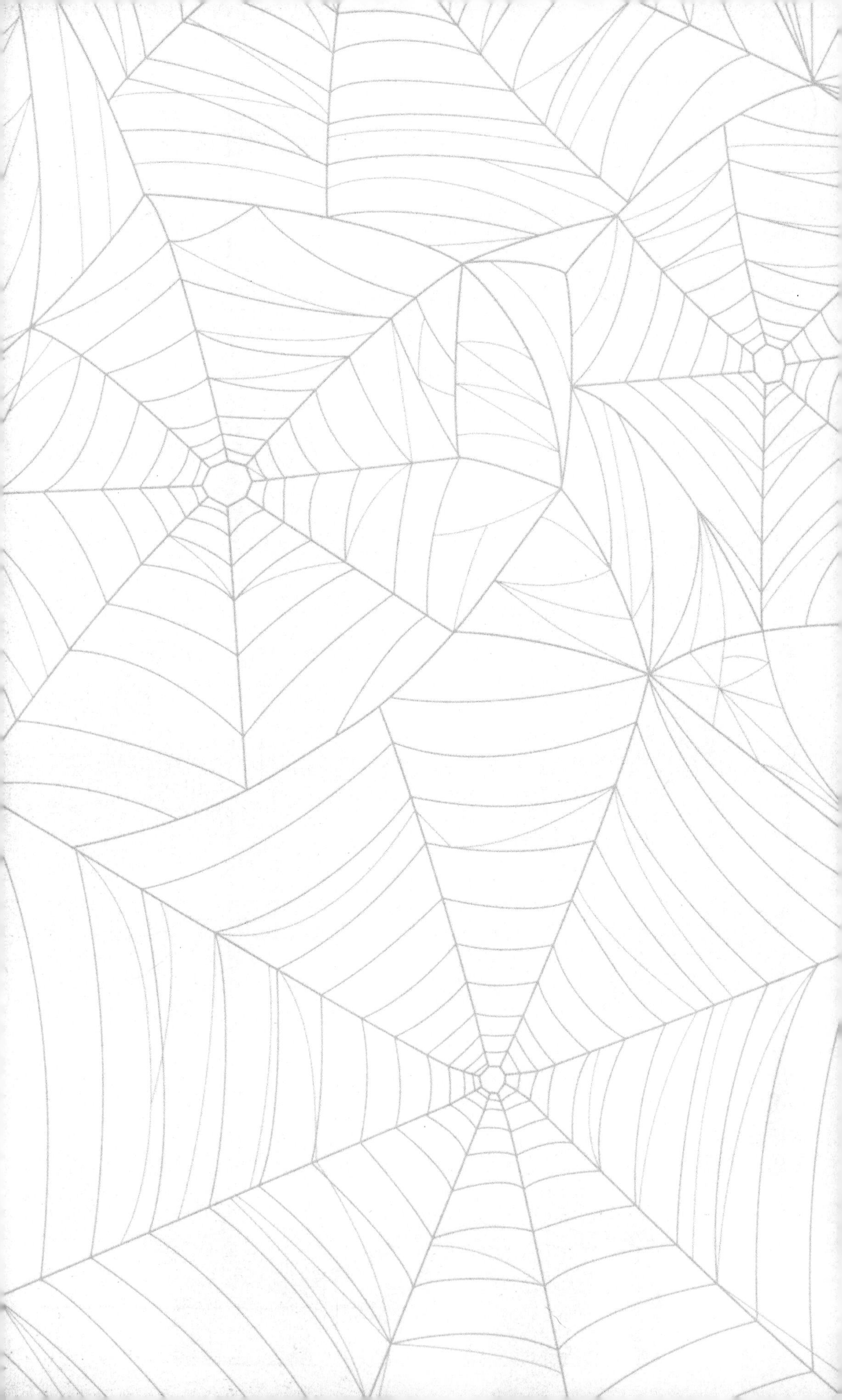

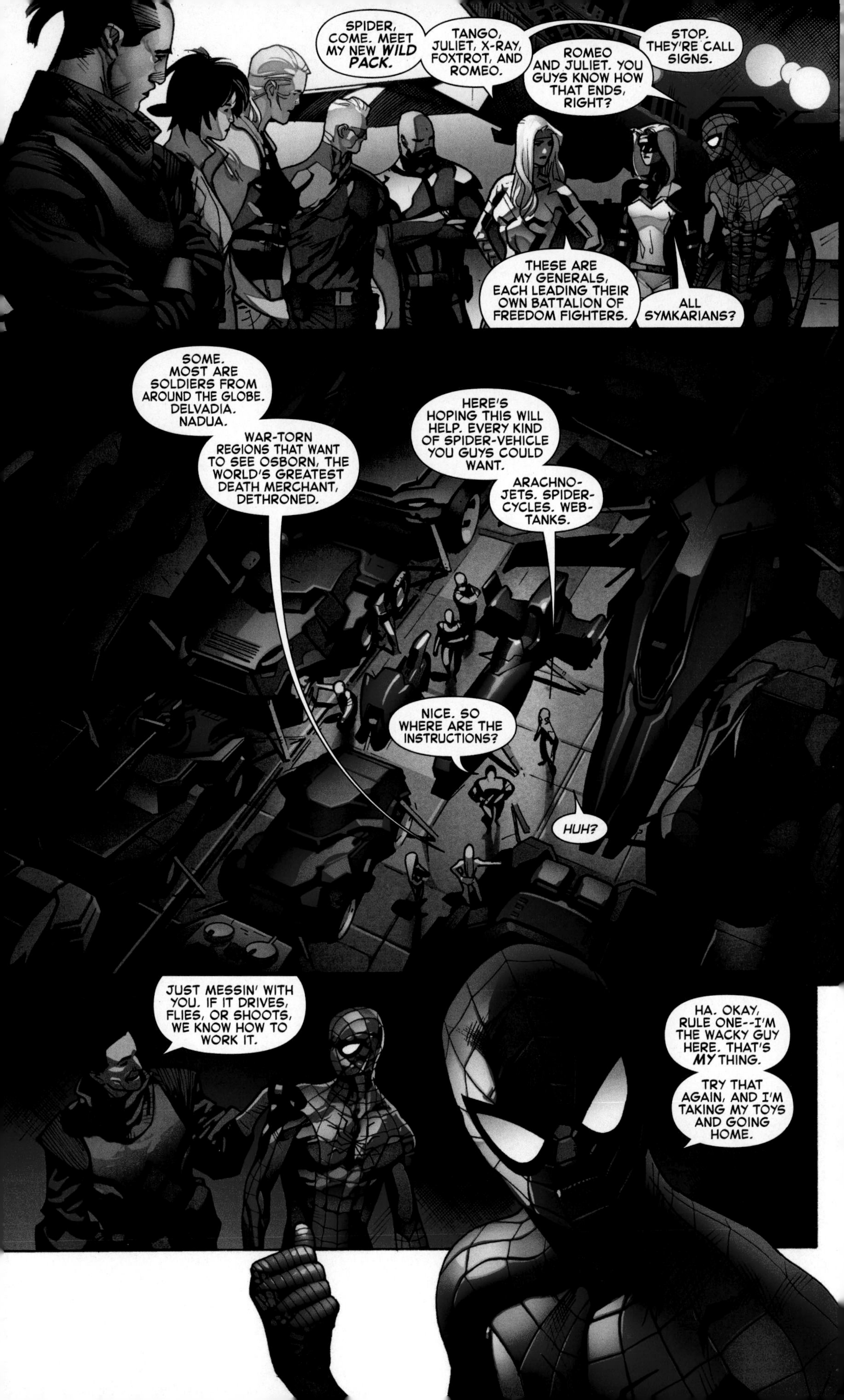
SPIDER, COME. MEET MY NEW WILD PACK.
TANGO, JULIET, X-RAY, FOXTROT, AND ROMEO.
ROMEO AND JULIET. YOU GUYS KNOW HOW THAT ENDS, RIGHT?
STOP. THEY'RE CALL SIGNS.
THESE ARE MY GENERALS, EACH LEADING THEIR OWN BATTALION OF FREEDOM FIGHTERS.
ALL SYMKARIANS?
SOME. MOST ARE SOLDIERS FROM AROUND THE GLOBE. DELVADIA. NADUA.
WAR-TORN REGIONS THAT WANT TO SEE OSBORN, THE WORLD'S GREATEST DEATH MERCHANT, DETHRONED.
HERE'S HOPING THIS WILL HELP. EVERY KIND OF SPIDER-VEHICLE YOU GUYS COULD WANT.
ARACHNO-JETS. SPIDER-CYCLES. WEB-TANKS.
NICE. SO WHERE ARE THE INSTRUCTIONS?
HUH?
JUST MESSIN' WITH YOU. IF IT DRIVES, FLIES, OR SHOOTS, WE KNOW HOW TO WORK IT.
HA. OKAY, RULE ONE--I'M THE WACKY GUY HERE. THAT'S MY THING.
TRY THAT AGAIN, AND I'M TAKING MY TOYS AND GOING HOME.

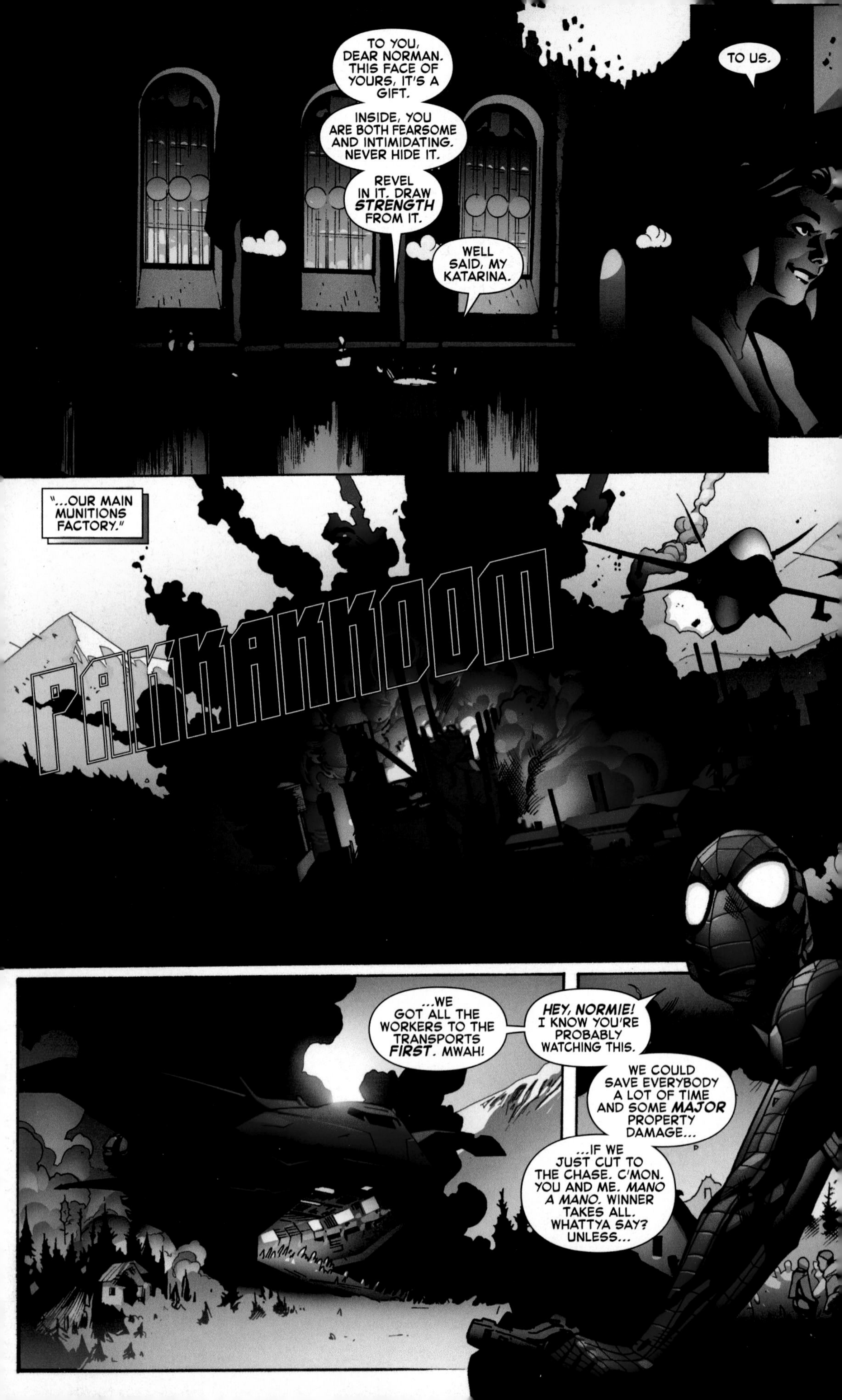
TO YOU, DEAR NORMAN. THIS FACE OF YOURS, IT'S A GIFT.
INSIDE, YOU ARE BOTH FEARSOME AND INTIMIDATING. NEVER HIDE IT.
REVEL IN IT. DRAW STRENGTH FROM IT.
TO US.
WELL SAID, MY KATARINA.
"...OUR MAIN MUNITIONS FACTORY."
PAKKAKKOOM
...WE GOT ALL THE WORKERS TO THE TRANSPORTS FIRST. MWAH!
HEY, NORMIE! I KNOW YOU'RE PROBABLY WATCHING THIS.
WE COULD SAVE EVERYBODY A LOT OF TIME AND SOME MAJOR PROPERTY DAMAGE...
...IF WE JUST CUT TO THE CHASE. C'MON. YOU AND ME. MANO A MANO. WINNER TAKES ALL. WHATTYA SAY? UNLESS...

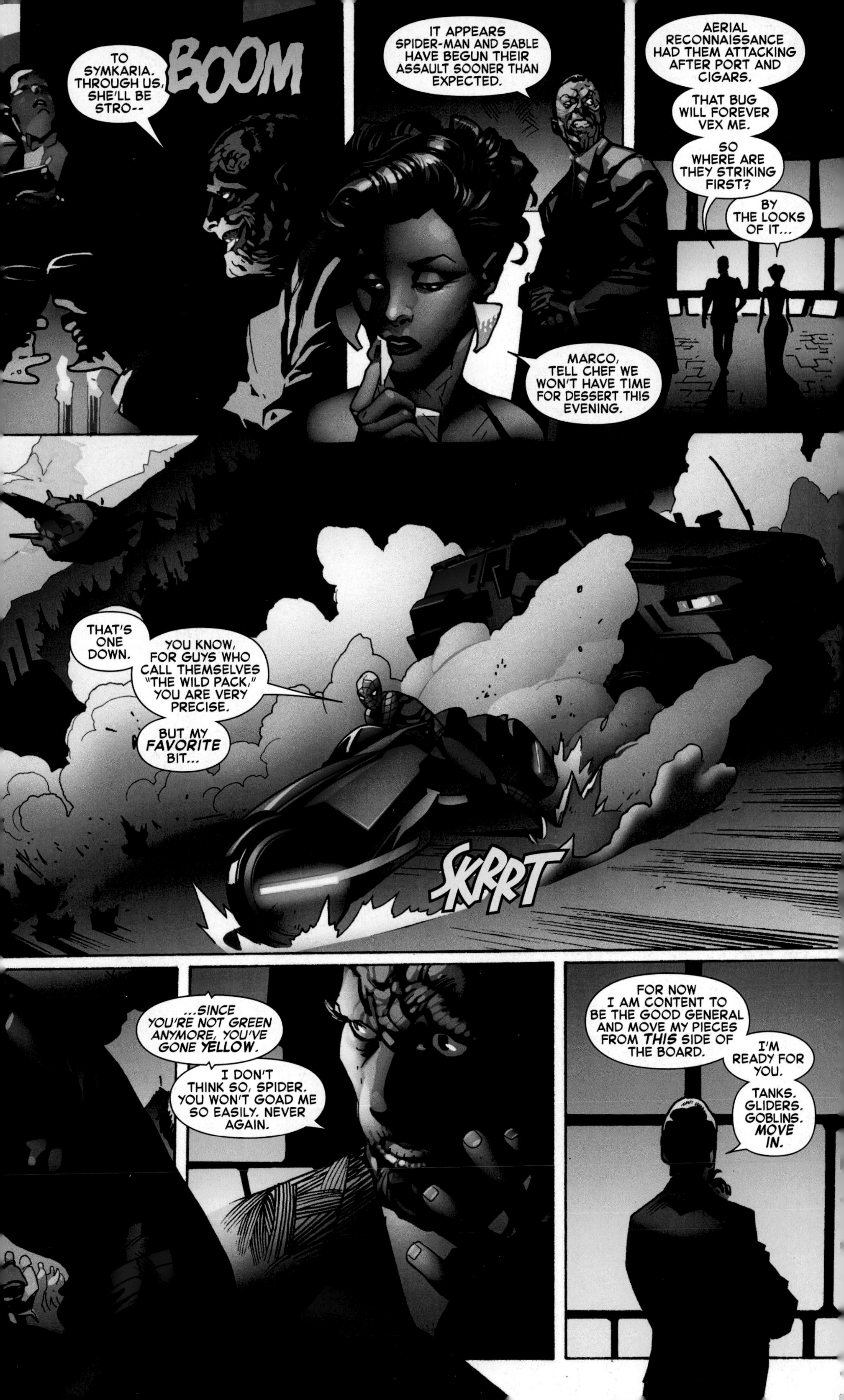
TO SYMKARIA. THROUGH US, SHE'LL BE STRO--
BOOM
IT APPEARS SPIDER-MAN AND SABLE HAVE BEGUN THEIR ASSAULT SOONER THAN EXPECTED.
MARCO, TELL CHEF WE WON'T HAVE TIME FOR DESSERT THIS EVENING.
AERIAL RECONNAISSANCE HAD THEM ATTACKING AFTER PORT AND CIGARS.
THAT BUG WILL FOREVER VEX ME.
SO WHERE ARE THEY STRIKING FIRST?
BY THE LOOKS OF IT...
THAT'S ONE DOWN.
YOU KNOW, FOR GUYS WHO CALL THEMSELVES "THE WILD PACK," YOU ARE VERY PRECISE.
BUT MY FAVORITE BIT...
SKRRT
...SINCE YOU'RE NOT GREEN ANYMORE, YOU'VE GONE YELLOW.
I DON'T THINK SO, SPIDER. YOU WON'T GOAD ME SO EASILY. NEVER AGAIN.
FOR NOW I AM CONTENT TO BE THE GOOD GENERAL AND MOVE MY PIECES FROM THIS SIDE OF THE BOARD.
I'M READY FOR YOU.
TANKS. GLIDERS. GOBLINS. MOVE IN.

TOOM TOOM TOOM

HAHAHAHA HAHAHA

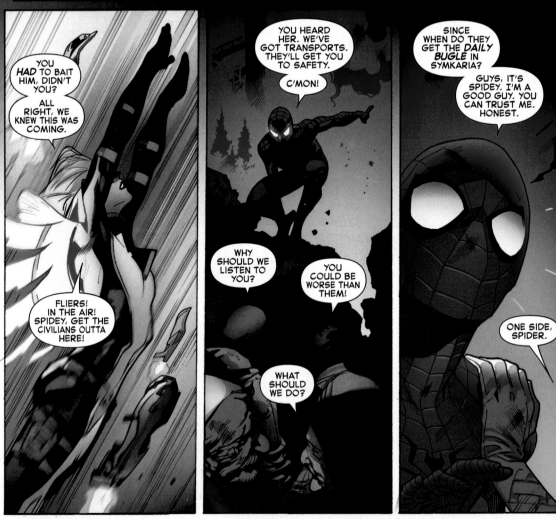

YOU *HAD* TO BAIT HIM, DIDN'T YOU?

ALL RIGHT, WE KNEW THIS WAS COMING.

FLIERS! IN THE AIR! SPIDEY, GET THE CIVILIANS OUTTA HERE!

YOU HEARD HER. WE'VE GOT TRANSPORTS. THEY'LL GET YOU TO SAFETY.

C'MON!

WHY SHOULD WE LISTEN TO YOU?

YOU COULD BE WORSE THAN THEM!

WHAT SHOULD WE DO?

SINCE WHEN DO THEY GET THE *DAILY BUGLE* IN SYMKARIA?

GUYS, IT'S SPIDEY. I'M A GOOD GUY. YOU CAN TRUST ME. HONEST.

ONE SIDE, SPIDER.

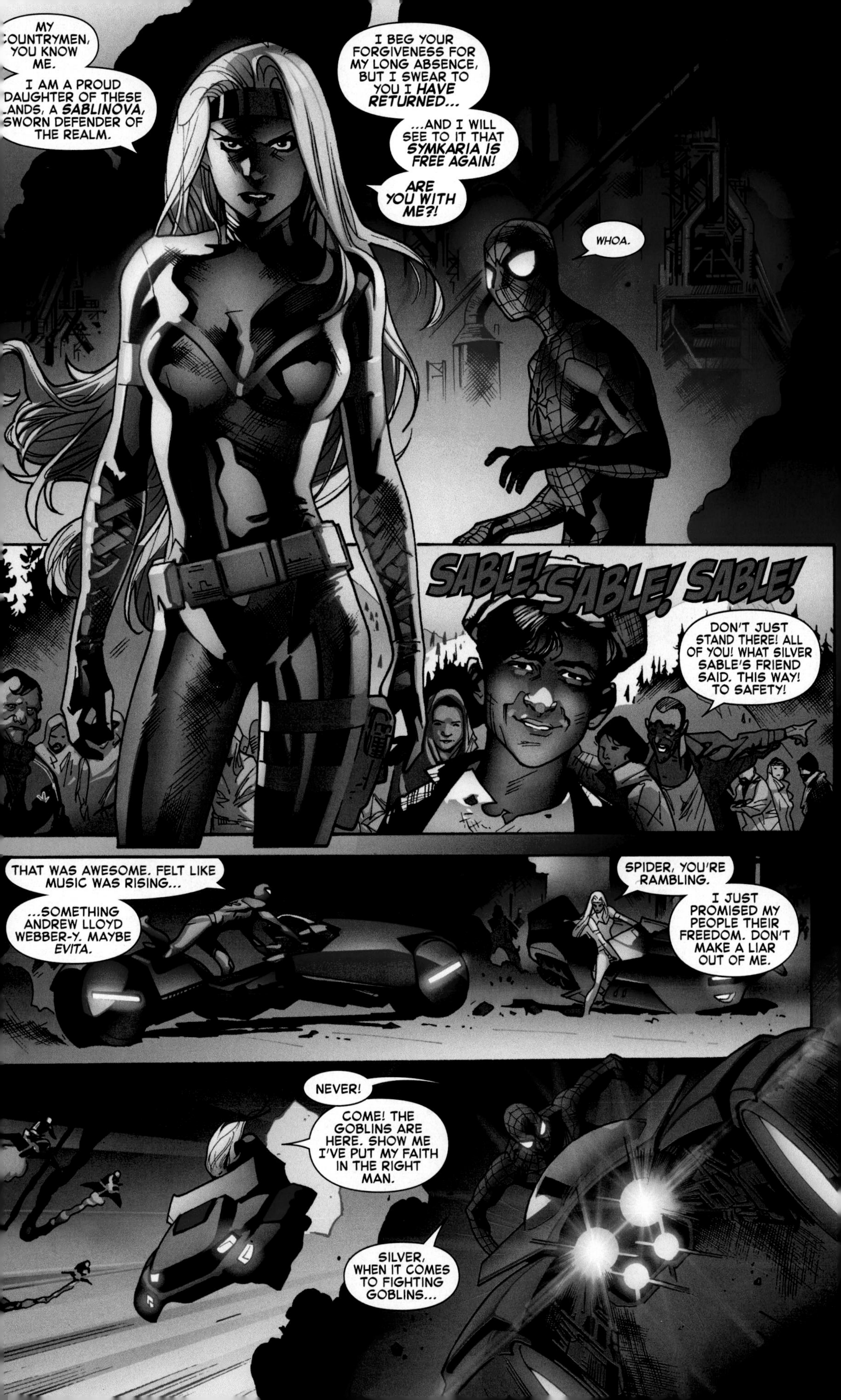

MY COUNTRYMEN, YOU KNOW ME.
I AM A PROUD DAUGHTER OF THESE LANDS, A SABLINOVA, SWORN DEFENDER OF THE REALM.
I BEG YOUR FORGIVENESS FOR MY LONG ABSENCE, BUT I SWEAR TO YOU I HAVE RETURNED...
...AND I WILL SEE TO IT THAT SYMKARIA IS FREE AGAIN!
ARE YOU WITH ME?!
WHOA.
SABLE! SABLE! SABLE!
DON'T JUST STAND THERE! ALL OF YOU! WHAT SILVER SABLE'S FRIEND SAID. THIS WAY! TO SAFETY!
THAT WAS AWESOME. FELT LIKE MUSIC WAS RISING...
...SOMETHING ANDREW LLOYD WEBBER-Y. MAYBE EVITA.
SPIDER, YOU'RE RAMBLING.
I JUST PROMISED MY PEOPLE THEIR FREEDOM. DON'T MAKE A LIAR OUT OF ME.
NEVER!
COME! THE GOBLINS ARE HERE. SHOW ME I'VE PUT MY FAITH IN THE RIGHT MAN.
SILVER, WHEN IT COMES TO FIGHTING GOBLINS...

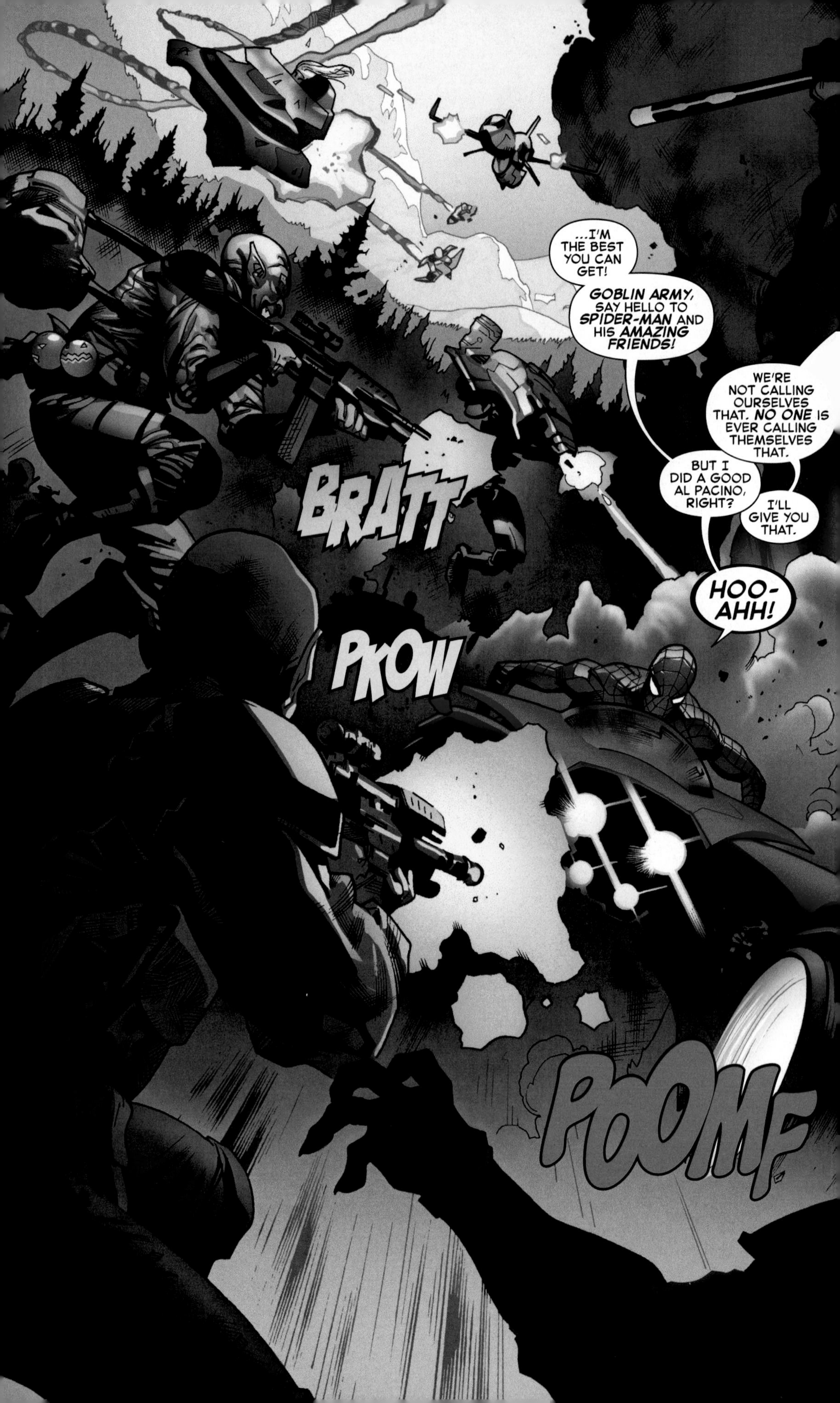

...I'M THE BEST YOU CAN GET!
GOBLIN ARMY, SAY HELLO TO SPIDER-MAN AND HIS AMAZING FRIENDS!
WE'RE NOT CALLING OURSELVES THAT. NO ONE IS EVER CALLING THEMSELVES THAT.
BUT I DID A GOOD AL PACINO, RIGHT?
I'LL GIVE YOU THAT.
HOO-AHH!
BRATT
PKOW
POOMF

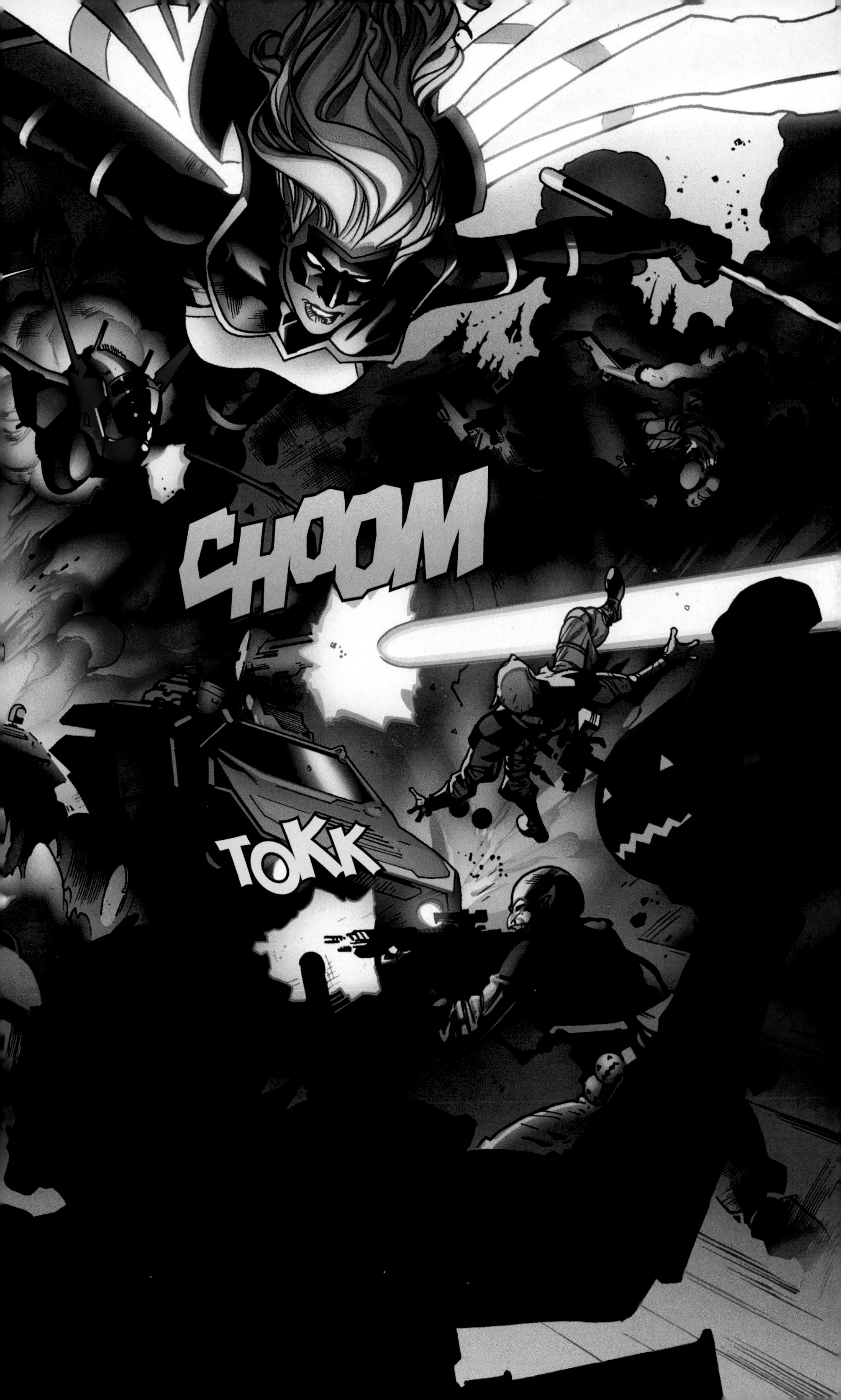
CHOOM
TOKK

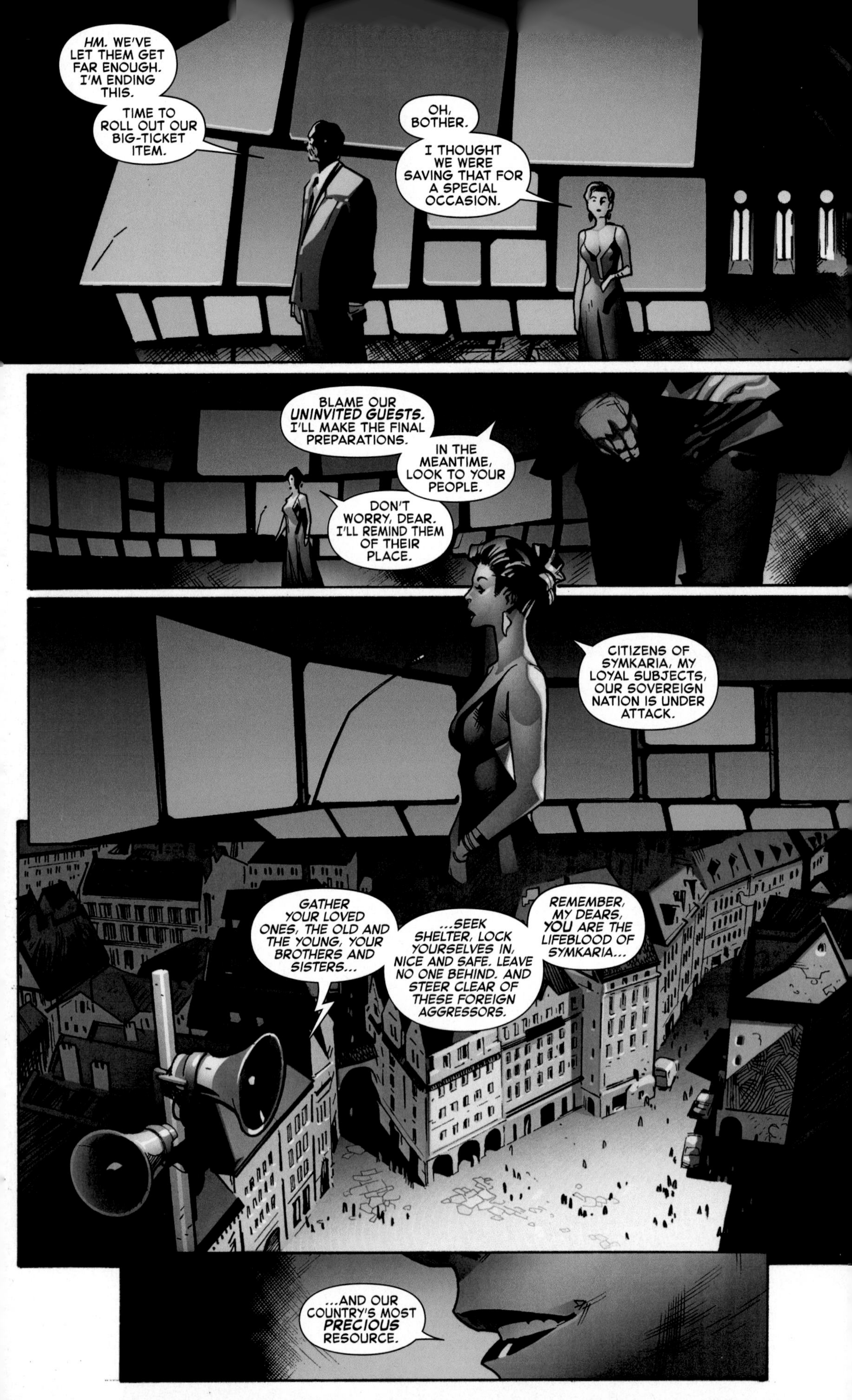
HM. WE'VE LET THEM GET FAR ENOUGH. I'M ENDING THIS.
TIME TO ROLL OUT OUR BIG-TICKET ITEM.
OH, BOTHER.
I THOUGHT WE WERE SAVING THAT FOR A SPECIAL OCCASION.
BLAME OUR UNINVITED GUESTS. I'LL MAKE THE FINAL PREPARATIONS.
IN THE MEANTIME, LOOK TO YOUR PEOPLE.
DON'T WORRY, DEAR. I'LL REMIND THEM OF THEIR PLACE.
CITIZENS OF SYMKARIA, MY LOYAL SUBJECTS, OUR SOVEREIGN NATION IS UNDER ATTACK.
GATHER YOUR LOVED ONES, THE OLD AND THE YOUNG, YOUR BROTHERS AND SISTERS...
...SEEK SHELTER, LOCK YOURSELVES IN, NICE AND SAFE. LEAVE NO ONE BEHIND. AND STEER CLEAR OF THESE FOREIGN AGGRESSORS.
REMEMBER, MY DEARS, YOU ARE THE LIFEBLOOD OF SYMKARIA...
...AND OUR COUNTRY'S MOST PRECIOUS RESOURCE.

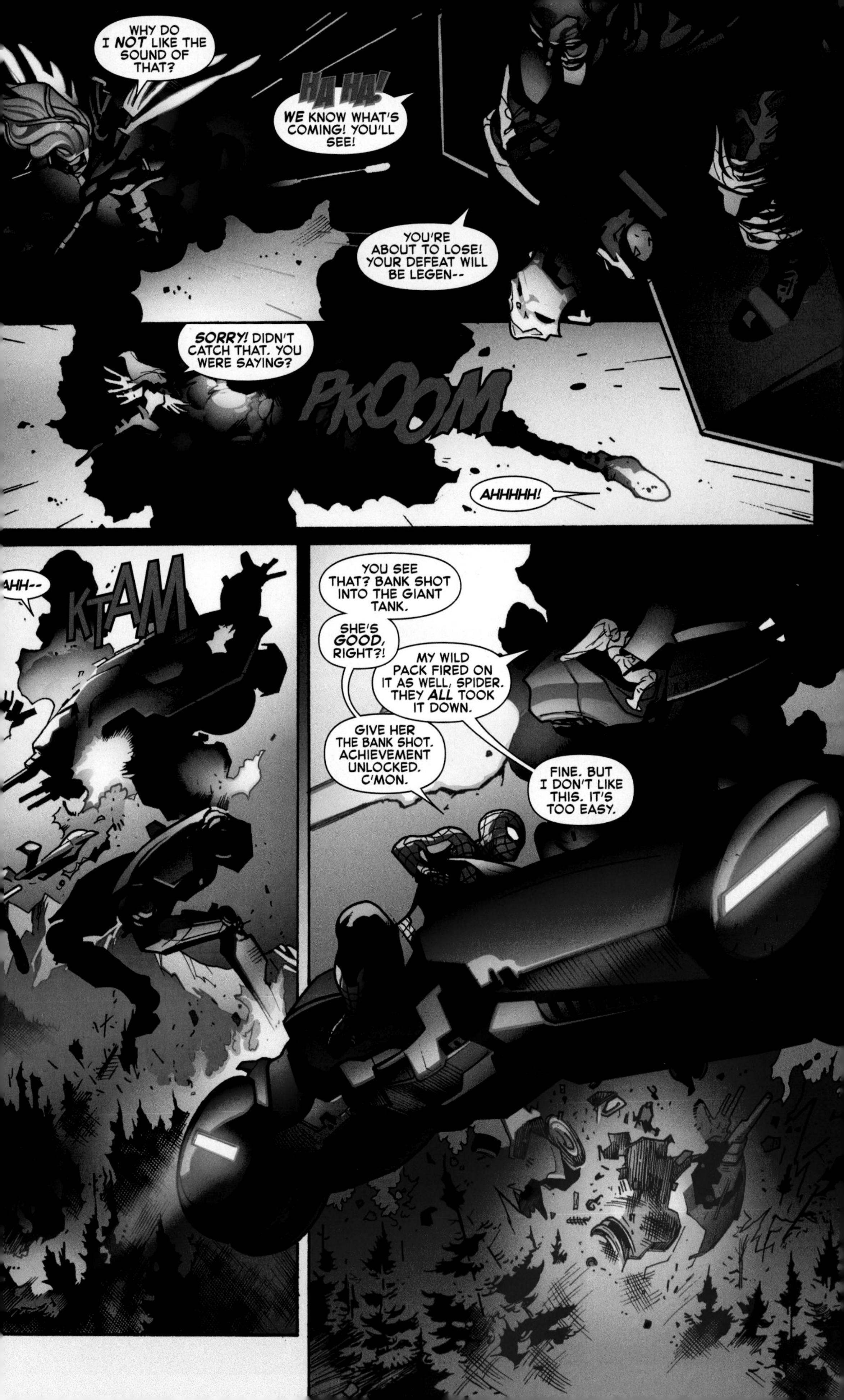

WHY DO I **NOT** LIKE THE SOUND OF THAT?
HA HA!
WE KNOW WHAT'S COMING! YOU'LL SEE!
YOU'RE ABOUT TO LOSE! YOUR DEFEAT WILL BE LEGEN--
SORRY! DIDN'T CATCH THAT. YOU WERE SAYING?
PKOOM
AHHHHH!
AHH--
KTAM
YOU SEE THAT? BANK SHOT INTO THE GIANT TANK.
SHE'S **GOOD**, RIGHT?!
MY WILD PACK FIRED ON IT AS WELL, SPIDER. THEY **ALL** TOOK IT DOWN.
GIVE HER THE BANK SHOT. ACHIEVEMENT UNLOCKED. C'MON.
FINE. BUT I DON'T LIKE THIS. IT'S TOO EASY.

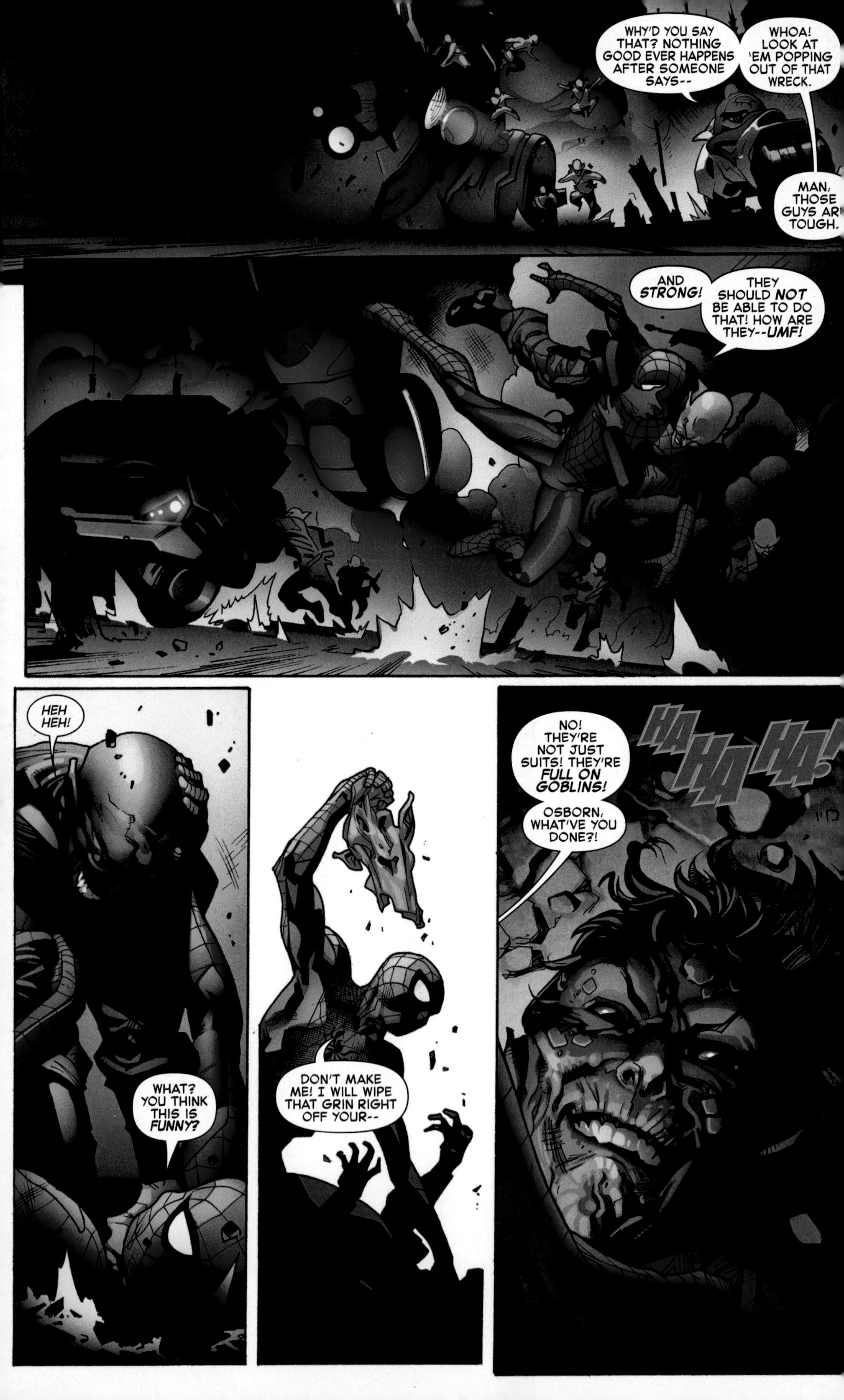
WHY'D YOU SAY THAT? NOTHING GOOD EVER HAPPENS AFTER SOMEONE SAYS--
WHOA! LOOK AT 'EM POPPING OUT OF THAT WRECK.
MAN, THOSE GUYS AR TOUGH.
AND STRONG!
THEY SHOULD NOT BE ABLE TO DO THAT! HOW ARE THEY--UMF!
HEH HEH!
WHAT? YOU THINK THIS IS FUNNY?
DON'T MAKE ME! I WILL WIPE THAT GRIN RIGHT OFF YOUR--
HA HA HA!
NO! THEY'RE NOT JUST SUITS! THEY'RE FULL ON GOBLINS!
OSBORN, WHAT'VE YOU DONE?!

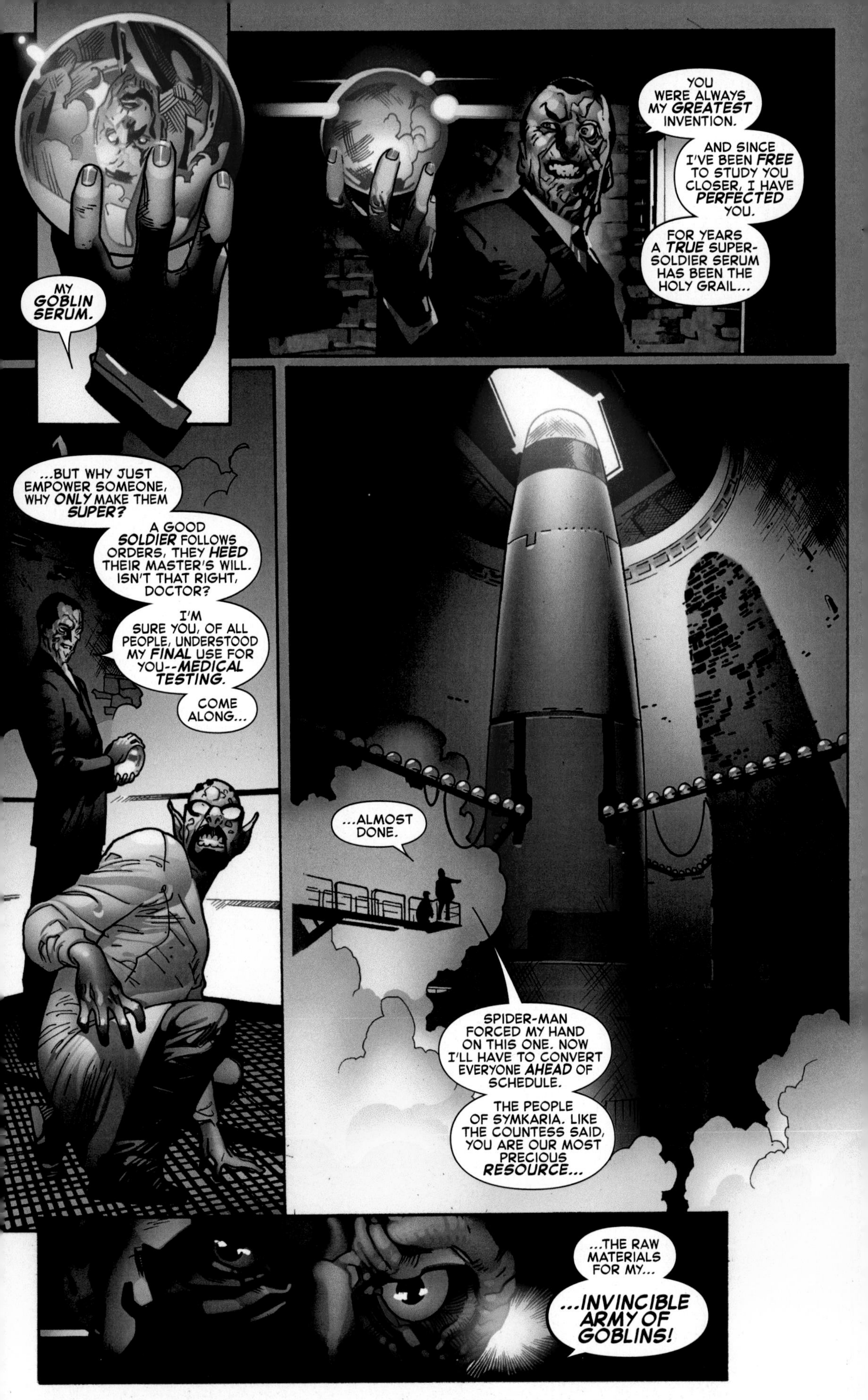
MY GOBLIN SERUM.
YOU WERE ALWAYS MY GREATEST INVENTION.
AND SINCE I'VE BEEN FREE TO STUDY YOU CLOSER, I HAVE PERFECTED YOU.
FOR YEARS A TRUE SUPER-SOLDIER SERUM HAS BEEN THE HOLY GRAIL...
...BUT WHY JUST EMPOWER SOMEONE, WHY ONLY MAKE THEM SUPER?
A GOOD SOLDIER FOLLOWS ORDERS, THEY HEED THEIR MASTER'S WILL. ISN'T THAT RIGHT, DOCTOR?
I'M SURE YOU, OF ALL PEOPLE, UNDERSTOOD MY FINAL USE FOR YOU--MEDICAL TESTING.
COME ALONG...
...ALMOST DONE.
SPIDER-MAN FORCED MY HAND ON THIS ONE. NOW I'LL HAVE TO CONVERT EVERYONE AHEAD OF SCHEDULE.
THE PEOPLE OF SYMKARIA. LIKE THE COUNTESS SAID, YOU ARE OUR MOST PRECIOUS RESOURCE...
...THE RAW MATERIALS FOR MY...
...INVINCIBLE ARMY OF GOBLINS!

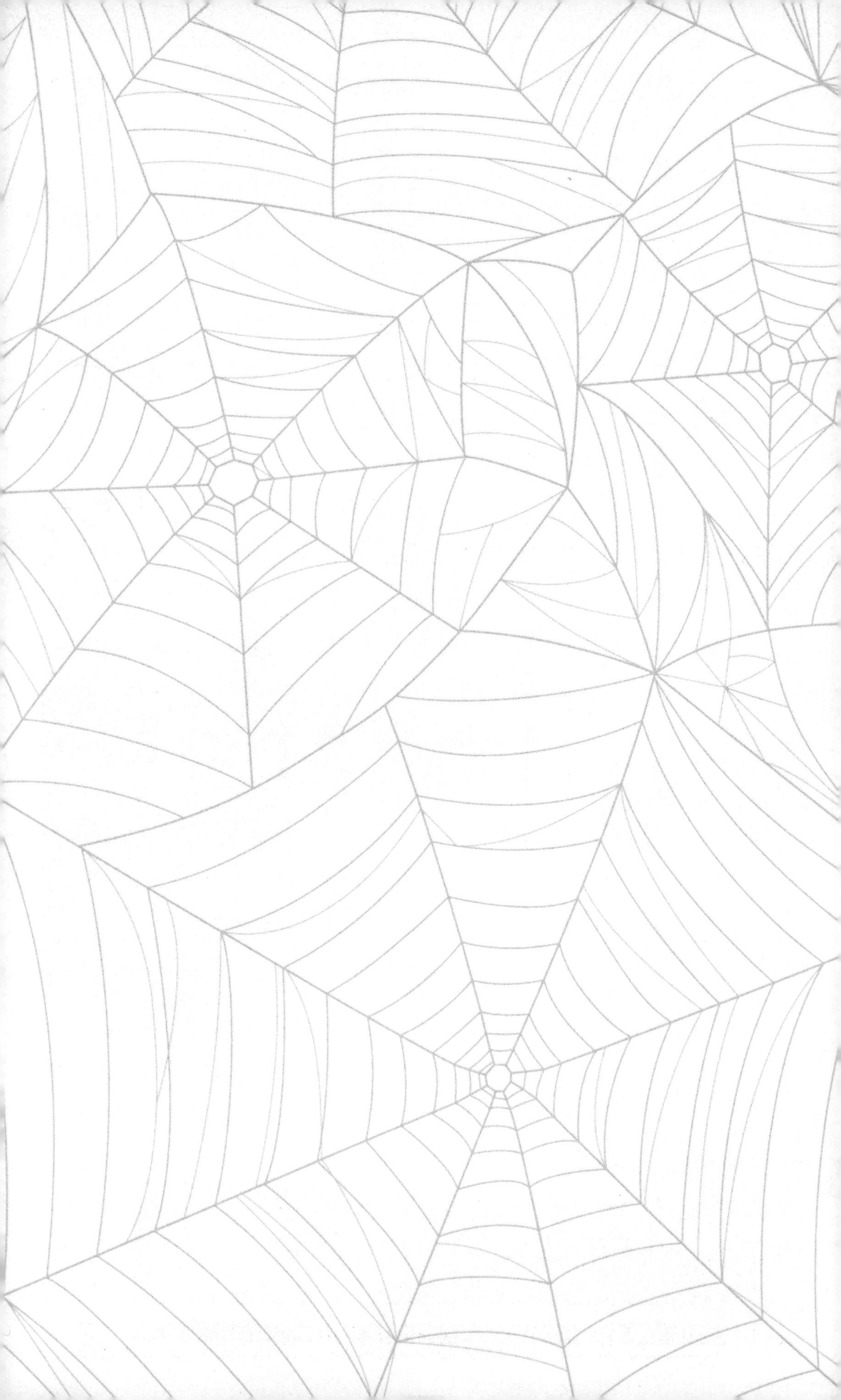

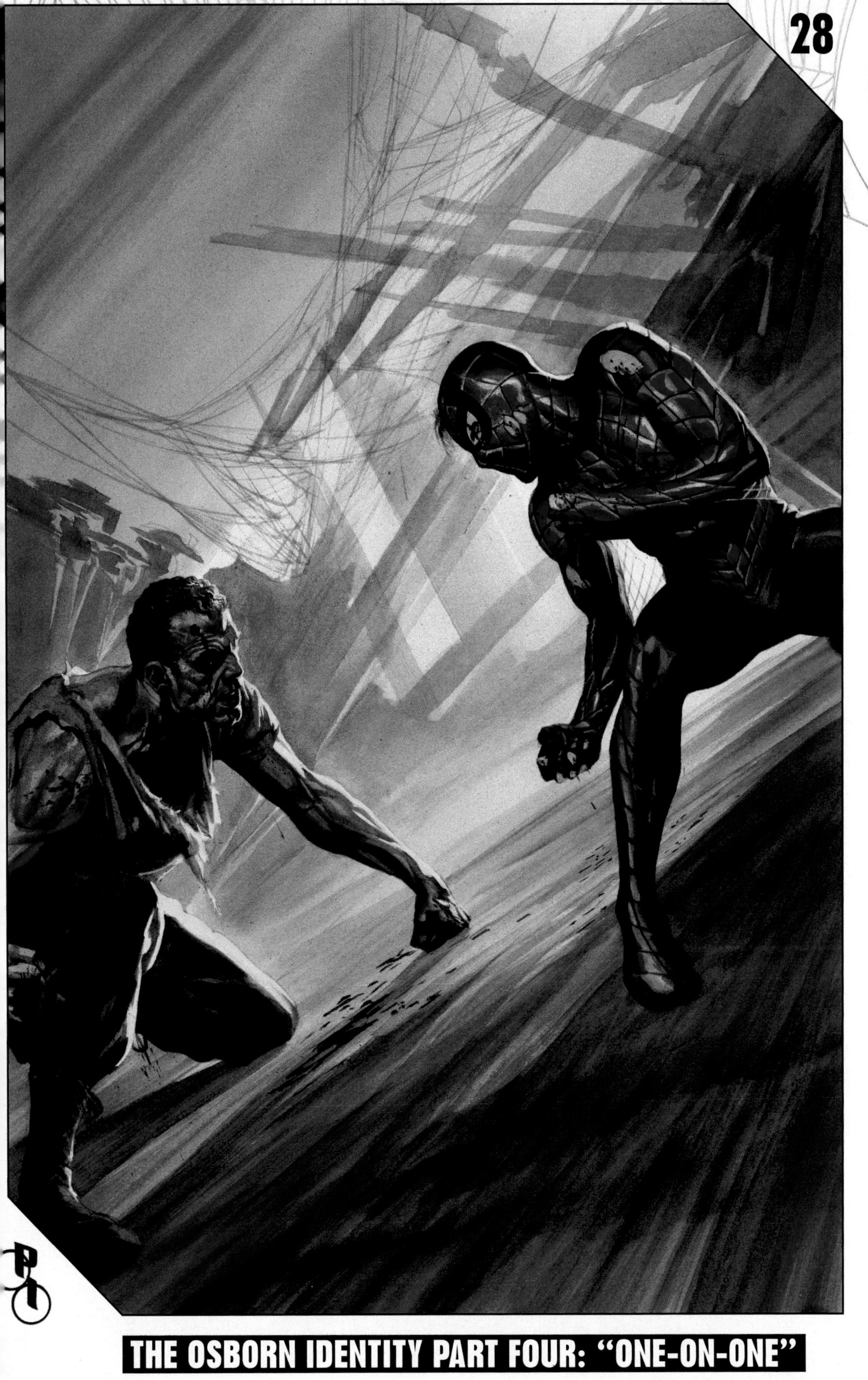

28

THE OSBORN IDENTITY PART FOUR: "ONE-ON-ONE"

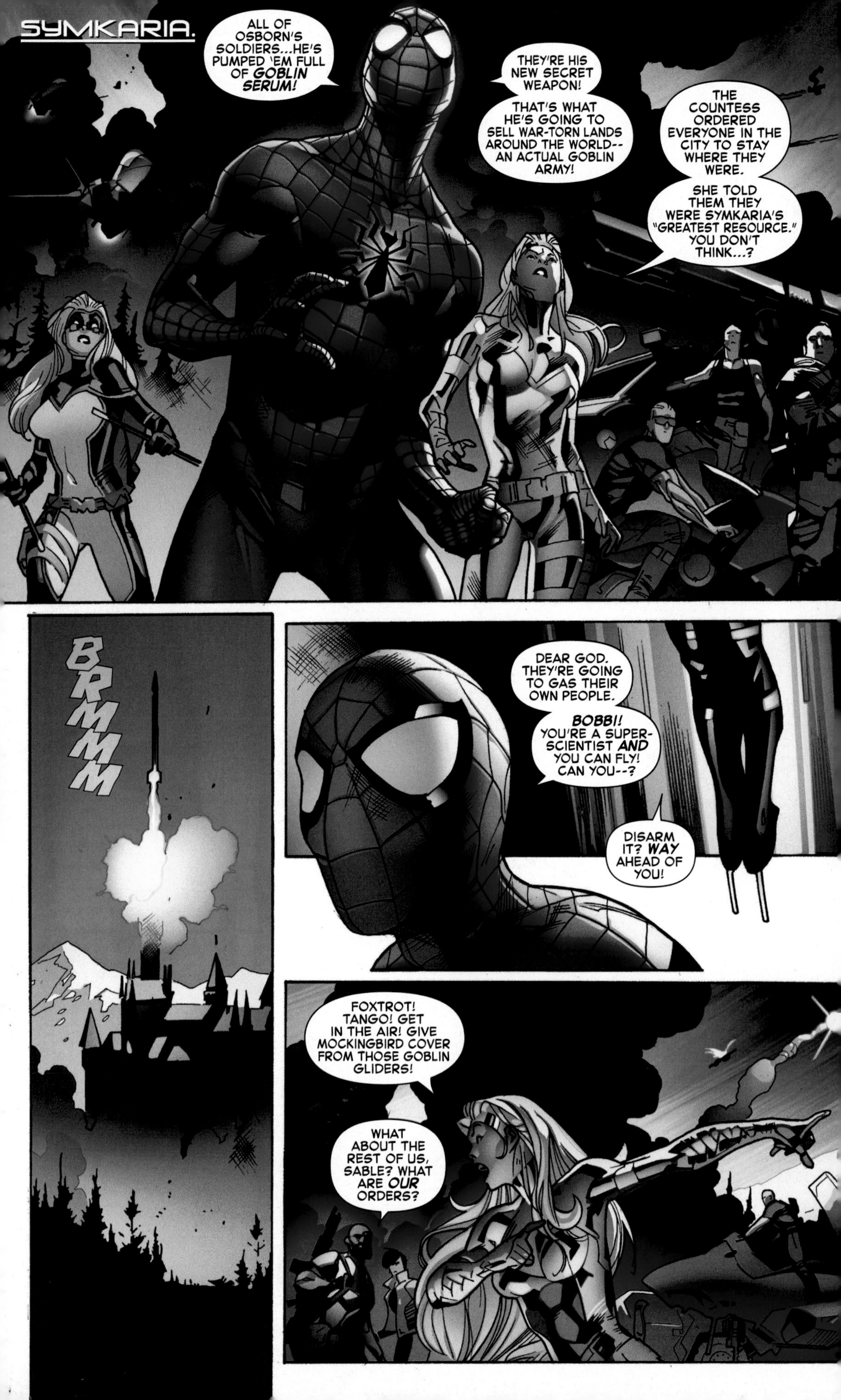

SYMKARIA.
ALL OF OSBORN'S SOLDIERS...HE'S PUMPED 'EM FULL OF GOBLIN SERUM!
THEY'RE HIS NEW SECRET WEAPON!
THAT'S WHAT HE'S GOING TO SELL WAR-TORN LANDS AROUND THE WORLD-- AN ACTUAL GOBLIN ARMY!
THE COUNTESS ORDERED EVERYONE IN THE CITY TO STAY WHERE THEY WERE.
SHE TOLD THEM THEY WERE SYMKARIA'S "GREATEST RESOURCE." YOU DON'T THINK...?
BRMMM
DEAR GOD. THEY'RE GOING TO GAS THEIR OWN PEOPLE.
BOBBI! YOU'RE A SUPER-SCIENTIST AND YOU CAN FLY! CAN YOU--?
DISARM IT? WAY AHEAD OF YOU!
FOXTROT! TANGO! GET IN THE AIR! GIVE MOCKINGBIRD COVER FROM THOSE GOBLIN GLIDERS!
WHAT ABOUT THE REST OF US, SABLE? WHAT ARE OUR ORDERS?

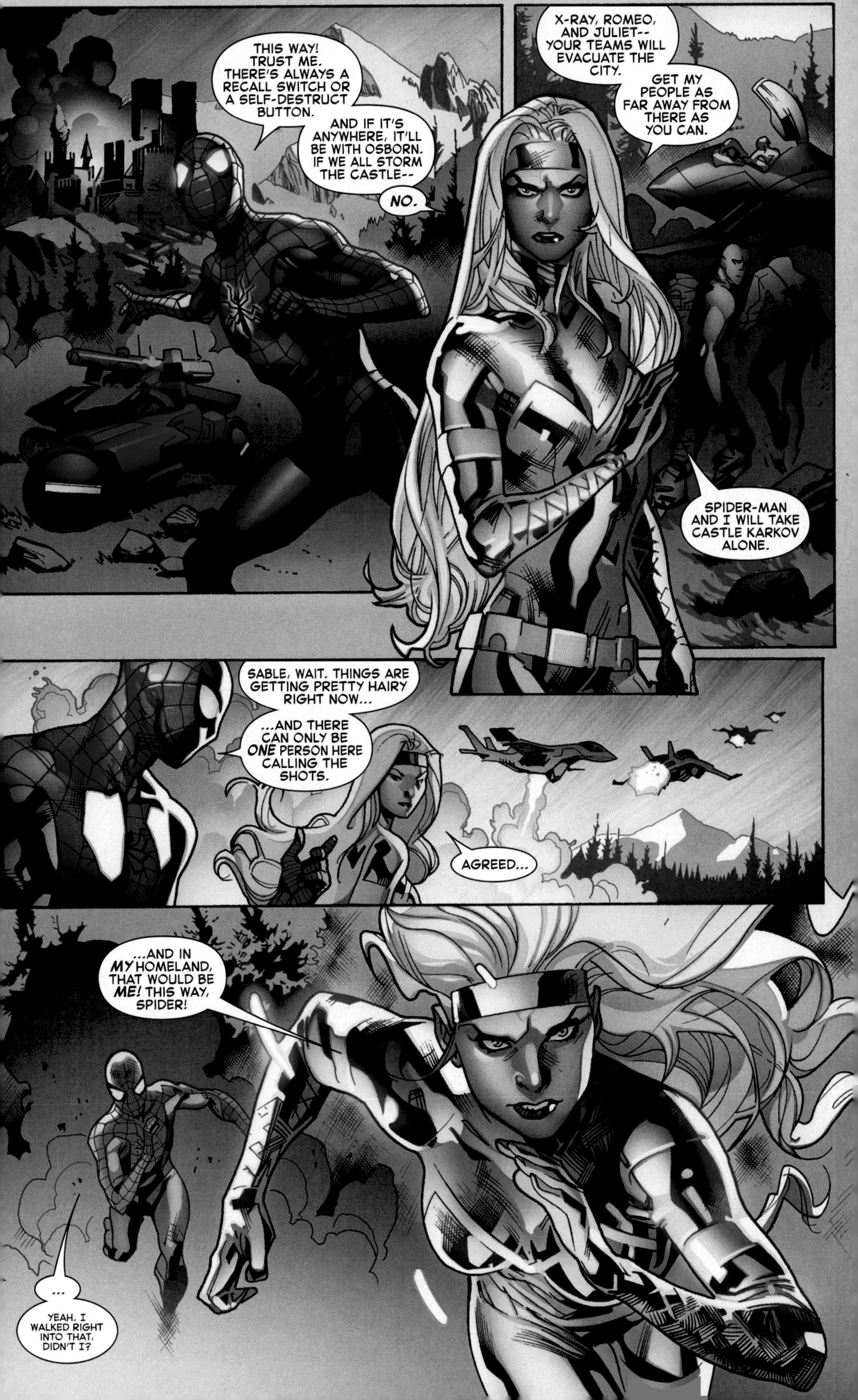

THIS WAY! TRUST ME. THERE'S ALWAYS A RECALL SWITCH OR A SELF-DESTRUCT BUTTON.
AND IF IT'S ANYWHERE, IT'LL BE WITH OSBORN. IF WE ALL STORM THE CASTLE--
NO.
X-RAY, ROMEO, AND JULIET-- YOUR TEAMS WILL EVACUATE THE CITY.
GET MY PEOPLE AS FAR AWAY FROM THERE AS YOU CAN.
SPIDER-MAN AND I WILL TAKE CASTLE KARKOV ALONE.
SABLE, WAIT. THINGS ARE GETTING PRETTY HAIRY RIGHT NOW...
...AND THERE CAN ONLY BE ONE PERSON HERE CALLING THE SHOTS.
AGREED...
...AND IN MY HOMELAND, THAT WOULD BE ME! THIS WAY, SPIDER!
...
YEAH. I WALKED RIGHT INTO THAT, DIDN'T I?

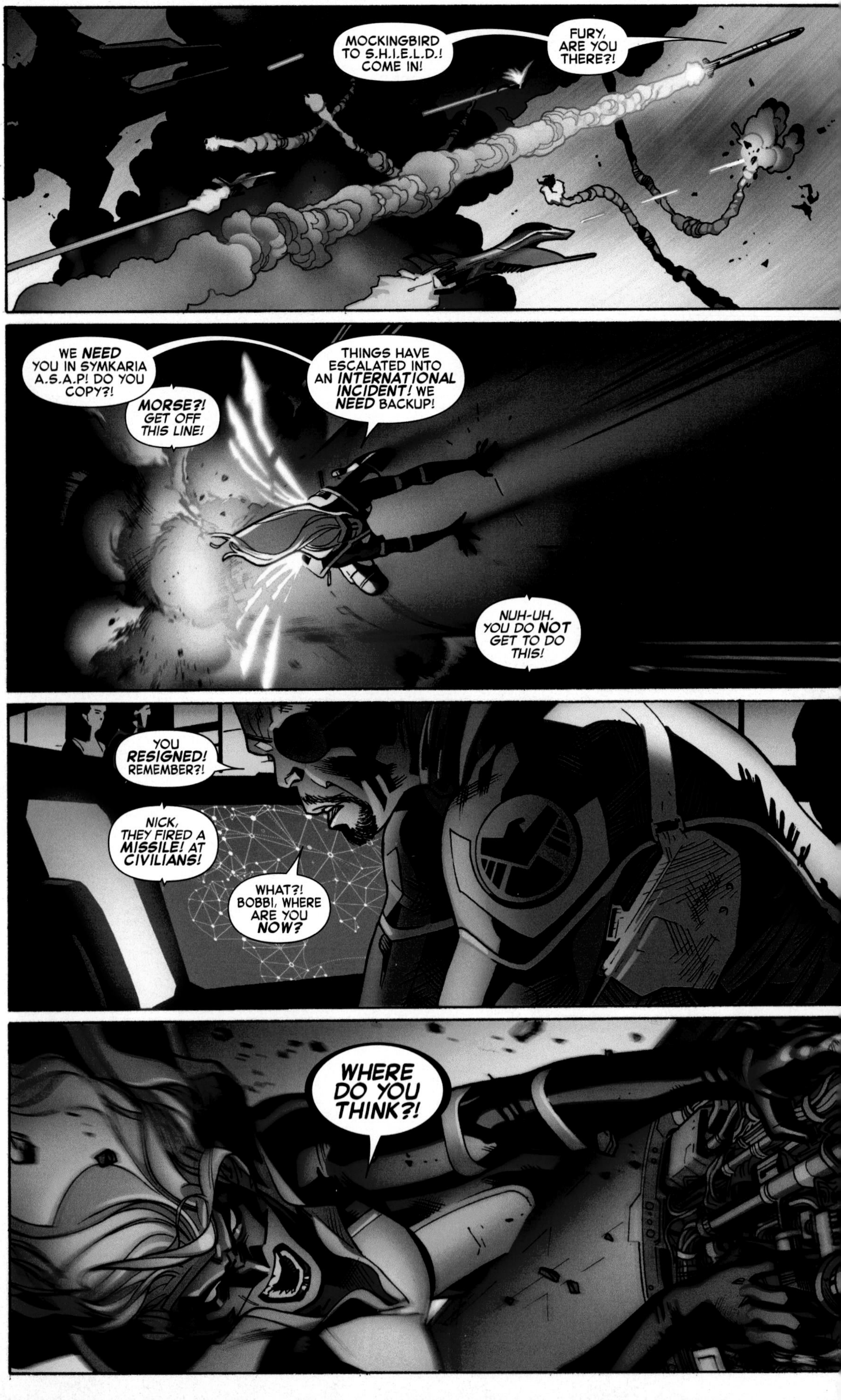

MOCKINGBIRD TO S.H.I.E.L.D.! COME IN!
FURY, ARE YOU THERE?!
WE NEED YOU IN SYMKARIA A.S.A.P! DO YOU COPY?!
THINGS HAVE ESCALATED INTO AN INTERNATIONAL INCIDENT! WE NEED BACKUP!
MORSE?! GET OFF THIS LINE!
NUH-UH. YOU DO NOT GET TO DO THIS!
YOU RESIGNED! REMEMBER?!
NICK, THEY FIRED A MISSILE! AT CIVILIANS!
WHAT?! BOBBI, WHERE ARE YOU NOW?
WHERE DO YOU THINK?!

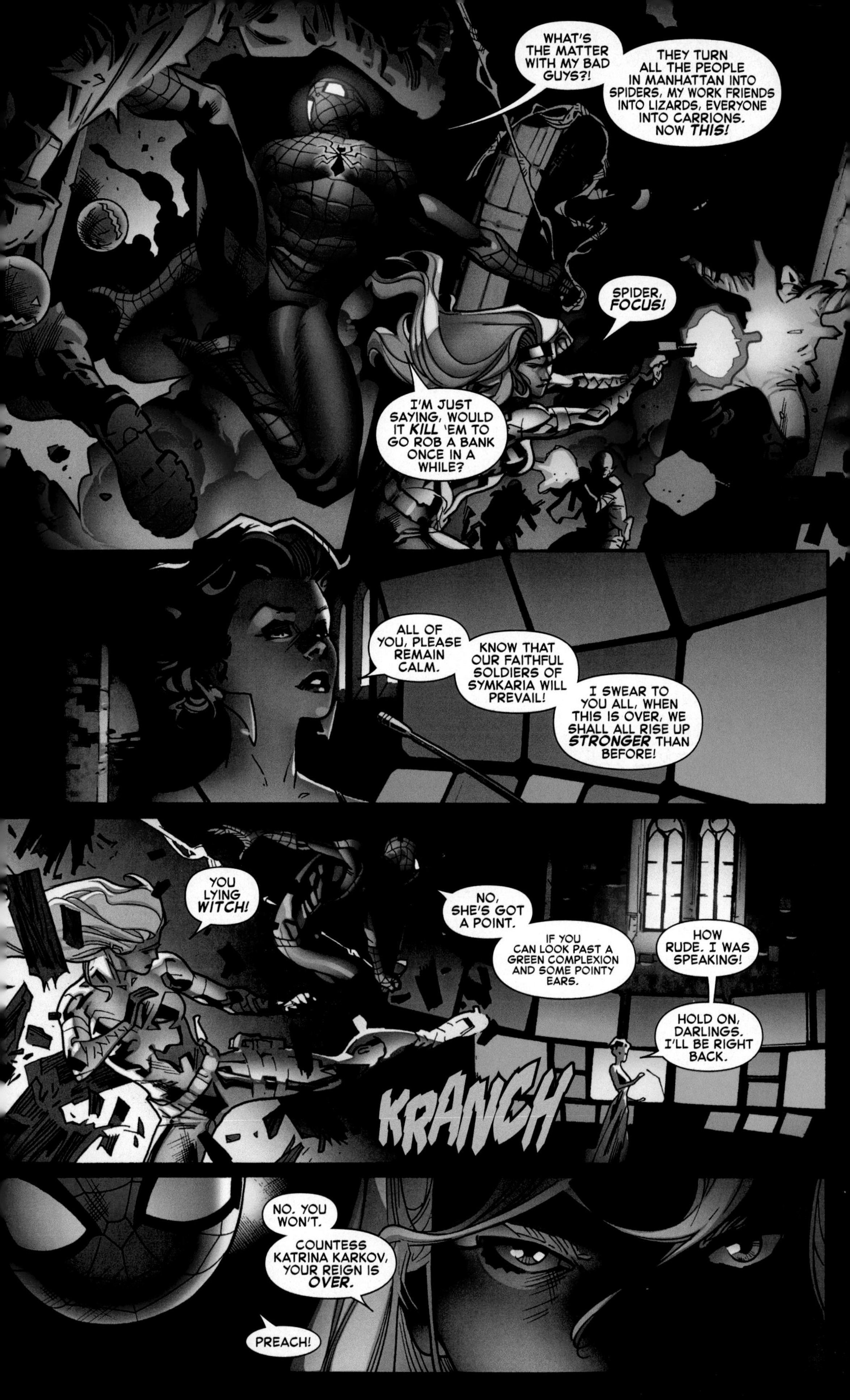
WHAT'S THE MATTER WITH MY BAD GUYS?!
THEY TURN ALL THE PEOPLE IN MANHATTAN INTO SPIDERS, MY WORK FRIENDS INTO LIZARDS, EVERYONE INTO CARRIONS. NOW THIS!
SPIDER, FOCUS!
I'M JUST SAYING, WOULD IT KILL 'EM TO GO ROB A BANK ONCE IN A WHILE?
ALL OF YOU, PLEASE REMAIN CALM.
KNOW THAT OUR FAITHFUL SOLDIERS OF SYMKARIA WILL PREVAIL!
I SWEAR TO YOU ALL, WHEN THIS IS OVER, WE SHALL ALL RISE UP STRONGER THAN BEFORE!
YOU LYING WITCH!
NO, SHE'S GOT A POINT.
IF YOU CAN LOOK PAST A GREEN COMPLEXION AND SOME POINTY EARS.
HOW RUDE. I WAS SPEAKING!
HOLD ON, DARLINGS. I'LL BE RIGHT BACK.
KRANCH
NO. YOU WON'T.
COUNTESS KATRINA KARKOV, YOUR REIGN IS OVER.
PREACH!

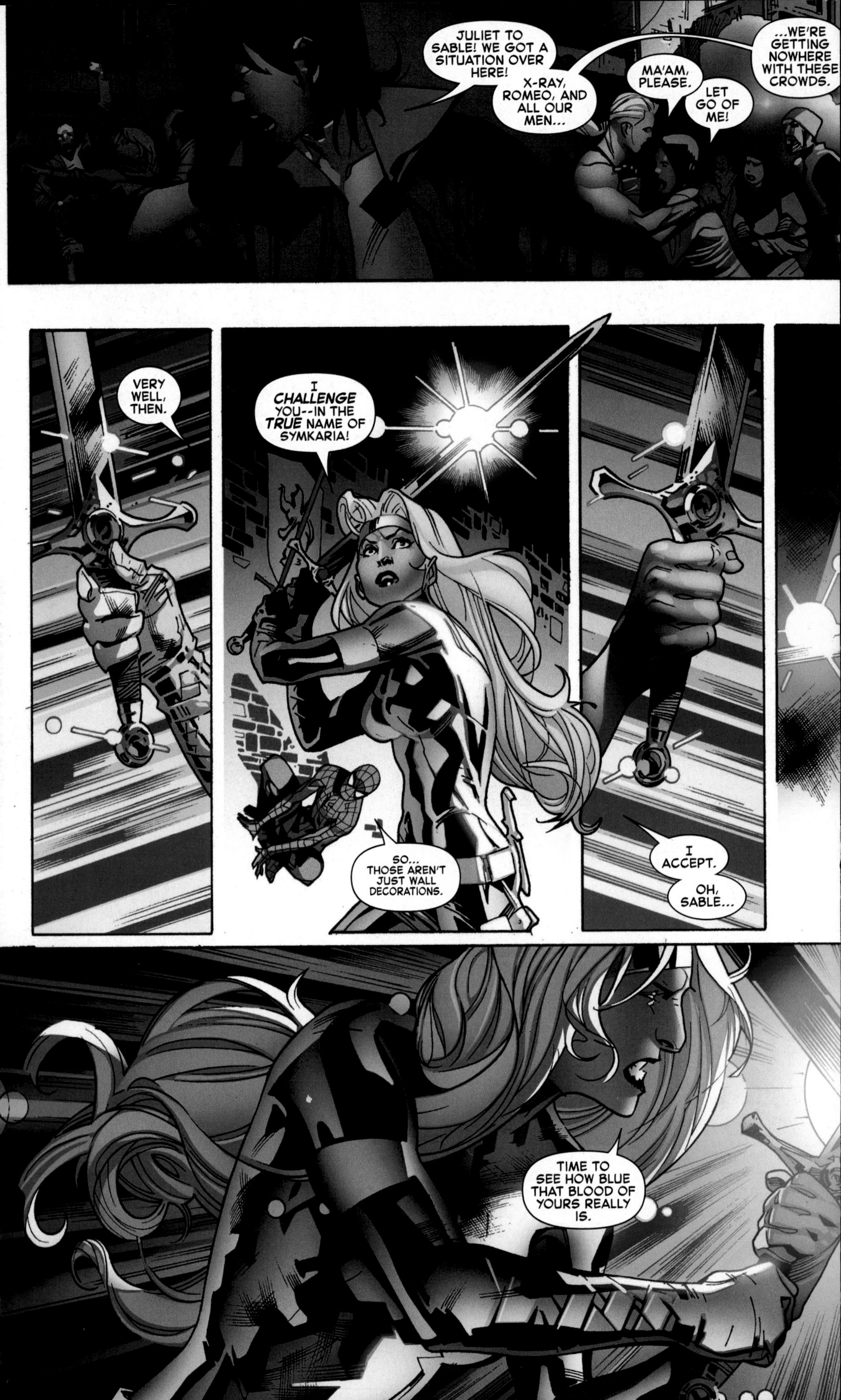
JULIET TO SABLE! WE GOT A SITUATION OVER HERE!
X-RAY, ROMEO, AND ALL OUR MEN...
...WE'RE GETTING NOWHERE WITH THESE CROWDS.
MA'AM, PLEASE.
LET GO OF ME!
VERY WELL, THEN.
I CHALLENGE YOU--IN THE TRUE NAME OF SYMKARIA!
SO... THOSE AREN'T JUST WALL DECORATIONS.
I ACCEPT.
OH, SABLE...
TIME TO SEE HOW BLUE THAT BLOOD OF YOURS REALLY IS.

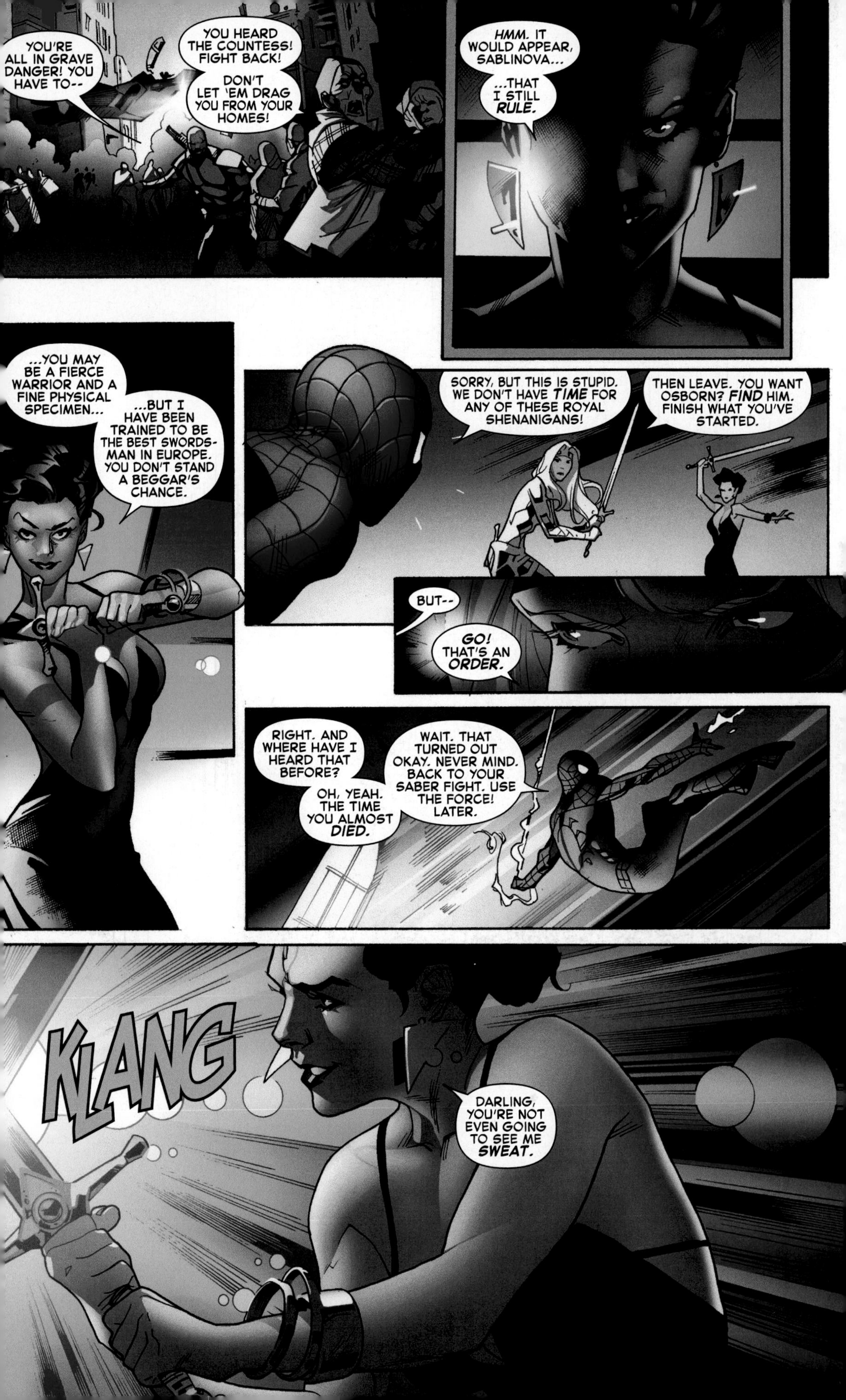
YOU'RE ALL IN GRAVE DANGER! YOU HAVE TO--
YOU HEARD THE COUNTESS! FIGHT BACK!
DON'T LET 'EM DRAG YOU FROM YOUR HOMES!
HMM. IT WOULD APPEAR, SABLINOVA...
...THAT I STILL RULE.
...YOU MAY BE A FIERCE WARRIOR AND A FINE PHYSICAL SPECIMEN...
...BUT I HAVE BEEN TRAINED TO BE THE BEST SWORDS-MAN IN EUROPE. YOU DON'T STAND A BEGGAR'S CHANCE.
SORRY, BUT THIS IS STUPID. WE DON'T HAVE TIME FOR ANY OF THESE ROYAL SHENANIGANS!
THEN LEAVE. YOU WANT OSBORN? FIND HIM. FINISH WHAT YOU'VE STARTED.
BUT--
GO! THAT'S AN ORDER.
RIGHT. AND WHERE HAVE I HEARD THAT BEFORE?
OH, YEAH. THE TIME YOU ALMOST DIED.
WAIT. THAT TURNED OUT OKAY. NEVER MIND. BACK TO YOUR SABER FIGHT. USE THE FORCE! LATER.
KLANG
DARLING, YOU'RE NOT EVEN GOING TO SEE ME SWEAT.

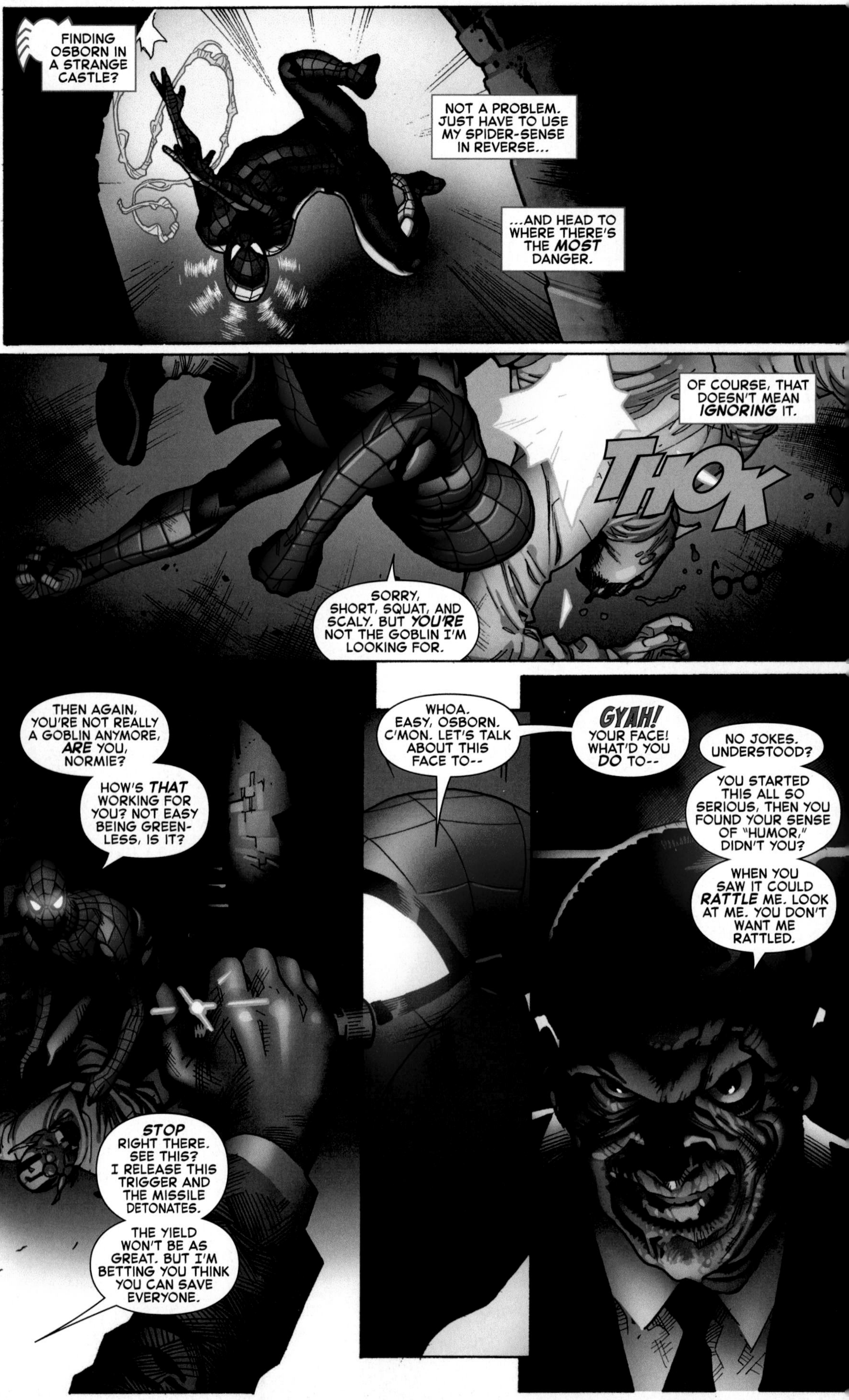

FINDING OSBORN IN A STRANGE CASTLE?
NOT A PROBLEM. JUST HAVE TO USE MY SPIDER-SENSE IN REVERSE...
...AND HEAD TO WHERE THERE'S THE MOST DANGER.
OF COURSE, THAT DOESN'T MEAN IGNORING IT.
THOK
SORRY, SHORT, SQUAT, AND SCALY. BUT YOU'RE NOT THE GOBLIN I'M LOOKING FOR.
THEN AGAIN, YOU'RE NOT REALLY A GOBLIN ANYMORE, ARE YOU, NORMIE?
HOW'S THAT WORKING FOR YOU? NOT EASY BEING GREEN-LESS, IS IT?
STOP RIGHT THERE. SEE THIS? I RELEASE THIS TRIGGER AND THE MISSILE DETONATES.
THE YIELD WON'T BE AS GREAT. BUT I'M BETTING YOU THINK YOU CAN SAVE EVERYONE.
WHOA. EASY, OSBORN. C'MON. LET'S TALK ABOUT THIS FACE TO--
GYAH! YOUR FACE! WHAT'D YOU DO TO--
NO JOKES. UNDERSTOOD?
YOU STARTED THIS ALL SO SERIOUS, THEN YOU FOUND YOUR SENSE OF "HUMOR," DIDN'T YOU?
WHEN YOU SAW IT COULD RATTLE ME. LOOK AT ME. YOU DON'T WANT ME RATTLED.

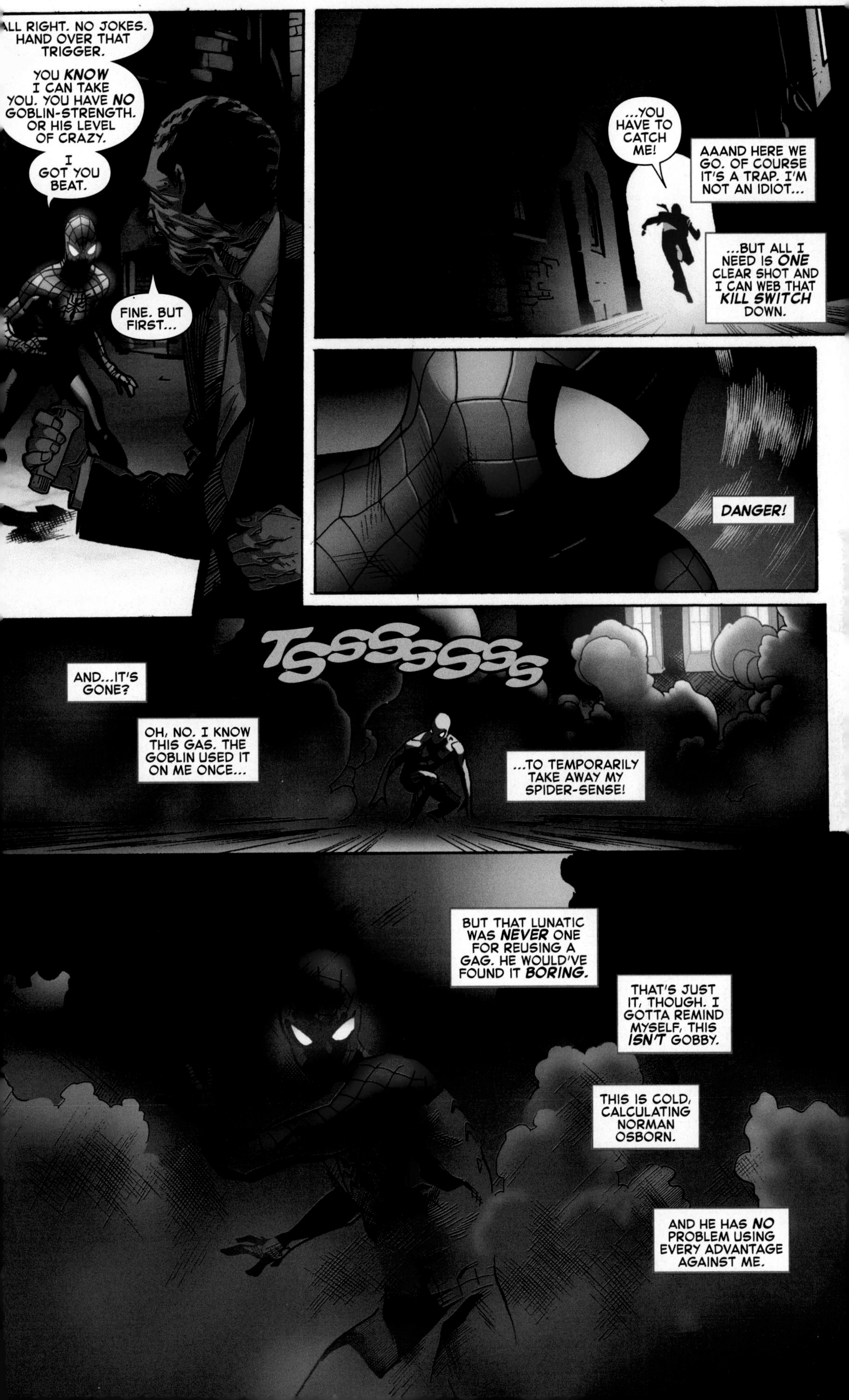
ALL RIGHT. NO JOKES. HAND OVER THAT TRIGGER.
YOU KNOW I CAN TAKE YOU. YOU HAVE NO GOBLIN-STRENGTH. OR HIS LEVEL OF CRAZY.
I GOT YOU BEAT.
FINE. BUT FIRST...
...YOU HAVE TO CATCH ME!
AAAND HERE WE GO. OF COURSE IT'S A TRAP. I'M NOT AN IDIOT...
...BUT ALL I NEED IS ONE CLEAR SHOT AND I CAN WEB THAT KILL SWITCH DOWN.
DANGER!
TSSSSSSSS
AND...IT'S GONE?
OH, NO. I KNOW THIS GAS. THE GOBLIN USED IT ON ME ONCE...
...TO TEMPORARILY TAKE AWAY MY SPIDER-SENSE!
BUT THAT LUNATIC WAS NEVER ONE FOR REUSING A GAG. HE WOULD'VE FOUND IT BORING.
THAT'S JUST IT, THOUGH. I GOTTA REMIND MYSELF, THIS ISN'T GOBBY.
THIS IS COLD, CALCULATING NORMAN OSBORN.
AND HE HAS NO PROBLEM USING EVERY ADVANTAGE AGAINST ME.

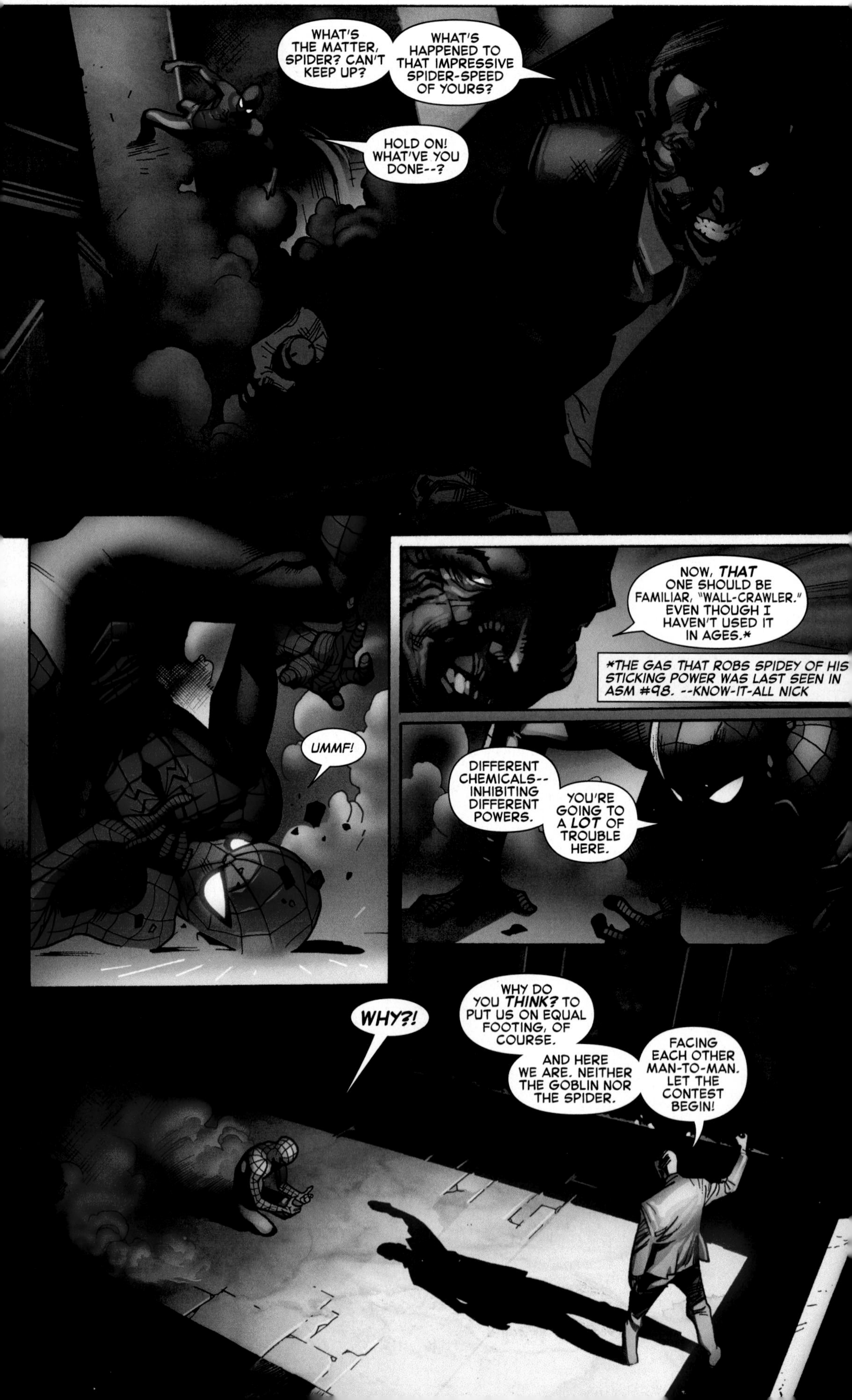

WHAT'S THE MATTER, SPIDER? CAN'T KEEP UP?
WHAT'S HAPPENED TO THAT IMPRESSIVE SPIDER-SPEED OF YOURS?
HOLD ON! WHAT'VE YOU DONE--?
UMMF!
NOW, THAT ONE SHOULD BE FAMILIAR, "WALL-CRAWLER." EVEN THOUGH I HAVEN'T USED IT IN AGES.*
*THE GAS THAT ROBS SPIDEY OF HIS STICKING POWER WAS LAST SEEN IN ASM #98. --KNOW-IT-ALL NICK
DIFFERENT CHEMICALS-- INHIBITING DIFFERENT POWERS.
YOU'RE GOING TO A LOT OF TROUBLE HERE.
WHY?!
WHY DO YOU THINK? TO PUT US ON EQUAL FOOTING, OF COURSE.
AND HERE WE ARE. NEITHER THE GOBLIN NOR THE SPIDER.
FACING EACH OTHER MAN-TO-MAN. LET THE CONTEST BEGIN!

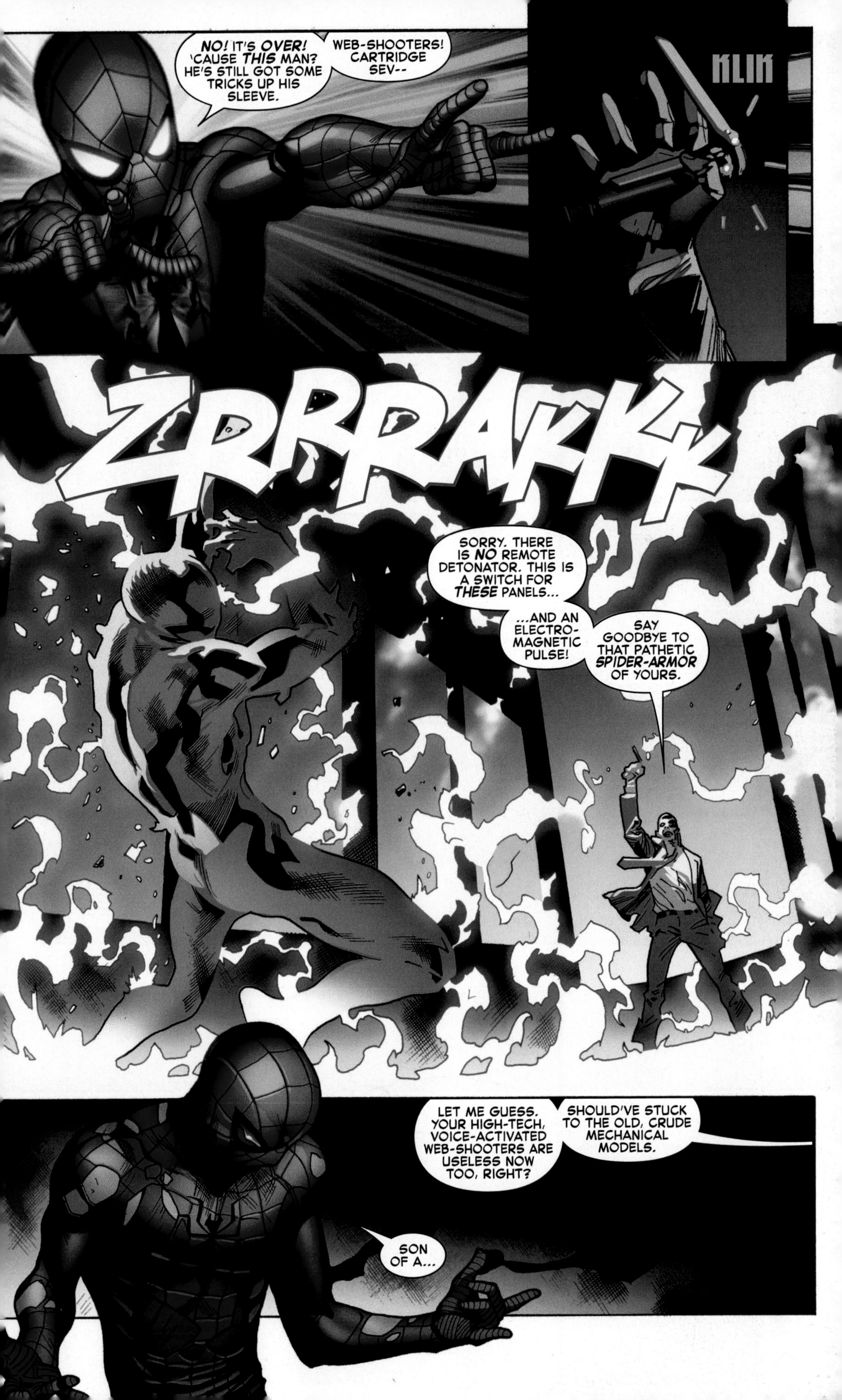

NO! IT'S OVER! 'CAUSE THIS MAN? HE'S STILL GOT SOME TRICKS UP HIS SLEEVE.
WEB-SHOOTERS! CARTRIDGE SEV--
KLIK
ZRRRAKKK
SORRY. THERE IS NO REMOTE DETONATOR. THIS IS A SWITCH FOR THESE PANELS...
...AND AN ELECTRO-MAGNETIC PULSE!
SAY GOODBYE TO THAT PATHETIC SPIDER-ARMOR OF YOURS.
LET ME GUESS. YOUR HIGH-TECH, VOICE-ACTIVATED WEB-SHOOTERS ARE USELESS NOW TOO, RIGHT?
SHOULD'VE STUCK TO THE OLD, CRUDE MECHANICAL MODELS.
SON OF A...

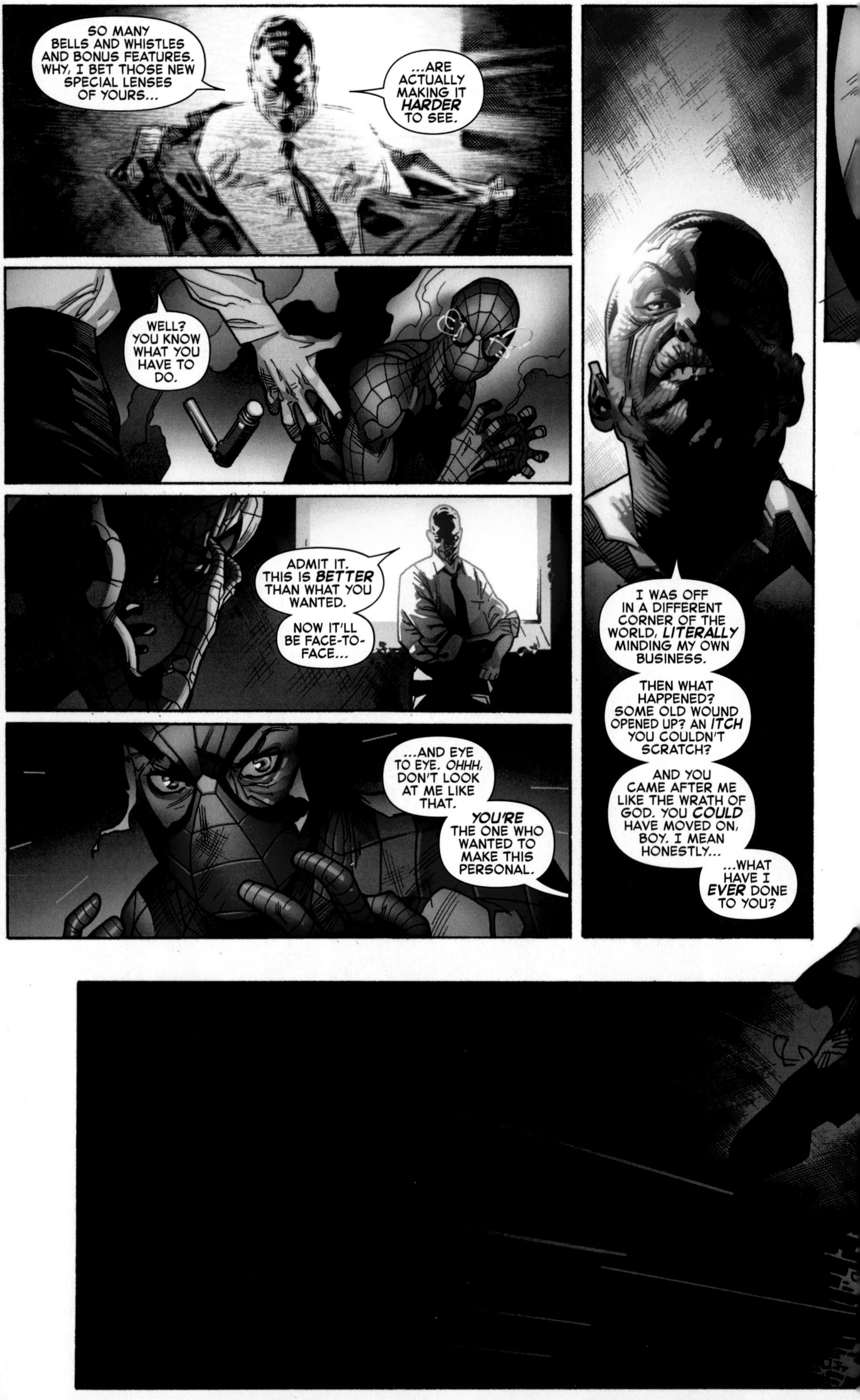

SO MANY BELLS AND WHISTLES AND BONUS FEATURES. WHY, I BET THOSE NEW SPECIAL LENSES OF YOURS...
...ARE ACTUALLY MAKING IT HARDER TO SEE.
WELL? YOU KNOW WHAT YOU HAVE TO DO.
ADMIT IT. THIS IS BETTER THAN WHAT YOU WANTED.
NOW IT'LL BE FACE-TO-FACE...
...AND EYE TO EYE. OHHH, DON'T LOOK AT ME LIKE THAT.
YOU'RE THE ONE WHO WANTED TO MAKE THIS PERSONAL.
I WAS OFF IN A DIFFERENT CORNER OF THE WORLD, LITERALLY MINDING MY OWN BUSINESS.
THEN WHAT HAPPENED? SOME OLD WOUND OPENED UP? AN ITCH YOU COULDN'T SCRATCH?
AND YOU CAME AFTER ME LIKE THE WRATH OF GOD. YOU COULD HAVE MOVED ON, BOY. I MEAN HONESTLY...
...WHAT HAVE I EVER DONE TO YOU?

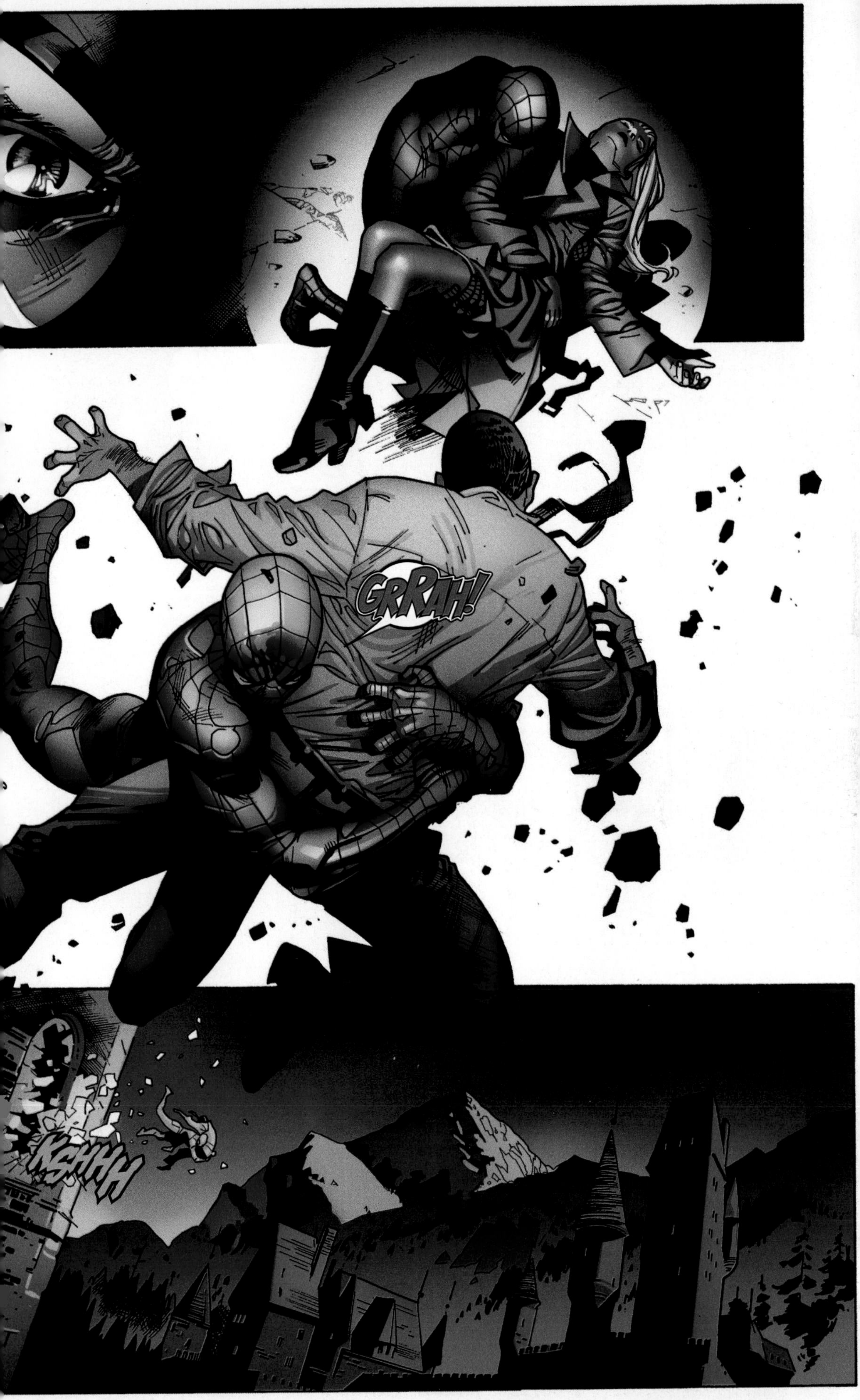
GRRAH!
KSHHH

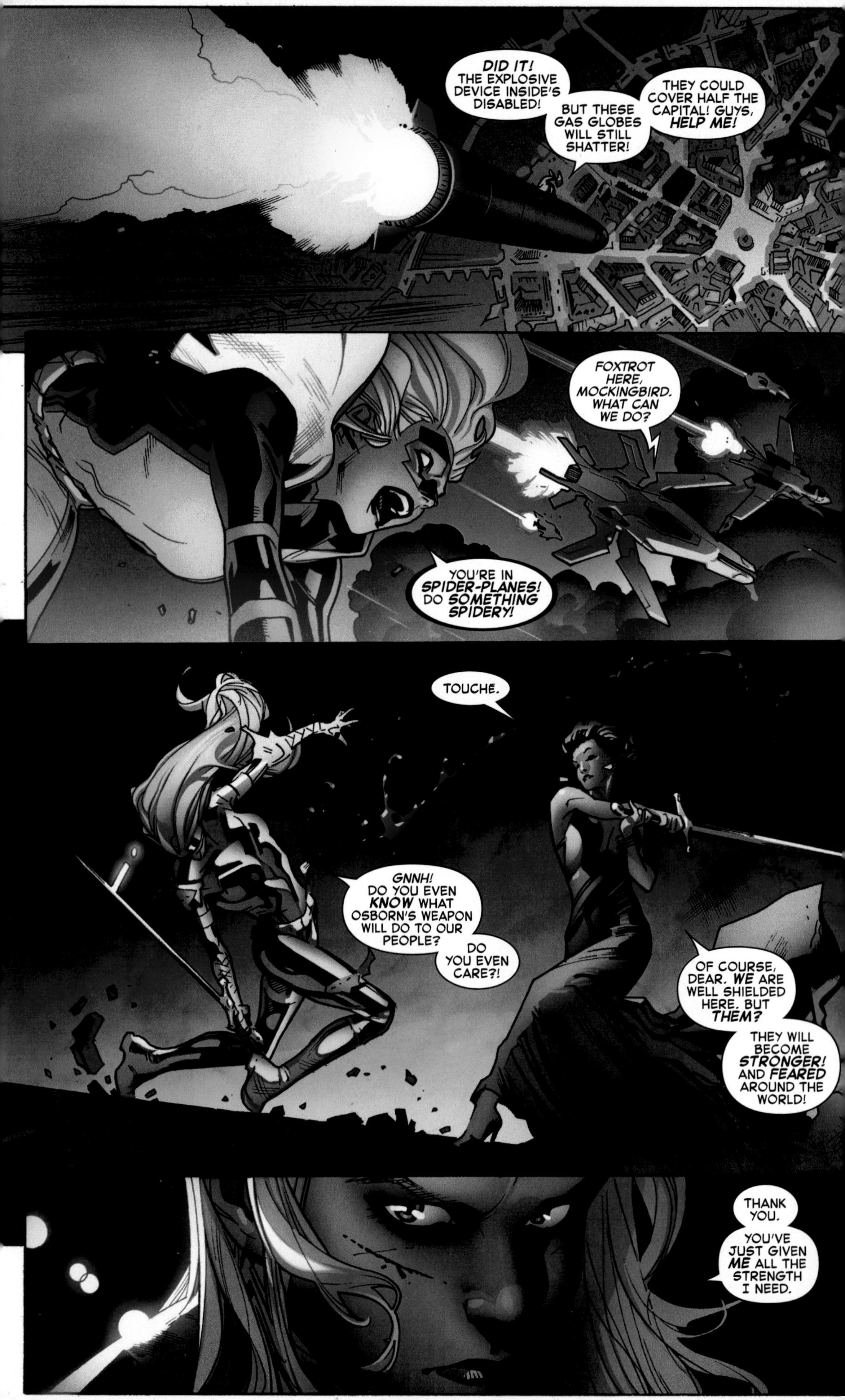

DID IT! THE EXPLOSIVE DEVICE INSIDE'S DISABLED!
BUT THESE GAS GLOBES WILL STILL SHATTER!
THEY COULD COVER HALF THE CAPITAL! GUYS, HELP ME!
FOXTROT HERE, MOCKINGBIRD. WHAT CAN WE DO?
YOU'RE IN SPIDER-PLANES! DO SOMETHING SPIDERY!
TOUCHE.
GNNH! DO YOU EVEN KNOW WHAT OSBORN'S WEAPON WILL DO TO OUR PEOPLE?
DO YOU EVEN CARE?!
OF COURSE, DEAR. WE ARE WELL SHIELDED HERE. BUT THEM?
THEY WILL BECOME STRONGER! AND FEARED AROUND THE WORLD!
THANK YOU.
YOU'VE JUST GIVEN ME ALL THE STRENGTH I NEED.

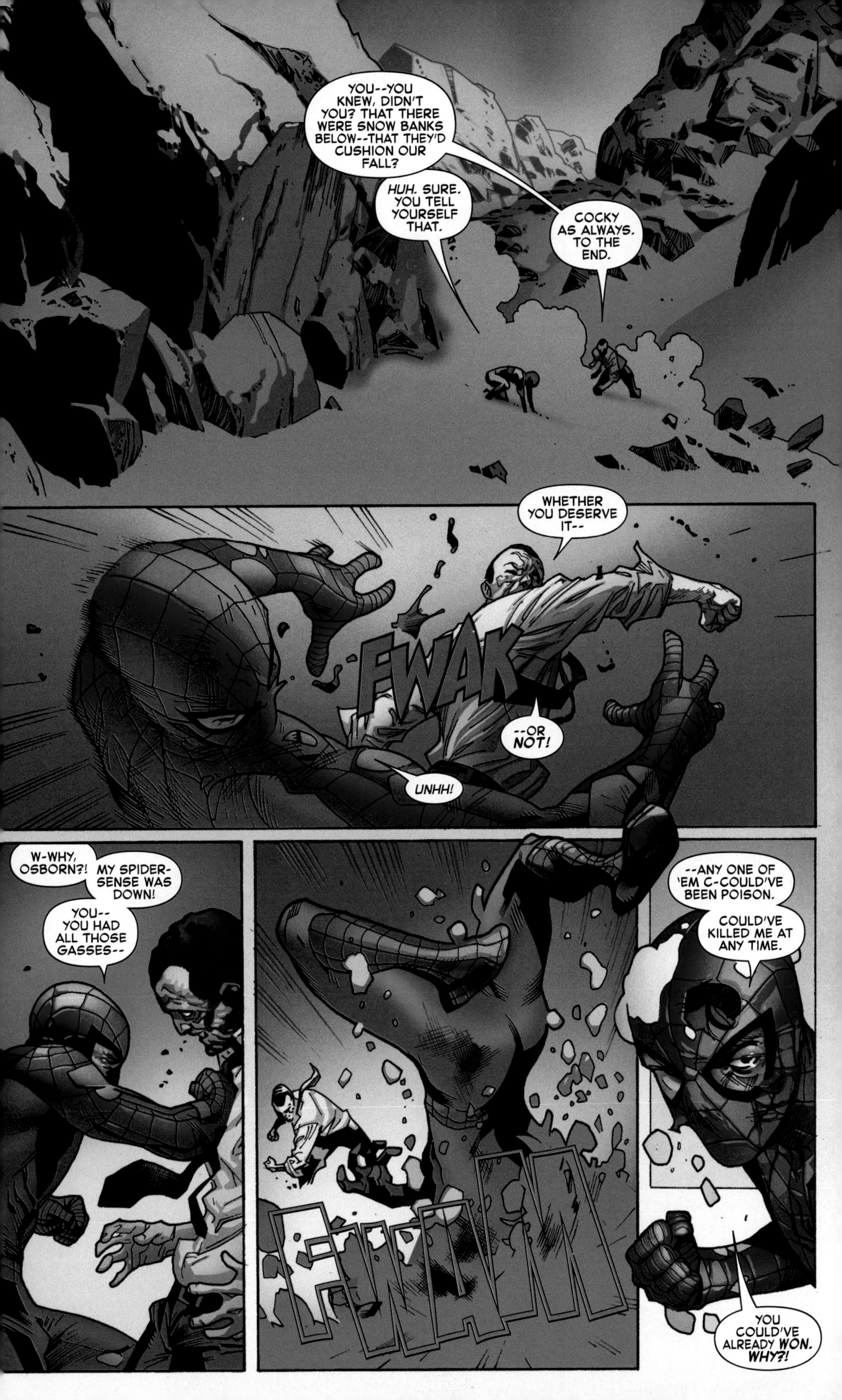
YOU--YOU KNEW, DIDN'T YOU? THAT THERE WERE SNOW BANKS BELOW--THAT THEY'D CUSHION OUR FALL?
HUH. SURE. YOU TELL YOURSELF THAT.
COCKY AS ALWAYS. TO THE END.
WHETHER YOU DESERVE IT--
FWAK
--OR NOT!
UNHH!
W-WHY, OSBORN?!
MY SPIDER-SENSE WAS DOWN!
YOU-- YOU HAD ALL THOSE GASSES--
--ANY ONE OF 'EM C-COULD'VE BEEN POISON.
COULD'VE KILLED ME AT ANY TIME.
FWAM
YOU COULD'VE ALREADY WON. WHY?!

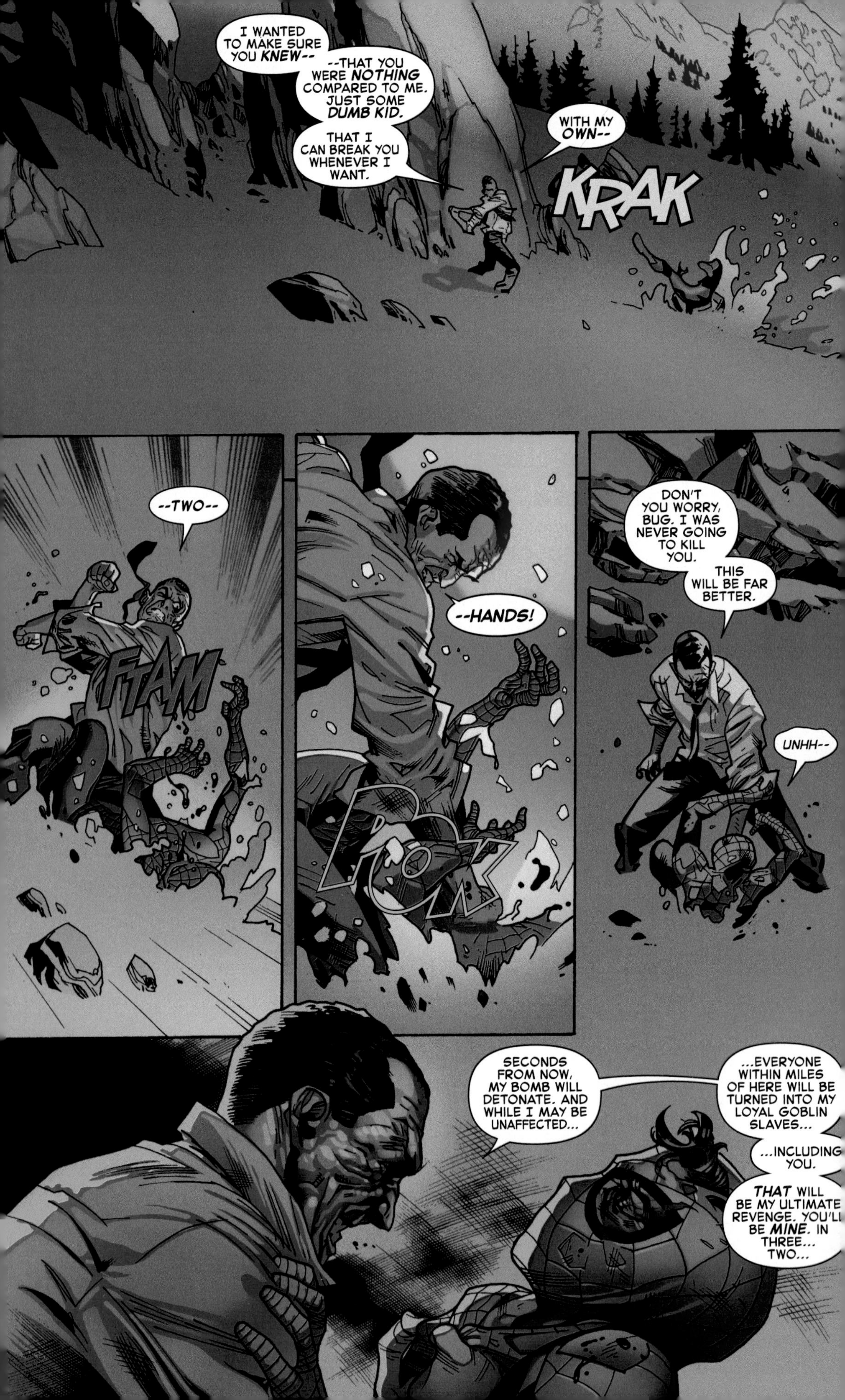
I WANTED TO MAKE SURE YOU KNEW--
--THAT YOU WERE NOTHING COMPARED TO ME. JUST SOME DUMB KID.
THAT I CAN BREAK YOU WHENEVER I WANT.
WITH MY OWN--
KRAK
--TWO--
FTAM
--HANDS!
DON'T YOU WORRY, BUG. I WAS NEVER GOING TO KILL YOU.
THIS WILL BE FAR BETTER.
UNHH--
SECONDS FROM NOW, MY BOMB WILL DETONATE. AND WHILE I MAY BE UNAFFECTED...
...EVERYONE WITHIN MILES OF HERE WILL BE TURNED INTO MY LOYAL GOBLIN SLAVES...
...INCLUDING YOU.
THAT WILL BE MY ULTIMATE REVENGE. YOU'LL BE MINE. IN THREE... TWO...

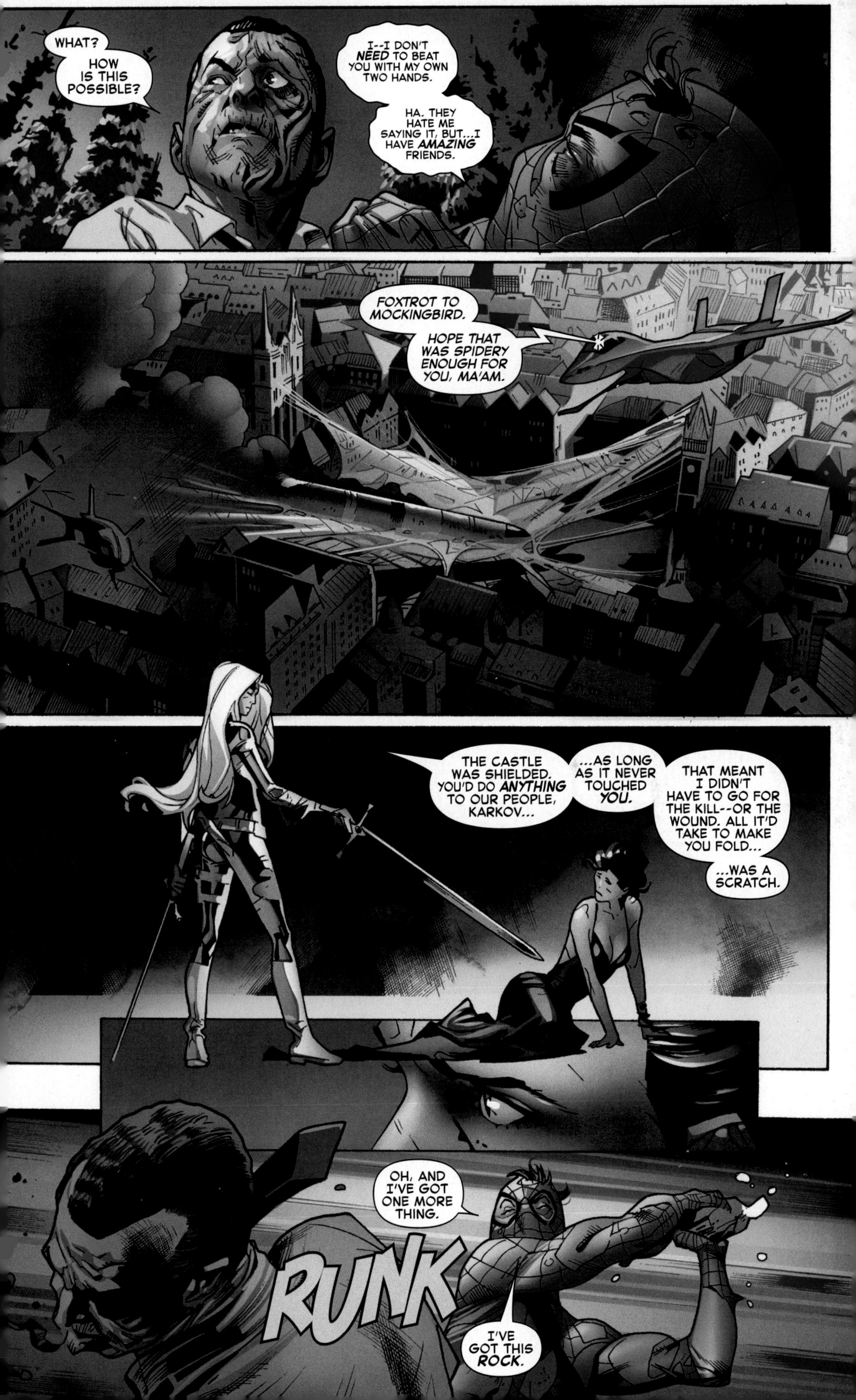
WHAT? HOW IS THIS POSSIBLE?
I--I DON'T NEED TO BEAT YOU WITH MY OWN TWO HANDS.
HA. THEY HATE ME SAYING IT, BUT...I HAVE AMAZING FRIENDS.
FOXTROT TO MOCKINGBIRD.
HOPE THAT WAS SPIDERY ENOUGH FOR YOU, MA'AM.
THE CASTLE WAS SHIELDED. YOU'D DO ANYTHING TO OUR PEOPLE, KARKOV...
...AS LONG AS IT NEVER TOUCHED YOU.
THAT MEANT I DIDN'T HAVE TO GO FOR THE KILL--OR THE WOUND. ALL IT'D TAKE TO MAKE YOU FOLD...
...WAS A SCRATCH.
OH, AND I'VE GOT ONE MORE THING.
RUNK
I'VE GOT THIS ROCK.

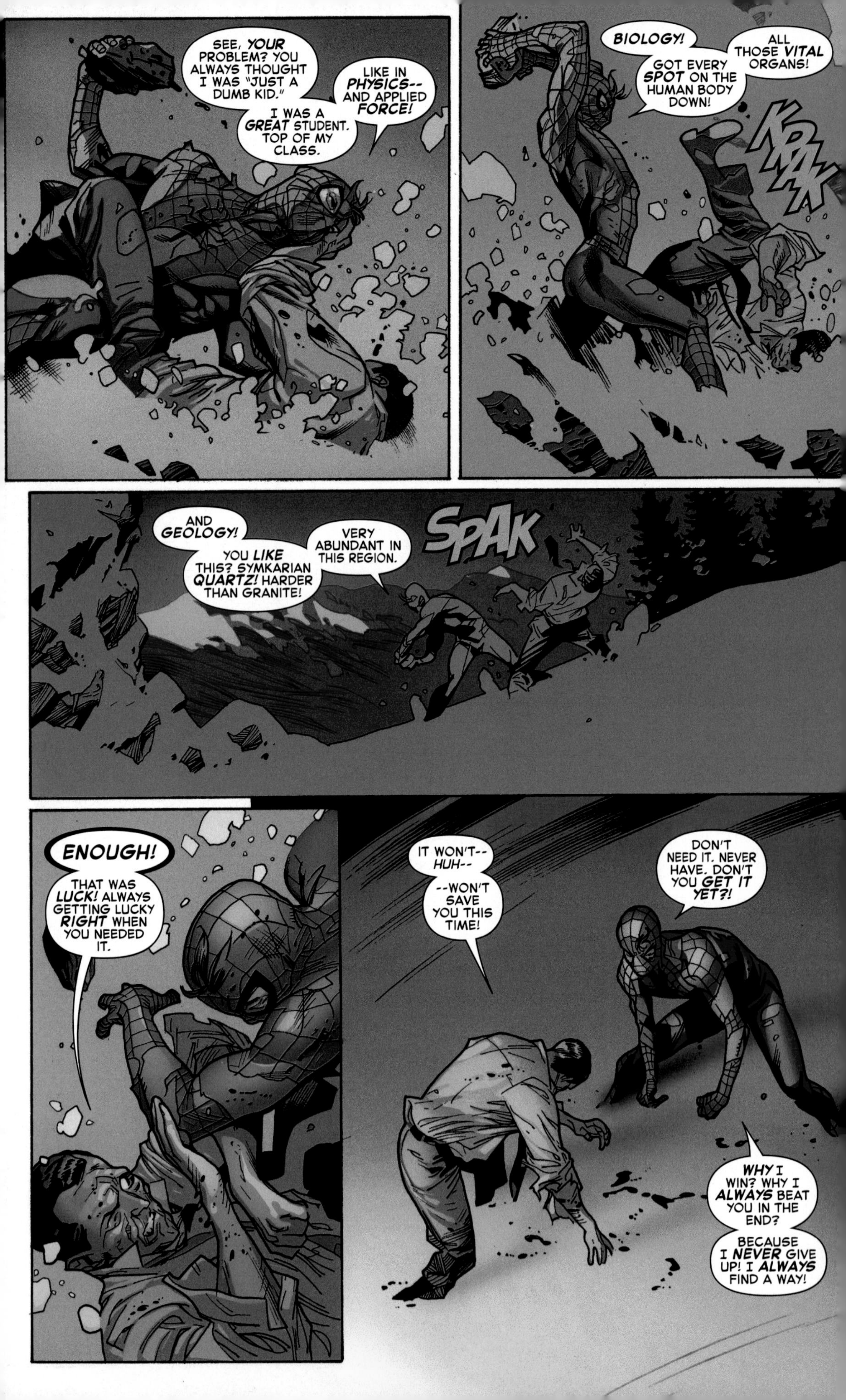
SEE, YOUR PROBLEM? YOU ALWAYS THOUGHT I WAS "JUST A DUMB KID."
I WAS A GREAT STUDENT. TOP OF MY CLASS.
LIKE IN PHYSICS-- AND APPLIED FORCE!
BIOLOGY!
GOT EVERY SPOT ON THE HUMAN BODY DOWN!
ALL THOSE VITAL ORGANS!
KRAK
AND GEOLOGY!
YOU LIKE THIS? SYMKARIAN QUARTZ! HARDER THAN GRANITE!
VERY ABUNDANT IN THIS REGION.
SPAK
ENOUGH!
THAT WAS LUCK! ALWAYS GETTING LUCKY RIGHT WHEN YOU NEEDED IT.
IT WON'T-- HUH--
--WON'T SAVE YOU THIS TIME!
DON'T NEED IT. NEVER HAVE. DON'T YOU GET IT YET?!
WHY I WIN? WHY I ALWAYS BEAT YOU IN THE END?
BECAUSE I NEVER GIVE UP! I ALWAYS FIND A WAY!

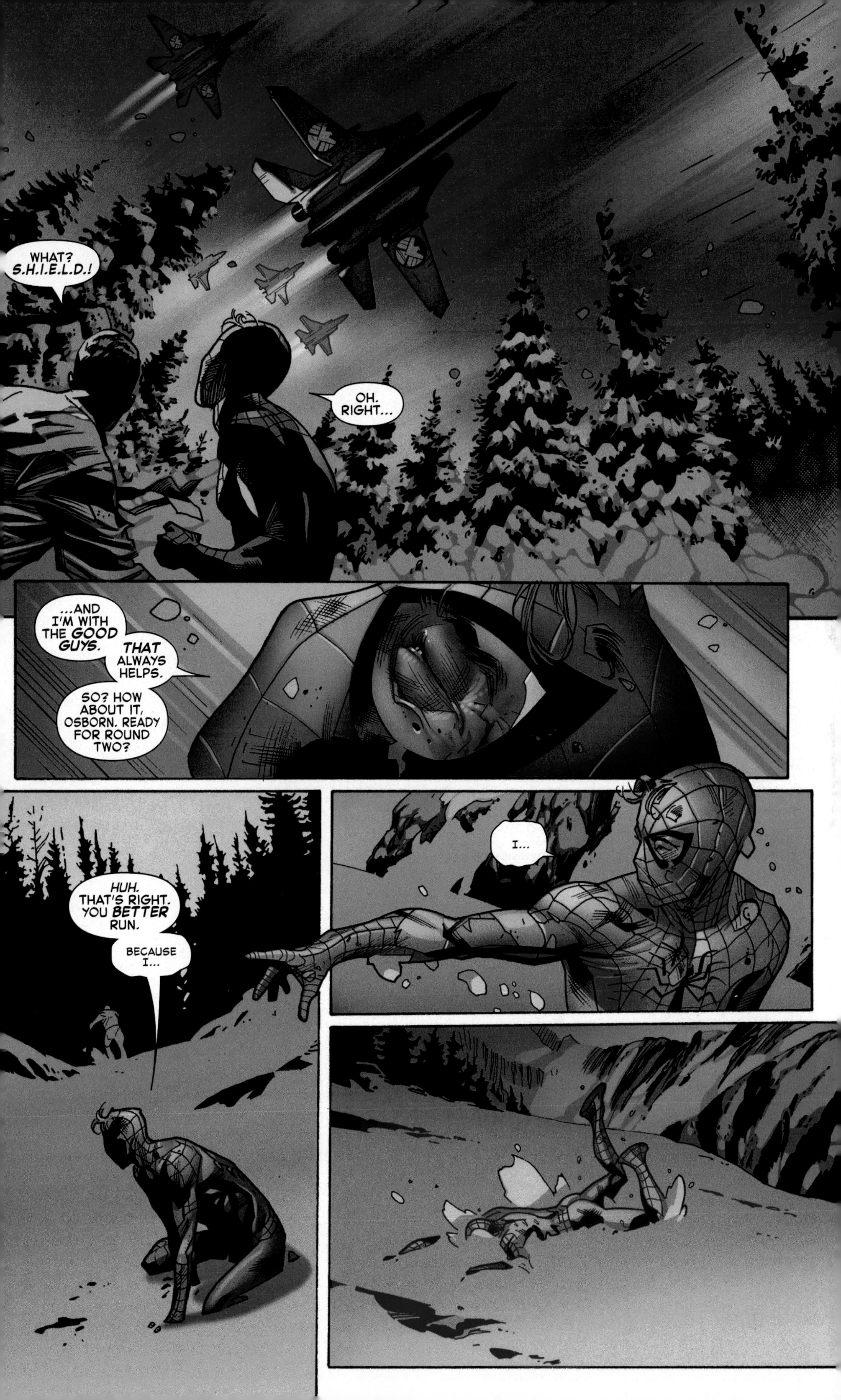
WHAT? S.H.I.E.L.D.!
OH. RIGHT...
...AND I'M WITH THE GOOD GUYS. THAT ALWAYS HELPS.
SO? HOW ABOUT IT, OSBORN. READY FOR ROUND TWO?
HUH. THAT'S RIGHT. YOU BETTER RUN.
BECAUSE I...
I...

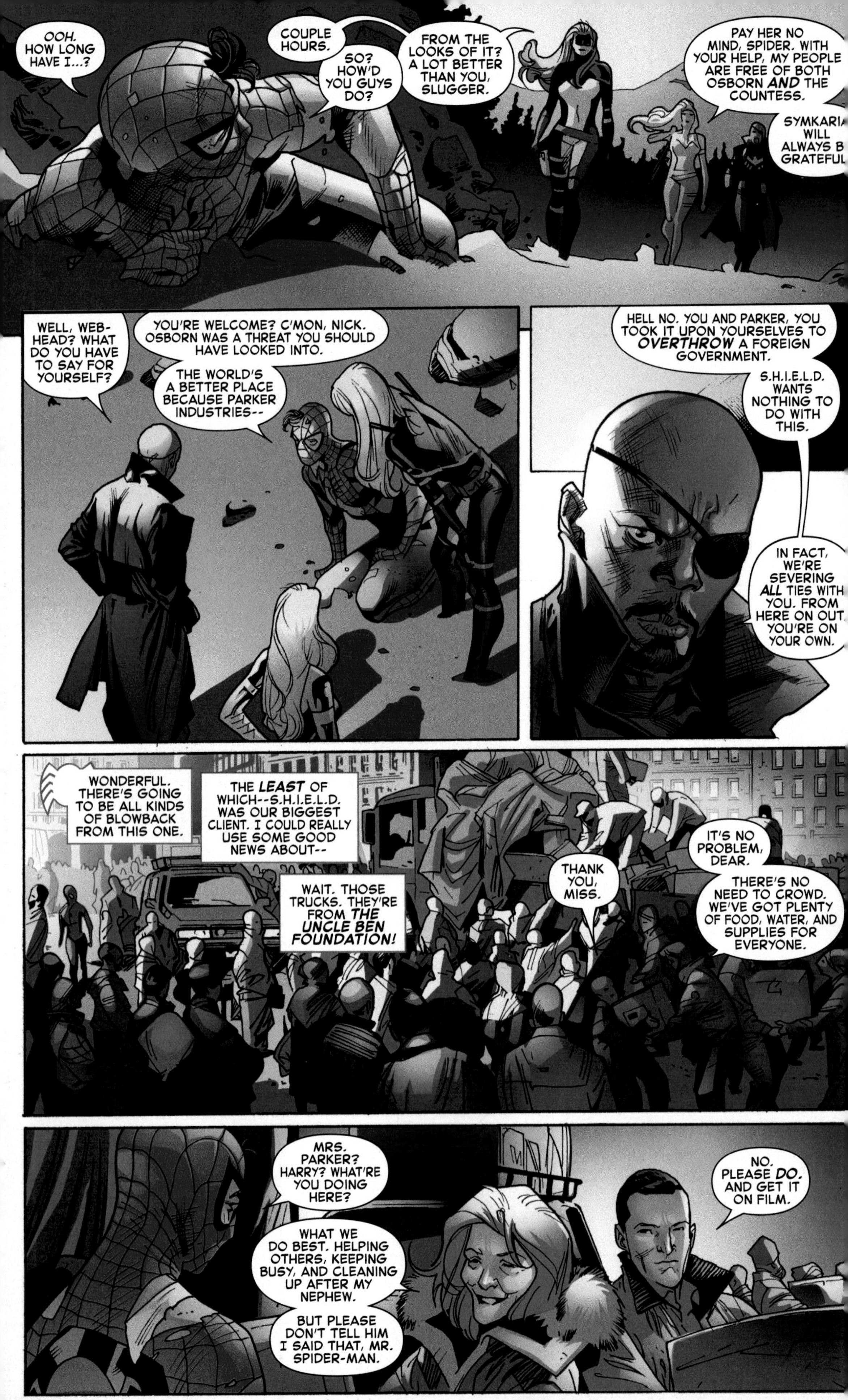

OOH. HOW LONG HAVE I...?
COUPLE HOURS.
SO? HOW'D YOU GUYS DO?
FROM THE LOOKS OF IT? A LOT BETTER THAN YOU, SLUGGER.
PAY HER NO MIND, SPIDER. WITH YOUR HELP, MY PEOPLE ARE FREE OF BOTH OSBORN AND THE COUNTESS.
SYMKARIA WILL ALWAYS B GRATEFUL
WELL, WEB-HEAD? WHAT DO YOU HAVE TO SAY FOR YOURSELF?
YOU'RE WELCOME? C'MON, NICK. OSBORN WAS A THREAT YOU SHOULD HAVE LOOKED INTO.
THE WORLD'S A BETTER PLACE BECAUSE PARKER INDUSTRIES--
HELL NO. YOU AND PARKER, YOU TOOK IT UPON YOURSELVES TO OVERTHROW A FOREIGN GOVERNMENT.
S.H.I.E.L.D. WANTS NOTHING TO DO WITH THIS.
IN FACT, WE'RE SEVERING ALL TIES WITH YOU. FROM HERE ON OUT, YOU'RE ON YOUR OWN.
WONDERFUL. THERE'S GOING TO BE ALL KINDS OF BLOWBACK FROM THIS ONE.
THE LEAST OF WHICH--S.H.I.E.L.D. WAS OUR BIGGEST CLIENT. I COULD REALLY USE SOME GOOD NEWS ABOUT--
WAIT. THOSE TRUCKS. THEY'RE FROM THE UNCLE BEN FOUNDATION!
THANK YOU, MISS.
IT'S NO PROBLEM, DEAR.
THERE'S NO NEED TO CROWD. WE'VE GOT PLENTY OF FOOD, WATER, AND SUPPLIES FOR EVERYONE.
MRS. PARKER? HARRY? WHAT'RE YOU DOING HERE?
WHAT WE DO BEST. HELPING OTHERS, KEEPING BUSY, AND CLEANING UP AFTER MY NEPHEW.
BUT PLEASE DON'T TELL HIM I SAID THAT, MR. SPIDER-MAN.
NO. PLEASE DO. AND GET IT ON FILM.

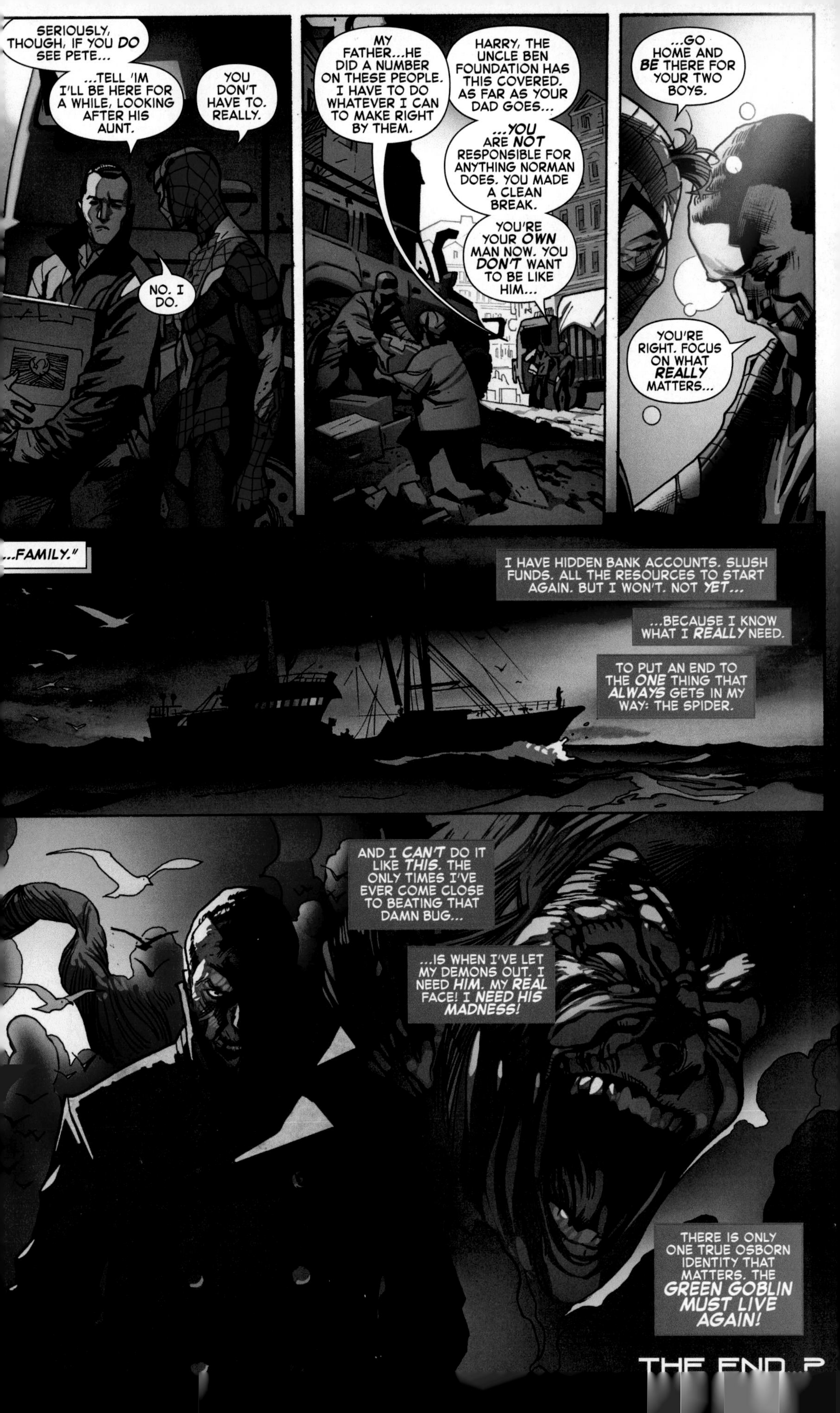
SERIOUSLY, THOUGH, IF YOU DO SEE PETE...
...TELL 'IM I'LL BE HERE FOR A WHILE, LOOKING AFTER HIS AUNT.
YOU DON'T HAVE TO. REALLY.
NO. I DO.
MY FATHER...HE DID A NUMBER ON THESE PEOPLE. I HAVE TO DO WHATEVER I CAN TO MAKE RIGHT BY THEM.
HARRY, THE UNCLE BEN FOUNDATION HAS THIS COVERED. AS FAR AS YOUR DAD GOES...
...YOU ARE NOT RESPONSIBLE FOR ANYTHING NORMAN DOES. YOU MADE A CLEAN BREAK.
YOU'RE YOUR OWN MAN NOW. YOU DON'T WANT TO BE LIKE HIM...
...GO HOME AND BE THERE FOR YOUR TWO BOYS.
YOU'RE RIGHT. FOCUS ON WHAT REALLY MATTERS...
...FAMILY."
I HAVE HIDDEN BANK ACCOUNTS. SLUSH FUNDS. ALL THE RESOURCES TO START AGAIN. BUT I WON'T. NOT YET...
...BECAUSE I KNOW WHAT I REALLY NEED.
TO PUT AN END TO THE ONE THING THAT ALWAYS GETS IN MY WAY: THE SPIDER.
AND I CAN'T DO IT LIKE THIS. THE ONLY TIMES I'VE EVER COME CLOSE TO BEATING THAT DAMN BUG...
...IS WHEN I'VE LET MY DEMONS OUT. I NEED HIM. MY REAL FACE! I NEED HIS MADNESS!
THERE IS ONLY ONE TRUE OSBORN IDENTITY THAT MATTERS. THE GREEN GOBLIN MUST LIVE AGAIN!
THE END ?

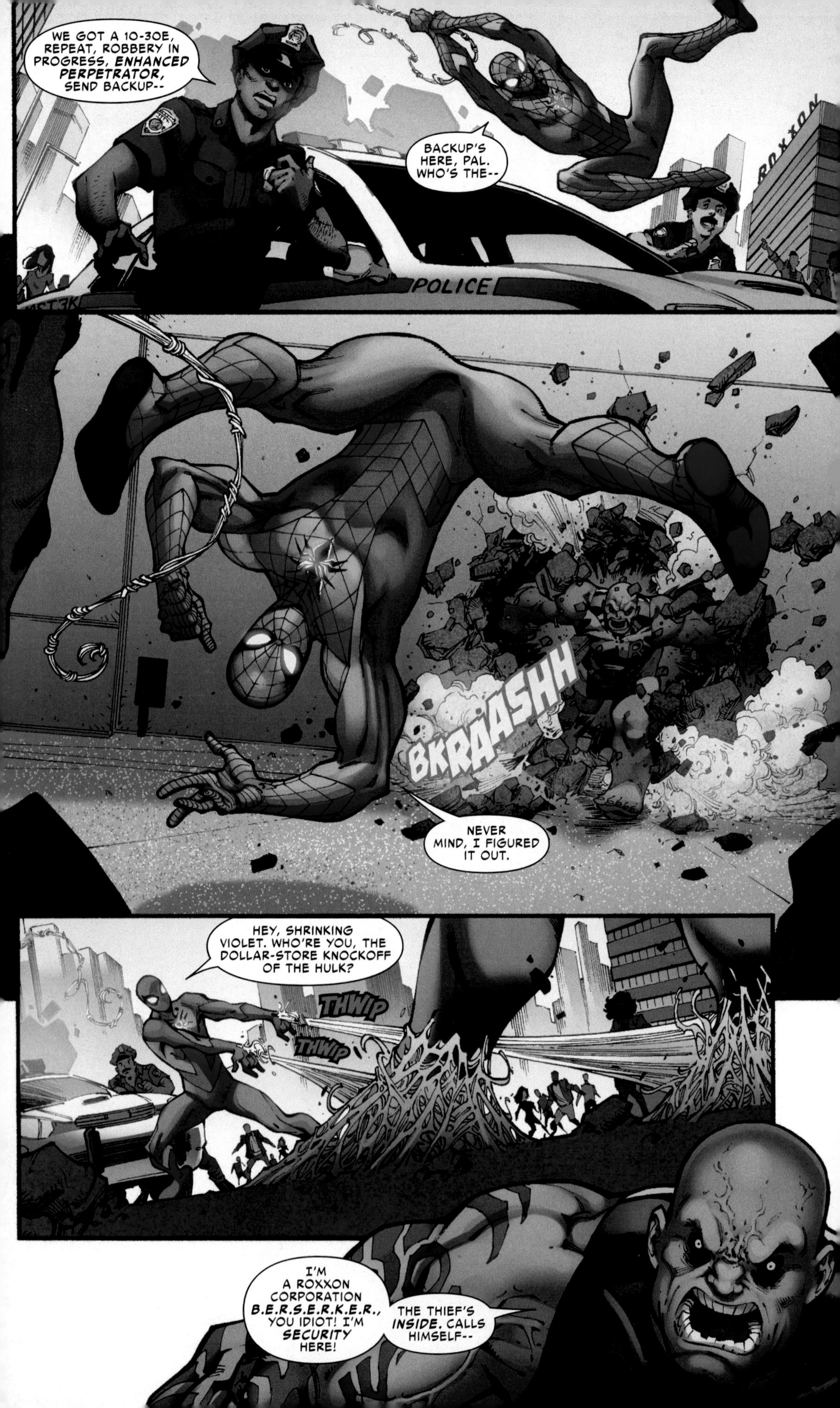

WE GOT A 10-30E, REPEAT, ROBBERY IN PROGRESS, ENHANCED PERPETRATOR, SEND BACKUP--
BACKUP'S HERE, PAL. WHO'S THE--
POLICE
ROXXON
BKRAASHH
NEVER MIND, I FIGURED IT OUT.
HEY, SHRINKING VIOLET. WHO'RE YOU, THE DOLLAR-STORE KNOCKOFF OF THE HULK?
THWIP
THWIP
I'M A ROXXON CORPORATION B.E.R.S.E.R.K.E.R., YOU IDIOT! I'M SECURITY HERE!
THE THIEF'S INSIDE. CALLS HIMSELF--

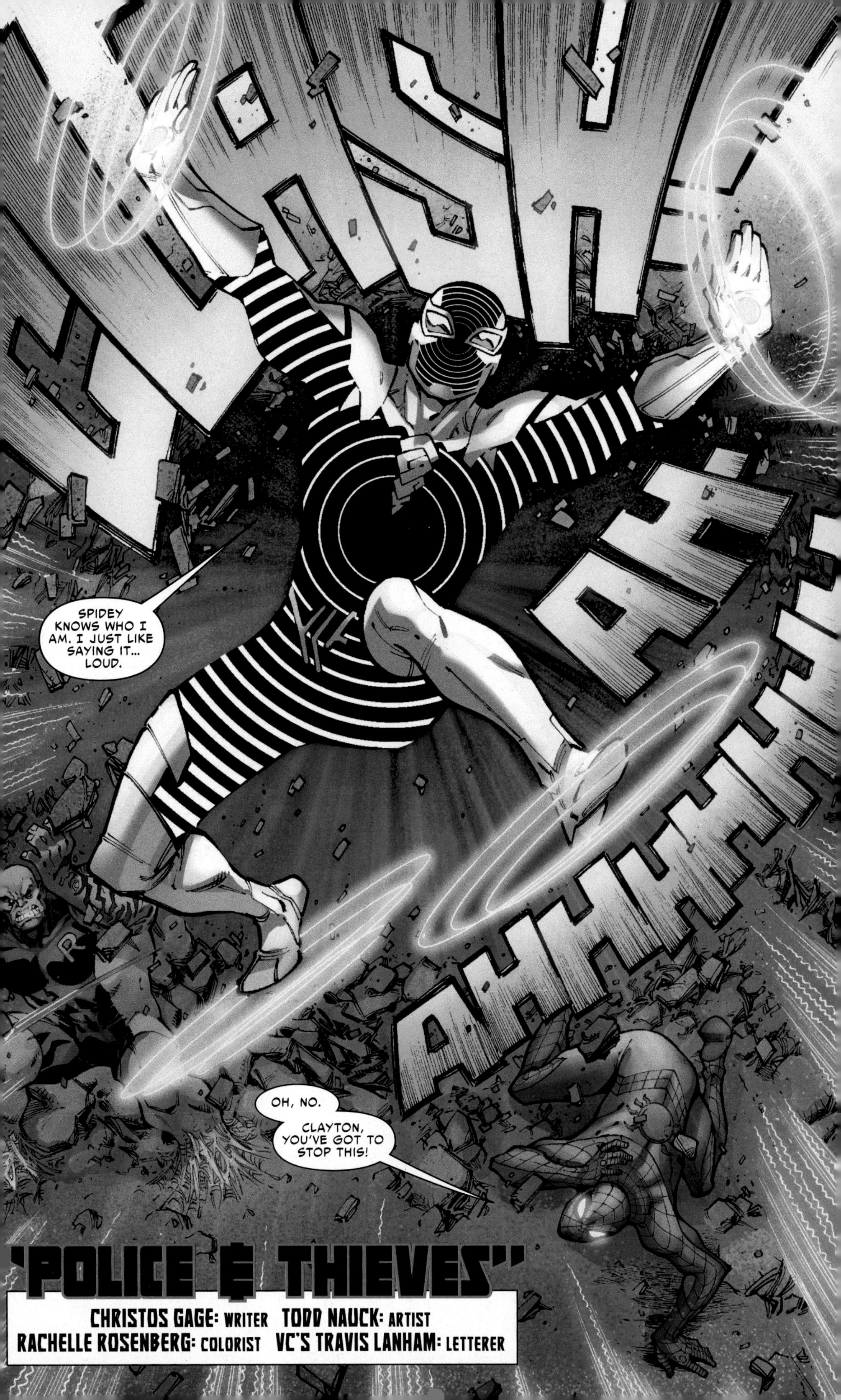

SPIDEY KNOWS WHO I AM. I JUST LIKE SAYING IT... LOUD.
AHHH
OH, NO.
CLAYTON, YOU'VE GOT TO STOP THIS!
"POLICE & THIEVES"
CHRISTOS GAGE: WRITER TODD NAUCK: ARTIST
RACHELLE ROSENBERG: COLORIST VC'S TRAVIS LANHAM: LETTERER

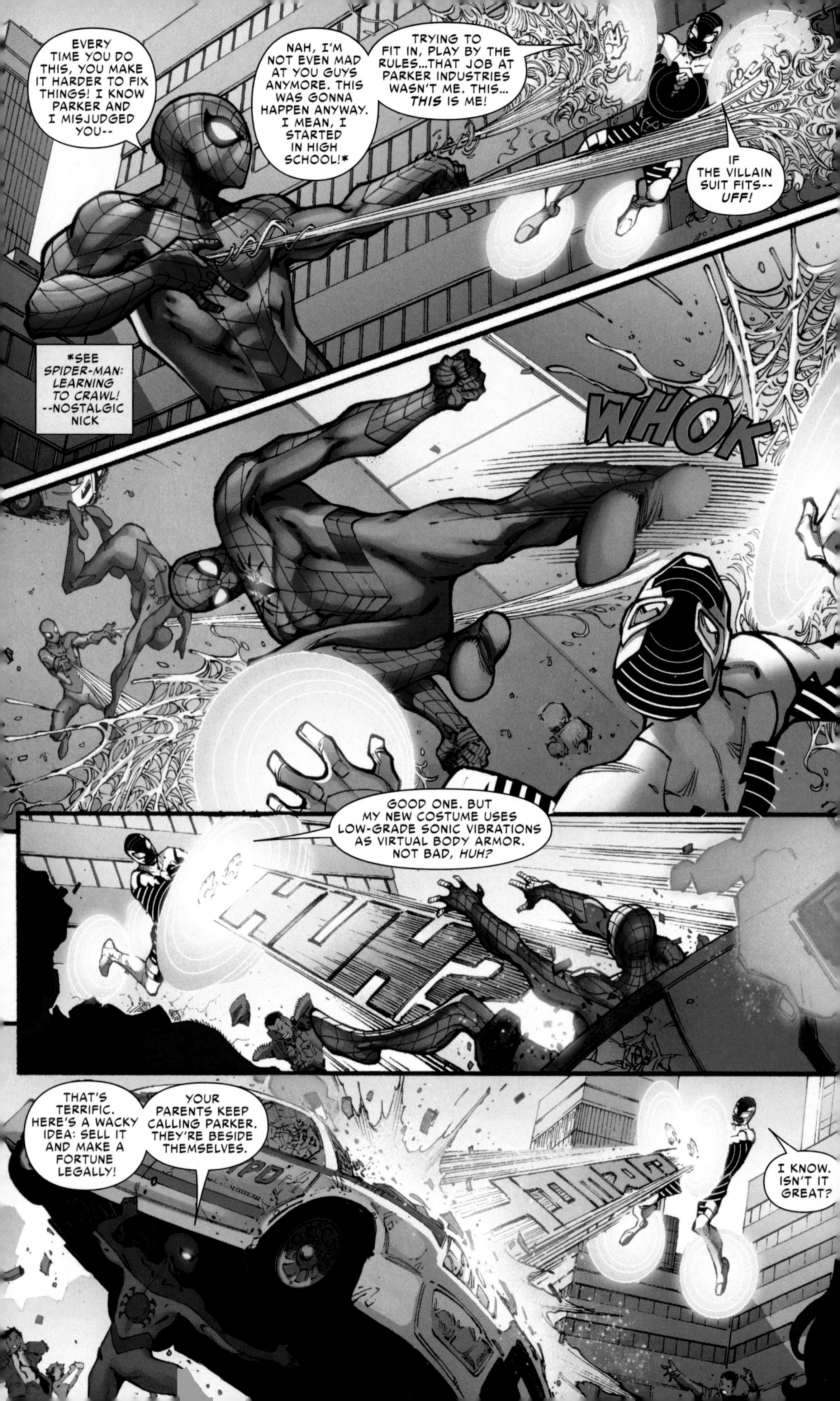
EVERY TIME YOU DO THIS, YOU MAKE IT HARDER TO FIX THINGS! I KNOW PARKER AND I MISJUDGED YOU--
NAH, I'M NOT EVEN MAD AT YOU GUYS ANYMORE. THIS WAS GONNA HAPPEN ANYWAY. I MEAN, I STARTED IN HIGH SCHOOL!*
TRYING TO FIT IN, PLAY BY THE RULES...THAT JOB AT PARKER INDUSTRIES WASN'T ME. THIS... *THIS* IS ME!
IF THE VILLAIN SUIT FITS-- *UFF!*
*SEE *SPIDER-MAN: LEARNING TO CRAWL!* --NOSTALGIC NICK
WHOK
GOOD ONE. BUT MY NEW COSTUME USES LOW-GRADE SONIC VIBRATIONS AS VIRTUAL BODY ARMOR. NOT BAD, *HUH?*
THAT'S TERRIFIC. HERE'S A WACKY IDEA: SELL IT AND MAKE A FORTUNE LEGALLY!
YOUR PARENTS KEEP CALLING PARKER. THEY'RE BESIDE THEMSELVES.
I KNOW. ISN'T IT GREAT?

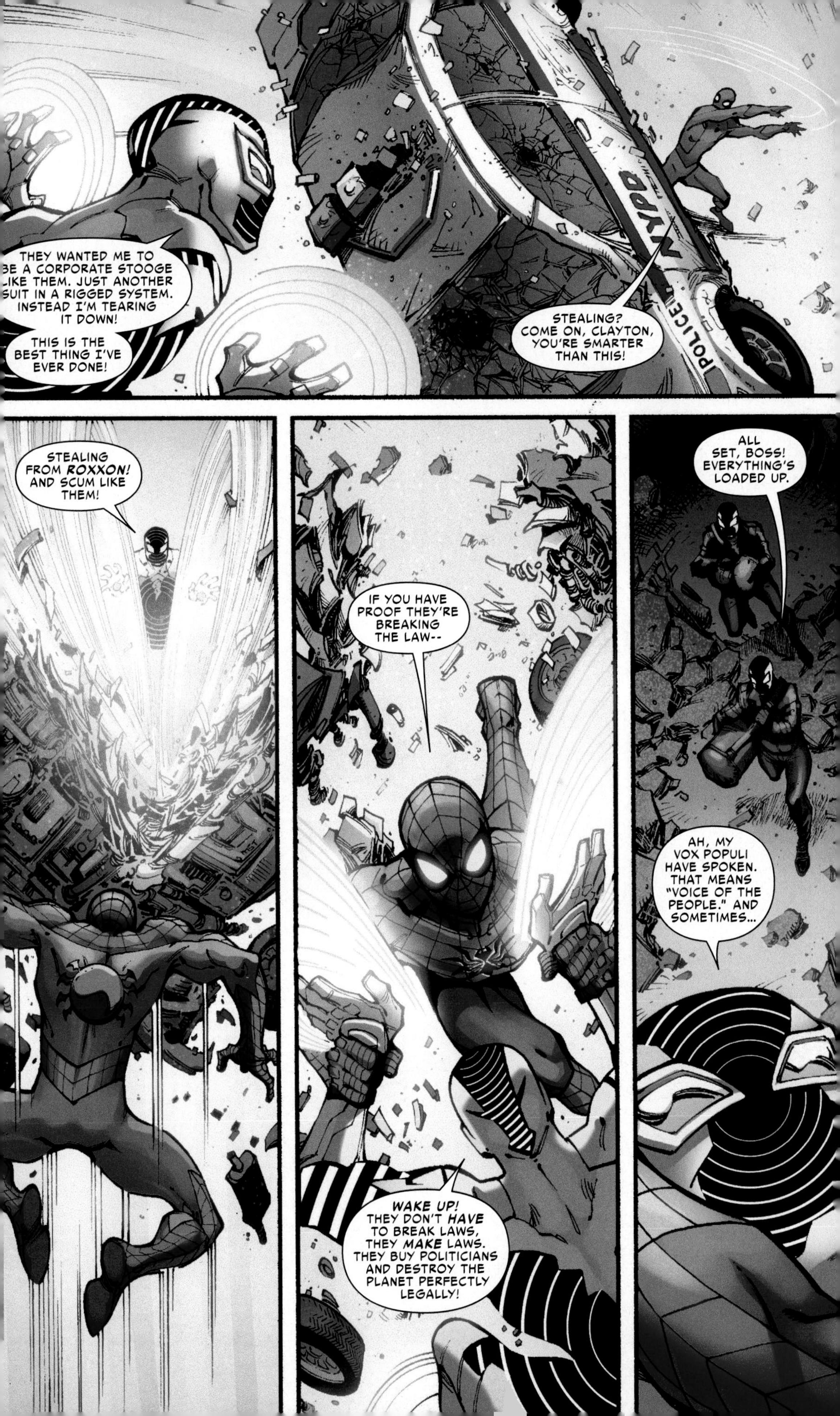

THEY WANTED ME TO BE A CORPORATE STOOGE LIKE THEM. JUST ANOTHER SUIT IN A RIGGED SYSTEM. INSTEAD I'M TEARING IT DOWN!
THIS IS THE BEST THING I'VE EVER DONE!
NYPD
POLICE
STEALING? COME ON, CLAYTON, YOU'RE SMARTER THAN THIS!
STEALING FROM *ROXXON!* AND SCUM LIKE THEM!
IF YOU HAVE PROOF THEY'RE BREAKING THE LAW--
WAKE UP! THEY DON'T *HAVE* TO BREAK LAWS, THEY *MAKE* LAWS. THEY BUY POLITICIANS AND DESTROY THE PLANET PERFECTLY LEGALLY!
ALL SET, BOSS! EVERYTHING'S LOADED UP.
AH, MY VOX POPULI HAVE SPOKEN. THAT MEANS "VOICE OF THE PEOPLE." AND SOMETIMES...

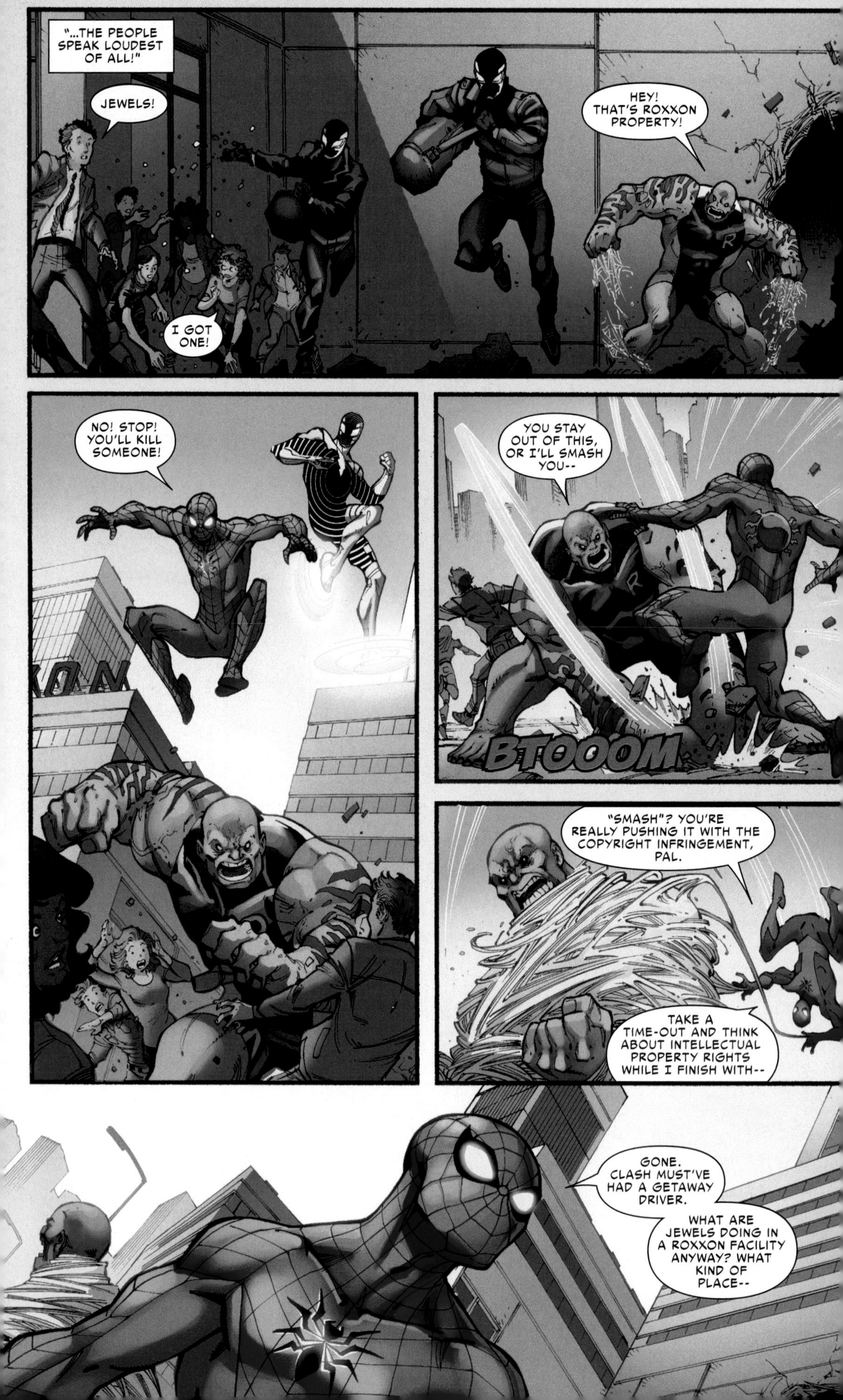
"...THE PEOPLE SPEAK LOUDEST OF ALL!"
JEWELS!
I GOT ONE!
HEY! THAT'S ROXXON PROPERTY!
NO! STOP! YOU'LL KILL SOMEONE!
YOU STAY OUT OF THIS, OR I'LL SMASH YOU--
BTOOOM
"SMASH"? YOU'RE REALLY PUSHING IT WITH THE COPYRIGHT INFRINGEMENT, PAL.
TAKE A TIME-OUT AND THINK ABOUT INTELLECTUAL PROPERTY RIGHTS WHILE I FINISH WITH--
GONE. CLASH MUST'VE HAD A GETAWAY DRIVER.
WHAT ARE JEWELS DOING IN A ROXXON FACILITY ANYWAY? WHAT KIND OF PLACE--

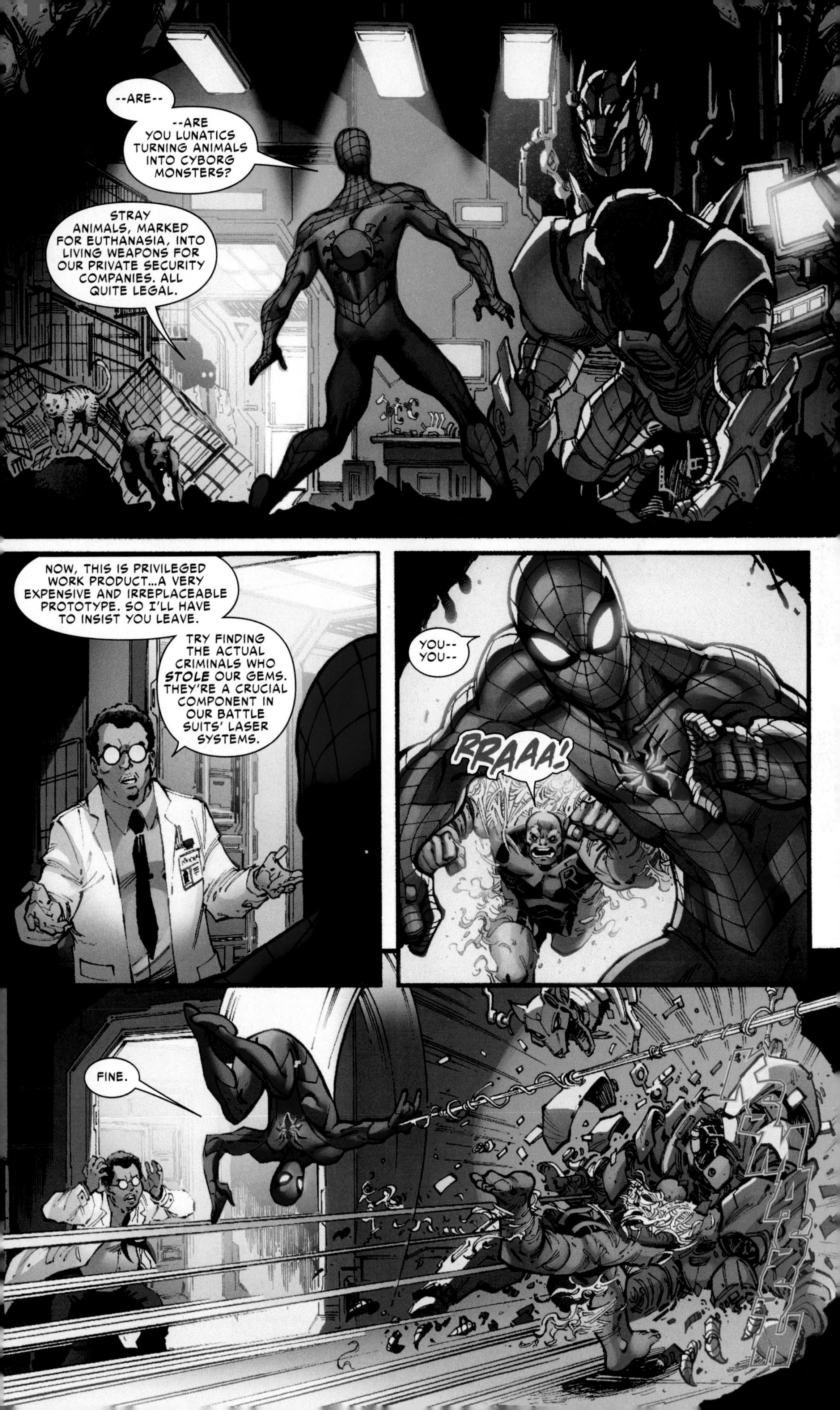

--ARE--
--ARE YOU LUNATICS TURNING ANIMALS INTO CYBORG MONSTERS?
STRAY ANIMALS, MARKED FOR EUTHANASIA, INTO LIVING WEAPONS FOR OUR PRIVATE SECURITY COMPANIES. ALL QUITE LEGAL.
NOW, THIS IS PRIVILEGED WORK PRODUCT...A VERY EXPENSIVE AND IRREPLACEABLE PROTOTYPE. SO I'LL HAVE TO INSIST YOU LEAVE.
TRY FINDING THE ACTUAL CRIMINALS WHO *STOLE* OUR GEMS. THEY'RE A CRUCIAL COMPONENT IN OUR BATTLE SUITS' LASER SYSTEMS.
YOU-- YOU--
RRAAA!
FINE.

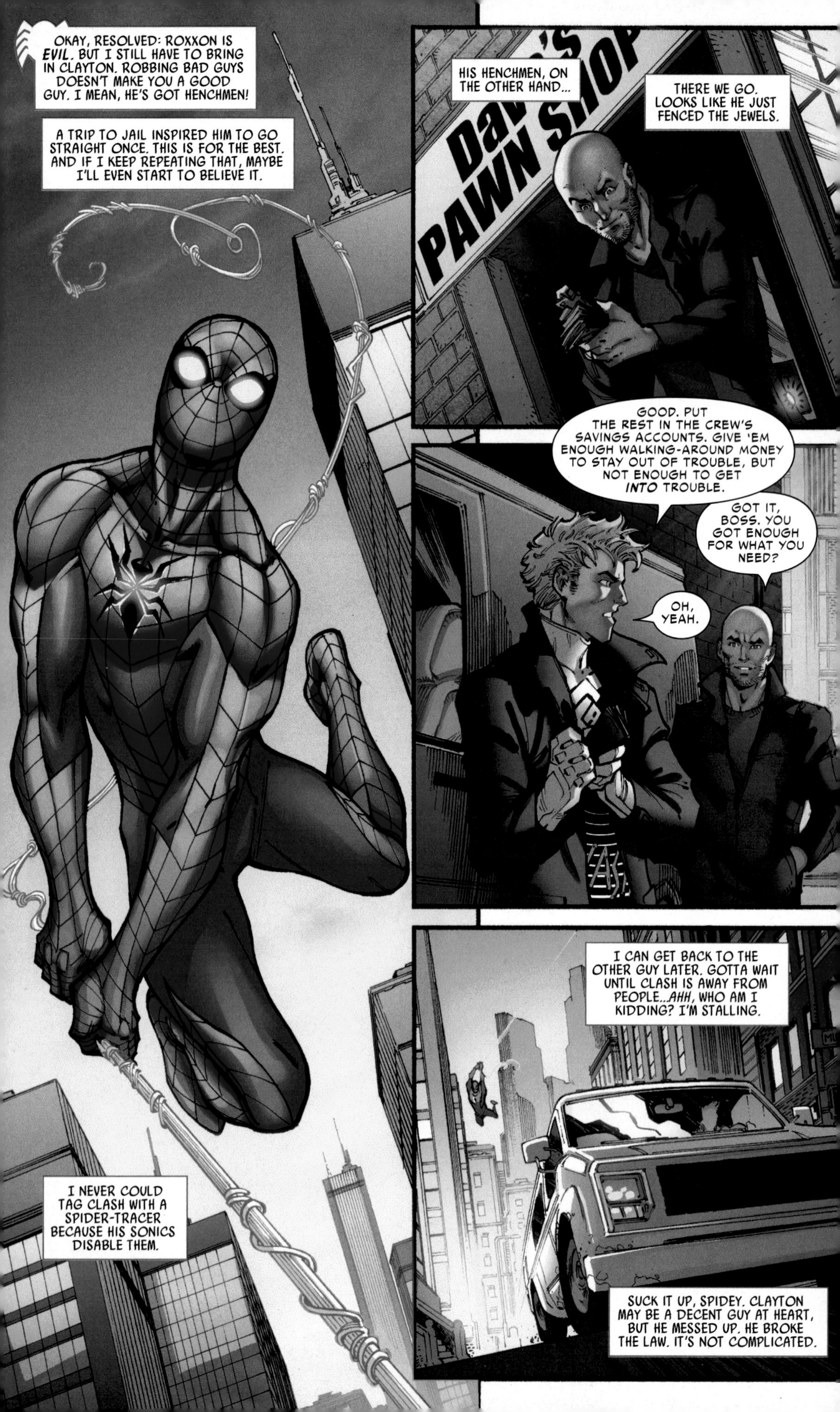

OKAY, RESOLVED: ROXXON IS EVIL. BUT I STILL HAVE TO BRING IN CLAYTON. ROBBING BAD GUYS DOESN'T MAKE YOU A GOOD GUY. I MEAN, HE'S GOT HENCHMEN!
A TRIP TO JAIL INSPIRED HIM TO GO STRAIGHT ONCE. THIS IS FOR THE BEST. AND IF I KEEP REPEATING THAT, MAYBE I'LL EVEN START TO BELIEVE IT.
I NEVER COULD TAG CLASH WITH A SPIDER-TRACER BECAUSE HIS SONICS DISABLE THEM.
HIS HENCHMEN, ON THE OTHER HAND...
THERE WE GO. LOOKS LIKE HE JUST FENCED THE JEWELS.
PAWN SHOP
GOOD. PUT THE REST IN THE CREW'S SAVINGS ACCOUNTS. GIVE 'EM ENOUGH WALKING-AROUND MONEY TO STAY OUT OF TROUBLE, BUT NOT ENOUGH TO GET INTO TROUBLE.
GOT IT, BOSS. YOU GOT ENOUGH FOR WHAT YOU NEED?
OH, YEAH.
I CAN GET BACK TO THE OTHER GUY LATER. GOTTA WAIT UNTIL CLASH IS AWAY FROM PEOPLE...AHH, WHO AM I KIDDING? I'M STALLING.
SUCK IT UP, SPIDEY. CLAYTON MAY BE A DECENT GUY AT HEART, BUT HE MESSED UP. HE BROKE THE LAW. IT'S NOT COMPLICATED.

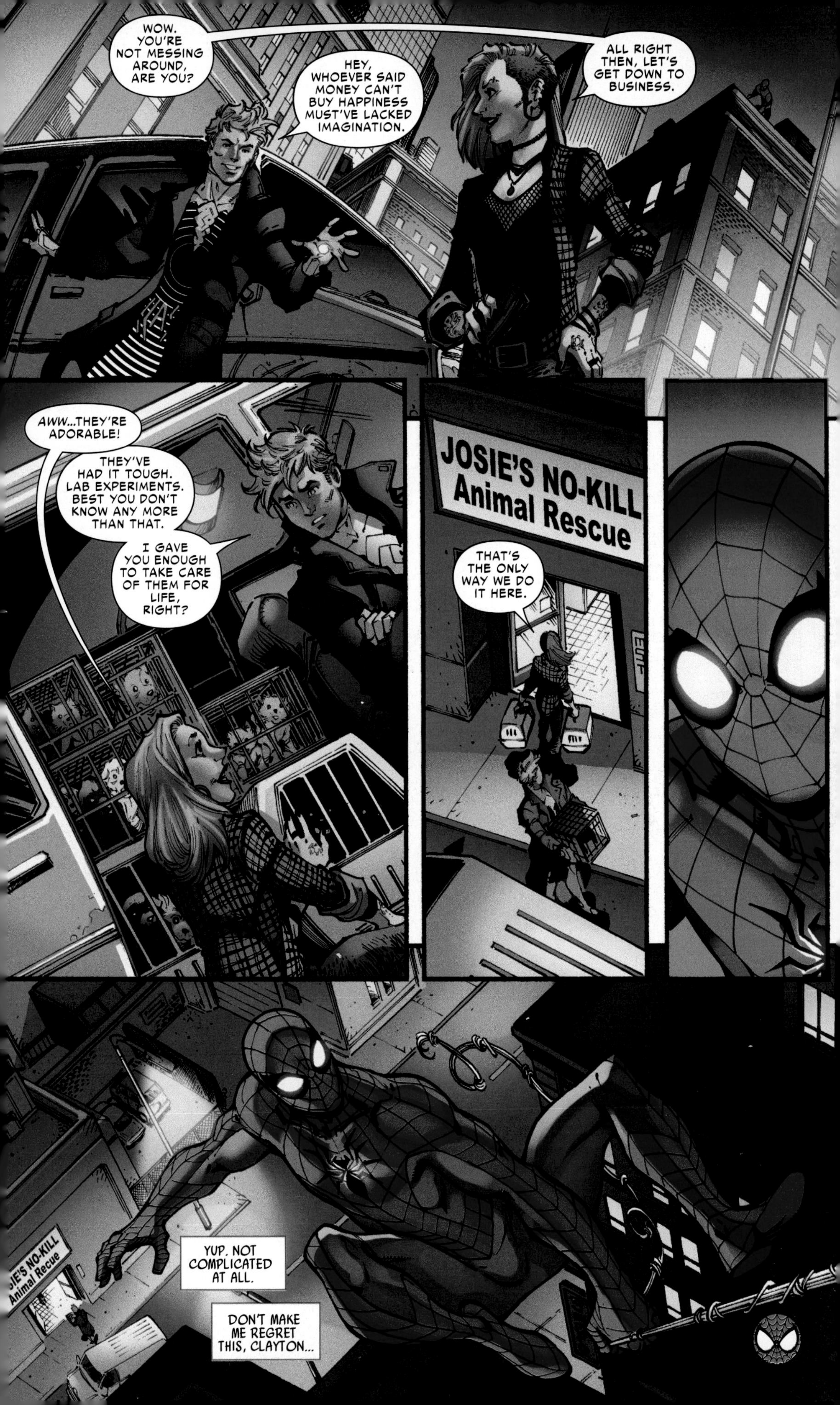
WOW. YOU'RE NOT MESSING AROUND, ARE YOU?
HEY, WHOEVER SAID MONEY CAN'T BUY HAPPINESS MUST'VE LACKED IMAGINATION.
ALL RIGHT THEN, LET'S GET DOWN TO BUSINESS.
AWW...THEY'RE ADORABLE!
THEY'VE HAD IT TOUGH. LAB EXPERIMENTS. BEST YOU DON'T KNOW ANY MORE THAN THAT.
I GAVE YOU ENOUGH TO TAKE CARE OF THEM FOR LIFE, RIGHT?
JOSIE'S NO-KILL Animal Rescue
THAT'S THE ONLY WAY WE DO IT HERE.
YUP. NOT COMPLICATED AT ALL.
DON'T MAKE ME REGRET THIS, CLAYTON...

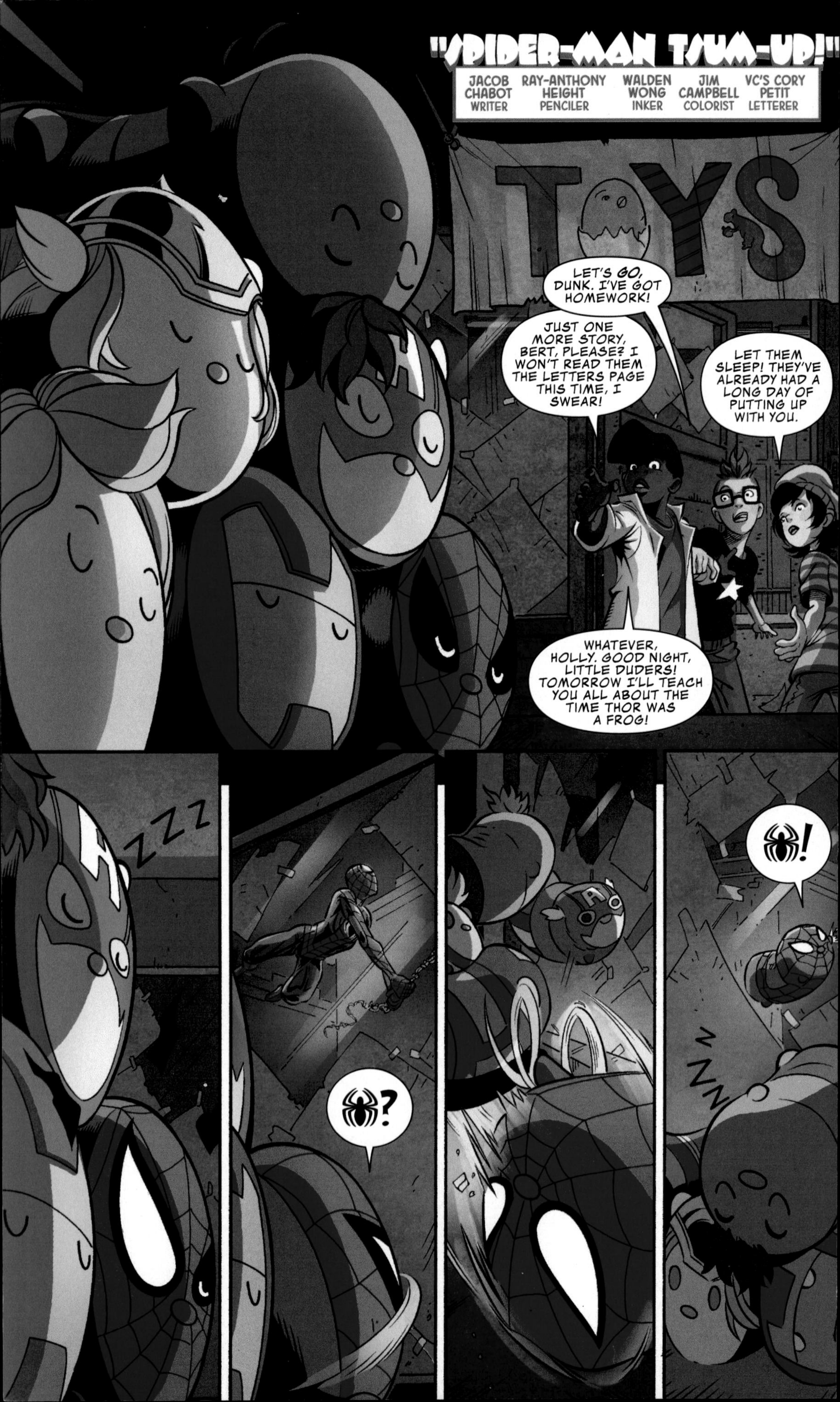
"SPIDER-MAN TSUM-UP!"
JACOB CHABOT WRITER
RAY-ANTHONY HEIGHT PENCILER
WALDEN WONG INKER
JIM CAMPBELL COLORIST
VC'S CORY PETIT LETTERER
TOYS
LET'S GO, DUNK. I'VE GOT HOMEWORK!
JUST ONE MORE STORY, BERT, PLEASE? I WON'T READ THEM THE LETTERS PAGE THIS TIME, I SWEAR!
LET THEM SLEEP! THEY'VE ALREADY HAD A LONG DAY OF PUTTING UP WITH YOU.
WHATEVER, HOLLY. GOOD NIGHT, LITTLE DUDERS! TOMORROW I'LL TEACH YOU ALL ABOUT THE TIME THOR WAS A FROG!
ZZZ
?
!
ZZZ

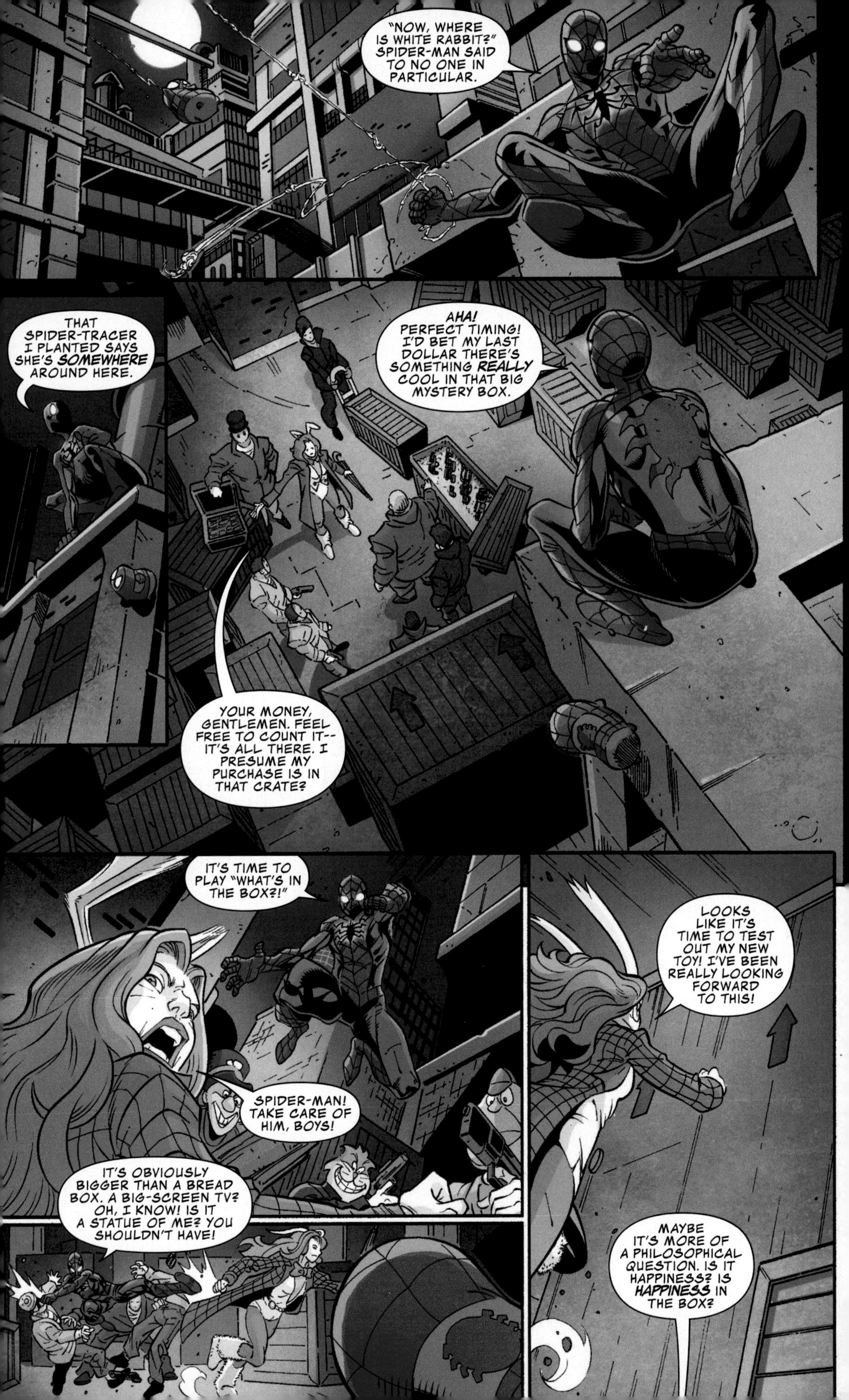
"NOW, WHERE IS WHITE RABBIT?" SPIDER-MAN SAID TO NO ONE IN PARTICULAR.
THAT SPIDER-TRACER I PLANTED SAYS SHE'S SOMEWHERE AROUND HERE.
AHA! PERFECT TIMING! I'D BET MY LAST DOLLAR THERE'S SOMETHING REALLY COOL IN THAT BIG MYSTERY BOX.
YOUR MONEY, GENTLEMEN. FEEL FREE TO COUNT IT-- IT'S ALL THERE. I PRESUME MY PURCHASE IS IN THAT CRATE?
IT'S TIME TO PLAY "WHAT'S IN THE BOX?!"
SPIDER-MAN! TAKE CARE OF HIM, BOYS!
LOOKS LIKE IT'S TIME TO TEST OUT MY NEW TOY! I'VE BEEN REALLY LOOKING FORWARD TO THIS!
IT'S OBVIOUSLY BIGGER THAN A BREAD BOX. A BIG-SCREEN TV? OH, I KNOW! IS IT A STATUE OF ME? YOU SHOULDN'T HAVE!
MAYBE IT'S MORE OF A PHILOSOPHICAL QUESTION. IS IT HAPPINESS? IS HAPPINESS IN THE BOX?

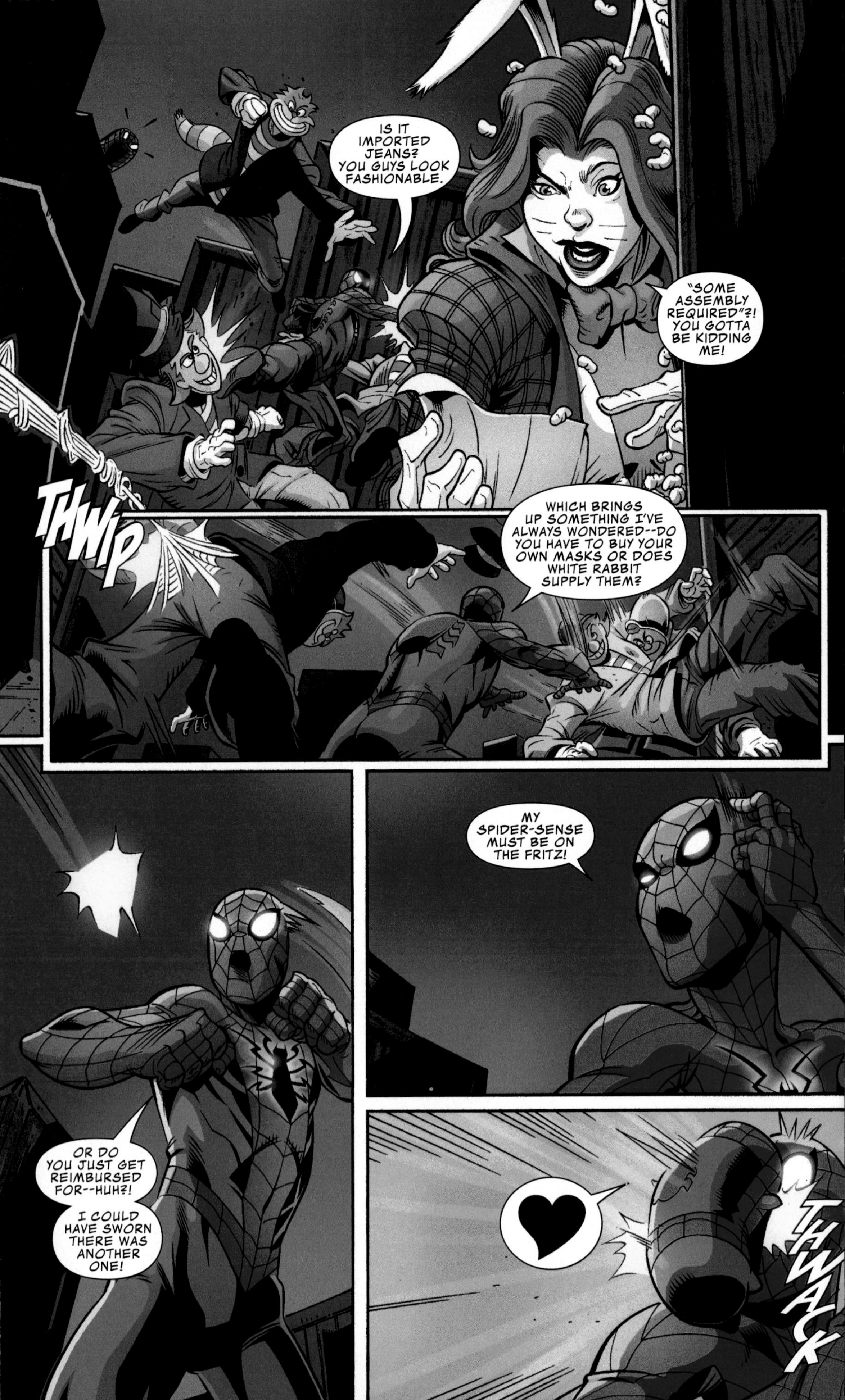
IS IT IMPORTED JEANS? YOU GUYS LOOK FASHIONABLE.
"SOME ASSEMBLY REQUIRED"?! YOU GOTTA BE KIDDING ME!
THWIP
WHICH BRINGS UP SOMETHING I'VE ALWAYS WONDERED--DO YOU HAVE TO BUY YOUR OWN MASKS OR DOES WHITE RABBIT SUPPLY THEM?
OR DO YOU JUST GET REIMBURSED FOR--HUH?!
I COULD HAVE SWORN THERE WAS ANOTHER ONE!
MY SPIDER-SENSE MUST BE ON THE FRITZ!
THWACK

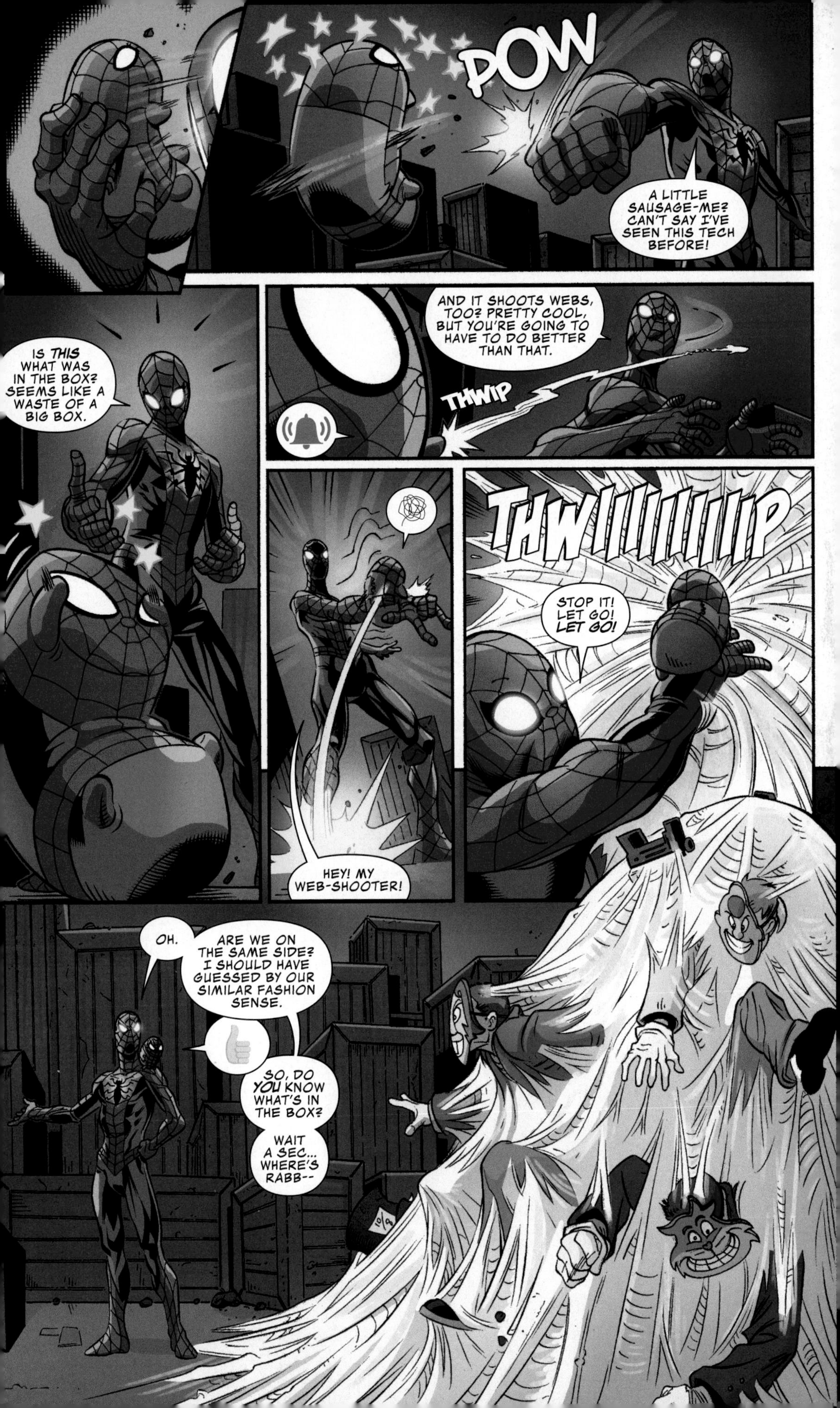
POW
A LITTLE SAUSAGE-ME? CAN'T SAY I'VE SEEN THIS TECH BEFORE!
IS *THIS* WHAT WAS IN THE BOX? SEEMS LIKE A WASTE OF A BIG BOX.
AND IT SHOOTS WEBS, TOO? PRETTY COOL, BUT YOU'RE GOING TO HAVE TO DO BETTER THAN THAT.
THWIP
HEY! MY WEB-SHOOTER!
THWIIIIIIIIIP
STOP IT! LET GO! *LET GO!*
OH.
ARE WE ON THE SAME SIDE? I SHOULD HAVE GUESSED BY OUR SIMILAR FASHION SENSE.
SO, DO *YOU* KNOW WHAT'S IN THE BOX?
WAIT A SEC... WHERE'S RABB--

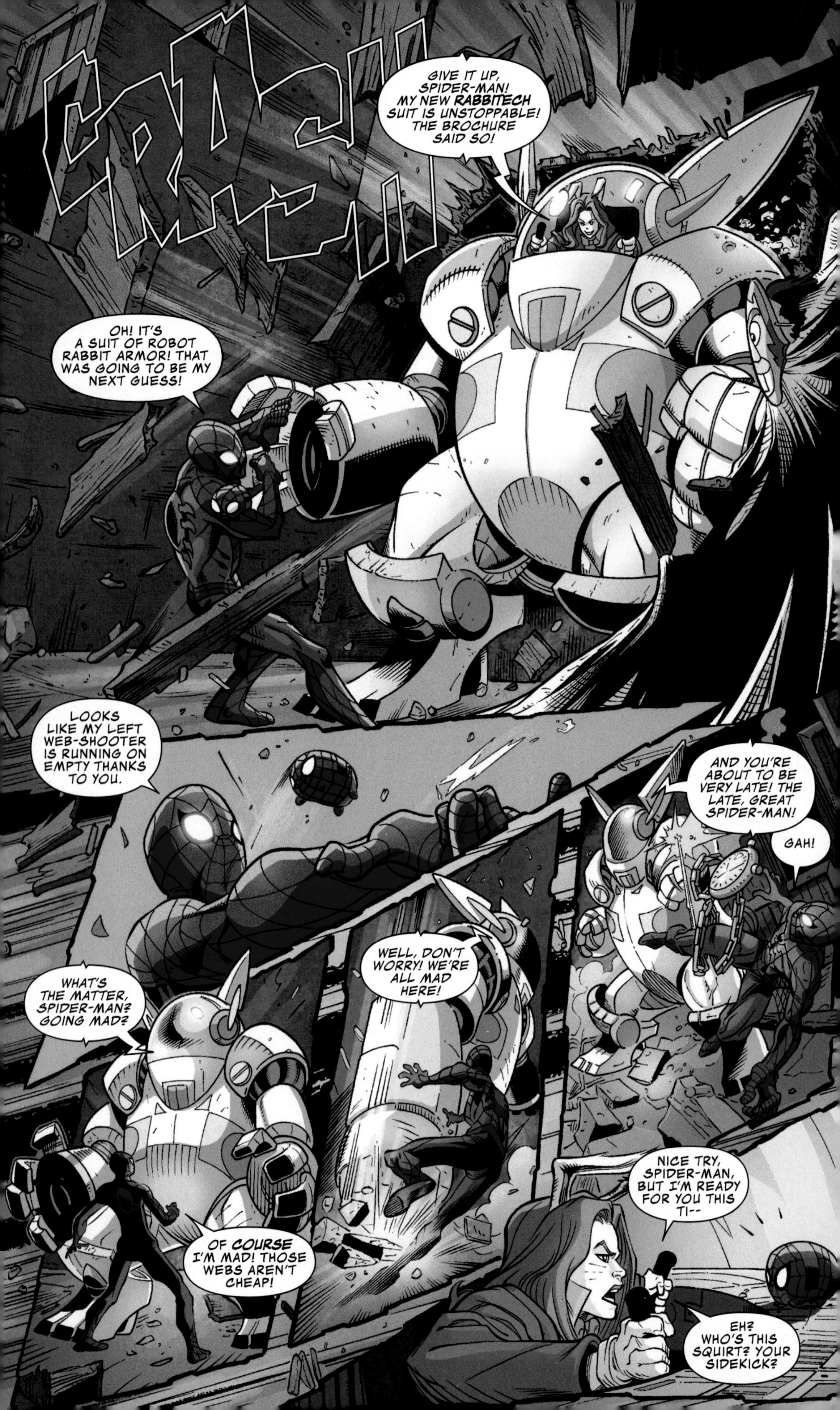

CRASH
GIVE IT UP, SPIDER-MAN! MY NEW **RABBITECH** SUIT IS UNSTOPPABLE! THE BROCHURE SAID SO!
OH! IT'S A SUIT OF ROBOT RABBIT ARMOR! THAT WAS GOING TO BE MY NEXT GUESS!
LOOKS LIKE MY LEFT WEB-SHOOTER IS RUNNING ON EMPTY THANKS TO YOU.
WHAT'S THE MATTER, SPIDER-MAN? GOING MAD?
OF **COURSE** I'M MAD! THOSE WEBS AREN'T CHEAP!
WELL, DON'T WORRY! WE'RE ALL MAD HERE!
AND YOU'RE ABOUT TO BE VERY LATE! THE LATE, GREAT SPIDER-MAN!
GAH!
NICE TRY, SPIDER-MAN, BUT I'M READY FOR YOU THIS TI--
EH? WHO'S THIS SQUIRT? YOUR SIDEKICK?

YOU SEE HIM, TOO? SO I'M *NOT* CRAZY! WAIT...I FORGET WHO I'M TALKING TO.

I'LL DEAL WITH *YOU* ONCE I FINISH CRUSHING DAD.

WHAT THE--

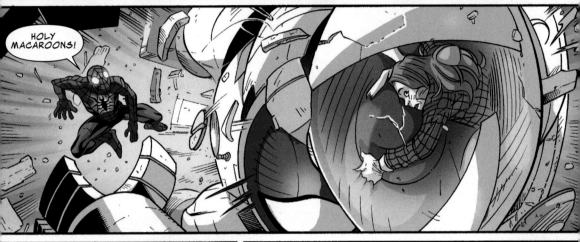

HOLY MACAROONS!

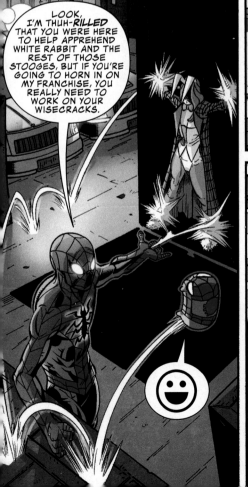

LOOK, I'M THUH-*RILLED* THAT YOU WERE HERE TO HELP APPREHEND WHITE RABBIT AND THE REST OF THOSE STOOGES, BUT IF YOU'RE GOING TO HORN IN ON MY FRANCHISE, YOU REALLY NEED TO WORK ON YOUR WISECRACKS.

UGH. WHO INVENTED SIX IN THE MORNING? IT'S BARELY LIGHT OUT!

DO YOU THINK SPIDER-MAN HAS TO MAKE HOMEROOM BY EIGHT? THAT GUY PROBABLY NEVER EVEN HAD TO GO TO SCHOOL! SOME GUYS HAVE ALL THE LUCK.

CHEER UP, GUYS! I BROUGHT DONU--

NO MORE TEAM-UPS

WHOA. WHAT HAPPENED TO *YOU?!*

🕷!

TSUM TSUM VOL. 2...*COMING TSUM!*

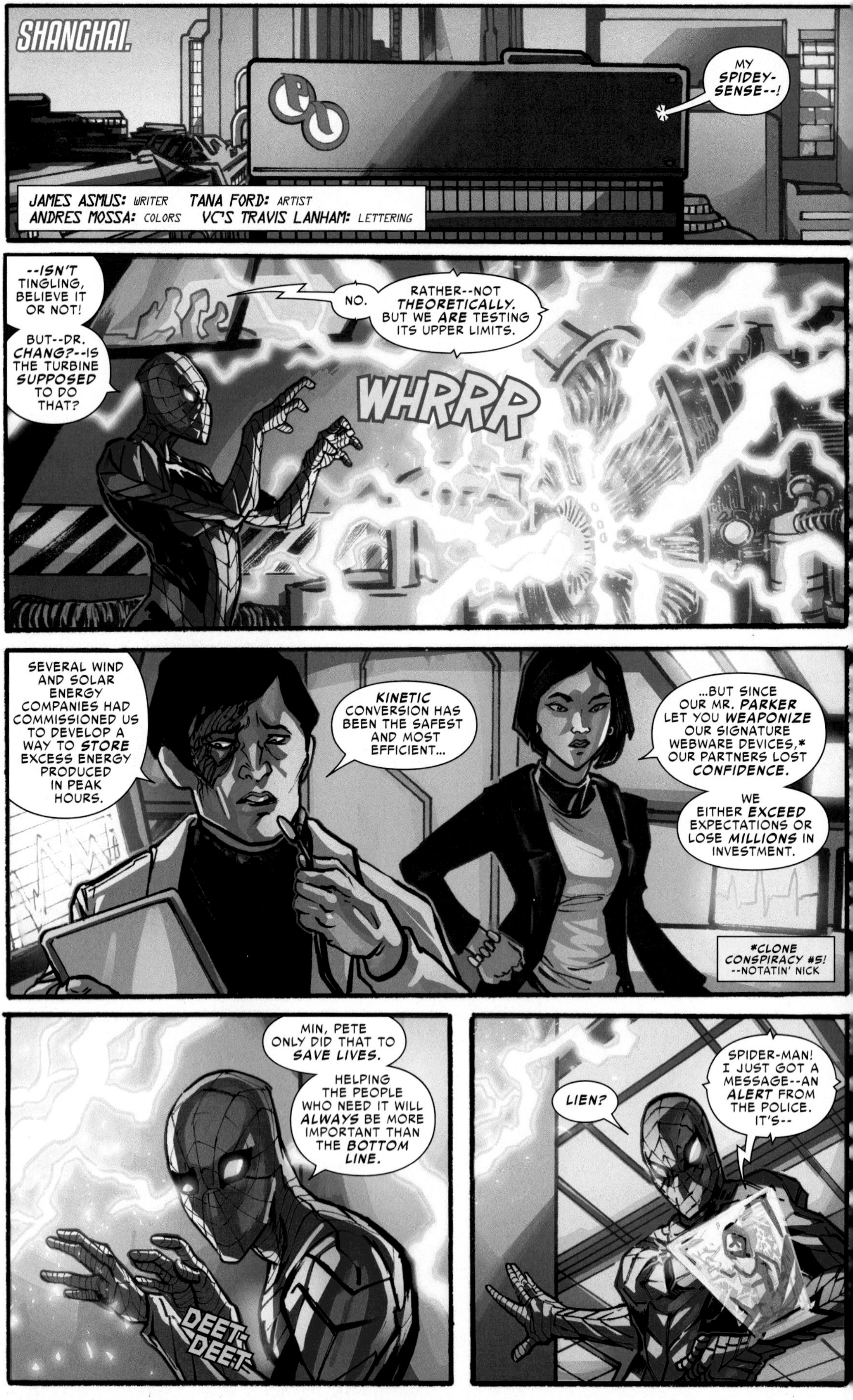
SHANGHAI.
MY SPIDEY-SENSE--!
JAMES ASMUS: WRITER TANA FORD: ARTIST
ANDRES MOSSA: COLORS VC'S TRAVIS LANHAM: LETTERING
--ISN'T TINGLING, BELIEVE IT OR NOT!
BUT--DR. CHANG?--IS THE TURBINE SUPPOSED TO DO THAT?
NO.
RATHER--NOT THEORETICALLY. BUT WE ARE TESTING ITS UPPER LIMITS.
WHRRR
SEVERAL WIND AND SOLAR ENERGY COMPANIES HAD COMMISSIONED US TO DEVELOP A WAY TO STORE EXCESS ENERGY PRODUCED IN PEAK HOURS.
KINETIC CONVERSION HAS BEEN THE SAFEST AND MOST EFFICIENT...
...BUT SINCE OUR MR. PARKER LET YOU WEAPONIZE OUR SIGNATURE WEBWARE DEVICES,* OUR PARTNERS LOST CONFIDENCE.
WE EITHER EXCEED EXPECTATIONS OR LOSE MILLIONS IN INVESTMENT.
*CLONE CONSPIRACY #5! --NOTATIN' NICK
MIN, PETE ONLY DID THAT TO SAVE LIVES.
HELPING THE PEOPLE WHO NEED IT WILL ALWAYS BE MORE IMPORTANT THAN THE BOTTOM LINE.
DEET-DEET
LIEN?
SPIDER-MAN! I JUST GOT A MESSAGE--AN ALERT FROM THE POLICE. IT'S--

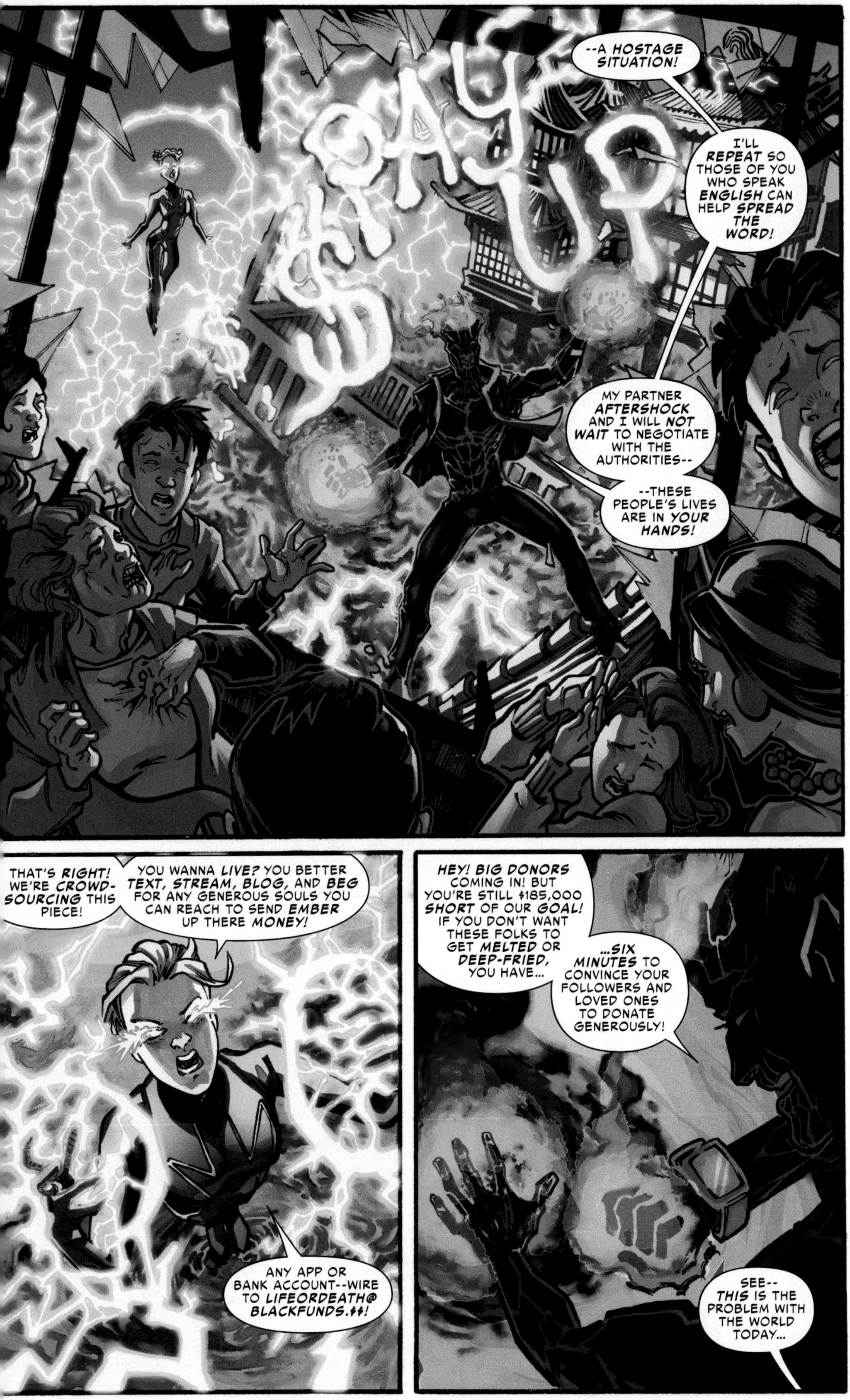
--A HOSTAGE SITUATION!
I'LL REPEAT SO THOSE OF YOU WHO SPEAK ENGLISH CAN HELP SPREAD THE WORD!
$PAY UP
MY PARTNER AFTERSHOCK AND I WILL NOT WAIT TO NEGOTIATE WITH THE AUTHORITIES--
--THESE PEOPLE'S LIVES ARE IN YOUR HANDS!
THAT'S RIGHT! WE'RE CROWD-SOURCING THIS PIECE!
YOU WANNA LIVE? YOU BETTER TEXT, STREAM, BLOG, AND BEG FOR ANY GENEROUS SOULS YOU CAN REACH TO SEND EMBER UP THERE MONEY!
ANY APP OR BANK ACCOUNT--WIRE TO LIFEORDEATH@BLACKFUNDS.¢¢!
HEY! BIG DONORS COMING IN! BUT YOU'RE STILL $185,000 SHORT OF OUR GOAL! IF YOU DON'T WANT THESE FOLKS TO GET MELTED OR DEEP-FRIED, YOU HAVE...
...SIX MINUTES TO CONVINCE YOUR FOLLOWERS AND LOVED ONES TO DONATE GENEROUSLY!
SEE--THIS IS THE PROBLEM WITH THE WORLD TODAY...

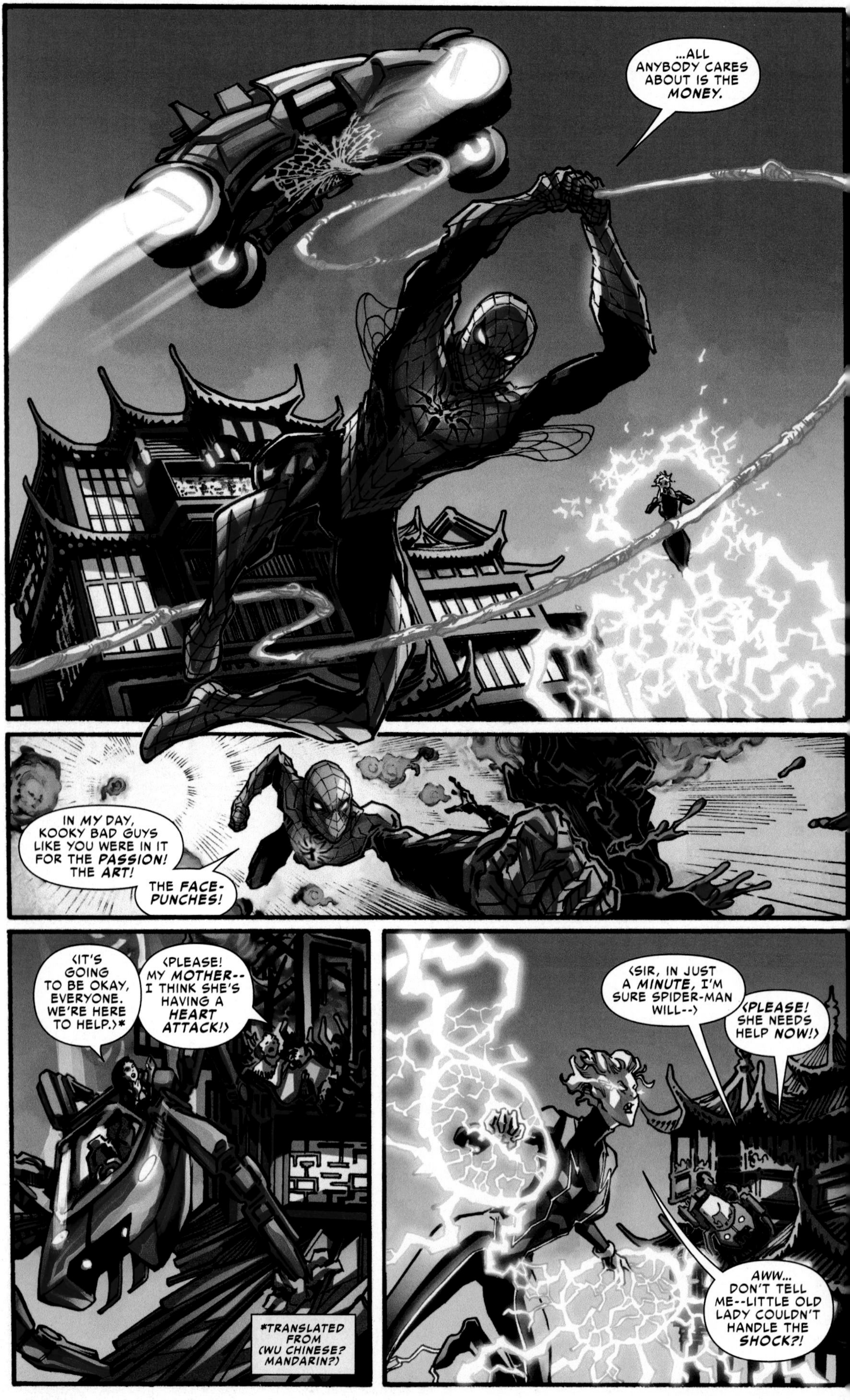
...ALL ANYBODY CARES ABOUT IS THE MONEY.
IN MY DAY, KOOKY BAD GUYS LIKE YOU WERE IN IT FOR THE PASSION! THE ART!
THE FACE-PUNCHES!
<IT'S GOING TO BE OKAY, EVERYONE. WE'RE HERE TO HELP.>*
<PLEASE! MY MOTHER-- I THINK SHE'S HAVING A HEART ATTACK!>
*TRANSLATED FROM (WU CHINESE? MANDARIN?)
<SIR, IN JUST A MINUTE, I'M SURE SPIDER-MAN WILL-->
<PLEASE! SHE NEEDS HELP NOW!>
AWW... DON'T TELL ME--LITTLE OLD LADY COULDN'T HANDLE THE SHOCK?!

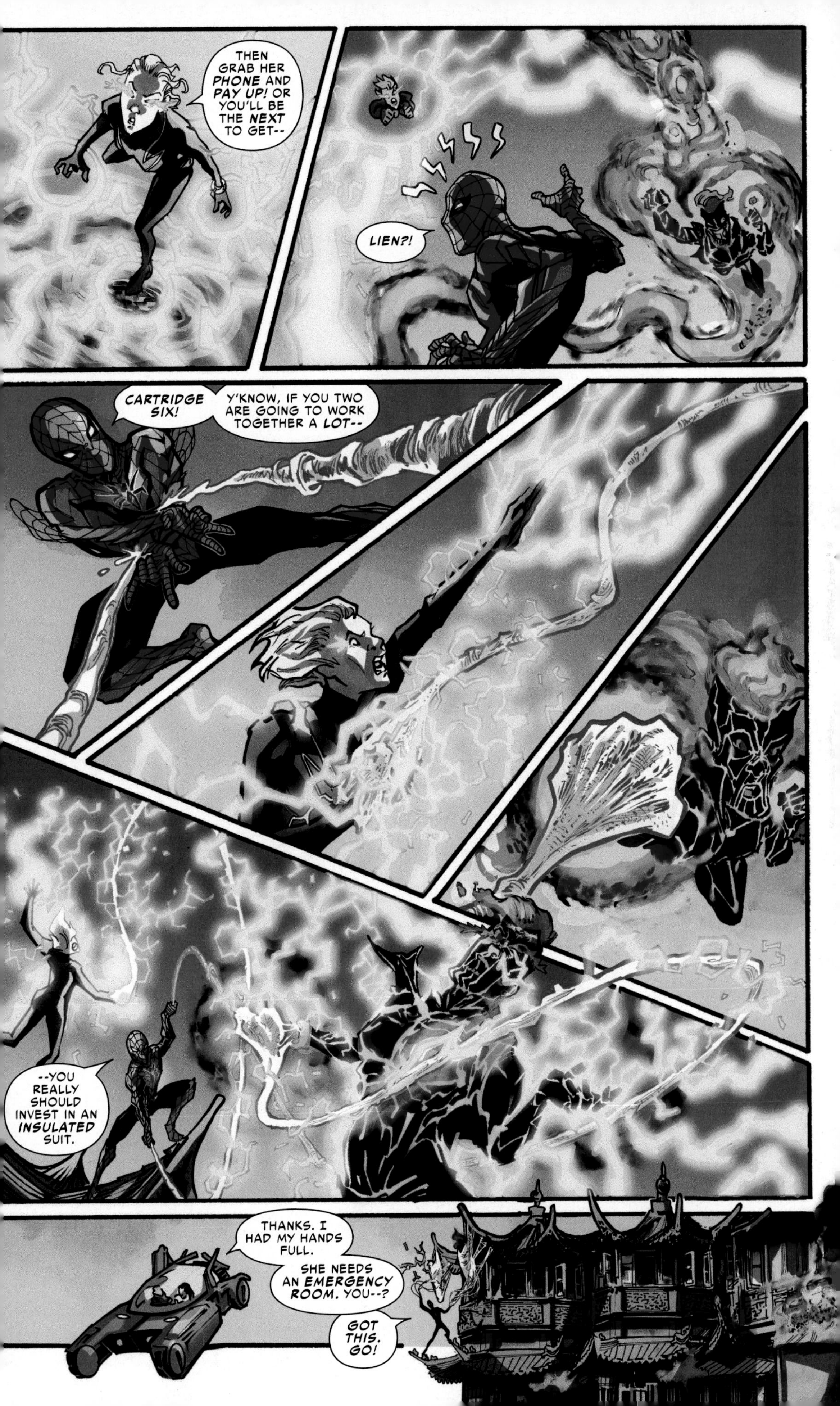
THEN GRAB HER PHONE AND PAY UP! OR YOU'LL BE THE NEXT TO GET--
LIEN?!
CARTRIDGE SIX!
Y'KNOW, IF YOU TWO ARE GOING TO WORK TOGETHER A LOT--
--YOU REALLY SHOULD INVEST IN AN INSULATED SUIT.
THANKS. I HAD MY HANDS FULL.
SHE NEEDS AN EMERGENCY ROOM. YOU--?
GOT THIS. GO!

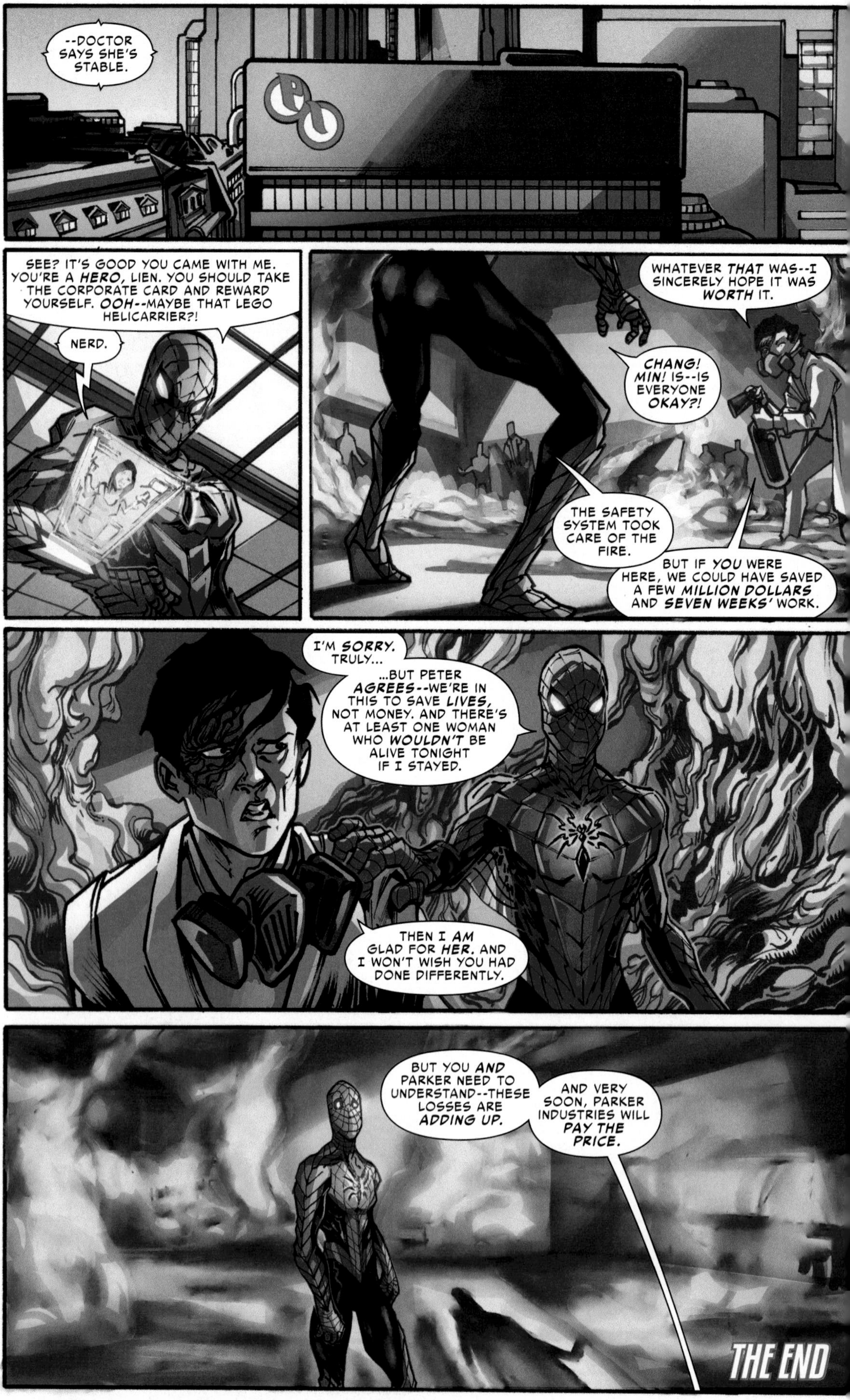
--DOCTOR SAYS SHE'S STABLE.
SEE? IT'S GOOD YOU CAME WITH ME. YOU'RE A HERO, LIEN. YOU SHOULD TAKE THE CORPORATE CARD AND REWARD YOURSELF. OOH--MAYBE THAT LEGO HELICARRIER?!
NERD.
WHATEVER THAT WAS--I SINCERELY HOPE IT WAS WORTH IT.
CHANG! MIN! IS--IS EVERYONE OKAY?!
THE SAFETY SYSTEM TOOK CARE OF THE FIRE.
BUT IF YOU WERE HERE, WE COULD HAVE SAVED A FEW MILLION DOLLARS AND SEVEN WEEKS' WORK.
I'M SORRY. TRULY...
...BUT PETER AGREES--WE'RE IN THIS TO SAVE LIVES, NOT MONEY. AND THERE'S AT LEAST ONE WOMAN WHO WOULDN'T BE ALIVE TONIGHT IF I STAYED.
THEN I AM GLAD FOR HER. AND I WON'T WISH YOU HAD DONE DIFFERENTLY.
BUT YOU AND PARKER NEED TO UNDERSTAND--THESE LOSSES ARE ADDING UP.
AND VERY SOON, PARKER INDUSTRIES WILL PAY THE PRICE.
THE END

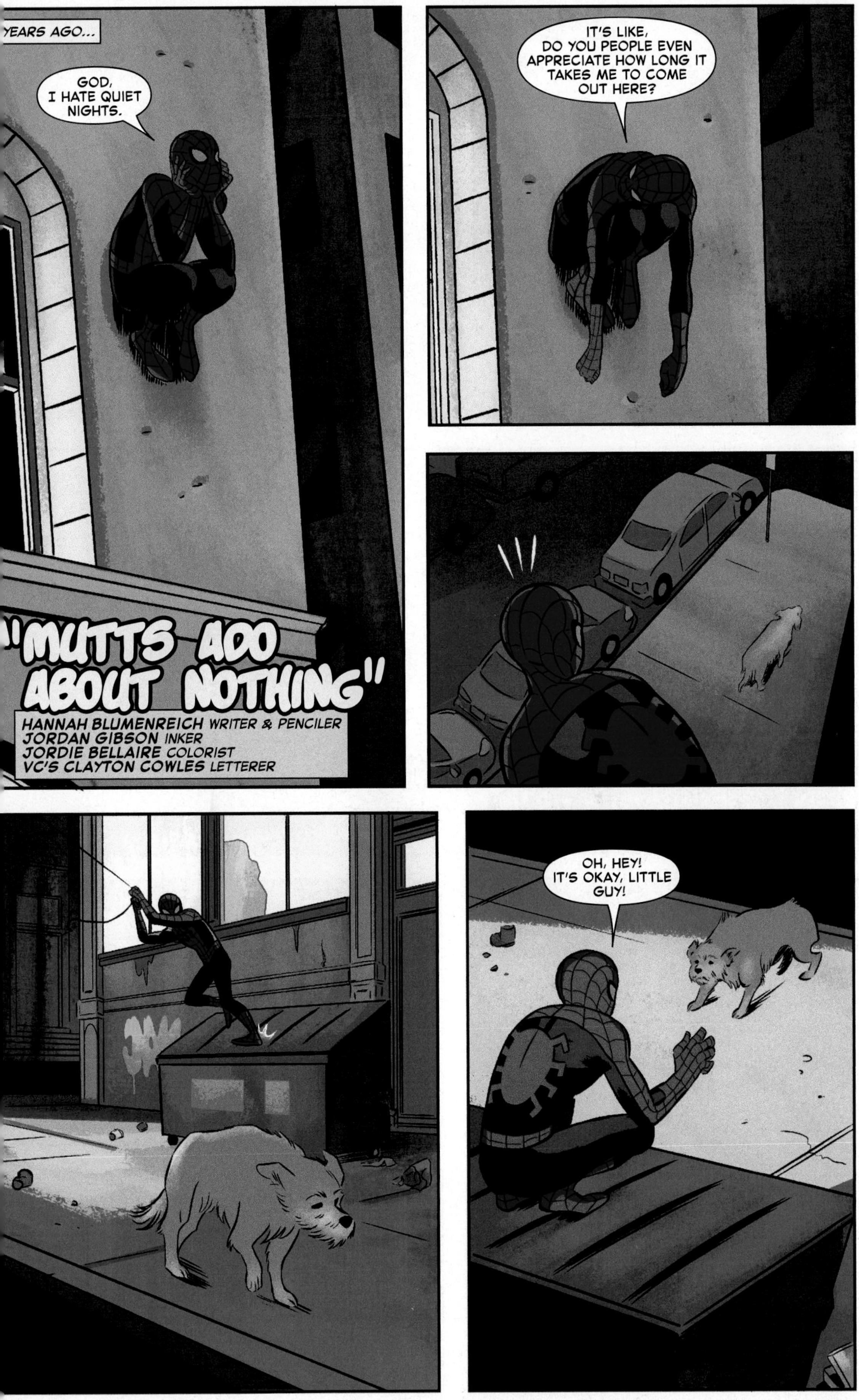

YEARS AGO...
GOD, I HATE QUIET NIGHTS.
"MUTTS ADO ABOUT NOTHING"
HANNAH BLUMENREICH WRITER & PENCILER
JORDAN GIBSON INKER
JORDIE BELLAIRE COLORIST
VC'S CLAYTON COWLES LETTERER
IT'S LIKE, DO YOU PEOPLE EVEN APPRECIATE HOW LONG IT TAKES ME TO COME OUT HERE?
OH, HEY! IT'S OKAY, LITTLE GUY!

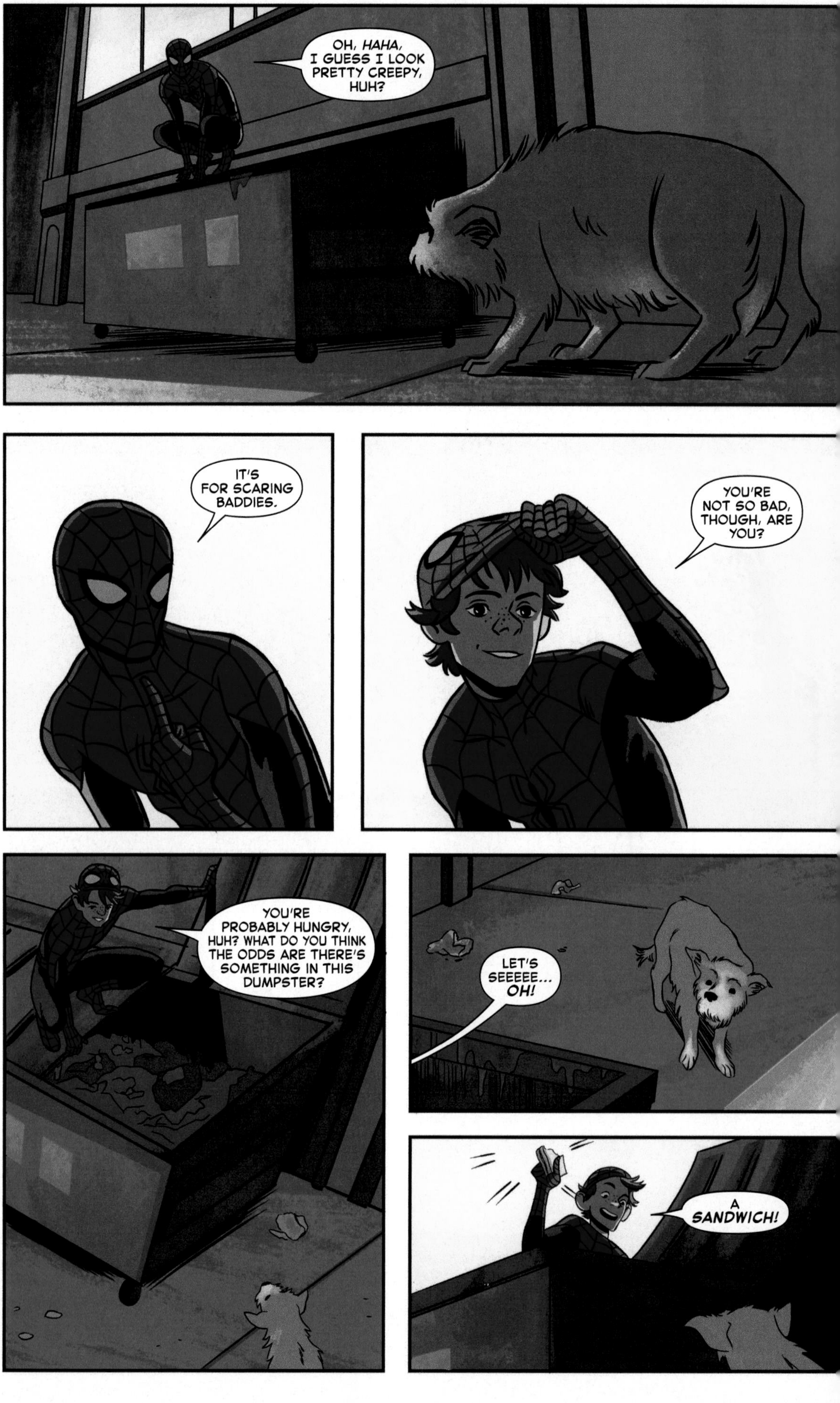

OH, *HAHA*, I GUESS I LOOK PRETTY CREEPY, HUH?
IT'S FOR SCARING BADDIES.
YOU'RE NOT SO BAD, THOUGH, ARE YOU?
YOU'RE PROBABLY HUNGRY, HUH? WHAT DO YOU THINK THE ODDS ARE THERE'S SOMETHING IN THIS DUMPSTER?
LET'S SEEEEE... *OH!*
A *SANDWICH!*

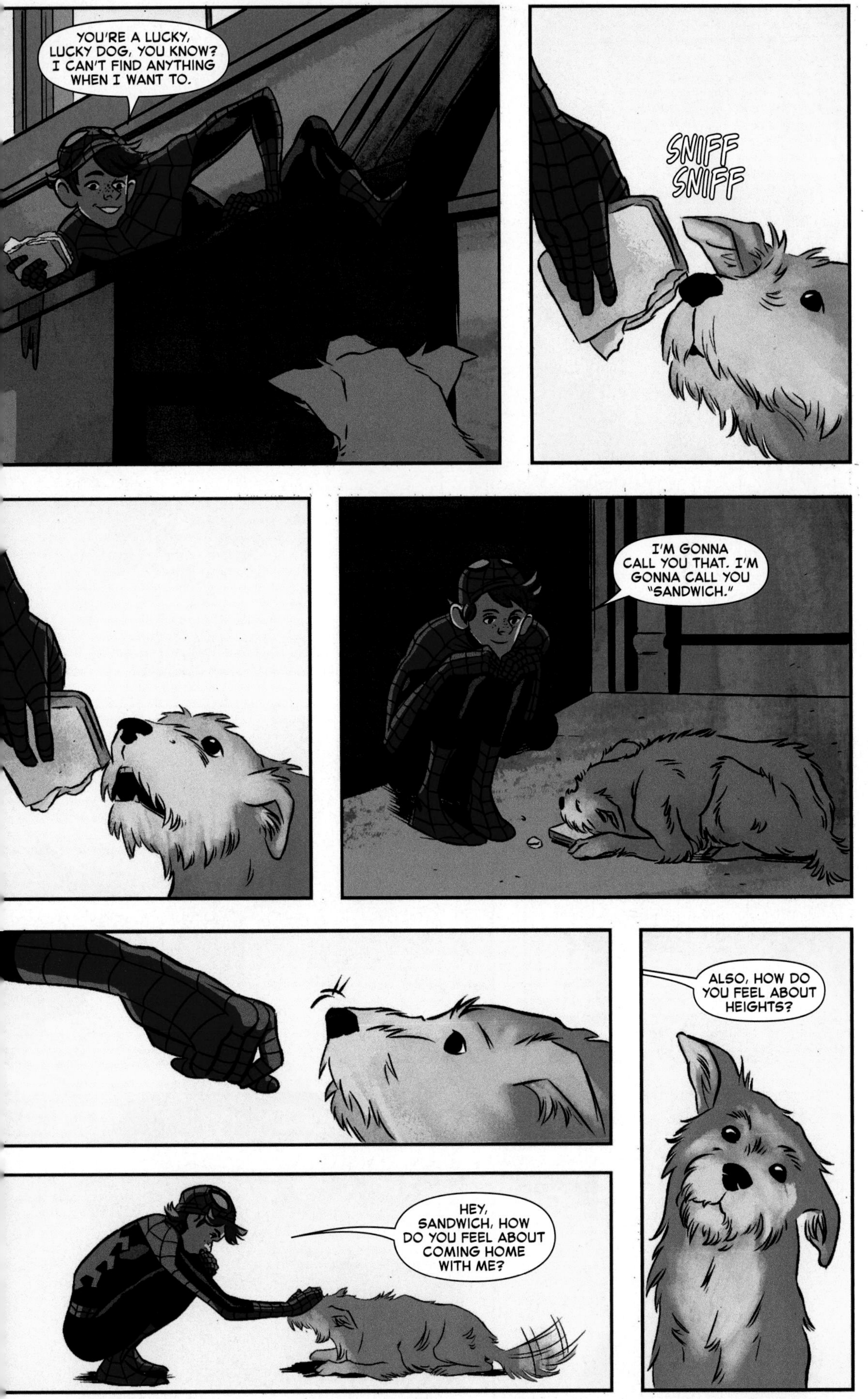
YOU'RE A LUCKY, LUCKY DOG, YOU KNOW? I CAN'T FIND ANYTHING WHEN I WANT TO.
SNIFF SNIFF
I'M GONNA CALL YOU THAT. I'M GONNA CALL YOU "SANDWICH."
HEY, SANDWICH, HOW DO YOU FEEL ABOUT COMING HOME WITH ME?
ALSO, HOW DO YOU FEEL ABOUT HEIGHTS?

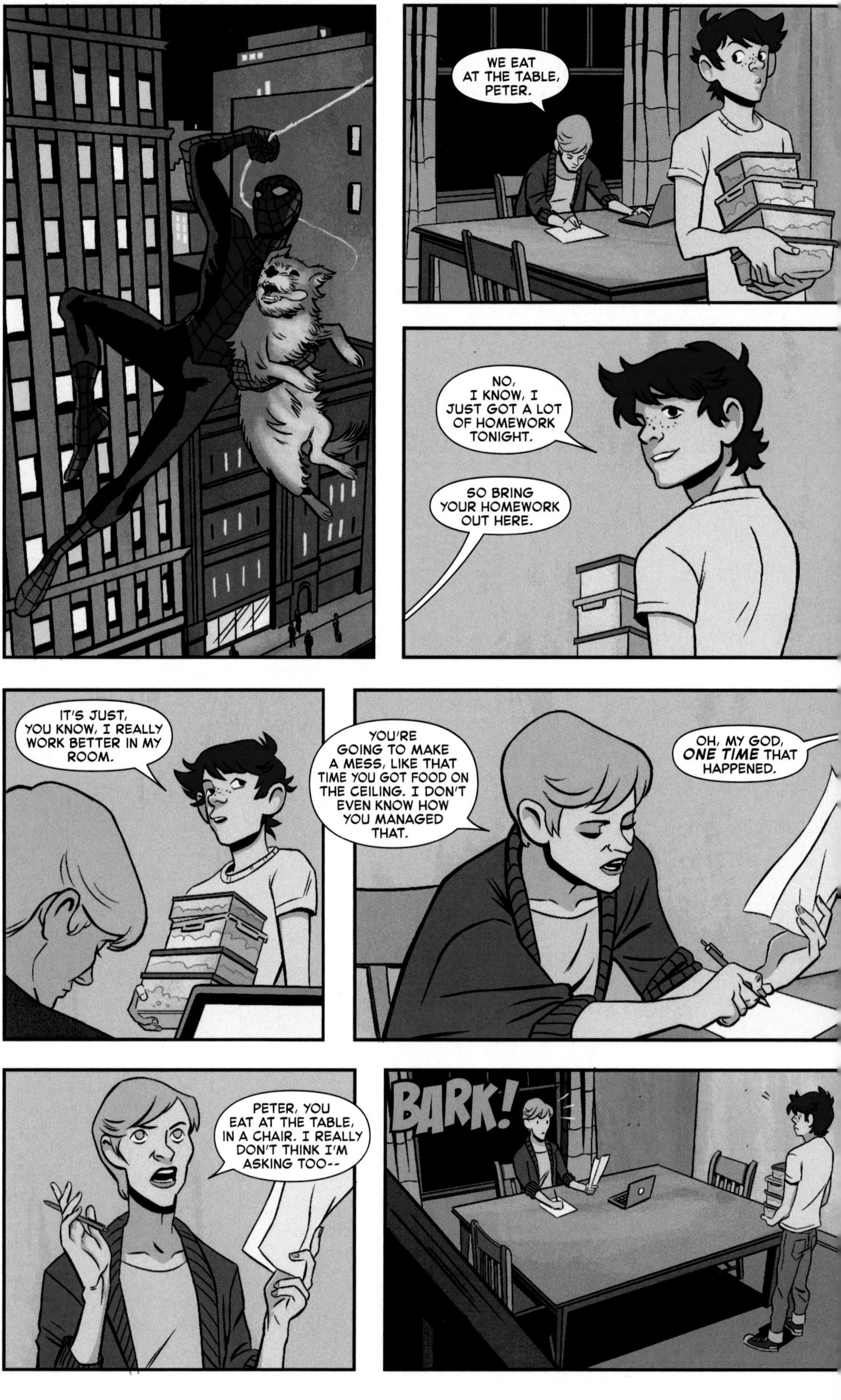

WE EAT AT THE TABLE, PETER.
NO, I KNOW, I JUST GOT A LOT OF HOMEWORK TONIGHT.
SO BRING YOUR HOMEWORK OUT HERE.
IT'S JUST, YOU KNOW, I REALLY WORK BETTER IN MY ROOM.
YOU'RE GOING TO MAKE A MESS, LIKE THAT TIME YOU GOT FOOD ON THE CEILING. I DON'T EVEN KNOW HOW YOU MANAGED THAT.
OH, MY GOD, ONE TIME THAT HAPPENED.
PETER, YOU EAT AT THE TABLE, IN A CHAIR. I REALLY DON'T THINK I'M ASKING TOO--
BARK!

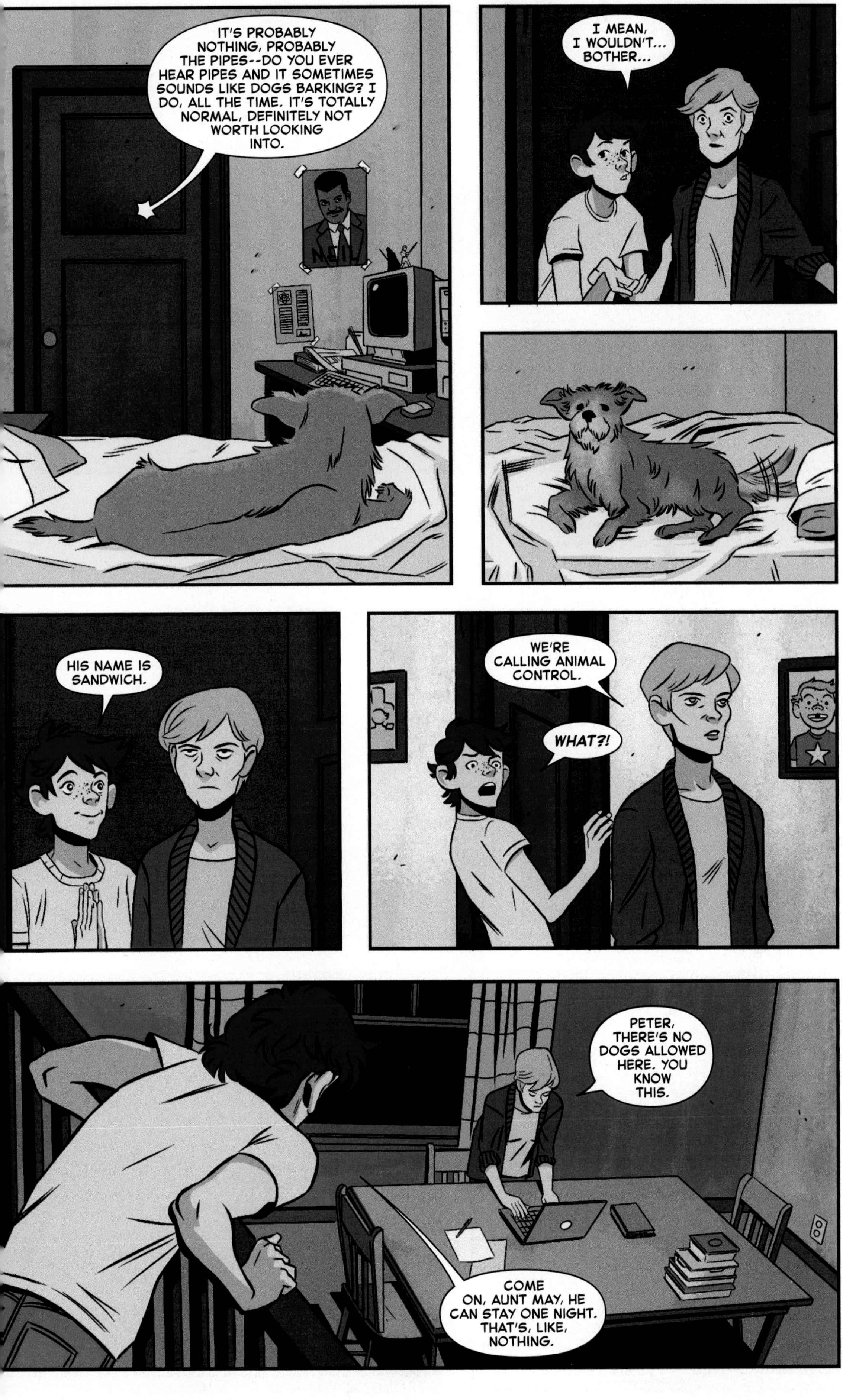
IT'S PROBABLY NOTHING, PROBABLY THE PIPES--DO YOU EVER HEAR PIPES AND IT SOMETIMES SOUNDS LIKE DOGS BARKING? I DO, ALL THE TIME. IT'S TOTALLY NORMAL, DEFINITELY NOT WORTH LOOKING INTO.
NEIL
I MEAN, I WOULDN'T... BOTHER...
HIS NAME IS SANDWICH.
WE'RE CALLING ANIMAL CONTROL.
WHAT?!
PETER, THERE'S NO DOGS ALLOWED HERE. YOU KNOW THIS.
COME ON, AUNT MAY, HE CAN STAY ONE NIGHT. THAT'S, LIKE, NOTHING.

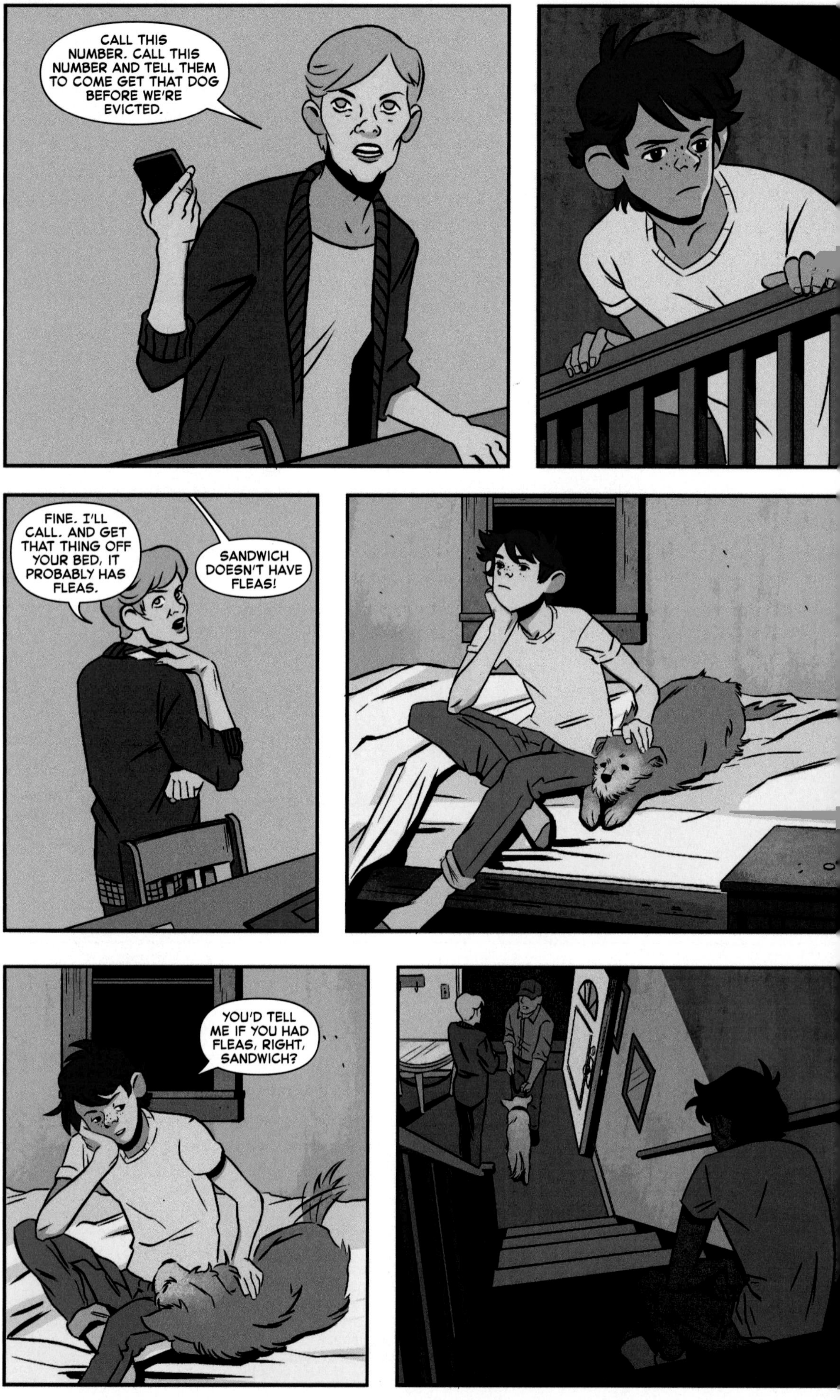
CALL THIS NUMBER. CALL THIS NUMBER AND TELL THEM TO COME GET THAT DOG BEFORE WE'RE EVICTED.
FINE. I'LL CALL. AND GET THAT THING OFF YOUR BED, IT PROBABLY HAS FLEAS.
SANDWICH DOESN'T HAVE FLEAS!
YOU'D TELL ME IF YOU HAD FLEAS, RIGHT, SANDWICH?

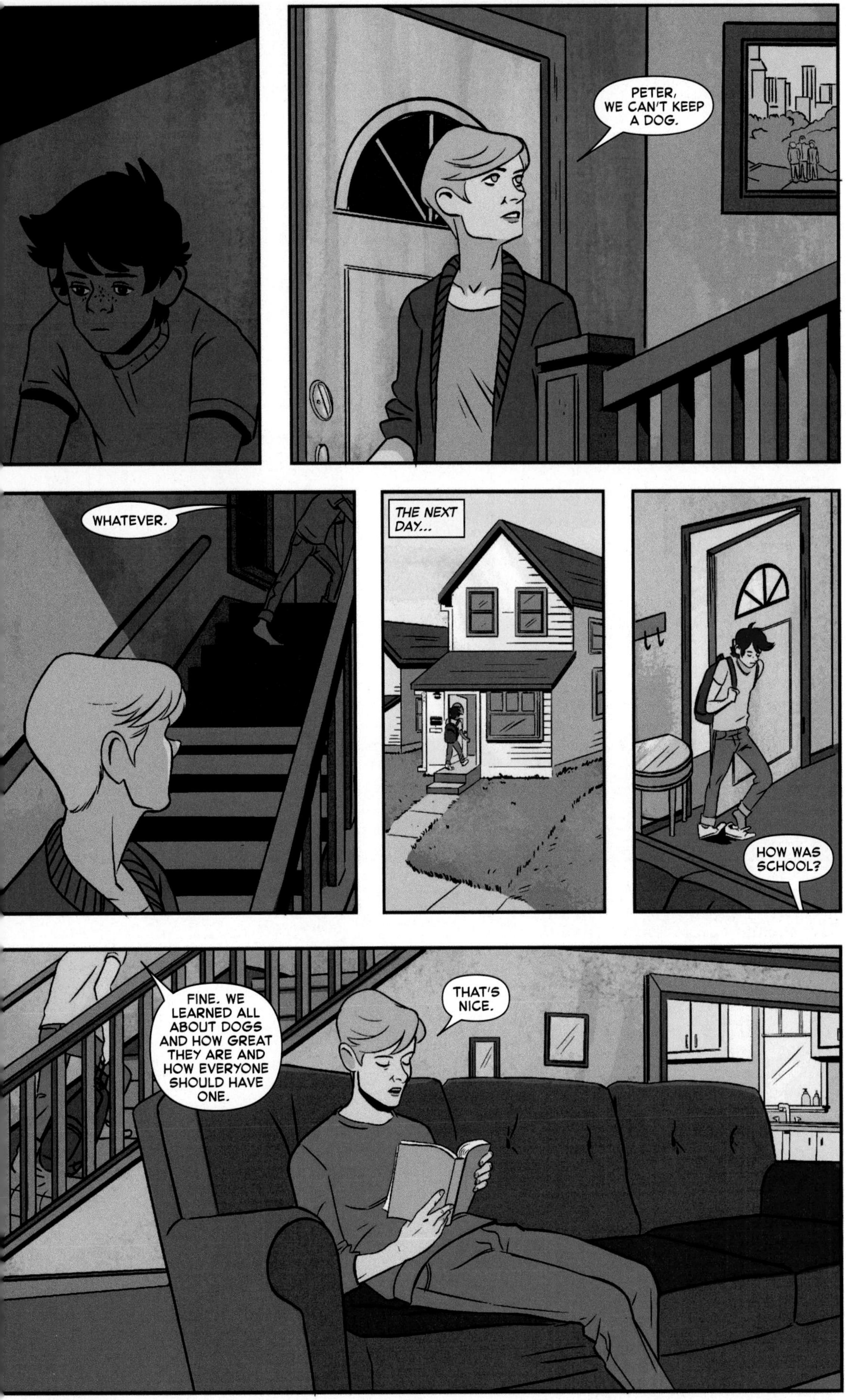
PETER, WE CAN'T KEEP A DOG.
WHATEVER.
THE NEXT DAY...
HOW WAS SCHOOL?
FINE. WE LEARNED ALL ABOUT DOGS AND HOW GREAT THEY ARE AND HOW EVERYONE SHOULD HAVE ONE.
THAT'S NICE.

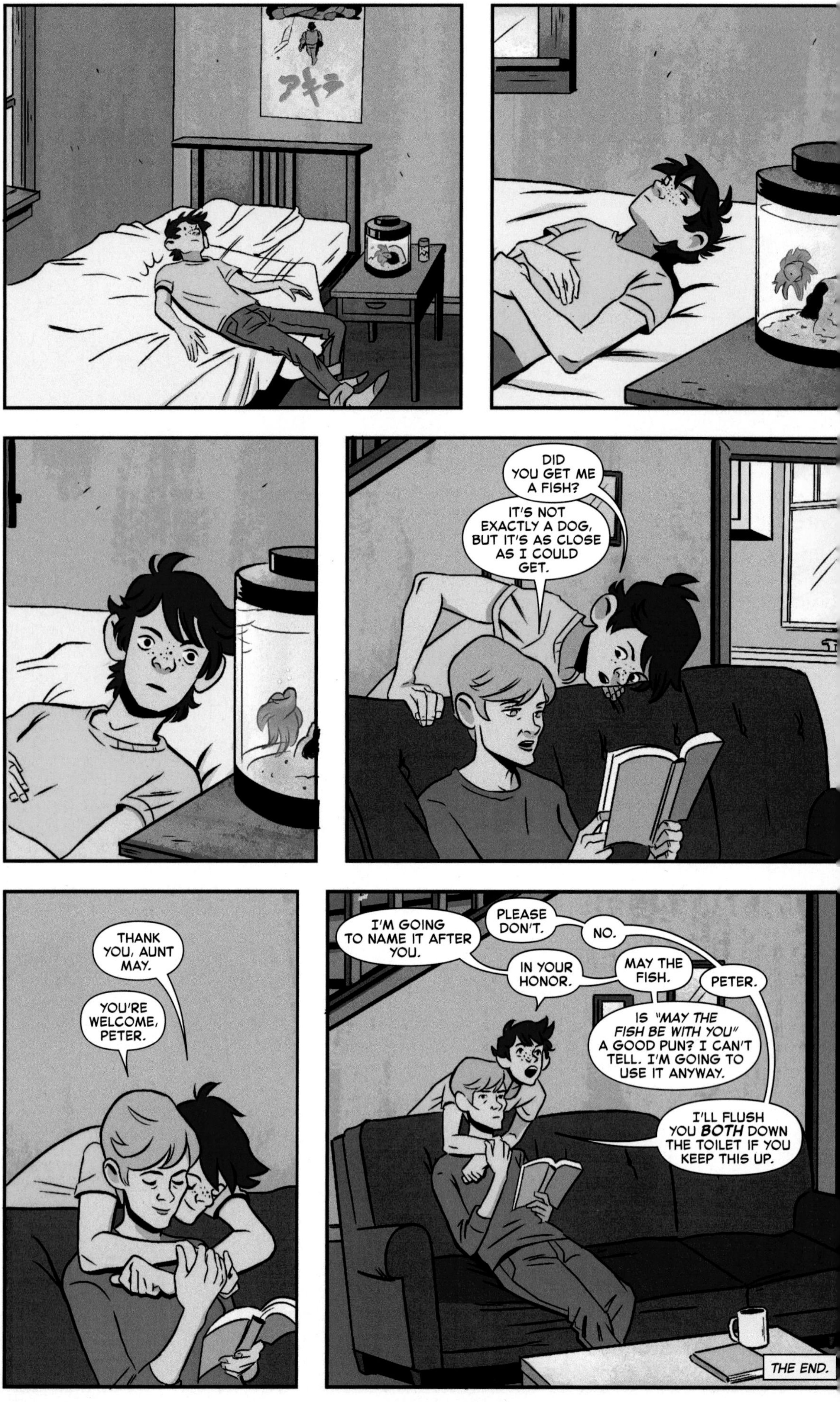
アキラ
DID YOU GET ME A FISH?
IT'S NOT EXACTLY A DOG, BUT IT'S AS CLOSE AS I COULD GET.
THANK YOU, AUNT MAY.
YOU'RE WELCOME, PETER.
I'M GOING TO NAME IT AFTER YOU.
PLEASE DON'T.
IN YOUR HONOR.
NO.
MAY THE FISH.
PETER.
IS "MAY THE FISH BE WITH YOU" A GOOD PUN? I CAN'T TELL. I'M GOING TO USE IT ANYWAY.
I'LL FLUSH YOU BOTH DOWN THE TOILET IF YOU KEEP THIS UP.
THE END.

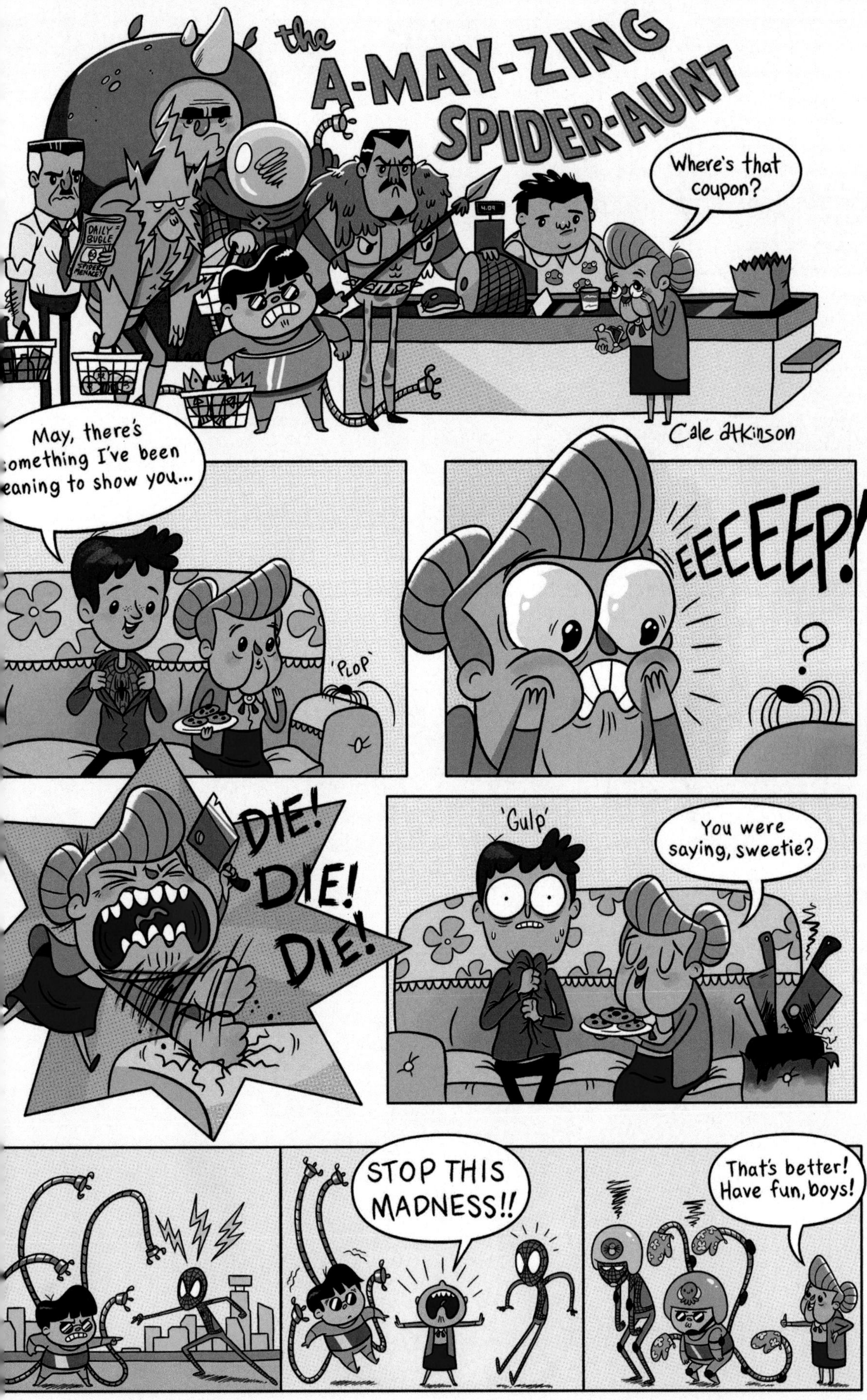
the
A-MAY-ZING
SPIDER-AUNT
DAILY BUGLE
SPIDER MENACE!
4.09
Where's that coupon?
Cale Atkinson
May, there's something I've been meaning to show you...
'PLOP'
EEEEEP!
?
DIE! DIE! DIE!
'Gulp'
You were saying, sweetie?
STOP THIS MADNESS!!
That's better! Have fun, boys!

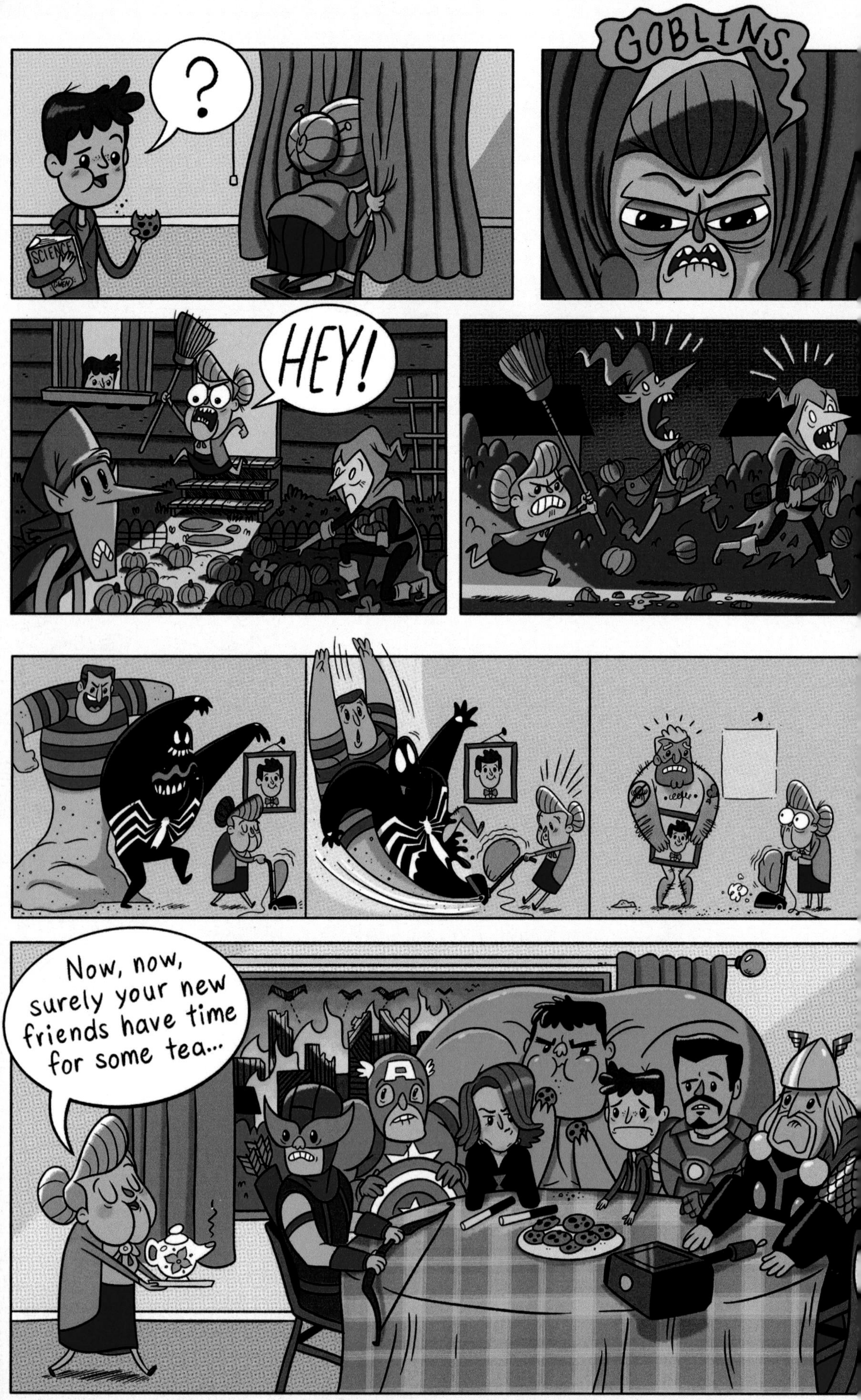
?
SCIENCE
GOBLINS.
HEY!
Now, now, surely your new friends have time for some tea...

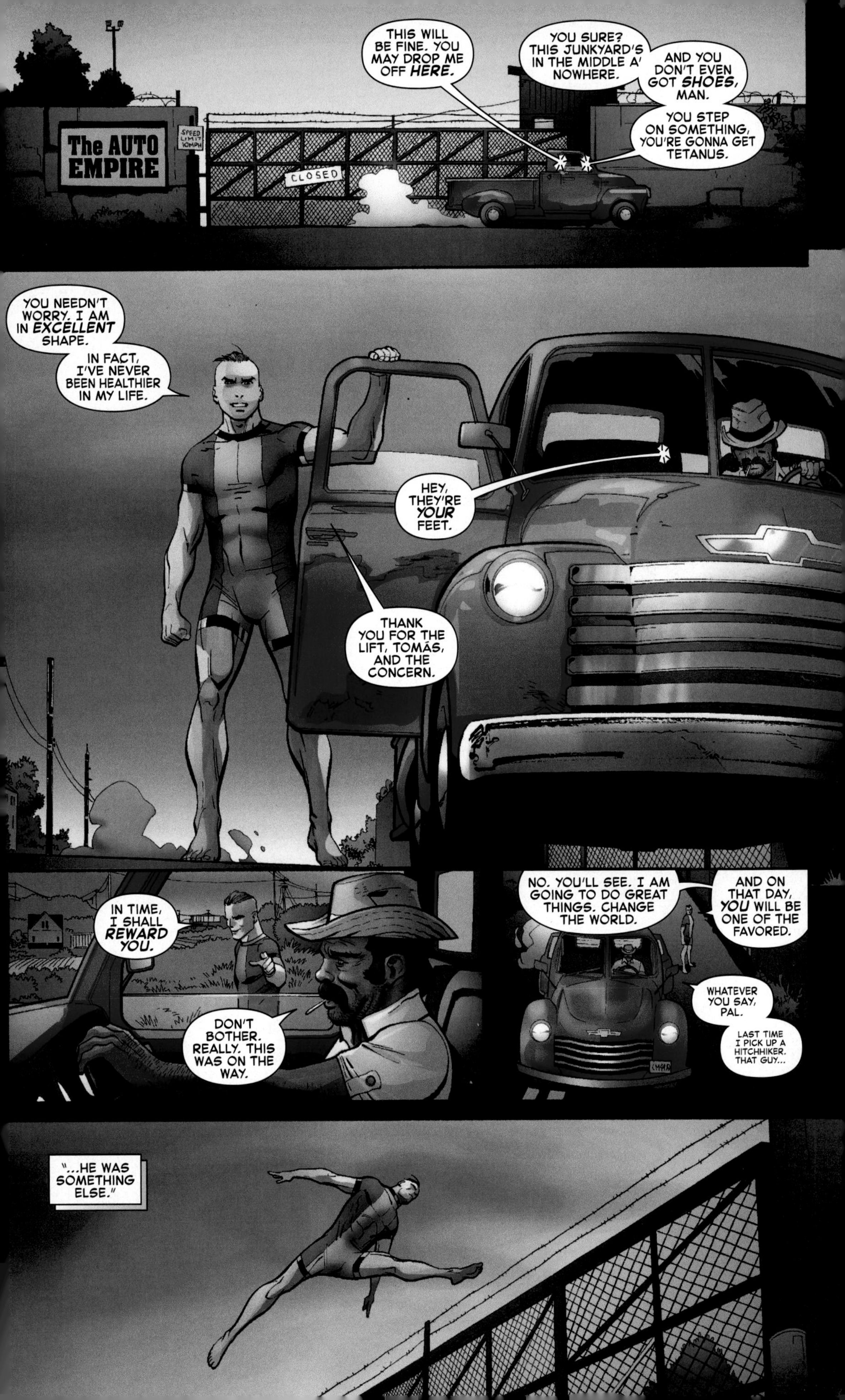
THIS WILL BE FINE. YOU MAY DROP ME OFF HERE.
YOU SURE? THIS JUNKYARD'S IN THE MIDDLE A' NOWHERE.
AND YOU DON'T EVEN GOT SHOES, MAN.
YOU STEP ON SOMETHING, YOU'RE GONNA GET TETANUS.
The AUTO EMPIRE
SPEED LIMIT 10MPH
CLOSED
YOU NEEDN'T WORRY. I AM IN EXCELLENT SHAPE.
IN FACT, I'VE NEVER BEEN HEALTHIER IN MY LIFE.
HEY, THEY'RE YOUR FEET.
THANK YOU FOR THE LIFT, TOMÁS, AND THE CONCERN.
IN TIME, I SHALL REWARD YOU.
DON'T BOTHER. REALLY. THIS WAS ON THE WAY.
NO. YOU'LL SEE. I AM GOING TO DO GREAT THINGS. CHANGE THE WORLD.
AND ON THAT DAY, YOU WILL BE ONE OF THE FAVORED.
WHATEVER YOU SAY, PAL.
LAST TIME I PICK UP A HITCHHIKER. THAT GUY...
"...HE WAS SOMETHING ELSE."

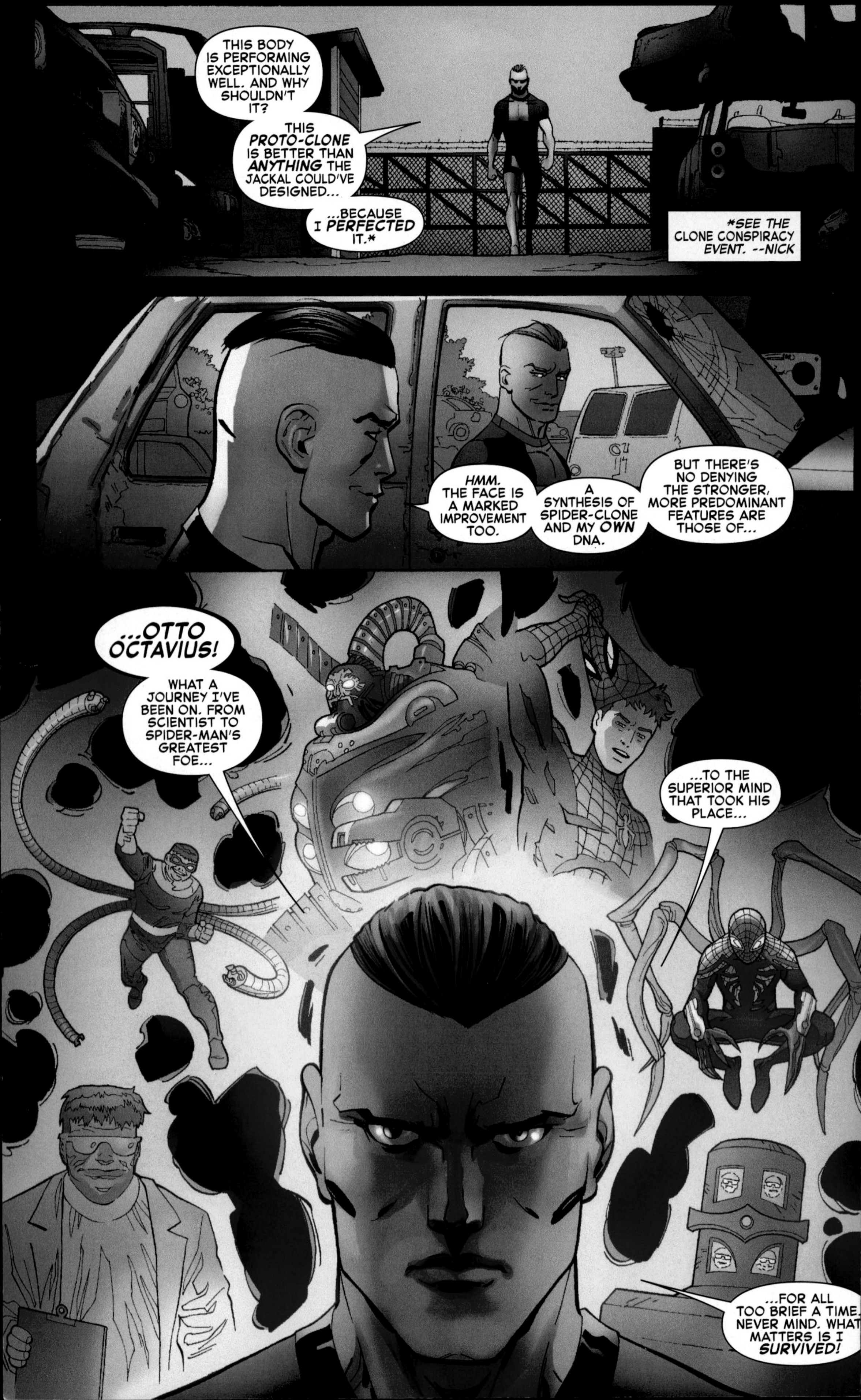
THIS BODY IS PERFORMING EXCEPTIONALLY WELL. AND WHY SHOULDN'T IT?
THIS *PROTO-CLONE* IS BETTER THAN *ANYTHING* THE JACKAL COULD'VE DESIGNED...
...BECAUSE I *PERFECTED* IT.*
*SEE THE CLONE CONSPIRACY EVENT. --NICK
HMM. THE FACE IS A MARKED IMPROVEMENT TOO.
A SYNTHESIS OF SPIDER-CLONE AND MY *OWN* DNA.
BUT THERE'S NO DENYING THE STRONGER, MORE PREDOMINANT FEATURES ARE THOSE OF...
...OTTO OCTAVIUS!
WHAT A JOURNEY I'VE BEEN ON. FROM SCIENTIST TO SPIDER-MAN'S GREATEST FOE...
...TO THE SUPERIOR MIND THAT TOOK HIS PLACE...
...FOR ALL TOO BRIEF A TIME. NEVER MIND. WHAT MATTERS IS I *SURVIVED!*

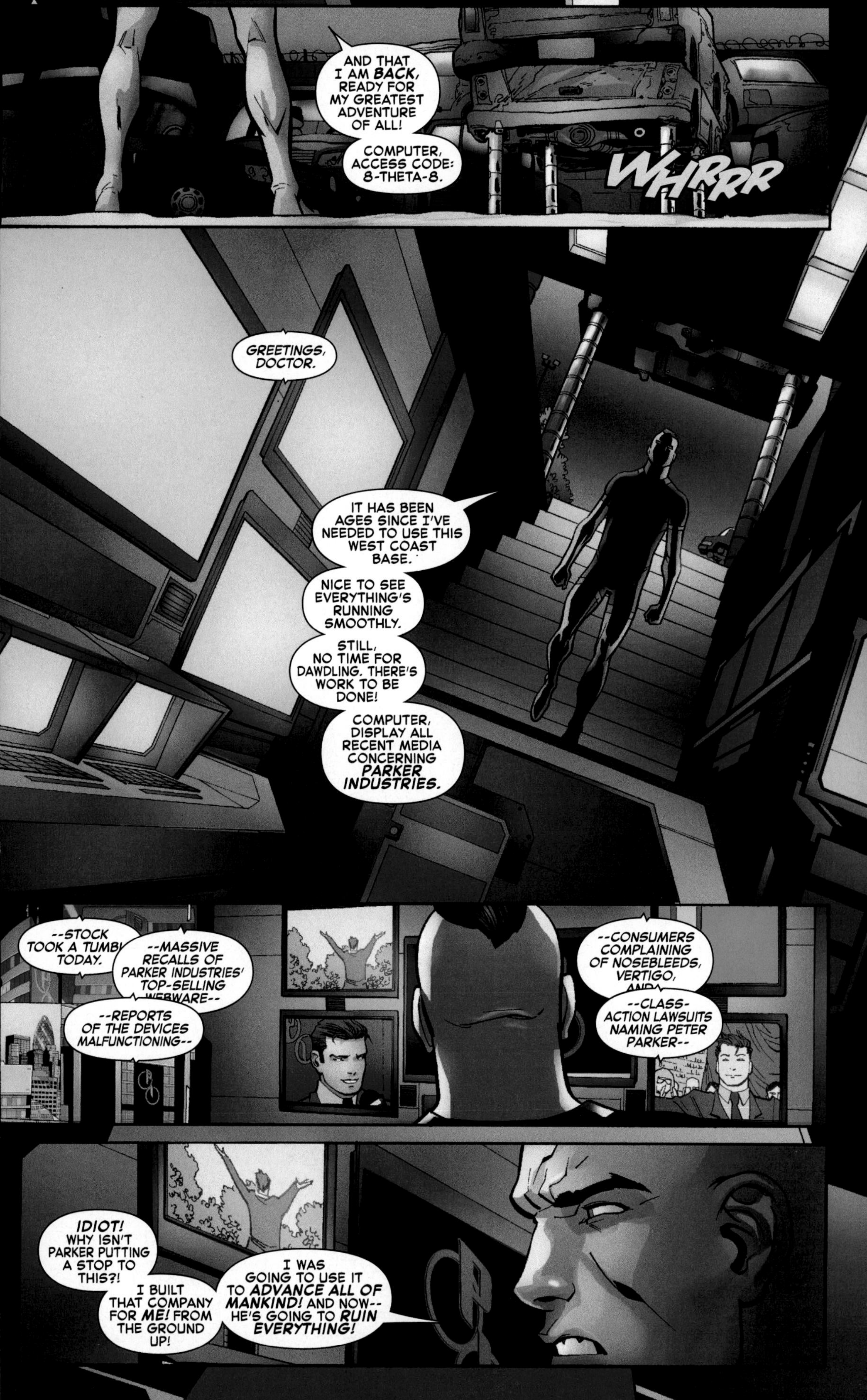
AND THAT I AM BACK, READY FOR MY GREATEST ADVENTURE OF ALL!
COMPUTER, ACCESS CODE: 8-THETA-8.
WHRRR
GREETINGS, DOCTOR.
IT HAS BEEN AGES SINCE I'VE NEEDED TO USE THIS WEST COAST BASE.
NICE TO SEE EVERYTHING'S RUNNING SMOOTHLY.
STILL, NO TIME FOR DAWDLING. THERE'S WORK TO BE DONE!
COMPUTER, DISPLAY ALL RECENT MEDIA CONCERNING PARKER INDUSTRIES.
--STOCK TOOK A TUMBL TODAY.
--MASSIVE RECALLS OF PARKER INDUSTRIES' TOP-SELLING WEBWARE--
--REPORTS OF THE DEVICES MALFUNCTIONING--
--CONSUMERS COMPLAINING OF NOSEBLEEDS, VERTIGO, AND
--CLASS-ACTION LAWSUITS NAMING PETER PARKER--
IDIOT! WHY ISN'T PARKER PUTTING A STOP TO THIS?!
I BUILT THAT COMPANY FOR ME! FROM THE GROUND UP!
I WAS GOING TO USE IT TO ADVANCE ALL OF MANKIND! AND NOW--HE'S GOING TO RUIN EVERYTHING!

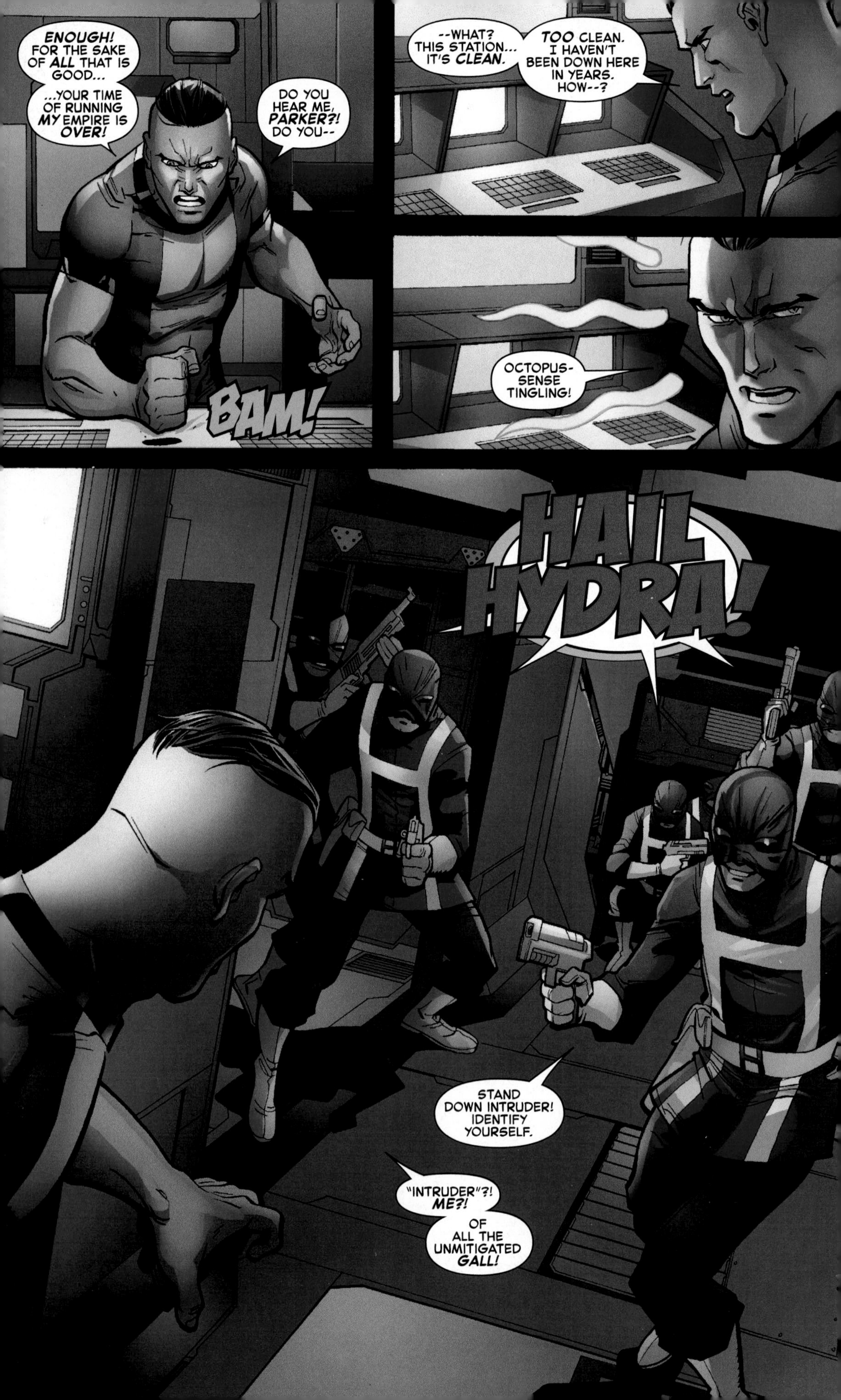
ENOUGH! FOR THE SAKE OF ALL THAT IS GOOD...
...YOUR TIME OF RUNNING MY EMPIRE IS OVER!
DO YOU HEAR ME, PARKER?! DO YOU--
BAM!
--WHAT? THIS STATION... IT'S CLEAN.
TOO CLEAN. I HAVEN'T BEEN DOWN HERE IN YEARS. HOW--?
OCTOPUS-SENSE TINGLING!
HAIL HYDRA!
STAND DOWN INTRUDER! IDENTIFY YOURSELF.
"INTRUDER"?! ME?!
OF ALL THE UNMITIGATED GALL!

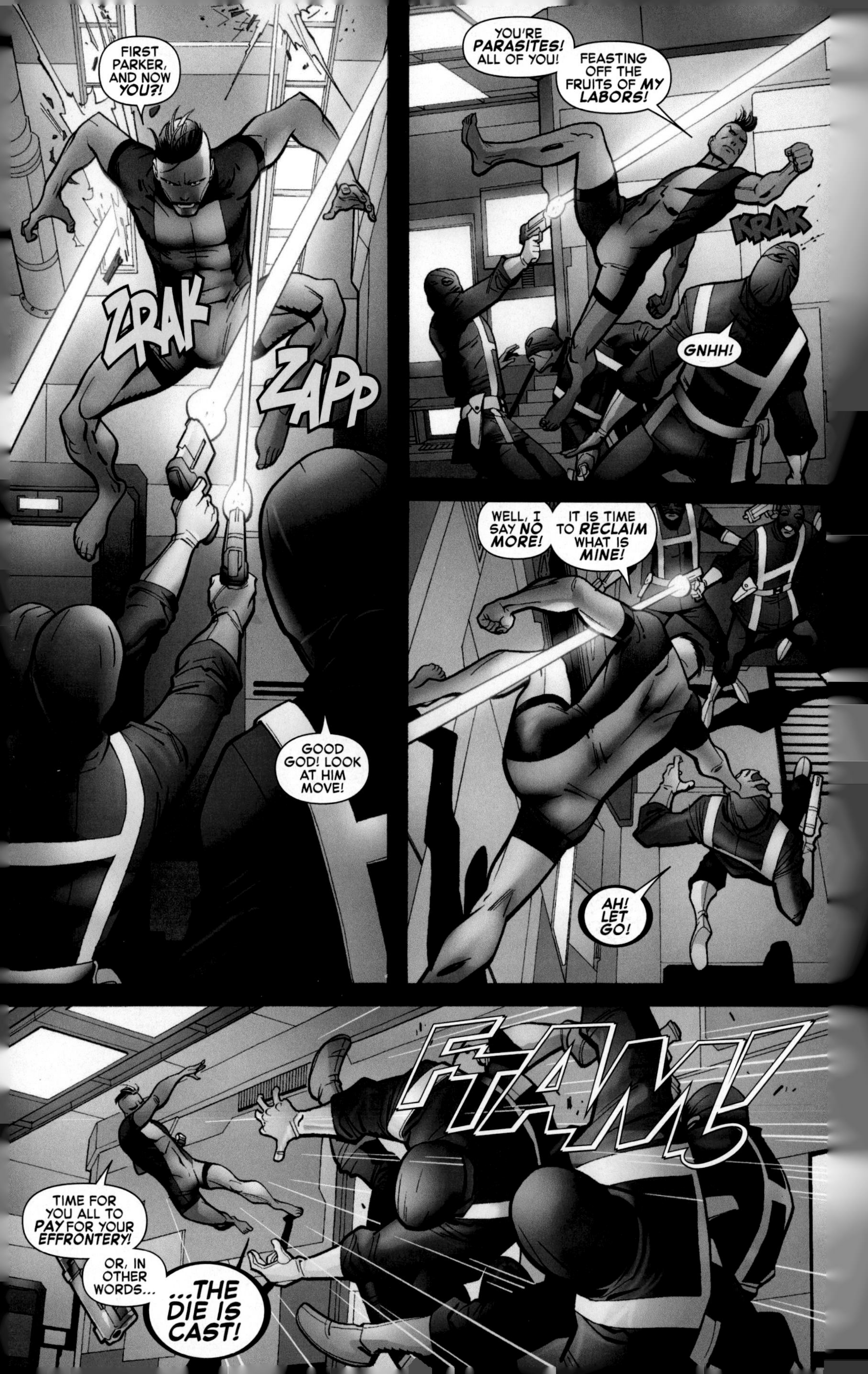

FIRST PARKER, AND NOW YOU?!
ZRAK
ZAPP
GOOD GOD! LOOK AT HIM MOVE!
YOU'RE PARASITES! ALL OF YOU!
FEASTING OFF THE FRUITS OF MY LABORS!
KRAK
GNHH!
WELL, I SAY NO MORE!
IT IS TIME TO RECLAIM WHAT IS MINE!
AH! LET GO!
FTAM!
TIME FOR YOU ALL TO PAY FOR YOUR EFFRONTERY!
OR, IN OTHER WORDS...
...THE DIE IS CAST!

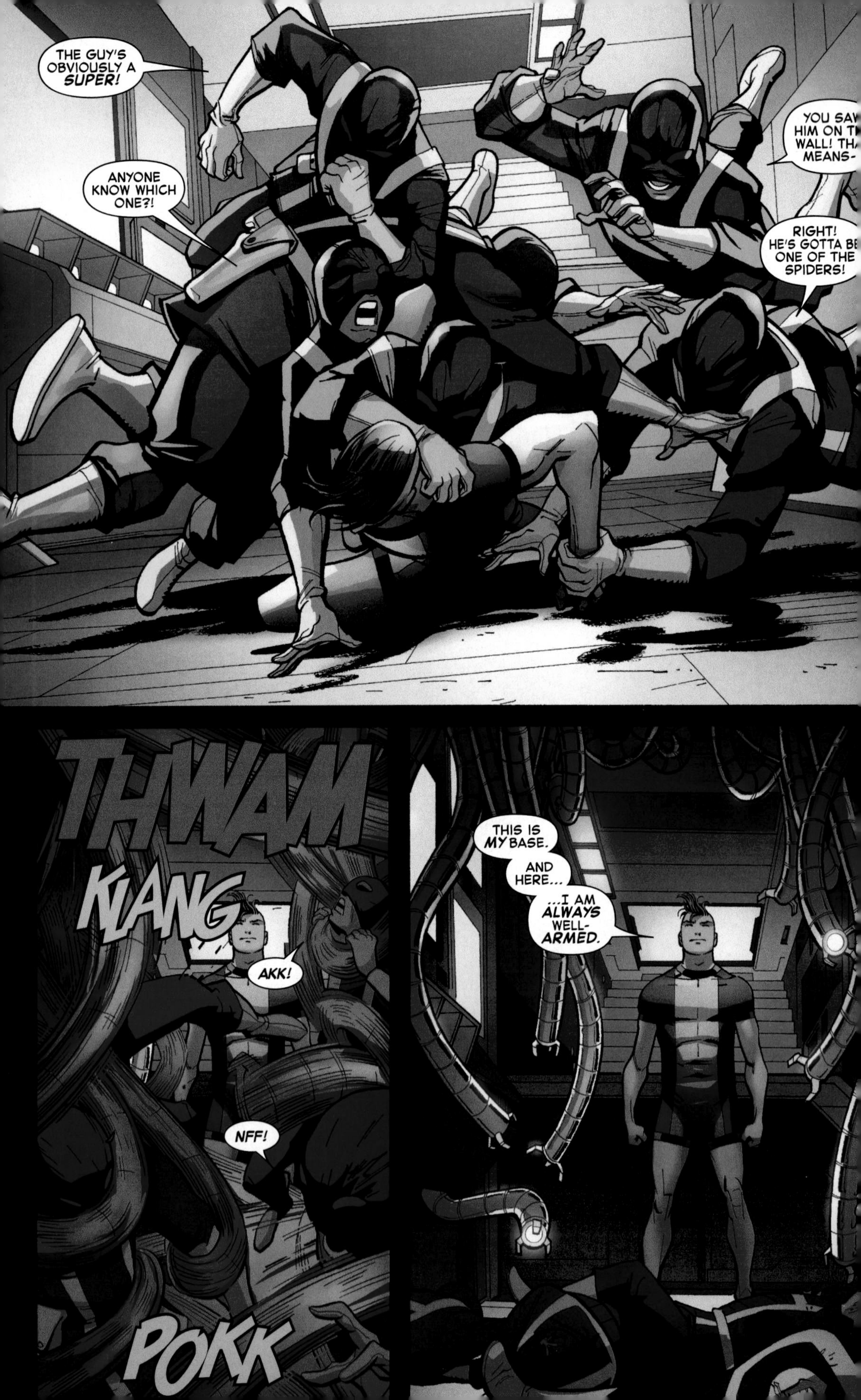
THE GUY'S OBVIOUSLY A SUPER!
ANYONE KNOW WHICH ONE?!
YOU SAW HIM ON TH WALL! THA MEANS-
RIGHT! HE'S GOTTA BE ONE OF THE SPIDERS!
THWAM
KLANG
AKK!
NFF!
POKK
THIS IS MY BASE.
AND HERE...
...I AM ALWAYS WELL-ARMED.

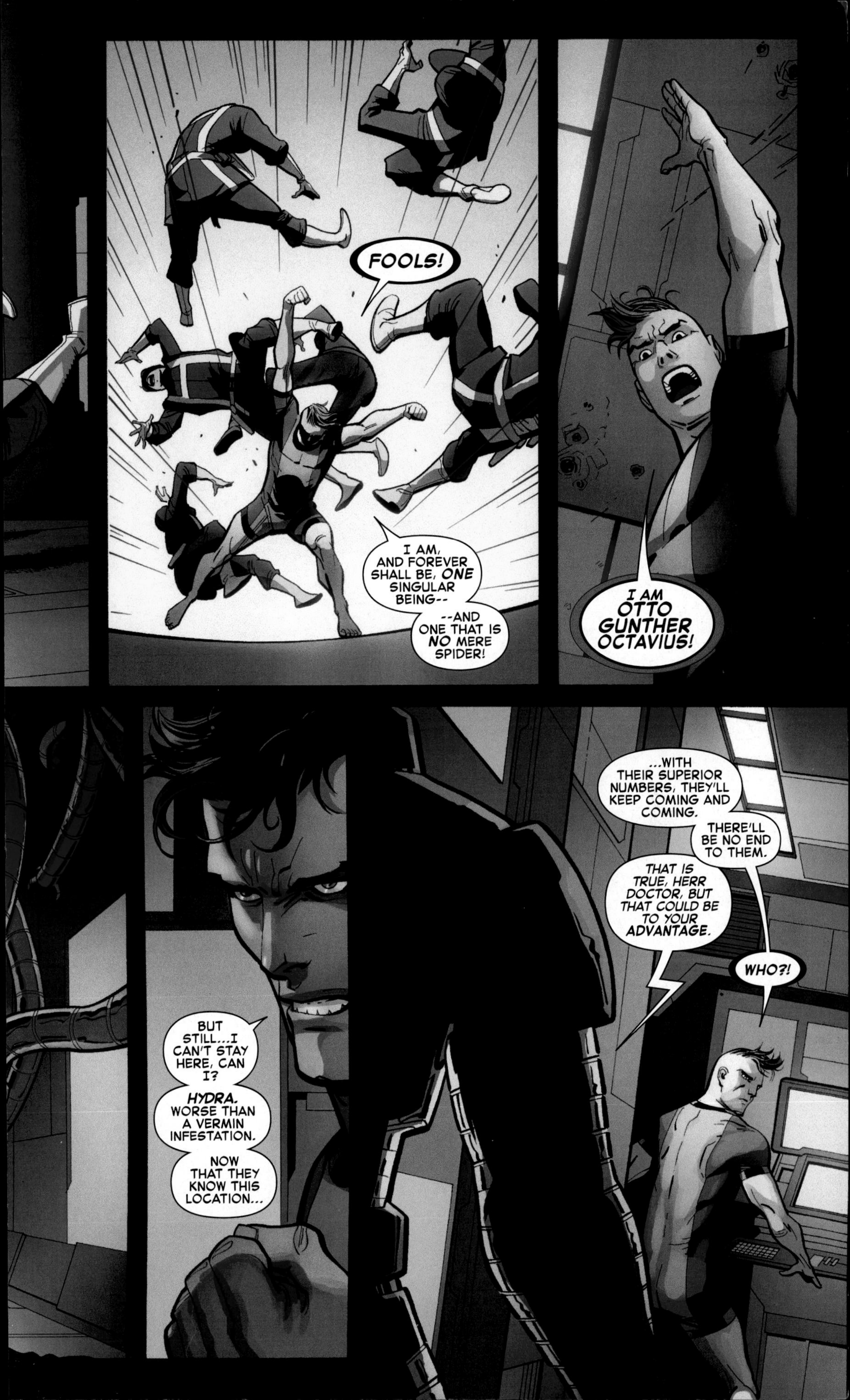
FOOLS!
I AM, AND FOREVER SHALL BE, ONE SINGULAR BEING--
--AND ONE THAT IS NO MERE SPIDER!
I AM OTTO GUNTHER OCTAVIUS!
BUT STILL...I CAN'T STAY HERE, CAN I?
HYDRA. WORSE THAN A VERMIN INFESTATION.
NOW THAT THEY KNOW THIS LOCATION...
...WITH THEIR SUPERIOR NUMBERS, THEY'LL KEEP COMING AND COMING.
THERE'LL BE NO END TO THEM.
THAT IS TRUE, HERR DOCTOR, BUT THAT COULD BE TO YOUR ADVANTAGE.
WHO?!

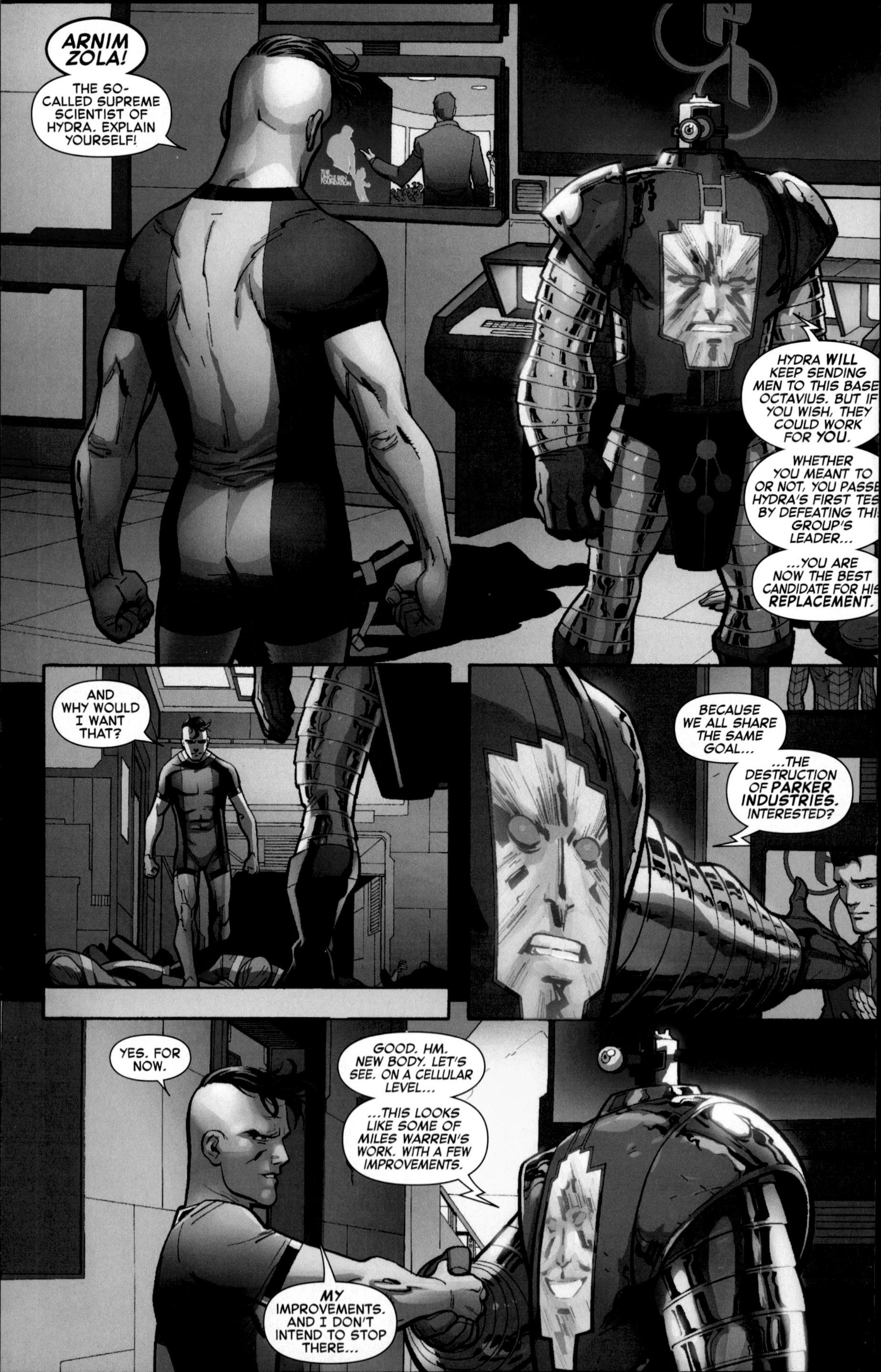
ARNIM ZOLA!
THE SO-CALLED SUPREME SCIENTIST OF HYDRA. EXPLAIN YOURSELF!
THE UNCLE BEN FOUNDATION
HYDRA WILL KEEP SENDING MEN TO THIS BASE OCTAVIUS. BUT IF YOU WISH, THEY COULD WORK FOR YOU.
WHETHER YOU MEANT TO OR NOT, YOU PASSE HYDRA'S FIRST TES BY DEFEATING THIS GROUP'S LEADER...
...YOU ARE NOW THE BEST CANDIDATE FOR HIS REPLACEMENT.
AND WHY WOULD I WANT THAT?
BECAUSE WE ALL SHARE THE SAME GOAL...
...THE DESTRUCTION OF PARKER INDUSTRIES. INTERESTED?
YES. FOR NOW.
GOOD. HM. NEW BODY. LET'S SEE. ON A CELLULAR LEVEL...
...THIS LOOKS LIKE SOME OF MILES WARREN'S WORK. WITH A FEW IMPROVEMENTS.
MY IMPROVEMENTS. AND I DON'T INTEND TO STOP THERE...

"...MY MIND IS RACING WITH ALL KINDS OF NEW POSSIBILITIES.

"WITH THE HELP OF THESE NEW MINIONS...

"...THE *VAST* RESOURCES AT HYDRA'S DISPOSAL, AND *MY* UNPARALLELED DESIGNS...

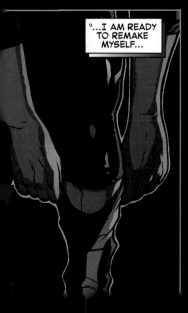

"...I AM READY TO REMAKE MYSELF...

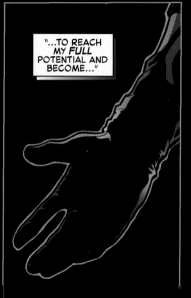

"...TO REACH MY *FULL* POTENTIAL AND BECOME..."

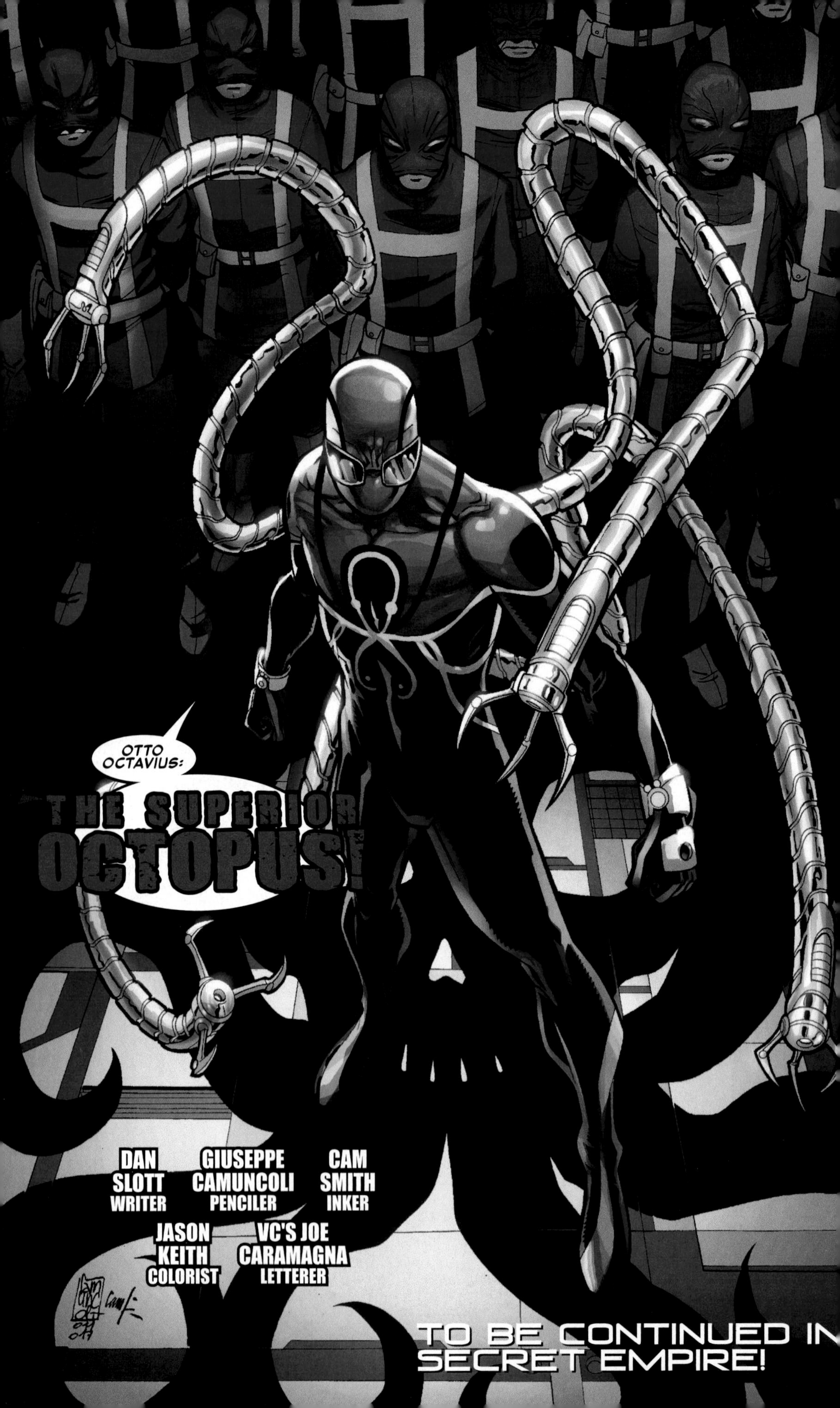

OTTO OCTAVIUS:
THE SUPERIOR OCTOPUS!
DAN SLOTT WRITER
GIUSEPPE CAMUNCOLI PENCILER
CAM SMITH INKER
JASON KEITH COLORIST
VC'S JOE CARAMAGNA LETTERER
TO BE CONTINUED IN SECRET EMPIRE!

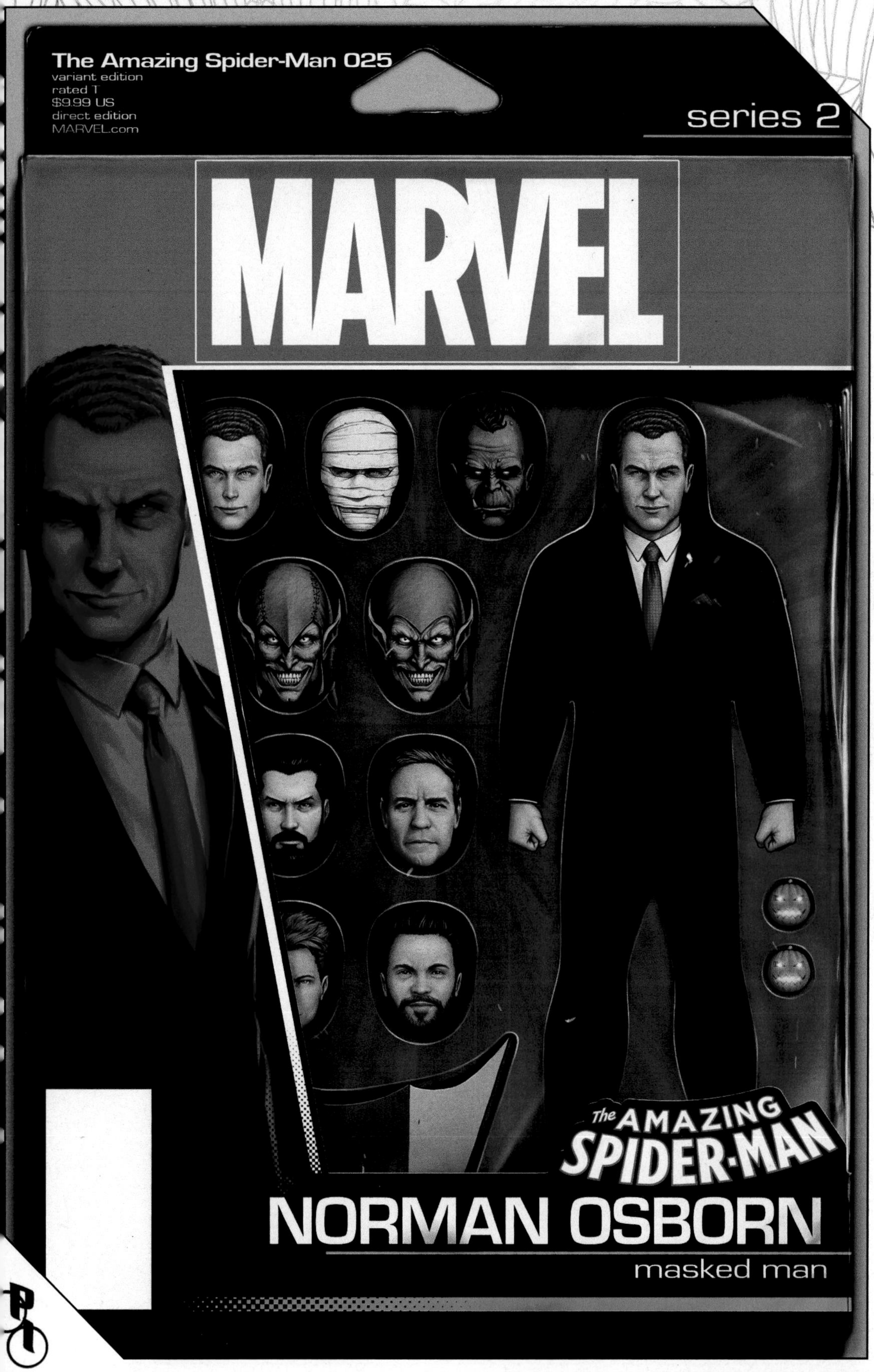
The Amazing Spider-Man 025
variant edition
rated T
$9.99 US
direct edition
MARVEL.com
series 2
MARVEL
The AMAZING SPIDER-MAN
NORMAN OSBORN
masked man

#25 ACTION FIGURE VARIANT BY JOHN TYLER CHRISTOPHER

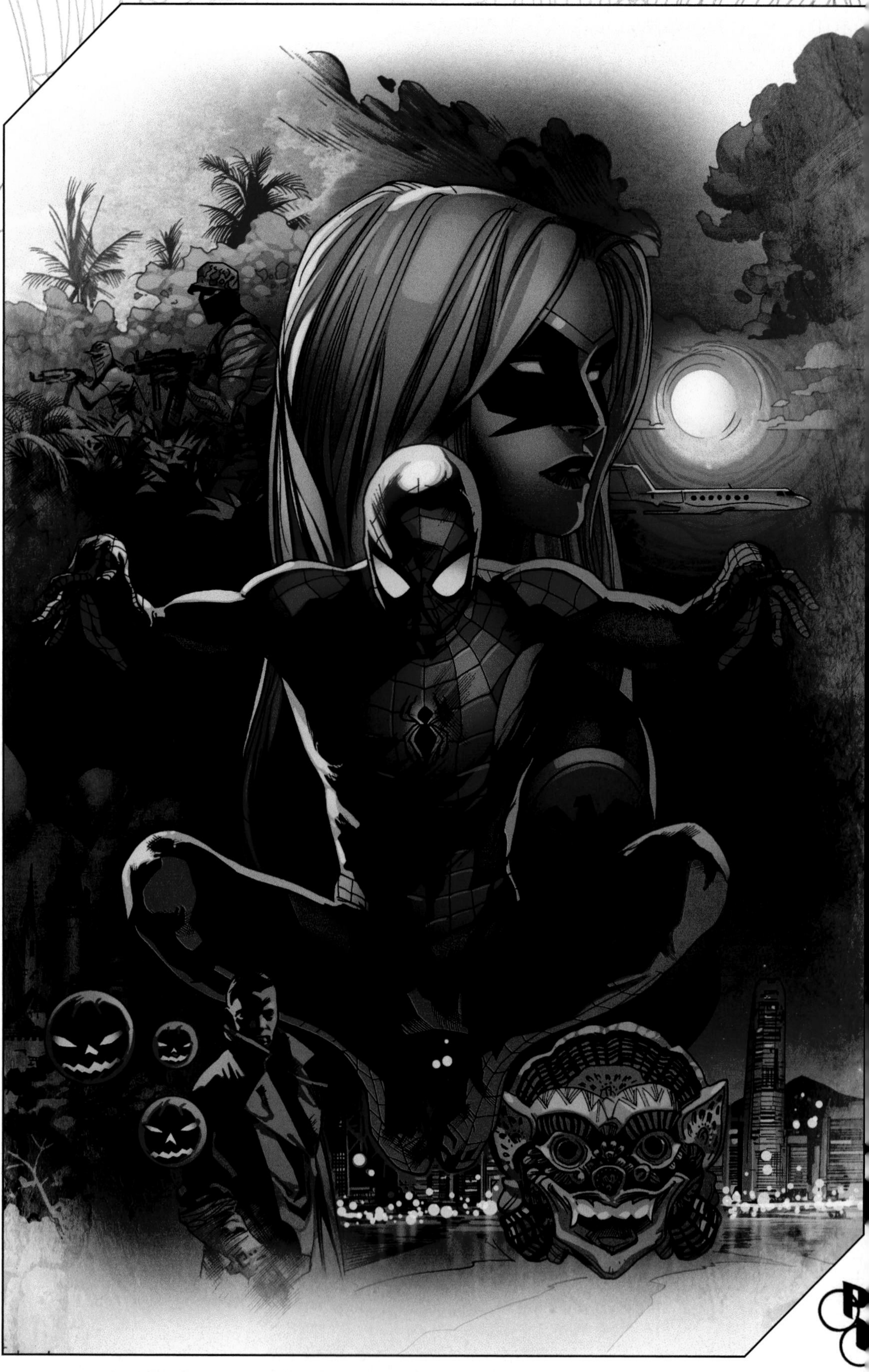

#25 VARIANT BY STUART IMMONEN, WADE VON GRAWBADGER & MARTE GRACIA

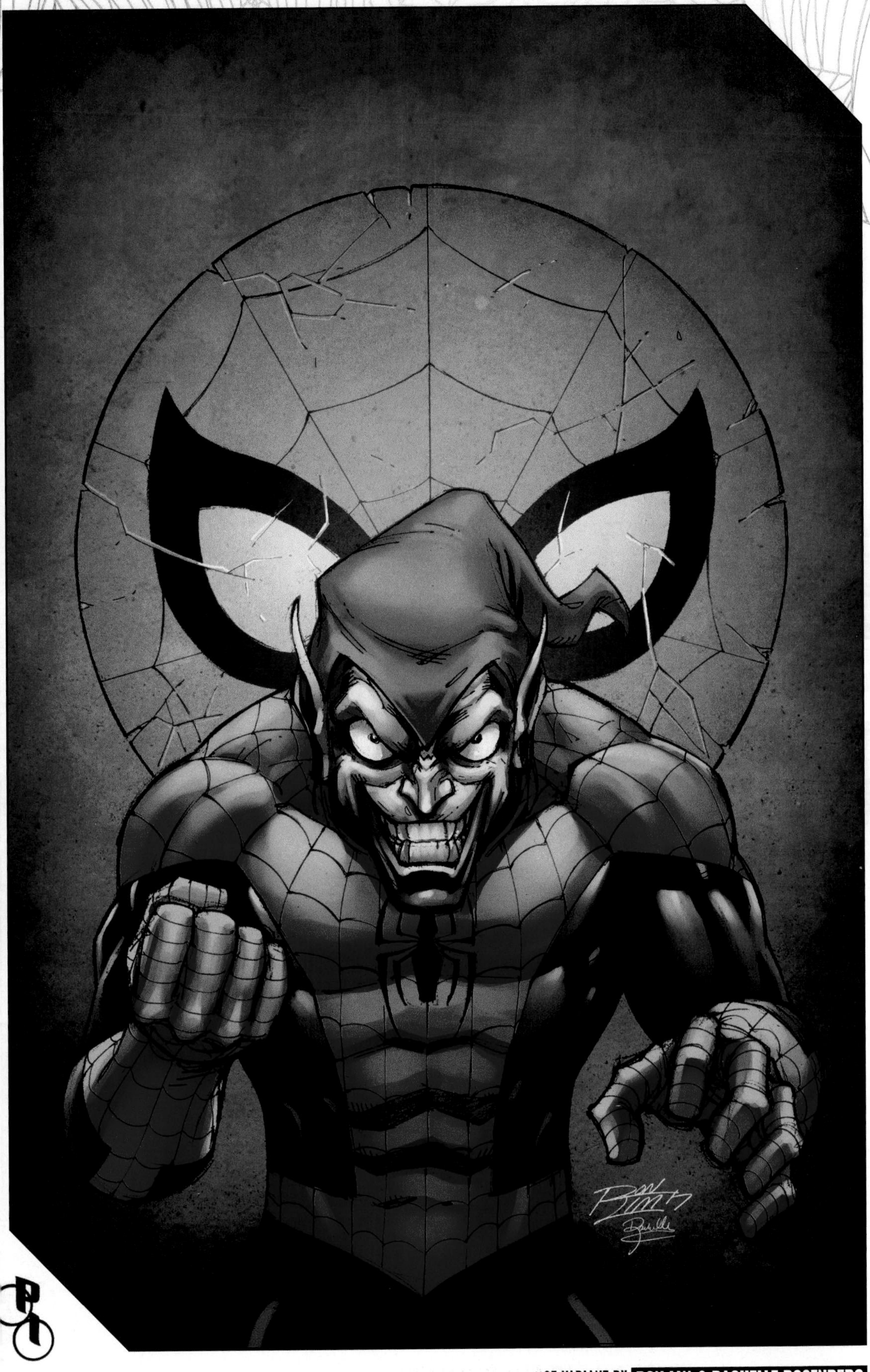

#25 VARIANT BY RON LIM & RACHELLE ROSENBERG

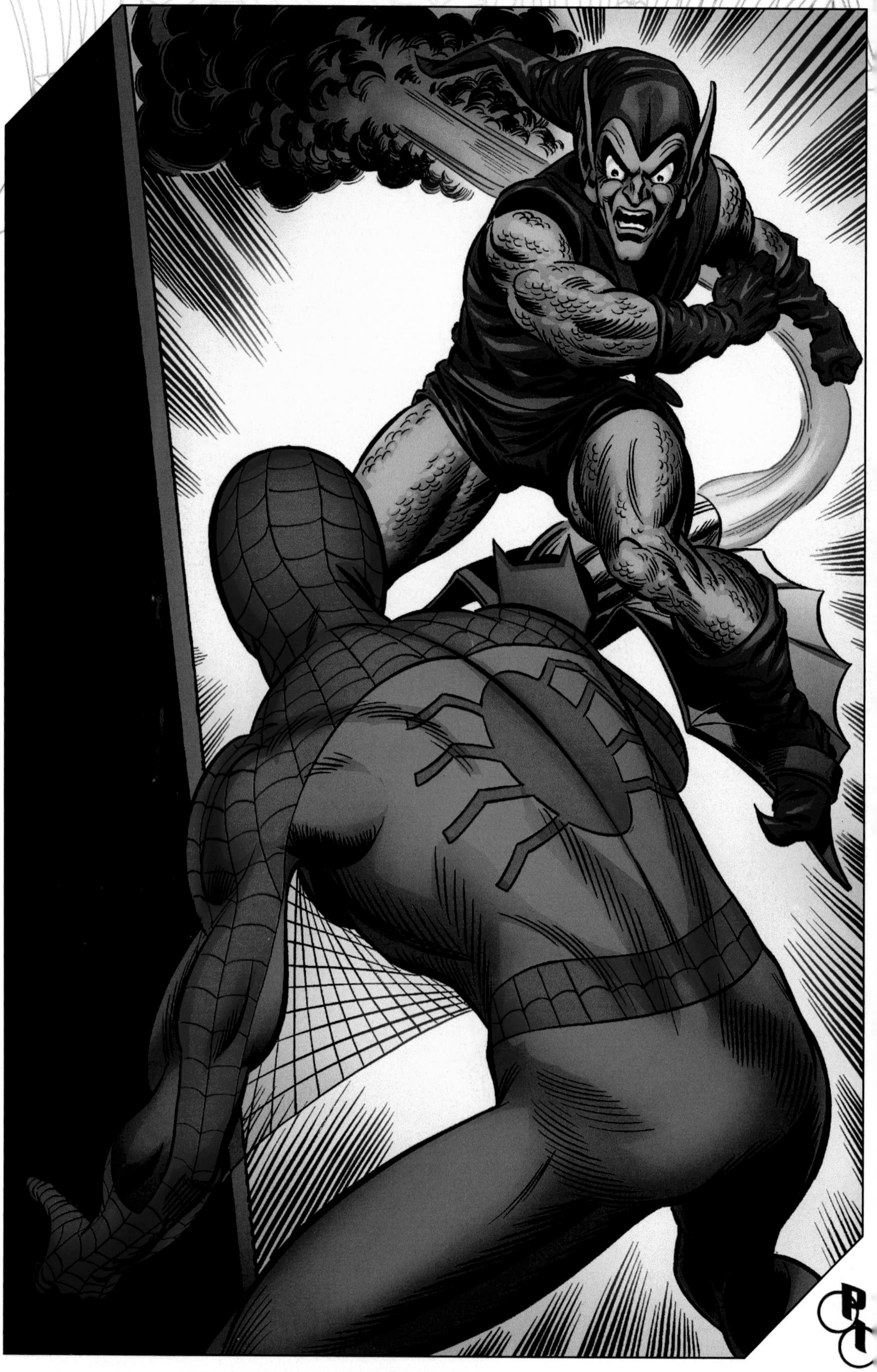

#25 REMASTERED VARIANT BY **GIL KANE, JOHN ROMITA SR. & JASON KEITH**

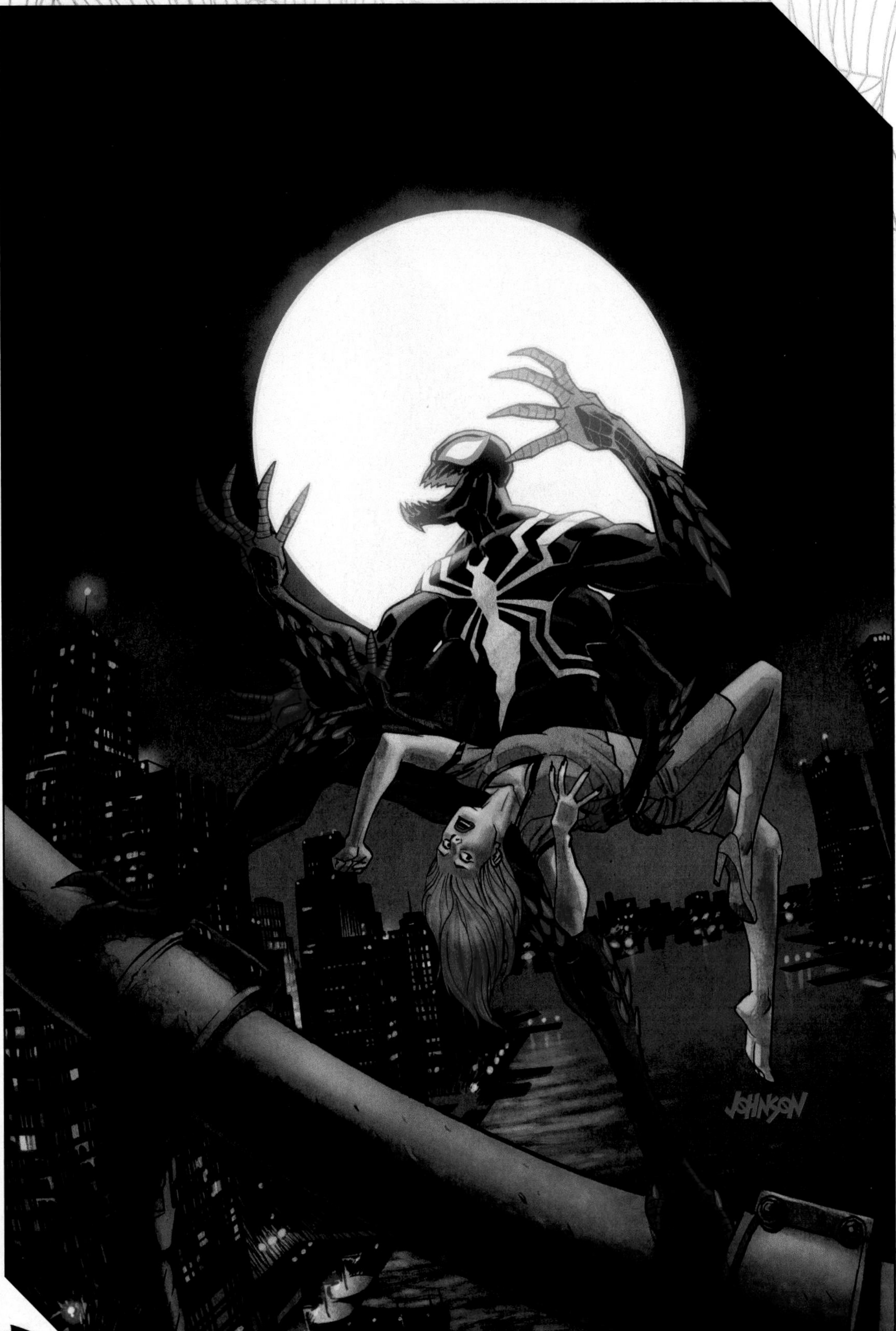
JOHNSON

#25 VENOMIZED VARIANT BY **DAVE JOHNSON**

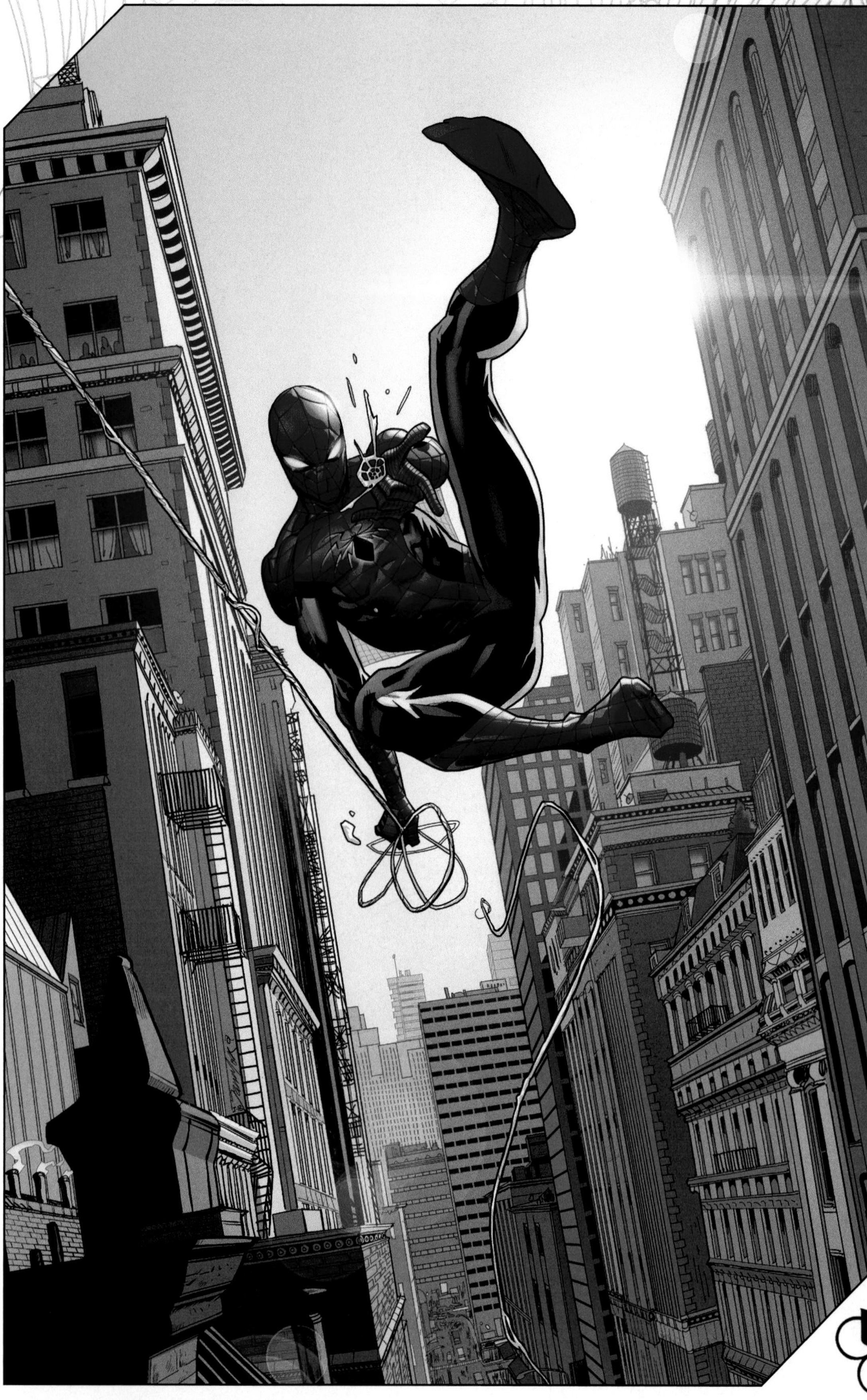

#26 VARIANT BY **DANIEL MORA & JUSTIN PONSOR**

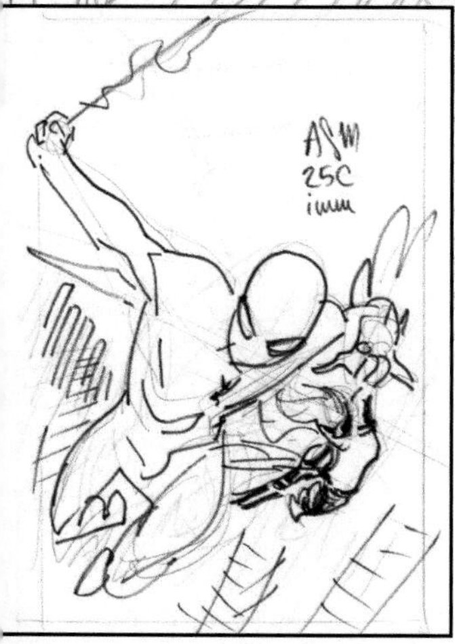
ASM
25C
imm

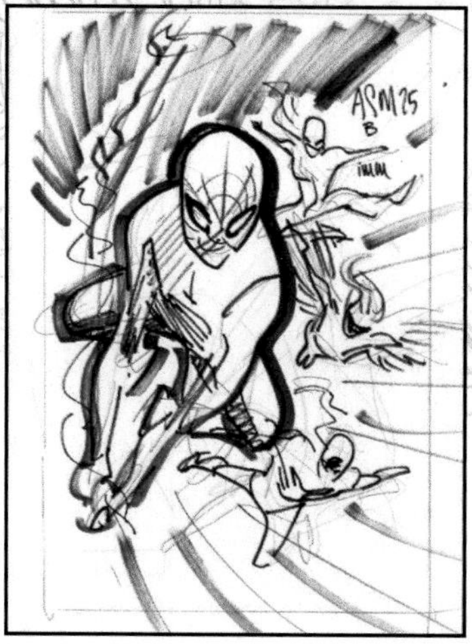
ASM 25
B
imm

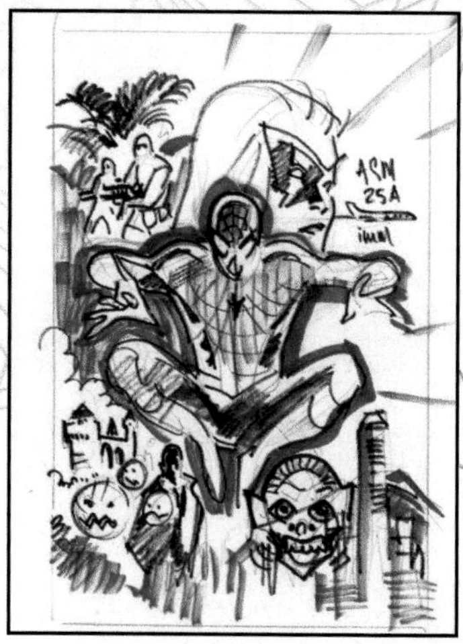
ASM
25A
imm

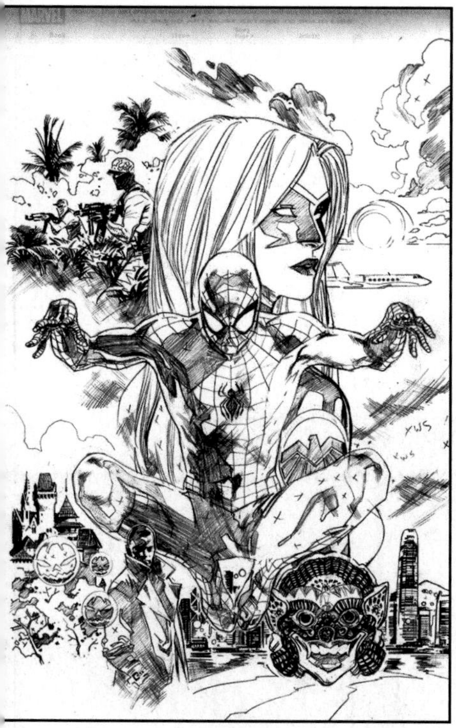

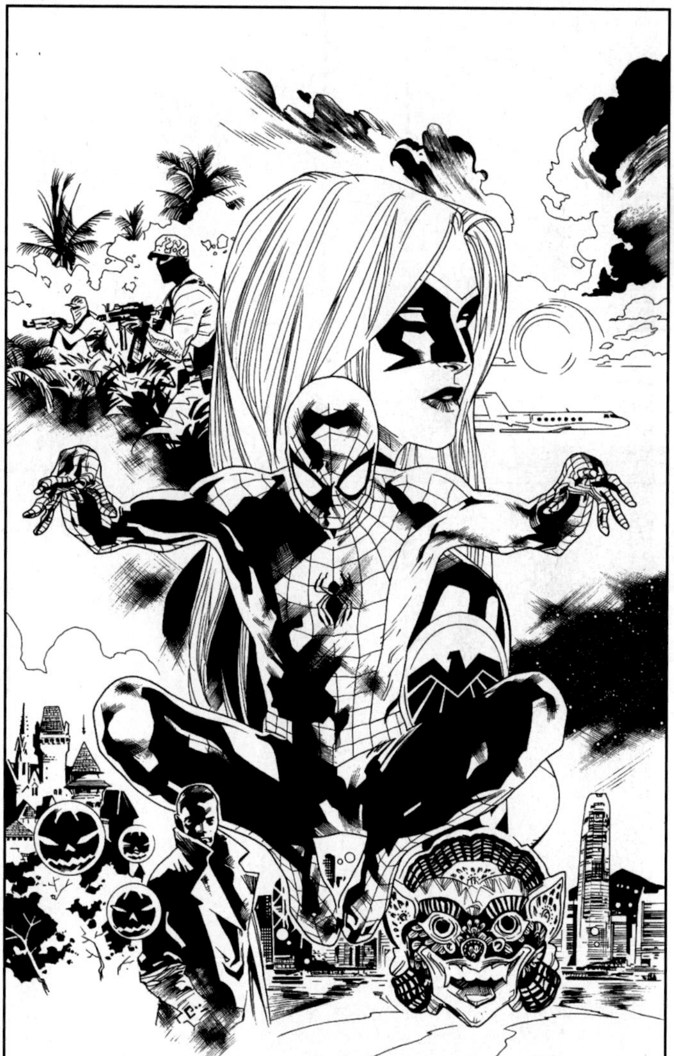

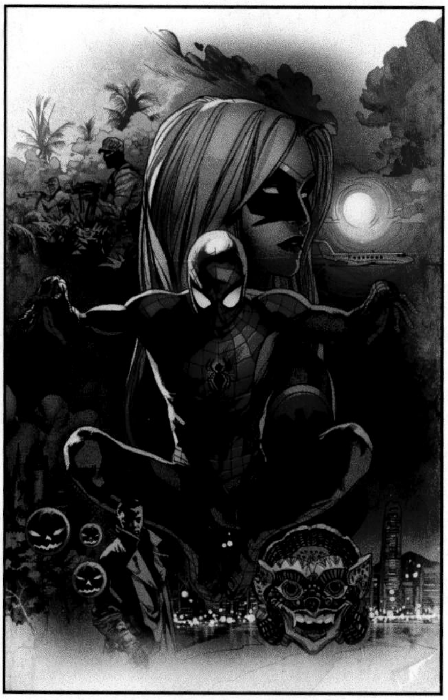

#25 VARIANT COVER PROCESS BY
STUART IMMONEN,
WADE VON GRAWBADGER
& MARTE GRACIA

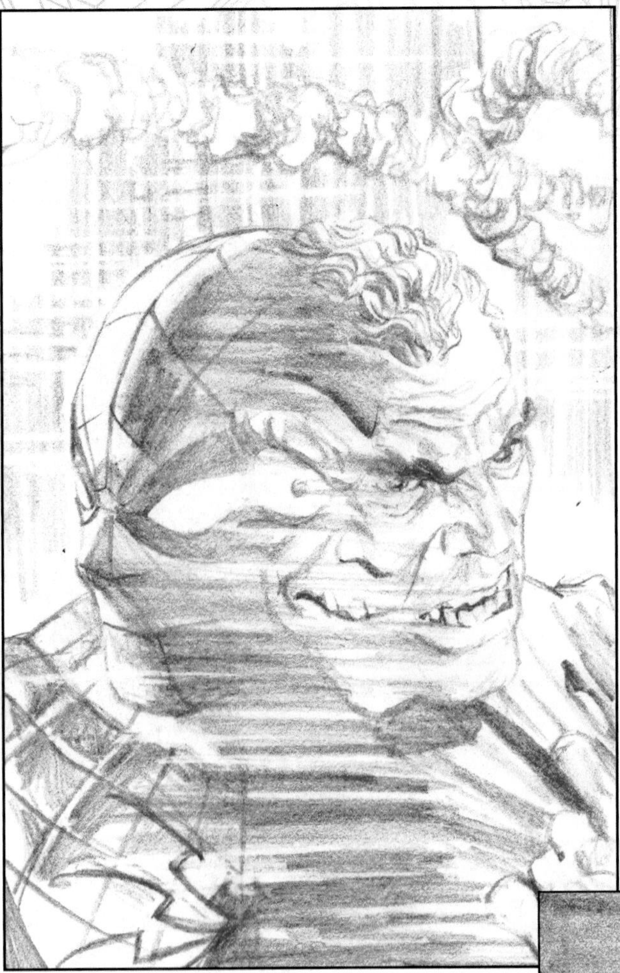

#25 COVER PROCESS BY
ALEX ROSS

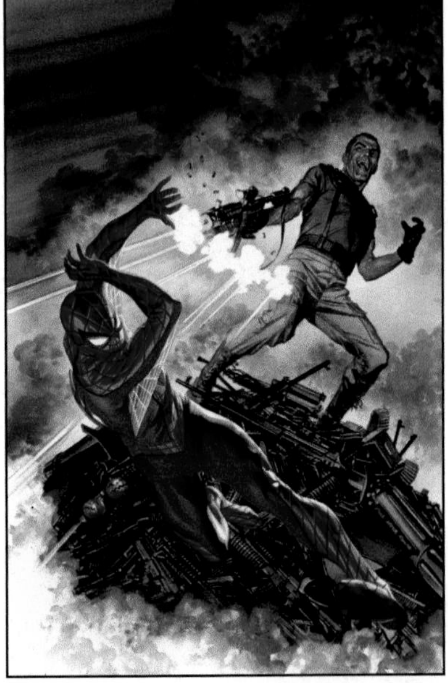

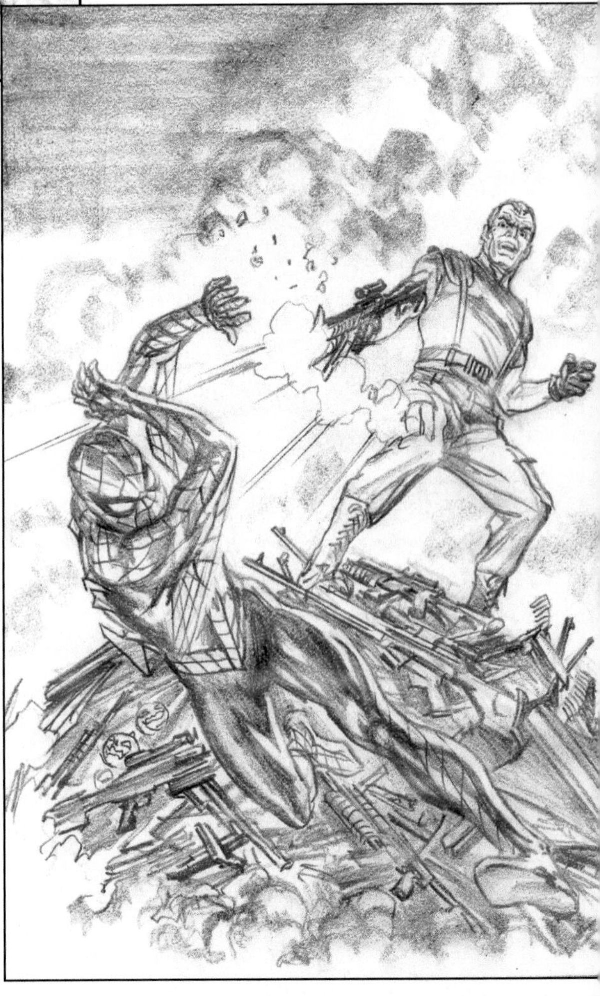

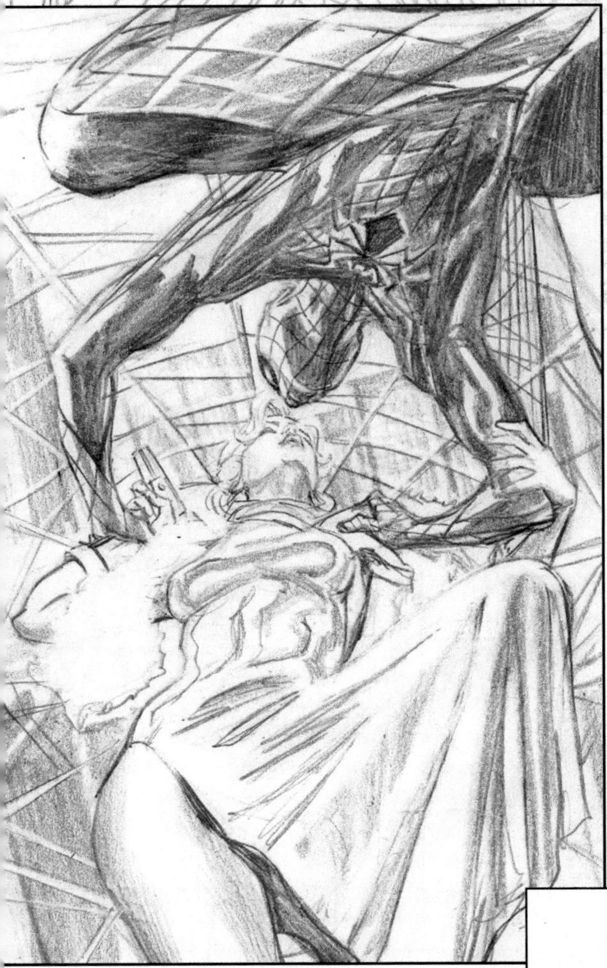

#26 COVER PROCESS BY
ALEX ROSS

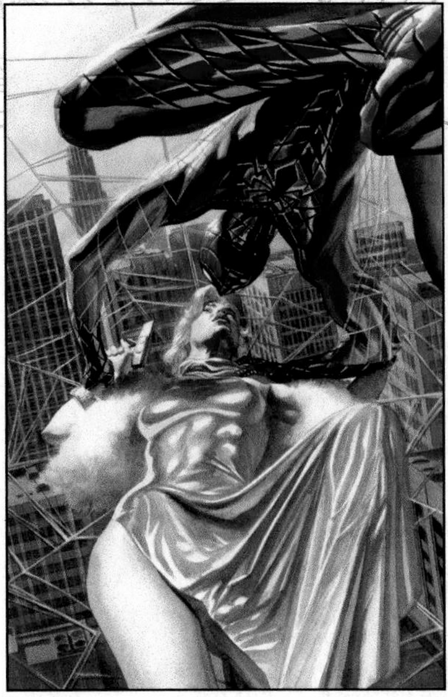

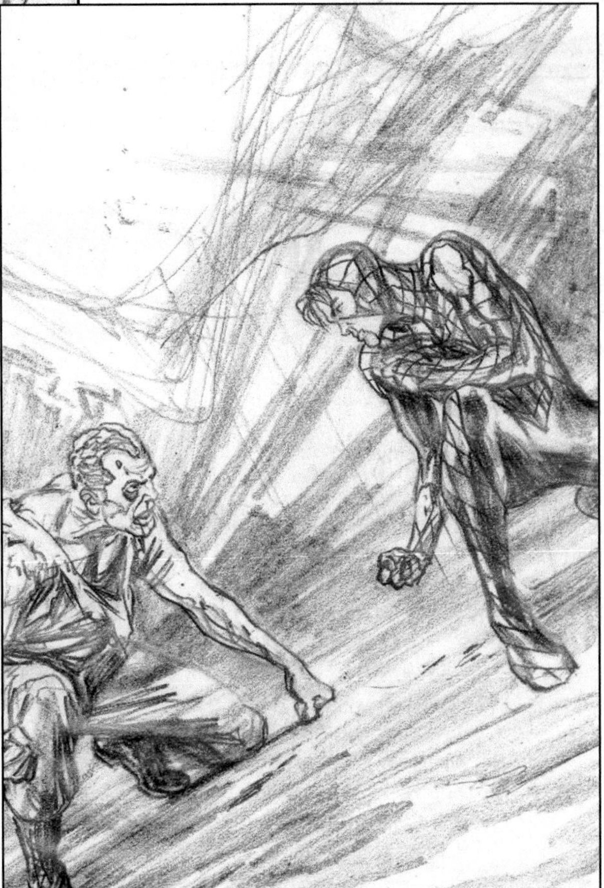

#28 COVER PROCESS BY
ALEX ROSS

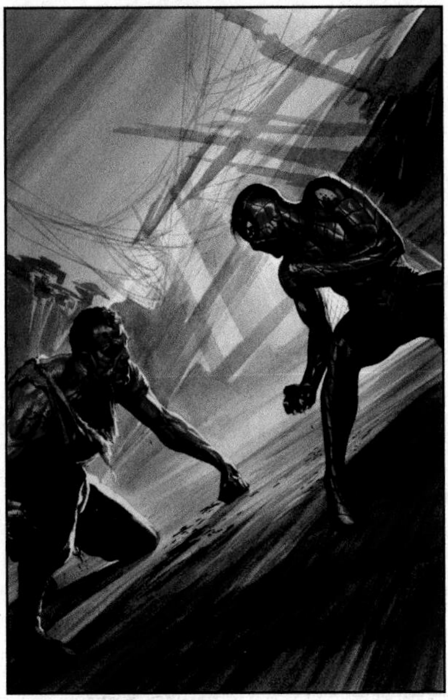

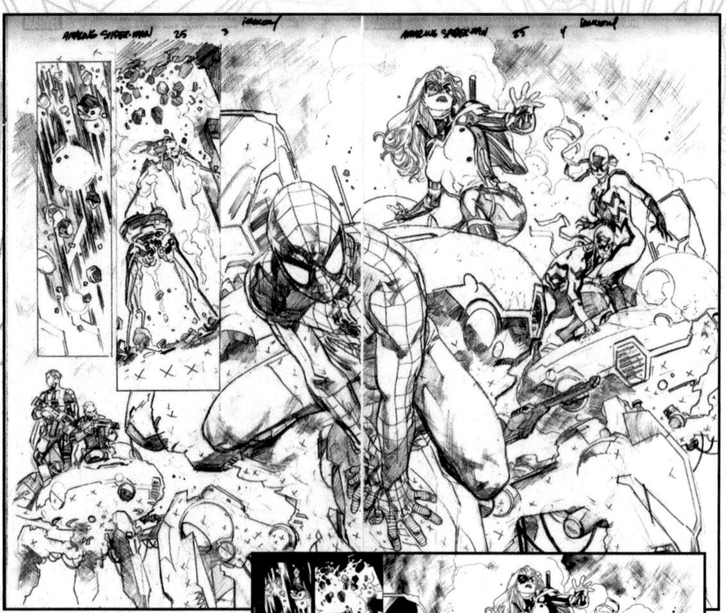

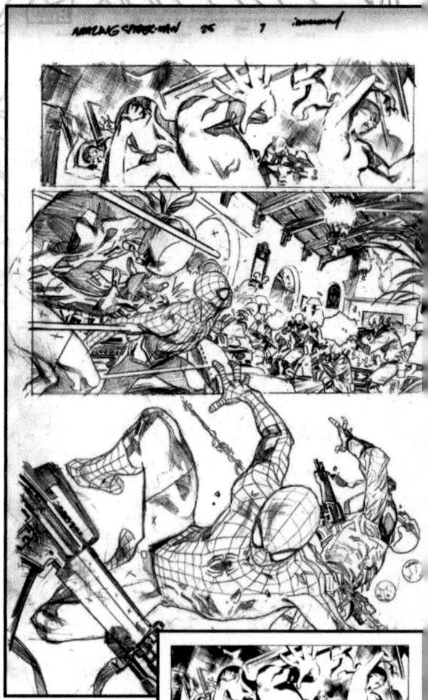

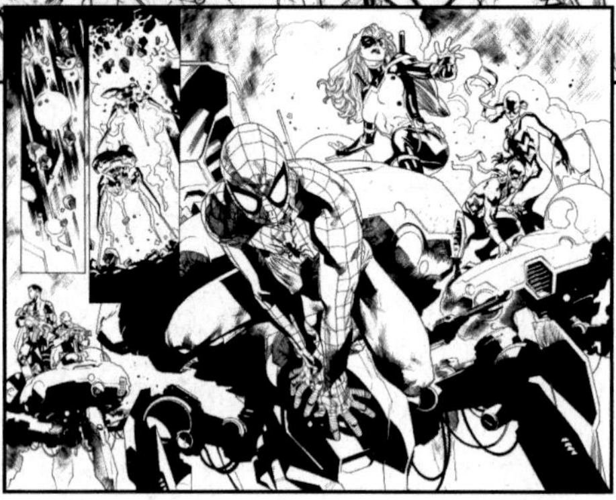

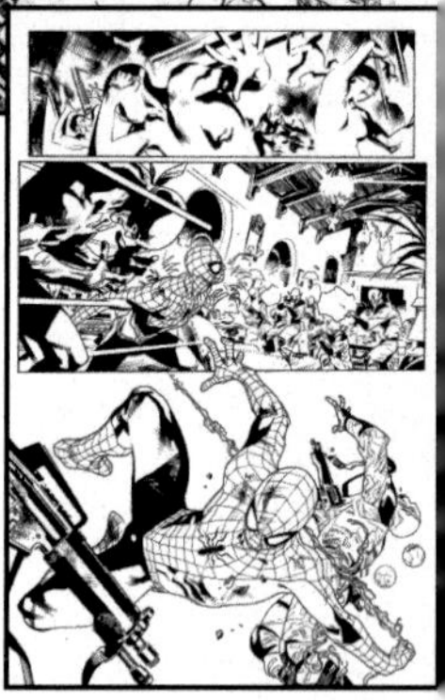

#25 PENCILS BY
STUART IMMONEN

INKS BY
WADE VON
GRAWBADGER

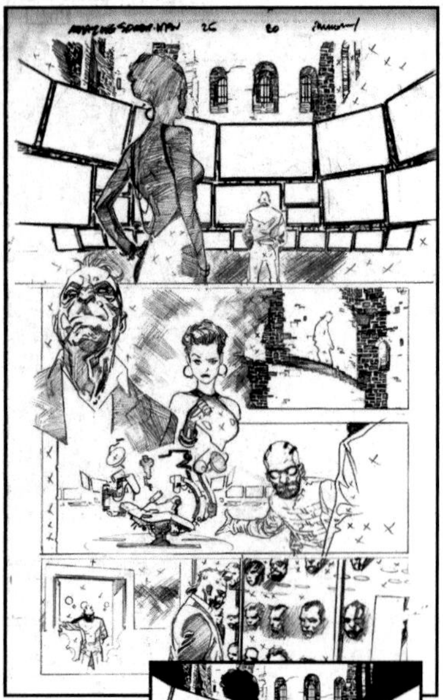

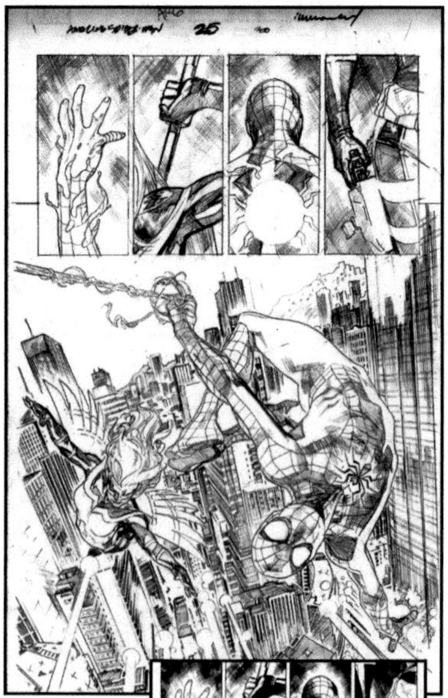

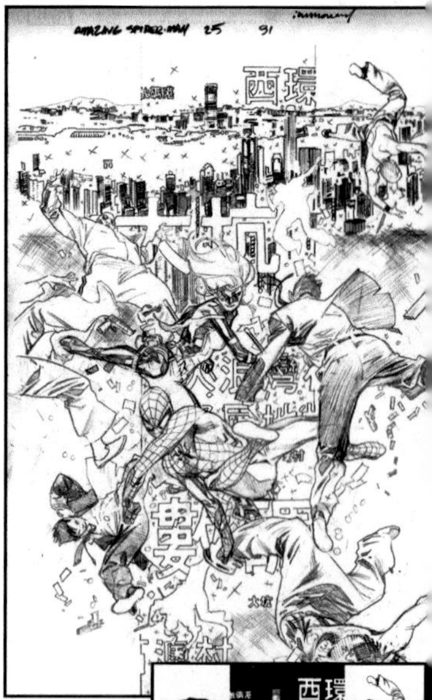

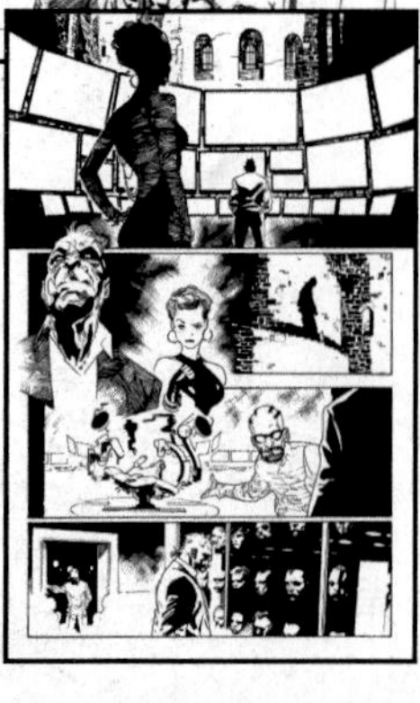

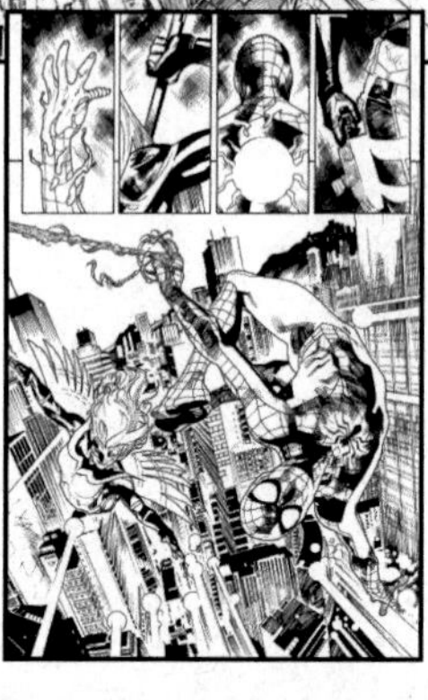

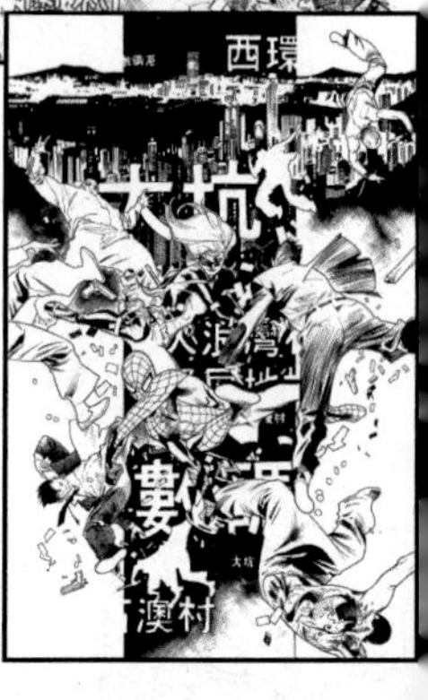